Bev B

York

Boom, Bust & Echo

Boom, Bust & Echo

How to Profit from the
Coming Demographic Shift

David K. Foot
with Daniel Stoffman

Macfarlane Walter & Ross
Toronto

Macfarlane Walter & Ross
37A Hazelton Avenue
Toronto Canada M5R 2E3

CANADIAN CATALOGUING IN PUBLICATION DATA

Foot, David K.
Boom, bust & echo:
how to profit from the coming demographic shift

Includes index.

ISBN 0-921912-97-8

1. Social prediction – Canada.
2. Economic forecasting – Canada.
3. Canada – Social conditions – 1971–   .
4. Canada – Economic conditions – 1991–   .
5. Canada – Population. I. Stoffman, Daniel. II. Title.

HN103.5.F66 1996   303.4971   C96-930590-7

The publisher gratefully acknowledges the support
of the Canada Council and the Ontario Arts Council

Printed and bound in Canada

Contents

Contents

Acknowledgments

This book got its start six years ago when Margaret Wente, then editor of *Report on Business Magazine*, assigned Daniel Stoffman to write an article on the work of David Foot. The article was so popular, and so frequently reprinted, that it was obvious a need existed for a fuller explanation of the impact of demographics on Canadian life. We are indebted to Catherine Dowling for her efficient research assistance; to Tom McCormack and David Cork for generously sharing their knowledge; to Wimmy Leung, whose research formed part of the basis for Chapter 10; to our agent, Dean Cooke, and publishers Jan Walter and Gary Ross for their enthusiastic support of the project; and to Judy Stoffman for her encouragement and invaluable advice.

Two-Thirds of Everything

I n 1985, tennis was booming in Canada. Tennis clubs had waiting lists, public courts were crowded even on weekdays, and sporting goods dealers had trouble keeping up with demand for the latest graphite racquets. The sport was gaining new adherents daily.

But as the 1990s progressed, something unexpected happened: the waiting lists evaporated at the tennis clubs. The managements of these clubs found themselves doing what would have been unthinkable a few years earlier — advertising for new members. By mid-decade, participation in tennis is down substantially. Those who oversee and promote the sport have expressed bewilderment.

They shouldn't be surprised. What has happened to tennis was not only predictable, it was inevitable. Because of the combination of a low fertility rate and increasing life expectancy, the Canadian population is aging, which means simply that the average age of Canadians is increasing. And older people don't play tennis as much as younger people.

The tennis boom started in the early 1970s when most of the baby-boomers, who make up a third of the total Canadian population, were in their teens and 20s. Those are prime tennis-playing years. In the mid-1990s, the boomers are in their 30s and 40s, with the oldest among them pushing 50. Those are prime years for leaving tennis racquets in basements and closets. Of course, many middle-aged and older people still play tennis just as they always have. A former governor general of Canada, Roland Michener, for example, was still playing in his 90s. Nevertheless, the reality is that the average 90-year-old and the average 40-year-old are both less likely to pick up a tennis racquet than the average 20-year-old. The tennis boom was predictable in 1970 to anyone who understood demographics. And the decline in participation was just as predictable in 1970 as it is obvious in the mid-1990s.

Demography, the study of human populations, is the most powerful — and most underutilized — tool we have to understand the past and to foretell the future. Demographics affect every one of us as individuals, far more than most of us have ever imagined. They also play a pivotal role in the economic and social life of our country. Yet because demographic facts seem so obvious once they are pointed out, many people are inclined to resist them. Life, they say, can't possibly be that simple. By refusing to accept the obvious, they make life more complicated and unpredictable than it has to be.

Demographics explain about two-thirds of everything. They tell us a great deal about which products will be in demand in five years, and they accurately predict school enrolments many years in advance. They allow us to forecast which drugs will be in fashion ten years down the road, as well as what sorts of crimes will be on the increase. They help us to know when houses will go up in value, and when they will go down.

If more of our decision-makers understood demographics, Canada would be a better place to live because it would run more smoothly and more efficiently. Had Ontario Hydro's forecasters, for example, understood demographics, they would have been less likely to squander $8 billion in 1977 on the unnecessary Darlington nuclear power station. Similarly, private developers would have fewer offices and condominium units standing empty in the mid-1990s. School boards, if they used demographics, would not open new elementary schools just when they should be expanding high schools instead. Yet school boards across Canada often do things like that, just as hospital managements close maternity wards and then have to reverse themselves when births pick up a couple of years later.

Demographics are about everyone, and that's why this book is for everyone. Demographics tell you, as an individual, a great deal about who you are, where you've been, and where you're going. If, for example, you were lucky enough to be born in 1937 and you've been successful, it wouldn't hurt to learn a little humility. You haven't had much competition, because few people were born in Canada in 1937. That demographic good fortune probably had as much to do with your success as you did.

On the other hand, perhaps you had the misfortune to enter the world in 1961, one of the worst years in this century to be born. You're one of a huge crowd of late baby-boomers, also known as Generation X. The mass of older boomers who preceded you are occupying most of the best jobs and have pushed the price of real estate way up, perhaps out of your reach. Chances are that life has been a struggle for you. And your parents, the lucky people who were born in 1937 or thereabouts, probably don't understand how tough that struggle has been. For your own peace of mind, you need to understand that some of the setbacks you have experienced may relate more to demographics than to any personal failings. The more knowledge you have about those demographic realities, the better prepared you are to cope with them — and perhaps find a way to turn them to your own advantage.

Anyone involved in planning for the future needs to understand demographics. That's true whether you're planning your own personal future or that of a school system, a hospital, a chain of restaurants, or a multinational corporation. It is simply not possible to do any competent planning without a knowledge of demographics — not only demographics in general, but Canadian demographics in particular, because the Canadian population structure is unique.

Demographics are critically important for business. They probably won't alter a company's financial results from one financial quarter to the next. But the management of a business that fails to pay attention to demographics for five years may wake up to find itself in a different business than it thought it was in — or not in business at all.

In 1993, a major cosmetics company noticed some market developments that senior management found puzzling. Demand for certain products, such as bright lipsticks, was falling dramatically while demand for others, especially skin care products, was rising. Even men were starting to buy skin creams. What, they wanted to know, was going on? Was this just a passing fad, or were new long-term trends emerging that they needed to know about? The company had already done plenty of research. It had a sophisticated grasp of certain demographic facts, such as how the ethnicity, geographic location, and income levels of its customers related to product preferences. But it had missed the aging trend.

Like its influence on tennis, the impact of aging on behaviour at the cosmetics counter is glaringly obvious — once it's been pointed out. What this company needed to understand was that the number of potential customers in their 30s and 40s was rising, while the number in their teens and 20s was falling, and that this was not a temporary phenomenon but rather a long-term trend that would influence the company's sales figures for many years to come. It had to accept the reality that, try as it might through advertising or in-store promotion, it could not alter the fact that a 38-year-old is less likely to wear certain kinds of lipstick than an 18-year-old. The 38-year-old, on the other hand, is much more likely than the 18-year-old to buy an expensive skin cream.

Moreover, a huge number of males are now moving into middle age. Because this market is so large, it is now worthwhile for cosmetics companies to launch new products designed for men. Not only are there more middle-aged men than before, but boomer males seem more willing than their predecessors to spend money on their appearance. This new development in the cosmetics marketplace is one of the effects of demographics: because the baby boom was so large, a cult of youth dominated North America when the boomers were young. The appeal of this youth culture was so strong that middle-aged boomers are clinging more tenaciously than previous generations to a youthful image.

These demographically driven market shifts have important implications that require careful consideration for any company in the intensely competitive cosmetics industry. What happens to marketing strategy? Do you shift some dollars to men's magazines and to media that appeal to older women, and take dollars away from vehicles aimed at young women and teenagers? What about your sales force? Who has more credibility behind the counter: a gorgeous 22-year-old who has never had to worry about her perfect skin, or a gorgeous 52-year-old who still looks great because, she says, she knows how to apply the right products?

Fortunately for this company, it had a product mix that could be adjusted to fit these changes in the marketplace with comparative ease. In fact, population aging is a boon for the cosmetics business in general because, as people get older, they become susceptible to the lure of products that promise to perpetuate a youthful appearance and they are more likely to be able to afford them.

Other industries are not so fortunate. The beer industry, for example, used to aim its marketing strategy at sports-minded young men, who are consumers of large volumes of relatively inexpensive brands of beer. It stuck to this strategy even as its customers grew older, less fascinated with sports, and more inclined to sip a high-quality specialty beer than to guzzle a run-of-the-mill mass-market brand. Fortunately for consumers, the inertia of the large companies allowed the microbreweries to establish a foothold in a shrinking market by producing different products. The beer market was going to flatten regardless of what marketing strategy the beermakers adopted, but the transition could have been much less painful had the big companies anticipated demographic change rather than reacting to it long after it had already occurred.

That's what this book is all about: giving you, the reader, the power to anticipate demographic change. But it's important to understand that these are long-term trends. The farther ahead in the future you are looking, the more relevant demographics will be to you. If, for example, you are a businessperson whose chief preoccupation is this year's bottom line, the book won't be of much use to you. But if you are a strategic thinker interested in the well-being of your organization, including its bottom line, three years and more into the future, this book is for you.

If demographics explain about two-thirds of everything, what are some things they can't explain? Electoral politics is one. At first glance, this might seem surprising, because conventional wisdom is that people get more conservative as they get older. If that were true, population aging would be a convenient explanation for the success of right-of-centre political parties in recent years. The problem with that thesis is that political scientists can find no direct relationship between age and Canadian voting patterns. Moreover, the Canadian electorate in recent years has become increasingly volatile, with the result that it is harder than ever for governments of any political stripe to get re-elected. Yet demographic trends are predictable precisely because they are not volatile. That's why they won't help anyone place a winning bet on the next election.

However, while demographics won't predict electoral outcomes, they can be most useful in predicting electoral issues. For example, daycare was a big issue in federal elections during the 1980s when the large baby-boom generation was busy producing children. By the 1990s, most of those children were past the need for daycare, with the predictable result that much less was heard about this issue in the 1993 federal election that carried the Liberals to power.

Demographic projections aren't always as straightforward as some of the examples cited so far. Sometimes several trends come into play at once, making forecasts difficult. For example, the fertility rate — the average number of children per woman — declined during the 1960s and 1970s. That might have prompted a prediction that families would be moving into smaller houses during the 1980s and 1990s because they would have fewer people to accommodate. That hasn't happened, because countervailing trends were operating at the same time. One was a rise in family incomes, resulting in part from the entry of more women into the workforce. More people can now afford the individual privacy that a larger house offers. Moreover, an important demographic trend — the huge number of baby-boomers competing for the small number of senior management jobs — has meant that many people are finding themselves working harder than ever and having to take work home. Many others have left large organizations and established their own businesses operated out of home offices. As a result, yesterday's five-bedroom house has become today's three-bedroom, two-office house.

Demography makes use of a wide range of data, including the size of a given population, its birth and death rates, the number of immigrants it attracts and the number of emigrants it loses, the geographical dispersal of its members, and its ethnic composition. But when it comes to predicting behaviour, the most useful demographic variable is the age composition of the population. Who is more likely to join a gang that "swarms" people and steals their basketball jackets, a senior citizen or a teenager? Who is more likely to attend a chamber music concert, an 11-year-old or a 51-year-old? Because age is so powerful a predictor of human behaviour, the answers to these questions are blatantly obvious. If you know how many people of each age are around today, you can make a reliable forecast about how those same people will behave tomorrow.

This book does exactly that. What kinds of foods will people buy and what kinds of cars will they drive? Where will they choose to live? Which investments will they favour? These and many other things can be confidently predicted simply on the basis of readily available data on the age of Canadians.

The two keys to these forecasts are the number of people in each age group and the probability that each person will participate in a given behaviour. Express the number of people doing a certain thing as a percentage of the number of people in the population and you get the activity participation rate for the society as a whole. Probability and participation rate are the same thing, except that probability applies to an individual while participation rate applies to a whole society. Multiply the participation rate by the population, and you get the actual number of people who are bowling or buying houses or having heart attacks or whatever else you may want to measure. (See Appendices I and II for more on demographic forecasting.)

Participation rates are not 100% predictable because they are affected by such transient economic factors as recessions, income levels, and unemployment rates. They are also affected by such social factors as marital status and ethnicity. But they are two-thirds predictable

7

because of the age factor. Age is the best forecasting tool because it is guaranteed to change. A person's ethnicity will remain the same ten years hence. Her employment status may or may not remain the same. The one thing that is certain is that she will be ten years older.

How stable are these participation rates? In other words, how likely is it that a 45-year-old in 2005 will behave the same as a 45-year-old in 1995? Very likely. Occasionally, behaviours do change: the decline in smoking when the public finally understood its lethal impact on health is a prime example. But in most cases, participation rates of the various age groups in different activities are quite stable over time. That is what allows us to use demographics to predict future trends in retailing, recreation, and a host of other human activities.

In fact, age is a proxy for many of the socioeconomic variables that differentiate human beings. A 30-year-old, for example, is more likely to be married than a 20-year-old. A 40-year-old probably has a higher income than a 30-year-old. For this reason, focussing on age captures many other factors and simplifies the analytical process.

Analyzing human behaviour according to age has the great advantage of allowing us to know what is actually going on instead of living in a fog of misconception. Most journalists look at the total participation in an activity — crime, for example — and then exclaim in print, "It's going up!" or "It's going down!" But these changes, if based on the population as a whole, may be misleading, reflecting only the changing age composition of society. In an aging society, the number of crimes goes down because older people don't commit as many crimes as younger ones. A drop in the overall crime rate, therefore, may have no connection to any change in behaviour, the economy, social attitudes, or law enforcement techniques. It may be unrelated to anything at all except a decline in the number of people in the crime-prone youth age groups. On the other hand, the appearance of a higher crime rate among a particular age group would signify genuine change.

The ability to forecast undesirable outcomes, such as a rise in certain kinds of crime or increased use of hard drugs, highlights another important use of demographics — making predictions in the hope that they will be wrong. If we know, through demographic analysis, that certain things are likely to occur, then we can take steps to prevent or at least mitigate those outcomes. When that happens, a demographer can only be delighted to have his forecast proven wrong.

Canada's demographics are unique. Canada's population pyramid (see Figure 1) contains a massive bulge, representing the huge generation of baby-boomers born in the 20 years from 1947 to 1966. By comparison, the Depression and World War II generations that preceded the baby boom are small, as is the baby bust that followed it. But the most recently arrived group, the offspring of the boomers or the baby-boom echo, is comparatively large. That is why this book is called *Boom, Bust & Echo*. The different behaviours of these different demographic groups, and the interplay among them, are what make Canadian demographics so useful as an analytical and forecasting tool.

Because of these wide variations in the size of the different age groups in Canadian society, changes in social and economic behaviour resulting from the aging process are more evident in Canada than in European countries that have not had such sharp fluctuations in birth rates. On the other hand, much of the thinking in this book can be applied equally to the United States, which also experienced a baby boom, a baby bust, and a baby-boom echo.

In popular discussion of demographic issues, much confusion results from the frequent misunderstanding of two key demographic terms: fertility rate and birth rate. The fertility rate is the average number of children born to women over their lifetimes. The birth rate is the total number of births divided by the size of the population. It's important to grasp this distinction. For example, many people know that Canada's fertility rate, which for most of the last decade has been 1.7 babies per woman, is below the 2.1 babies per woman needed to replace the population. (You need two children to replace yourself and your partner. The extra tenth of a baby is needed to compensate for women who don't have any children and for children who don't live into adulthood.) Knowing that the fertility rate is less than replacement, many people assume the Canadian population is in danger of precipitous decline. That's why low fertility is often offered as a rationale for maintaining high immigration levels.

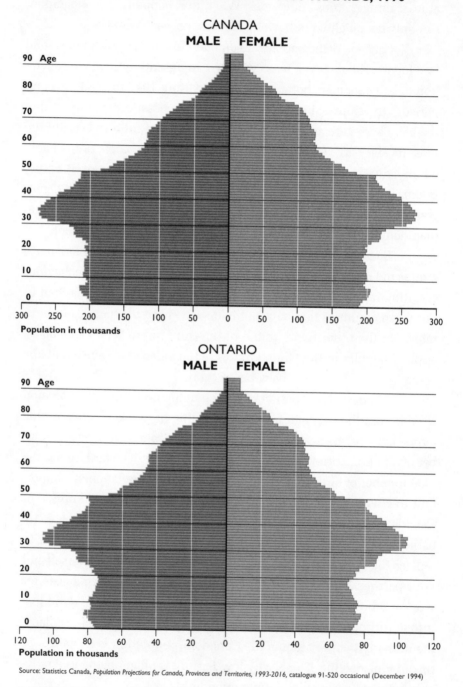

FIGURE 1: CANADA'S POPULATION PYRAMIDS, 1996

CANADA
MALE   FEMALE

Population in thousands

ONTARIO
MALE   FEMALE

Population in thousands

Source: Statistics Canada, *Population Projections for Canada, Provinces and Territories, 1993-2016,* catalogue 91-520 occasional (December 1994)

But despite below-replacement fertility, the Canadian population would be increasing even without *any* immigration because Canada has one of the highest birth rates among industrialized countries. That's because Canada during the 1980s had a higher percentage than other advanced countries of women in their prime childbearing years. We have, in other words, a high birth rate and a low fertility rate at the same time.

The analysis in this book is based, in large part, on statistical facts like these. In this way, it is different from the work of other authors who attempt to forecast economic and social trends. John Naisbitt, for example, analyzes the content of newspapers and other publications to find out where the world is headed. Faith Popcorn relies on focus groups. Allan Gregg uses public opinion surveys. These are all legitimate forecasting methods that often result in important insights. This book, however, is built on a different foundation: demographic facts. In this approach, an analysis of historical data is used as a jumping-off point into the future. Once you've read this book, you'll know enough to analyze demographic data yourself.

But before you can do that, you need to grasp the most basic demographic fact of all: every year each person gets a year older. Many sophisticated and educated people have great difficulty understanding the significance of this one simple fact. That's why phrases such as "population aging" are so often misunderstood. If, for example, you think population aging means that senior citizens are about to become the dominant group in society and if you start a business based on that assumption, you may go broke. If you had checked the birth figures for the 1930s, you would have known that, in the late 1990s, the ranks of seniors will be growing very slowly. In fact, the real era of "grey power" is 20 years away, and in the meantime, there are far more promising markets to tempt retailers and far more pressing social issues for all of us to worry about than a non-existent preponderance of seniors.

HOW TO READ THIS BOOK

This chapter and the next, which describes the various cohorts that compose the Canadian population, provide the basic knowledge of

Canadian demographics necessary for an understanding of everything that follows. Once you have read these two introductory chapters, we encourage you to read the rest of the book in whatever order suits best. Because different readers have different interests, each chapter has been written as a self-contained whole. If you're not interested in real estate, for example, you can skip the chapter on that subject with no loss of understanding of the chapters that follow. But it's important to note that many ideas and themes recur throughout the book. For that reason, readers are encouraged to take advantage of the cross-chapter references, which are a guide to the places in the book where each idea is fully explained.

Chapter 1

Boomers and Other Cohorts

Each of us is a member of a "cohort." The baby boom is a cohort that includes everyone born during a 20-year span of sustained high numbers of births in Canada. It also includes those born elsewhere during those same years but now living in Canada. The other cohorts in Canada span shorter periods of time.

Most of us think of ourselves as individuals and underestimate how much we have in common with fellow members of our cohort. And of course each of us *is* an individual. The 70-year-old who continues a lifelong pursuit of rock climbing while most in her age group have switched to more sedate recreations is a unique individual. So is the 12-year-old who prefers opera to rock music. But the chances are good that the young opera lover will rent his first apartment, buy his first car, and get married at about the same age as his peers. The timing of those events in his life will be determined largely by demographics. Before we can understand what demographics have in store for him and for all of us, we need to know the various cohorts that make up the Canadian population. Let's take a look at them now.

PRE–WORLD WAR I (BORN 1914 AND EARLIER)

Forget about the outmoded notion of "senior citizens" as one unified group sharing many characteristics in common. It's no longer true, if it ever was. An 85-year-old has no more in common with a 65-year-old than a 45-year-old has with a 25-year-old. They are different people, from different generations, with different interests, different financial circumstances, and different preoccupations and needs.

The most senior of seniors — the over-80-year-olds — constitute the one segment of the over-65 population that is currently growing rapidly because they were born in the first decade and a half of this century, when a high birth rate accompanied a booming Canadian economy. During this period, Canada also welcomed the largest concentrated influx of immigration in its history as part of a policy to settle the prairie provinces. Although the over-80s have a higher death rate than people in younger age groups, they are a growing cohort in the sense that those turning 80 during the 1990s are more numerous than their predecessors in the over-80 category. In 1996, 627,000 members of this cohort, born both in Canada and elsewhere, are living in Canada.

Because women, on average, live six years longer than men, most of this group is female. In their productive years, few women had independent careers outside the household and so they had little income of their own. They were married to men who didn't have transferable pensions. Not surprisingly, therefore, most of them are poor. Their greatest needs are appropriate housing and good health care. And their tragedy is that not enough of us are paying attention to them. As a society, we should be searching for innovative ways to combine housing with health care and related support services so that these women can conclude their lives in dignity and comfort. But the public sector is too preoccupied with deficit-cutting to think about imaginative solutions to social problems, and the senior seniors are too poor to interest the private sector.

The increase over the next decade in the number of elderly widows in our society is going to have a major impact on a younger group of people — people in their 50s and 60s who will be taking on the responsibility of caring for elderly, and increasingly ill, mothers. Traditionally, this is a task that falls to daughters more than to sons. Some women will be shouldering this new obligation on top of major responsibilities at work.

Imagine a vice-president of a large corporation in Toronto, preparing for a crucial meeting. She's an ambitious and talented woman who doesn't plan on making vice-president her final stop on the corporate ladder. She has her eye on the CEO's job, and this meeting is an important step in that direction. Then she gets an urgent call from Saskatoon, saying her mother has just broken her hip. Forget the big meeting: Mom needs her now more than ever, and she's on the next plane to Saskatoon. For the next few years, a great deal of her time and energy will be devoted to her mother. Because of real-life scenarios like this, many women who have the ability to make it to the top in business and government are not going to get there.

WORLD WAR I (1915 TO 1919)

It's always an advantage to be part of a small cohort. That's why even a small difference in one's date of birth can make a big difference in life. If you were born in 1910, you were part of a big cohort. If you were born in 1917, you were part of a smaller group. That in itself was no guarantee of success, but it was an important advantage. It meant you were in a smaller class at school and therefore had more attention from the teacher. And when it was time to go out to work, there were fewer competitors for what jobs were available.

During World War I, many Canadian men went off to battle and, as a result, many Canadian women stopped having babies. That's why people born in the last half of the teens of this century have enjoyed the lifelong advantage of having little peer-group competition. On the other hand, they entered the workforce while Canada was still in the grip of the Great Depression and jobs were few. After that, their careers were disrupted by World War II. Even so, they were better off than those born a few years earlier, who were part of a larger group and had to establish careers during the Depression. In 1996, 589,000 members of this cohort live in Canada. In general, people born in the second part of the teens have done better than those born just before.

THE ROARING TWENTIES (1920 TO 1929)

When the boys came home from the war, they quickly made up for lost time, with the result that lots of babies were produced during the 1920s. These offspring of the Roaring Twenties are young seniors in the mid-1990s and, despite the lifelong disadvantage of being part of a large cohort, they've had a pretty good run. Some of them went overseas to fight in World War II, which had the result of reducing competition for jobs for those who remained in Canada.

Moreover, because of the war effort the economy was growing, and so the 1920s kids had a better chance to get established than those born in the 1910s. The Roaring Twenties generation also helped to produce the baby boom that began in 1947. The boomers proceeded to drive up the price of the real estate and other assets that the kids of both the 1910s and 1920s owned. So, in general, these people have done well but, because they were members of a large flock, numbering almost 2 million in 1996, not as well as the favoured group that followed them.

THE DEPRESSION BABIES (1930 TO 1939)

In hard economic times, many Canadians couldn't afford children, and so fertility declined. The lucky ones who were born then became the golden group of Canadian society. Although they had a tough start, they have subsequently lived a life of incredible good fortune. These are the people entering senior citizenship during the mid-1990s, and yet again their timing is flawless: they are going to have free banking, reduced theatre ticket prices, and all the other breaks our society gives to seniors, because it will be several years yet before the dispensers of these perks wake up and realize that today's youngest seniors are the cohort least in need of such advantages.

The Depression kids haven't always had it easy. The 1930s were a time of hardship for everyone, including young children. They lived through World War II, hardly a carefree time to be alive. Because of their youth, they didn't have to serve in the war. But once the war ended, everything went their way. Entering the workforce during the postwar reconstruction of the 1950s, they never had to worry about finding a job. On the contrary, they had their choice of jobs. They never had to worry about being promoted; rather, they were promoted faster than they ever expected to be. Because they were doing so well, they went out and got more of everything, including kids. The Depression kids gave us the baby boom because they could afford a house full of children on only one salary.

Most of them had three or four children, and that was the best investment they could have made. Their kids sent real estate prices into the stratosphere in the 1980s, and subsequently they boosted the value of their parents' stock market holdings. Recently, some Depression kids have been cashing in these assets, using the proceeds to bolster their retirement nest eggs as well as for travel.

In 1996, 2.5 million Depression kids are living in Canada and still doing pretty well for themselves. They are holding down many of the senior jobs in this country — in government, in business, in major educational and other institutions. Some of them are smart and capable and some of them aren't. Few of them realize how much they owe their success to being part of a small cohort that has always been in the right place at the right time.

WORLD WAR II (1940 TO 1946)

For those who postponed having children because of the Depression, the biological clock was running out by the end of the 1930s and the early years of the 1940s. Then the war kick-started the economy — and the fertility rate. Canada, away from the main arenas of war, was a pretty good place to be. Canadians had plenty of food and jobs were plentiful. And so maternity wards started to fill up again. These war-time babies, the pre-boomers, number 2.2 million in 1996. They aren't as prosperous as the 1930s generation before them because more of them were born during each year. (The total number of Depression kids is larger because their cohort spans ten years, compared with only seven for the children of World War II.) On the other hand, the war babies haven't had nearly as much peer-group competition as those born in the following decade; so by comparison with everyone except the Depression kids, they've done extremely well.

Why did Canada experience a decline in births during World War I and an increase in births during World War II? A larger percentage of Canadian men went overseas during World War I than in World War II, and many more lost their lives: 60,661 in World War I, compared with 42,042 in World War II. Moreover, in August 1918, almost as many Canadians were killed by a worldwide influenza epidemic as fell victim to enemy fire during the war. Both calamities reduced the numbers of Canadians in the child-producing age groups. Another reason for the difference was that while World War I followed a period of prosperity and high fertility, World War II followed the Depression. People had been postponing having families in the 1930s, and those in a position to start having children during World War II were eager to do so. Yet another reason was that Canada's economy got a bigger boost from World War II than from World War I. During World War II Canada became a major producer of ships, cargo carriers, aircraft, tanks, and other military vehicles. As a result, Canadian incomes rose, and rising incomes always mean increased demand for everything, including children.

THE BABY BOOM (1947 TO 1966)

Even people with no knowledge of demographics have heard of the group born from 1947 to 1966. These are the baby-boomers. Some members of this particular cohort seem to think they are pretty special. To hear them talk, you'd think they were the most innovative and creative bunch of people Canada had ever seen, infusing all of society with new ways of thinking and new ways of doing things. This is nonsense. In fact, when they were 20, baby-boomers weren't much different from the 20-year-olds who had preceded them. And now that many of them are in their late 40s, they are behaving just as middle-aged people have always behaved.

The only thing special about the baby-boomers is that there are so many of them. It seems hard to imagine now, but at the height of the boom, Canadian women were averaging four offspring each. Canada produced more than 400,000 new Canadians in each year of the baby boom, peaking at 479,000 in 1959. But examining Canadian births alone isn't sufficient to define the baby boom. The largest single-year age group in Canada in the mid-1990s is those born in 1961, even though 3,600 fewer people were born here in that year than in 1959. That's because the 1961 group includes immigrants born in that year somewhere else. The most important demographic fact about 35-year-olds is how many of them there are in Canada in 1996, not how many people were born in Canada in 1961. The baby boom, both those born in Canada and those born elsewhere, totals 9.8 million people in 1996, almost 33% of the Canadian population.

Canada's was the loudest baby boom in the industrialized world. In fact, only three other Western countries — the United States, Australia, and New Zealand — had baby booms. Part of the reason was that these four countries were immigrant receivers, and immigrants tend to be in their 20s, the prime childbearing years. The U.S. boom started earlier, in 1946, and it also ended earlier, in 1964. That's why American periodicals in 1996 are full of articles about baby-boomers turning 50, an event that will be delayed until 1997 in Canada.

At its peak in 1957, the U.S. boom hit 3.7 children per family, nearly half a baby fewer than Canadian women were producing at the peak of the Canadian boom. The Americans started their boom earlier because more of their war effort was in the Pacific, and the Pacific war wound down sooner. The U.S. troops were brought home in 1945 and kids started appearing in 1946. Canadian troops came home later, so Canadian births did not leap upwards until 1947. As for the Australians, they never got much higher than three babies per woman, but they compensated by continuing their boom ten years longer than Canada did. That happened because Australians were slower to adopt the birth-control pill and because Australian women were slower than their North American counterparts to enter the work-force in large numbers.

Because the Canadian baby boom was so big, Canadian boomers are a slightly more important factor in Canadian life than American boomers are in American life. Fully one-third of Canadians today are boomers, and for that reason alone, when they get interested in a particular product or idea, we all have to sit up and take notice. It's not that the product or idea is so great, it's just that everyone seems to be talking about it. The result is that phenomena such as the return to "family values" are often mistakenly identified as new social trends rather than the predictable demographic events they really are. (There is nothing new or remarkable about 35-year-olds raising families being interested in family values.)

Why did the baby boom happen? A likely explanation is that during those 20 years, Canadians knew they could afford large families. The postwar economy was robust, the future seemed full of promise, and young couples wanted to share that bright future with a big family. A second reason was the high immigration levels that prevailed during the 1950s; immigrants tend to be people of childbearing age, and they made an important contribution to the boom. The combination of two ingredients — lots of people in their high fertility years and high incomes — is a surefire recipe for filling up maternity wards. But you need both: immigration levels were raised in the early years of the 1990s but the fertility rate didn't respond because incomes were falling, and Canadians, immigrants and non-immigrants alike, didn't think they could afford extra mouths to feed.

Why did the boom end? Towards the end of the 1960s, an increasing number of women were pursuing higher education or entering the workforce. As a result, they were postponing childbirth and deciding to have fewer children. The introduction of the birth-control pill made this easier than ever to achieve. The more rapid acceptance of the pill in the United States may explain why the American boom ended before Canada's.

Like the seniors, the boomers break down into separate subgroups. The front-end boomer, pushing 50, with a bulging waistline and equally bulging Registered Retirement Savings Plan, doesn't share much in the way of cultural attitudes or life experiences with the Generation-Xer, in his early 30s, whose career hasn't yet got off the ground and who has trouble scraping up rent money every month. But as boomers, they have one very important thing in common: they are part of a huge cohort. For the front-end boomers, this was an advantage they could exploit. For the back-end boomers of Generation X, it is the cause of most of their problems.

It's important to grasp this point because the mass media have thoroughly confused it. Newspaper articles often mix up Generation X with the baby-bust generation that followed it. Well into the 1990s, the media are still calling Gen-Xers "twenty-somethings" even though most of them have already celebrated their 30th birthdays. Some writers are so confused they seem to think Generation X is the children of the boomers. But it isn't. Most boomers weren't yet old enough to have children when Generation X came along. To clarify matters, we'll look at the characteristics of each subgroup of boomers in turn.

The front-end boomers have done pretty well for themselves. There are a lot of them, so they had to compete for jobs when they entered the workforce over the 1960s. But the entry of vast numbers of younger baby-boomers into the marketplace through the 1970s and 1980s created wonderful opportunities for the front-enders already entrenched in business and government. New products, new services, new government programs, new universities — it was a period of seemingly endless expansion. The front-end boomers got there first, so they are the ones in good jobs now in both the public and private sectors. They understand the needs of the baby boom because they are the leading edge of it.

Those born towards the end of the 1950s also understand the baby boom but, unlike the front-enders, they are less well positioned to profit from that knowledge. Generally, most members of this boomer subgroup have just managed to get a house. But that house is in the suburbs, and during the first part of the 1990s, its value crashed as the peak of the boom passed through its prime purchasing years. Most of these people are in a career, but that career seems to be going nowhere because the rungs ahead of them are clogged with older boomers who are still 15 to 20 years from retirement.

Things are tough for the late-1950s group, but not nearly as bad as for the back end that arrived just after them. These are the 2.6 million people born from 1960 to 1966. They are the same age as the characters in Douglas Coupland's novel *Generation X*, which gave the early-1960s group its name. Many of them are still living at home with their parents because, faced with horrendous obstacles in the labour market, they haven't been able to get their careers on track. That is why, while front-end boomers were earning 30% more than their fathers by age 30, back-enders were making 10% less than their fathers at the same age.

Gen-Xers' life experience has led them to distrust any sort of large institution, whether in the public or private sector. It didn't take them long to learn that, in an overcrowded world, they had no choice but to "look out for number one." On their first day in kindergarten, the Gen-Xers discovered there weren't enough seats for them. In elementary school, many of them were squeezed into portables. They have been part of a crowd ever since. Whether it was trying to enrol in a ballet class, get into a summer camp, or find a part-time job, waiting lists have been a way of life for Generation X.

The millions of baby-boomers who preceded them drove up rents, drove up house prices, and claimed all the best jobs and opportunities. As if that weren't enough, the Gen-Xers entered the labour market in the late 1970s and early 1980s, just when a brutal recession gripped the Canadian economy. In the best of circumstances, there would have been few jobs; in the recession there were virtually none. And when economic recovery finally began to create new demand for labour, the Gen-Xers were told they were too old for entry-level jobs and too short of experience for more senior ones. Is it any wonder we have 30-year-olds living at home in the mid-1990s?

One of the worst things the Gen-Xers have to cope with is their parents — the Depression generation. These are the 55-to-60-year-olds sitting at the top of the corporate ladder, approaching the end of very successful careers, and unable to fathom why their 30-year-old offspring are living at home. Tension is tremendous in these families. Often the father is certain that his own success is based solely on his own merit while he sees his son's failure as a result of lack of drive and ambition.

THE BABY BUST (1967 TO 1979)

The commercial introduction of the birth-control pill in 1961 and the rising participation of women in the labour market led to declining fertility over the 1960s. The result was a decline in births and a smaller cohort, often called the baby bust. In 1996, 5.4 million Canadians are in this cohort. The baby-busters have done pretty well so far, especially the younger ones. They have been able to get into just about any school or summer camp they wanted. They had no difficulty finding babysitting, lawn-mowing, and other part-time jobs in high school, unlike their older brothers and sisters, who had less opportunity to earn money while in high school because they had so many competitors. During the 1990s, university entry standards have been falling, making it easier for busters to get into the school of their choice.

There is good reason for the twenty-something of the mid-1990s to be both more realistic and more idealistic than the thirty-something of Generation X. In fact, the baby-busters resemble the front-end boomers, who could espouse idealistic causes during the 1960s safe in the knowledge that a good job and a prosperous lifestyle would be there for the taking once they were ready for those bourgeois things. But the back-end boomers, as we have seen, had no choice but to look out for their own best interests. They were less idealistic than their elders, not because they were worse people but because they couldn't afford to be idealistic. In contrast, the baby-busters have had a pretty good life so far, and when the world has treated you well, you have the luxury of being able to pay attention to social issues, such as peace, the environment, and AIDS, and therefore are more inclined to do so.

That's not to say there are no similarities between the Gen-Xers and the baby-busters. Both groups started their working careers in tough economic times when corporations were more interested in trimming payrolls than in hiring new staff. As a result, the older baby-busters face the same problems and frustrations that Generation X knows so well. But when the economy turns around, the 20-year-old with minimal experience will have better prospects than the 30-year-old with minimal experience. That's partly because employers usually prefer younger people for entry-level positions, because they are cheaper and more adaptable; partly because there are fewer busters than Gen-Xers; and partly because the busters are better equipped than the Gen-Xers with the computer skills that today's job market demands.

THE BABY-BOOM ECHO (1980 TO 1995)

These are the children of the boomers. The boomers were already having children in the 1970s, but by 1980 enough of them were reproducing to produce a mini-boom of their own. The boomers, however, never matched the reproductive prowess of their parents. At its peak, in 1990, the echo produced 406,000 babies from a population of 27.7 million, compared with 479,000 from a population of only 17.5 million in 1959. This generation is most noticeable in Ontario and western Canada. Quebec and the Atlantic provinces (except for Halifax) haven't had much of a baby-boom echo because so many of their boomers moved to Ontario and the western provinces and had their children there. So the echo won't have as much impact on society in eastern Canada as it will in Ontario and the west.

As of 1996, there are 6.9 million members of the echo generation. The boomers haven't finished having children, but over the remaining years of the decade the echo will dwindle to an end. This is predictable because most boomer women are past their prime childbearing years. Even if these women now decide they want big families, they won't be able to have them because they are too old.

What is the outlook for the echo kids? It won't be quite as smooth sailing as the baby-busters have had, but it won't be as disastrous as for Generation X either. These echo kids are part of a large cohort and that's always bad news. They crowded nurseries in the 1980s, pushed elementary school enrolments up in the late 1980s, and are about to do the same for high school enrolments in the mid-1990s. Like the baby boom, the echo has a front end, born in the 1980s, that will have an easier ride than its back end, born in the first half of the 1990s. The latter group, Generation X-II, will experience the familiar disadvantages of arriving at the rear of a large cohort. Think of a cohort as a group of people all wanting to get into the same theatre to see the same show. There is no reserved seating. So who claims the best seats? The ones who get there first. The back end of the echo generation, Gen X-II, will have a life experience similar to that of its parents, the first Generation X. Just as the first Gen-Xers have done, Gen X-II will have to scramble.

However, Gen X-II should be better prepared than its parents were to cope with high youth unemployment and other difficulties associated with a large cohort. That's because these kids have their Gen-X parents to teach them. By contrast, the original Generation X was the offspring of a small cohort that wasn't equipped to prepare them for the difficult world they encountered when they left home in the early 1980s.

THE FUTURE (1995 TO 2010)

These are the millennium kids, the generation that is following the baby-boom echo. The women producing them are the baby-busters, a cohort 19% smaller in each year than the baby-boomers and 45% smaller in total. Because of immigration, the millennium kids won't necessarily be 45% fewer than the echo kids, but they will definitely be a smaller group. As a result, as this book goes to press, we see another small, and therefore favoured, cohort emerging from Canada's maternity wards.

Chapter 2

The Real Estate Meltdown

One of the most melancholy sights in any Canadian city is the Incredible Hulk. Started in 1988, the Bay-Adelaide Centre, to give the building its official name, was going to be the brightest jewel in Toronto's glittering new downtown. That was a big boast indeed, because the boom in commercial construction that reshaped Toronto's skyline over the 1970s and 1980s was truly a sight to behold. The Royal Bank Plaza with its gold-sheathed exterior, the 72-storey First Canadian Place that was the Commonwealth's tallest building, and of course the soaring CN Tower — all these and many more transformed Toronto from Hogtown into what its boosters loved to call "the world's newest great city."

At a cost of $1 billion, the Bay-Adelaide Centre was to have two new office towers, including one of 57 stories, and a new urban park. In the middle of the 1990s, the park is there and so is an underground garage. But what was to be an ultra-modern office tower is a six-storey bunker, its raw concrete exterior streaked and filthy. It has no roof and empty holes where its windows should be. It looks more like war damage than what one would expect to see in the financial heart of Canada. But it wasn't bombs that destroyed the Incredible Hulk. It was a shortage of demand for office space. After months of dithering, the developers finally accepted the reality that hardly anyone wanted to rent space in their beautiful towers, certainly not at the rents needed to make the project economically viable. The construction crews were sent home.

The Incredible Hulk is usually explained away as the most visible symbol of the worst economic downturn since the Great Depression. But that's not all it is. More important, it is a costly lesson in demographic reality. The truth is that, even if the recession had not hit central Canada with the fury it did, Toronto did not need a new 57-storey office tower in the first years of the 1990s.

Real estate is about places for people to live in and work in. That's why real estate is driven far more by demographics than by economics. A growing population requires more goods and services and more people to provide them. The new labour-force entrants need new places to work in. But the late 1980s and early 1990s were years when the new entrants to the labour force were the baby-busters, those born in the years after the baby boom ended in 1966. There are fewer baby-busters than boomers, and that's why the demand for office space declined in the late 1980s.

Factors other than demographics do play some part in the success or failure of a real estate venture. Location, quality, property taxation, and economic cycles are all important. But the significance of these factors is consistently overrated by the industry itself, which is why many real estate companies that were big players ten years ago have become small players or have gone out of business. These companies failed because their owners ignored the overwhelming power of demographics. They understood the sophisticated intricacies of big-time real estate transactions, but they did not understand the obvious: if you erect a new office tower when hardly anyone is entering the labour force, you take a huge risk. If you build a building for the busters, chances are it's going to be a bust.

The Incredible Hulk is best viewed as a symbol not of the recession, but of the entire Canadian real estate industry for the rest of the 1990s. Because most of the needs of the boomers are filled, real estate is no longer a growth industry. That means it is a much better place to lose money than to make it in the 1990s. If you're a boomer who thinks your house is going to be your pension plan, think again. And if you're a real estate investor, unless you pick your spots brilliantly, you're not likely to make any money.

Let's put this in demographic context. The baby boom started in 1947 and ended in 1966. The typical Canadian enters the labour force at about the age of 20. During two momentous decades, from 1967 to 1986, more than one-third of the Canadian population entered the labour force and subsequently the housing market. In doing so, they transformed the skylines of Canada's cities. Until the boomers decided to leave home, Vancouver's West End consisted of rows of graceful old frame houses, and the only building more than three stories high was the Sylvia Hotel on English Bay. Now the Sylvia is dwarfed by a forest of highrise apartments in one of the most densely populated neighbourhoods in North America. Many would dispute whether this represents progress, just as others mourned the loss of many old buildings that fell to the wrecker's ball in the construction frenzy that reshaped the central cores of Montreal, Toronto, Calgary, and other Canadian and American cities.

Developers were not among the mourners. It was no accident that Canada, with the world's biggest baby boom, briefly boasted one of the world's great development industries. Olympia & York was the biggest office developer in the world, and others such as Campeau Corp., Trizec, and Bramalea made their mark right across North America. If these companies had paid attention to demographics, they would have known the boom could not continue. Just because there is a 30-year trend in an industry doesn't mean that trend will continue forever. That is especially true when the demographic realities that underlie the trend change significantly. In the case of commercial real estate, it was predictable at least 25 years ago that demand for new office space would stall over the last half of the 1980s because of the slowdown in labour-force growth. Yet even after the signs of drooping demand had begun to appear, developers continued to plan new office towers. Because they didn't understand demographics, they continued building for the future — a future when there would be fewer new workers needing new space to work in.

The recession of the first half of the 1990s loaded the deck even more against real estate because companies became more interested in firing than hiring. And at the same time, other factors were at work, with ominous implications. While the boomers were applying for their first jobs in the 1960s and 1970s, major Canadian employers had little incentive to automate, because armies of affordable workers were streaming onto the labour market every year. Why pay for expensive new machines when human labour can do the work for less? In the mid-1990s, the supply of new workers is shrinking at the same time as labour-saving equipment is dropping in price and rising in quality and effectiveness. These developments give employers every reason to embrace technology.

How does this affect the real estate industry? A computer requires less space than a person and it never insists on having its own office. Moreover, computers in combination with new communications technologies make it possible for people to work at home, with only occasional forays to the office. All these trends have contributed to cooling down demand for new office space. And of course, we have deregulation, globalization, and downsizing, three catchwords that translate into fewer jobs in both public and private sectors. When Bell Canada announces it will slash 10,000 people from its workforce shortly after a federal budget deems 45,000 civil servants surplus, then it's clear that our office towers will get emptier before they start to fill up again.

The one Canadian city where construction cranes are still in evidence at this writing is Vancouver. That's because Vancouver has faster population growth than the rest of the country, as a result of migration from other parts of Canada and abroad. But Vancouverites would do well to avoid smugness. British Columbia has had severe recessions in the past and it will not be immune from them in the future. Moreover, the prosperity of the real estate industry and that of the rest of us are not one and the same thing. A mere increase in a city's size doesn't mean that the incomes and well-being of the people who live there also increase. If it did, then the citizens of huge cities such as Mexico City and Calcutta would be wealthier than those of smaller ones such as Vancouver and Geneva. Economic growth can and does occur in the context of a stable population and in the absence of construction cranes. The point is simply that without large numbers of new labour-force entrants and a high rate of new family formation, real estate is a lousy investment.

What is true of commercial real estate is equally true of residential real estate. During those same two momentous decades — 1967 to 1986 — about 9 million Canadians left their parents' homes and set up households of their own. Inevitably, this created a phenomenal boom in residential real estate. It was just as inevitable that once the boomers were housed, the boom would end.

To understand the future of residential real estate in Canada, we need to understand the normal behaviour of people, baby-boomers or anyone else, when they enter the housing market. You leave your parents' house at the same time you enter the labour force, about age 20. But you don't buy a house then because you can't afford it and you are not ready to settle down anyway. So you rent. Over the next ten to fifteen years, you find a partner and establish a family. So you buy a house. In another ten years or so, in your 40s, you may be ready to move up to a better house or to renovate the one you have. You're also primed, if you can afford it, to buy a country property.

The movement of the huge baby-boom generation through these cycles has driven the real estate industry in Canada since 1967, Canada's centennial year. That year is fondly remembered for Montreal's wonderful Expo 67. But an even more significant event was going unnoticed at about the same time: the first boomers were tumbling out of the family nest and into the housing market. Only a third of them had left home by 1975 but their impact was already enormous: apartment vacancy rates everywhere were in free fall, triggering an explosion in rents that in turn led to rent controls in all ten provinces. Demand continued to increase through the 1970s, but rent controls killed the market's ability to respond. As a result, in those parts of urban Canada most sought after by young boomers, key money — a chunk of cash under the table — was required for the privilege of renting even the most dismal basement suite. For the next ten years, vacancy rates stayed down and rents stayed up.

Then came 1986, the year the last boomers left home. For rental housing in Canada, that was a key turning point because the baby-bust generation that followed is 45% smaller than the baby-boom cohort. So demand for accommodation, as was perfectly predictable, was about to drop. The inevitability of this development was independent of the recession that struck most of Canada in the 1990s. It would have happened even in an economic boom. By 1988, sure enough, vacancies were rising, especially at the high-priced end of the rental housing market, and through the 1990s we have continued to experience a falling rental market instead of a growing one. The recession, by forcing people to double up or live with their parents, aggravated the plight of the rental business.

No relief is in sight over the rest of the 1990s because the people entering the rental market are those born during the 1970s, and there aren't many of them. But there is a light at the end of the tunnel. The echo generation, which started in 1980, will venture out into the housing market around 2000. The echo kids are a comparatively large group, and so the demand for apartments to rent will start up again. Vacancy rates will drop and, by about 2005, unless governments impose rent controls again, we may see construction of new rental buildings in Canada. But it's important to note that this phenomenon will take place only in those parts of the country — Ontario, the west, and perhaps Halifax — that actually have an echo generation. Other parts of Canada have suffered an exodus of baby-boomers and, as a result, won't have a large group of boomer offspring needing apartments.

In real estate markets, factors other than demographics can sometimes delay the inevitable. That's what happened in the market for owner-occupied homes in the first years of the 1980s. The leading-edge members of the baby-boom generation were moving into their 30s, when their thoughts should have been turning to buying houses. That didn't happen. One reason was that all of Canada was mired in recession. Another was that we had outrageous interest rates. Yet another was that these same front-end boomers who should have been buying houses were occupying the best rent-controlled apartments and saw no immediate advantage to giving them up.

So the movement of front-end boomers out of rentals and into owner-occupied homes was delayed until the mid-1980s. By then, the first five years of boomers had accumulated enough money for a down-payment on a home. They had kids. They wanted backyards. The economy was growing again and interest rates were dropping.

And the housing market went crazy.

Those days of houses selling for more than their asking price and then doubling in value seem like ancient history in the mid-1990s. In fact, they should have lasted longer than they did. The housing market should have continued to show growth right through to the early 1990s, because the late boomers were still entering their house-buying years then. Price increases would inevitably have slowed down because the late boomers, the Gen-Xers, are less numerous and less well off than the front-enders, and making the jump from rental to owning was harder for them. But demand would have remained strong had it not been for the arrival in the early 1990s of a severe recession marked by high real interest rates that still haven't gone away. (The spread between interest rates and the rate of inflation, which is the "real" interest rate, is still relatively high in Canada, although actual interest rates have come down in recent years.)

As a result, many of the Gen-Xers — those born between 1960 and 1966 — continue to wait for a chance to buy their first house. Moreover, because of the uncertain economy, not much new housing has been built in the 1990s. That combination — lack of new supply plus pent-up demand — is a volatile one. It could result in one last mini-surge in house prices before the 1990s are over.

After that, houses will be what they were before the boomers entered the housing market, places to live in rather than investments. Boomers who think they will be able to sell their houses in, say, 2010 and live in luxury thereafter on the proceeds will be in for a surprise, because they are not going to realize profits anything like those the pre-boomers currently cashing in their houses are enjoying. That's because the advent of the baby-busters will put a damper on demand for owner-occupied accommodation just as it did for rental. The busters will see to it that supply of housing exceeds demand through the first decade of the new century. Only in the second decade of the 21st century, when the first members of the echo generation start house-hunting, will prices recover again.

What do demographics tell us about other real estate trends for the rest of the 1990s? They tell us that some kinds of real estate will continue to appreciate while other kinds will decline or stabilize. They also tell us that the movement back to the suburbs will continue and that the renovation business will pick up steam. Let's deal with each of these phenomena in turn.

"Real estate is turning into a stock market," observes David Cork, an Ottawa stockbroker for Scotia McLeod, who creates investment portfolios for his clients based on a keen appreciation of demographics. "On any given day, some stocks go up and some go down," he says. "In real estate, we are seeing the same thing."

In a genuine real estate boom, almost everything goes up in value. That's no longer true. In the 1990s and beyond, only those with the knowledge and insight to buy the right property in the right place at the right time can expect to turn a profit in real estate. This is already the case in Canada's healthiest major real estate market, the lower mainland of British Columbia. House price fluctuations in this part of Canada look very much like David Cork's stock market listings. In 1995, for example, a three-bedroom bungalow in suburban Richmond was off 11% while a similar house in the North Shore suburb of West Vancouver was up 11%. A four-bedroom executive home on the west side of Vancouver city rose in value by 4%, while a comparable house in suburban Maple Ridge lost 12% of its value. And so on.

These numbers suggest that if a commodity is desired by the baby-boomers, it is likely to go up in value, because the boomers are the largest group in society and one of the most affluent. Houses in certain parts of urban Canada are among the commodities that affluent boomers want. These front-end boomers are already living in, or aspire to live in, prestigious, long-established neighbourhoods such as those on the west side of Vancouver. Homes in such neighbourhoods tend to be older and may need costly repairs and renovations. But that is their only disadvantage. On the plus side, they are spacious and have large yards. They tend to be close to the downtown core, a crucial consideration for time-starved boomers. Finally, their size makes them

adaptable to the changes coming in the first decade of the next century, when the rental market will pick up while demand for large
family homes drops. Many big houses in central neighbourhoods will
then be converted into luxury flats. This phenomenon is already well
advanced in Toronto's Rosedale.

Homes in these good, inner-city districts will continue to enjoy
modest increases in value through the rest of the 1990s. Meanwhile,
once the Gen-Xers are accommodated, starter homes in the distant suburbs of the major cities will begin to decline in value or, at best, maintain stable prices. That's because the baby-bust generation, who will
make up much of the market for starter homes in the years after 2000,
is smaller than the boomers.

The slowdown in demand for starter homes means boomers
aspiring to move up won't be able to extract high prices for the homes
they are selling. That in turn will put a brake on prices of homes in
the boomer-occupied areas. And once the bulk of the baby boom is in
its retirement years, even homes in Canada's most desirable neighbourhoods — such as Shaughnessy (Vancouver), Rockcliffe Park
(Ottawa), and Forest Hill (Toronto) — will decline in value. The conclusion is clear: even in Canada's best urban neighbourhoods, the days
of rapid and huge increases in house prices are gone. The real estate
boom is over.

Younger people generally like the bright lights of the big city.
They want to be where the action is. That's why most rental accommodation is downtown or near colleges and universities. As the early
boomers moved out of their parents' homes in the late 1960s and
1970s, the inner city became the place to be, and we celebrated the
revival of Old Strathcona in Edmonton, Old Montreal, the Historic
Properties in Halifax, and False Creek in Vancouver. In Toronto,
affluent front-end boomers (also known as yuppies) transformed Cab-
bagetown into a new haven of chic, where drunks and street people
watched in amazement as renovators lavished huge sums on old
working-class houses. This was the ultimate in gentrification.

But did gentrification represent a value shift, as so many people assumed, a rejection of suburban conformity in favour of the free

and easy lifestyle of the inner city? Not really. In fact, it was just young people behaving as they always have, but because there were so many of them it looked like a new trend. Gradually, over the 1980s, growth switched back from the urban centres to the suburbs. Again, people were doing what comes naturally. The massive baby-boom generation was having kids and wanted bigger backyards as well as spacious garages for its minivans. So suburbanization replaced urbanization. This growth of the suburbs will continue through the 1990s.

But the impact of suburbanization should not be exaggerated. A major reason why Canada's three major cities — Toronto, Montreal, and Vancouver — consistently place near the top in global rankings of urban liveability is their relatively healthy downtown cores. In the United States, by contrast, the demographic phenomenon of boomers heading for the suburbs combined with severe social and racial problems to turn some large cities into urban doughnuts — a hole in the middle where the centre used to be, surrounded by a ring of thriving suburbs.

The cores of Canadian cities will remain healthy for four reasons. First, the large echo generation will move from the suburbs into the city centres in the first decade of the next century. Although there aren't enough echo kids to recreate the downtown boom of the 1970s and 1980s, there are enough of them to ensure that downtown remains alive. Second, Canada has high levels of immigration, and immigrants, as a group, tend to be younger than the Canadian-born. The housing preferences of young immigrants are the same as those of the young Canadian-born. Young new Canadians will settle in the inner city while their elders head for the burbs. Third, a small percentage of aging boomers — smaller than is commonly believed — will resist the call of the boondocks and trade in their large homes for downtown condos. These sophisticated older boomers will be a valuable addition to the mix that will keep our big cities good places to live as we head into the 21st century. Finally, Canada still has many young boomers — Generation X — without a lot of money. For them, buying an older house in a moderately priced downtown area and fixing it up may be more affordable than buying a newer house in a more expensive area.

The average age of first-time homebuyers is the early to middle 30s. This age varies by location, being lower in more affordable areas. The average age of those trading in their first home for something better is the middle 40s. That's where the front end of the baby boom is in the mid-1990s. Their kids, the echo generation that started arriving on the scene in 1980, are teenagers. Many of these kids are noisy and annoying — in other words, typical teenagers. They are demanding more space and more independence. Mom and Dad, who could use some peace and quiet, would love to give it to them. That means a bigger house where the two generations can practise peaceful coexistence. Expect a lot of action in the move-up market in the late 1990s as the boomers make space for their teenagers.

Some boomers will discover they can't get the price for their existing home that they need if they are to afford something much better. Instead, they will stay put and renovate or build an addition. The result will be boom times for the renovation business. The downturn in real estate in recent years has devastated the profession of architecture. Some firms have closed, others have downsized, and talented people have left the profession. No major rebound is in sight because real estate is no longer a growth industry. But architects who make quality renos a specialty have a good chance to prosper in the years to come. But the key word here is quality. These front-end boomers are a demanding lot and they won't tolerate shoddy workmanship. (See Chapter 5.) Architects and building contractors who can deliver good work on time will do well. The other kind won't.

A third response to the need for space is the second house, the cottage by the water or the condo near the ski slopes. Most Canadians live in large cities, but the call of the wild remains deeply ingrained in the Canadian psyche. As the boomers' kids move into their teen years, their parents' desire for a country retreat becomes more intense. Partly this desire is based on the hope that the pull of the recreational property will counteract the natural tendency of teens to drift away from the family as they begin the difficult process of becoming adults. Conversely, the second home is also a way to maintain family harmony through the strategy of providing more space.

Mom and Dad get some peace and quiet in the country while their teenagers enjoy the independence of being home alone in the noisy city for the weekend.

Whatever the motive, we know that the over-45 age group contains the largest group of owners of country properties, and we know that, in the 1990s, the baby-boomers are streaming into that age group. That's why leisure and recreational property will be a strong segment of the real estate market for the rest of the decade. This won't be a boom such as rental housing had in the 1970s or owner-occupied housing enjoyed in the 1980s. That's because, although everybody has to have a home base, only a relatively affluent minority can afford a second home in the country. But there will be enough of these to put considerable pressure on the price of recreational property located within a reasonable distance of our major cities. Currently only 8% of Canadian families own a leisure property. By the turn of the century, a significantly higher percentage of Canadians will own second homes.

While the biggest Canadian real estate companies were being hammered by recession during the first years of the 1990s, one company, Vancouver-based Intrawest Corp., continued to prosper. That was partly because most of Intrawest's assets are on the west coast, which has had rapid population growth and which avoided the worst of the recession. Another reason is that Intrawest's managers have a keener understanding of the realities of Canadian demographics than most of their competitors. Intrawest has always understood what the boomers needed and when they needed it. That's how it has managed to outperform the Toronto Stock Exchange's index of real estate companies by 700% since going public in 1990.

Because it knows where the boomers are headed, Intrawest has decided to concentrate on the resort business. "The last frontier of real estate in this century is vacation homes," says Joe Houssain, Intrawest's chairman. The managers in charge of developing the land around Intrawest's four-season resort at Mont Tremblant, in the Laurentians north of Montreal, have been surprised at the number of people interested in having their larger house near the mountain and keeping a smaller home in city — the reverse of the normal pattern.

Some of these people will be able to continue their working careers in a mountainside home office (sometimes called a "hoffice"), with occasional visits to see clients or other key contacts in Montreal. This is a variation on a trend that is going to accelerate through the 1990s and into the new century: the movement of the baby-boomers away from the urban areas.

This shift away from the big cities means that the outlook is very promising for Canada's smaller cities. Some early and pre-boomers in the B.C. lower mainland are already cashing in their city homes for big profits and moving to the interior of the province. This is an early manifestation of what will be an important trend by the next century, when large numbers of front-end boomers start to take early retirement. In Ontario, there will be a movement from greater Toronto to smaller cities to the east and west of the megalopolis, such places as Guelph to the west, Collingwood to the north, and Kingston to the east. These cities will have a chance to attract an influx of well-educated, affluent people who will expand the local tax base and make a positive contribution to the community, for example by supporting cultural and charitable causes. On the other hand, local municipalities will be faced with new costs associated with providing the serviced land and other requirements of an expanding population.

These retiring newcomers won't want to settle in the centres of their new small cities. Most will be looking for five-to-ten-acre lots in the suburbs. Others will be attracted by new residential communities built around golf courses. Their arrival will create a major challenge for local politicians and planners: how to expand without falling victim to the sort of urban sprawl that would destroy the small-city charm that is among these cities' chief assets. The front-end boomers will want a small-town atmosphere, but at the same time they are unwilling to give up such urban amenities as good restaurants and shopping. The cities with the best planners, who can figure out the best ways of balancing these conflicting demands, will win the contest to attract retiring boomers to the local tax rolls. Perhaps most important of all as the massive baby-boom generation enters its 50s and 60s will be health care facilities. Boomers are less likely to relocate to a community that lacks a top-notch hospital. Hospitals that are viewed as a financial burden in the mid-1990s will be an important economic development tool for some small cities and rural districts after the turn of the century. (See Chapter 9.) After 2010, many small communities will also be the sites of new retirement communities to house the World War II generation and the early boomers. (See Chapter 3.)

This demographics-driven movement back to small-town and rural Canada has important environmental implications. Rural land surrounding small cities is going to rise in value. Providing sewage, fire, and police services in formerly rural communities will be difficult. The pressure on farmland will increase. So will the pressure on forests and aquifers. These are priceless resources that must be protected for the generations to come. That should be done before the newcomers arrive, because once they are installed it will be much harder to impose new regulations. The time to start preparing for the movement of the boomers from the big cities to the small ones is the decade of the 1990s. Let's not wait to be surprised by the inevitable once again.

Chapter 3

Demographic Investing

D avid Cork, an Ottawa stockbroker and investment adviser, recommended early in the 1990s that his clients buy shares in U.S. Shoe, a company whose operations included Lenscrafters, a well-known retailer of eyeglasses. Cork, who bases his investment strategies on demographics, reasoned that rising sales by Lenscrafters would eventually push up the value of this under-performing stock for an obvious demographic reason: 80% of people over 40 need eyeglasses, and millions of baby-boomers across North America had already turned 40 or were about to. The market was undervaluing U.S. Shoe, Cork explained, because the market doesn't understand demographics.

The trouble was that the market continued not understanding demographics even after Cork's clients bought the stock. Although he explained that demographics are a long-term phenomenon, not a get-rich-quick scheme, his clients, watching the stock flounder several years after buying it, started to lose patience. Then in 1995, an Italian eyeglass manufacturer, Luxottica Group Spa., decided it wanted a piece of the growing North American market for eyeglasses and launched a takeover bid for U.S. Shoe. The stock doubled in value overnight and Cork's investors got their reward.

Because there are so many baby-boomers, they exert a dramatic impact on markets. The reason is simple: people of the same age tend to have the same needs at about the same time, eyeglasses being one example. Whether you are a boomer or not, you can make money by anticipating those needs. That is demographics-based investing.

Investors can choose among four kinds of assets: real estate, fixed-income investments (including bonds, treasury bills, and bank deposits), stocks, and collectibles (such as art, antiques, classic cars, stamps, and coins). In an aging population, stocks are the most promising. This chapter will examine the reasons why the stock market has a bright future in Canada and will suggest what sorts of stocks are most likely to do well as the population ages. There are plenty of potential U.S. Shoes out there. You just have to know how to spot them.

The case of Chrysler is instructive. The minivan, the wheels of the baby boom, turned Chrysler into a profitable carmaker. Yet at the time this new vehicle was being developed, Chrysler's stock was worth only US$2 and its management was begging for government help to fend off bankruptcy. At the same time, General Motors and Ford also had minivan prototypes in the planning stages. But Chrysler moved first, launching the MagicWagon in 1983. In the mid-1990s its stock has been trading at around US$50.

In North America, Chrysler was in the right place — the minivan — at the right time, just as the baby-boomers were producing children and needing roomier, but not too expensive, cars. Being in the right place at the right time has always been the secret to successful investing, but it's much easier said than done. The advantage of demographics is that they give us a road map to find that place and time. When you live in a country where almost a third of the population is reaching the same stage of life over the same 20-year period, then you own an investment road map drawn on a large scale.

In retrospect, it seems amazing that so many of us were surprised by the real estate boom of the 1970s and 1980s. Starting in the late 1960s and continuing for 20 years, more than 9 million people left their parents' homes and needed places of their own to live in. We knew they weren't all going to pitch tents on rural communes. We knew most of them would want apartments and houses in the major cities of Canada. We knew that the supply of land, and therefore of apartments and houses, in those cities was limited. Finally, we knew, or should have known, about the law of supply and demand, which states that if demand for a commodity increases faster than supply, the price of that commodity will rise. So when apartment rents and house prices soared, why was anyone taken by surprise?

The Canadian real estate boom was not only predictable, it was inevitable. (See Chapter 2.) People whose eyes were open to the obvious made fortunes buying and selling urban real estate in Canada. During that period, when the members of a generation as large as the entire population of Ontario were all singing the same tune — "Gimme shelter" — real estate was the best asset to invest in. But by the 1990s, most of the boomers had made their entry into the real estate market. As a result, demand dropped and the real estate market went flat. Those who were caught holding highly leveraged real estate investments were punished for ignoring demographic reality. When demand moves on, the bubble bursts. That too is demographics-based investing.

In a young population, money, like real estate, is a commodity in demand. In the 1970s and 1980s, some commentators expressed despair that Canadians, renowned for their tendency to save, had suddenly become big spenders. This was an example of how easily a phenomenon based purely on demographics can be mistaken for a value shift. In fact, people in their 40s and 50s were still saving during those decades. But at the same time, more than 9 million young adults were entering the job and housing markets and buying their first cars, furniture, and appliances while many of them were trying to pay off student loans. How and what were they supposed to save?

Just as the price of real estate went up because a huge number of people wanted it at the same time, so did the price of money. That's why we witnessed the incredible spectacle of Canadian banks paying double-digit interest rates on savings accounts. But by the mid-1990s, the baby-boom generation has bought most of the houses, appliances, and cars it needs. The baby-bust generation that is entering the labour and housing markets is smaller than the boom, and many busters aren't yet in a position to qualify for credit. As a result, the demand for money has flattened just as the real estate market has flattened, and interest rates have declined. Meanwhile, both public and private debt remain at record high and, to some, very worrisome levels.

Canadians are still great savers, and many older investors cling to the hope that the lucrative interest rates of 1981 will soon return. Demographics say that won't happen. Older people lend to younger people as well as to companies and governments. Through the 1970s and into the 1980s, many younger people were putting tremendous pressure on the money of a much smaller number of older people. But in the mid-1990s the peak-age baby-boomer is in his mid-30s and he's starting to pay down his mortgage. The baby boom as a group is paying off debt at a rapid clip and gradually transforming itself from a generation of borrowers to a generation of savers and lenders. The result is that debt levels will decline in the years ahead. At the same time, because both the boomers and the generations that preceded them will be competing to lend to a much smaller generation, the baby bust, interest rates will also decline.

What does this changed demographic environment mean for the future of interest rates? In answering that question, one should keep in mind that loan demand is not the only factor that determines interest rates. Government fiscal and monetary policies, domestic political uncertainty, and economic and political events outside Canada all play a part. But those are usually short-term phenomena. Over the long term, the composition and economic behaviour of the population are the most important determinants of the price of money. Demographics tell us that for the foreseeable future Canada will have more savers and fewer spenders, and that means the price of money — the interest rate — will decline.

We will be living in this low-interest-rate world for many years to come. But it does not follow that Canadians should or could abandon all fixed-income investments. In fact, in a period of falling interest rates, quality long-term bonds are an attractive investment that offer both safety and the possibility of capital gains. Moreover, most investors will want balanced portfolios that include such fixed-income instruments as guaranteed investment certificates (GICs) and federal treasury bills.

When you buy a treasury bill, you are lending money to the

government. And because bank deposits will outstrip dem
sumer and business loans, the banks will also find themselves .
money to the government. This is a positive development for Canaa..
because it means we will be able to repatriate much of our foreign
debt, which stood at $342 billion in 1995. When the government's
creditors are in Canada, the interest they earn is spent in Canada,
creating growth and employment. Moreover, if we don't need other
people's money, we won't need to raise our own rates whenever the
United States or some other foreign creditor raises its rates. In an inter-
dependent world of global capital flows, we will never have interest
rates made entirely in Canada. But as savers bring more of the national
debt back home, they will also increase Canadian control over Canadian interest rates.

Although low interest rates are good for the national treasury,
they are not good for people saving for retirement. If all a person's
money is in GICs paying 5% or less, her savings won't grow quickly
enough to deliver the income she will need to enjoy her retirement
years. Savers need to find investments that offer a higher rate of return.
That brings us to the stock market. The boomers are going to put an
ever larger portion of their retirement savings into stocks because,
given the low returns available on real estate and cash, they have no
acceptable alternative. And because they have little time and want
their money professionally managed, they will focus their attention on
quality mutual funds. Equity mutual funds are Canada's next investment boom.

The future doesn't just arrive suddenly one day. There are
always early warning signs. House prices in parts of urban Canada
spiked up as early as 1974, even though only a handful of front-end
boomers had yet acquired enough cash for a down-payment on a
house. That was the real estate boom announcing itself well before
it arrived in full force. Similarly, 1993 was an advance signal of the
future of equity mutual funds. Interest rates were lower and stocks
were enjoying a banner year. "GIC refugees" bailed out of fixed-income
investments and poured huge sums into equity funds. For many, this
was their first experience with an asset that carried the risk of loss of

capital. Sure enough, the next year saw a sub-par performance by the stock market, scaring some of the refugees back to GICs.

But as Canadians become older and more knowledgeable, they will learn that over the long term, common stocks outperform other investment vehicles. Moreover, dividends from stocks get more favourable tax treatment than interest from bonds or treasury bills. "The biggest risk Canadians have over the next 20 years is not to be invested," says David Cork. "In fact, over the last 100 years the biggest risk has always been not to be invested. The worry I have is that when the stock market takes off, it could be very rapid. It happened the same way with real estate. You didn't see a nice calm annual increase — it just took off. I think we are going to see that again."

To some, this sort of prediction will seem starry-eyed. But in the context of Canadian demographics and the Canadian investment environment, it is not far-fetched. In general, the incomes of people under 40 are completely committed to raising families and paying down debts, while people over 40 gradually have more discretionary income. By 2006, the entire 9.8-million-strong baby-boom generation will be in the 40-to-60 group of savers. Both the boomers and the World War II generation have two strong incentives in the mid-1990s to save for retirement: an unwillingness to be totally dependent on public or company pension plans, and the tax advantages available to those who invest in Registered Retirement Savings Plans (RRSPs). Regulations require 80% of an RRSP to be Canadian content, which greatly increases the demand for Canadian stocks. In an era of low interest rates, well-managed equity funds — some boasting average annual rates of return over ten years in the 10% range — are increasingly attractive as vehicles for RRSP investments.

The movement of Canadians' savings into mutual funds is already well under way. Between 1992 and 1995, the mutual fund industry's assets doubled to $137 billion, of which about 40% was in equity funds. The big banks set up mutual fund operations to grab a share of this fast-growing business, and other new players also arrived on the scene. The result was to present consumers with a wide and often confusing array of new investment products.

Jonathan Wellum, manager of the AIC Advantage Fund, which invests in money management companies, predicts that Canadians will have $500 billion invested in mutual funds by 2002. Wellum's investment strategy is based on the demographic fact that by 2000, half of the Canadian population will be 37 or over, and increasingly relying on the financial services provided by the companies that his fund holds. "That's savings age, a fabulous population distribution for wealth management companies," he says.

Cork sees one big difference between the real estate boom and the coming equity boom. Canadians were able to invest in billions of dollars worth of real estate located from St. John's to Victoria. But Canada has only one major stock market: the Toronto Stock Exchange. "Imagine if all of the boomers were going to affect one real estate market the way they are going to affect one stock market. We've seen the power they have. Now they are going to funnel money into one commodity — a very small number of stocks."

His point is that Canada has few powerful companies that qualify as blue-chip stocks. In the years to come, demand for such equities is likely to grow more quickly than supply, with results comparable to the real estate boom. The price of many stocks will outpace the earnings growth of the companies whose ownership they represent. In other words, stock prices will be more reflective of the demand for stocks than of the ability of a company to produce dividends. A similar phenomenon happened in Japan during the 1970s and 1980s, when savers who could not afford real estate and shunned the low returns offered by bank deposits pushed the price of stocks to astronomical levels. At that time, Japan, like the Canada of the near future, was a country with more savers than spenders. The reason was demographic: fertility in Canada declined in the late 1960s, but in Japan fertility declined in the late 1940s after two atomic bombs were dropped on the country.

Japanese stock prices eventually came down to earth with a thud as retired Japanese started to sell their equity holdings. Canadian stocks are no more likely than Japanese stocks to move in only one direction. That's why wise financial planners advise their clients to maintain balanced portfolios, whose proportion of equities diminishes as the investor approaches retirement.

The similarities between the investment environments of Japan in the 1970s and Canada in the 1990s should not be exaggerated. A major difference is that Canadian real estate, unlike Japanese real estate, is affordable to the average income earner, with the result that Canadians will continue to keep a large part of their assets in houses and cottages. Nevertheless, there is room for a major increase in stock buying by Canadians. Canadians contributed $19.2 billion to RRSPs in 1993, but that was only 20% of the $97.9 billion that they could have sheltered from taxes in that year. The reason RRSP contributions were not higher was that the majority of boomers under 40 were still paying down their mortgages and had nothing left over for RRSPs. That will change in the years ahead. RRSP contributions, as fast as they have been growing in the past few years, have the potential to grow five times faster. Much of that growth will be in equity funds.

For those interested in choosing their own stocks, the question remains: How do you spot a company that is poised to benefit from inevitable changes in consumer needs and desires caused by an aging population? When the baby boom was young, Japanese automakers grabbed a major share of the North American market by producing the cheap small cars young people needed. Then it was the turn of Chrysler and the minivan. Chrysler was a case of a company serving a broad market that came up with a new product that a large demographic cohort needed. Easier for investors to identify are those companies whose existing products and services are in increasing demand as the population ages. These include companies operating in such industries as financial services, pharmaceuticals, health care, and gambling.

In considering investments in industries like these, it must never be forgotten that demographics-based investing is not a way to get rich quick. Rather, it is a strategy for identifying long-term trends that will lead to long-term growth in various sectors of the economy. It is also a useful analytical tool for the investor. Suppose, for example, that your broker recommends a biotechnology stock whose main strength is some promising research into fertility. Techniques for boosting fertility have been a growth area for the past decade as women who delayed motherhood into their 30s found they needed help to conceive. In the mid-1990s, however, the baby-boom generation is pushing 40 and 50, and an increasing percentage of boomer women are too old to conceive, with or without fertility aids. A large percentage of the female population in other developed countries is also too old to have babies. As for the rest of the world, it needs help with birth control, not fertility. These facts don't necessarily doom a new fertility product to failure, but demographics tell us that such a product doesn't have the growth prospects in the future that it would have had ten years earlier.

Demographic analysis can help the investor, but a simplistic use of demographics can be dangerous. It must be kept in mind that in the Canadian context, population aging means increasing demand for goods and services required by *older* people, not *old* people. By 2000, the largest demographic cohort, the 9.8 million baby-boomers, will be 34 to 53. That's older, not old. In fact, by 2000, only 13% of Canada's population will be 65 or over. Many other developed countries will still be older than Canada. (See Chapter 11.) It must also be remembered that as the front-end boomers get older, increasing numbers of them will die. This will increase the relative importance of younger Canadians — Generation X (the back-end boomers), the baby bust, and the baby-boom echo — in Canadian society. Finally, let's not forget that Canada is a trading nation that sells its products all over the world. This means that a Canadian company whose products appeal mainly to young people is not necessarily a poor investment if it can export successfully to countries with young populations.

It is a sad fact but true that most people do more research before buying a car than before making an investment. In a time when governments are under severe pressure to weaken the public pension scheme, people who want to enjoy their golden years in comfort and style had better start accumulating some gold. To be successful, both investments and investment advisers should be chosen very carefully.

Some of these advisers charge commissions on every financial transaction. This gives them an incentive to trade securities in a client's portfolio frequently. But demographics-based investing is founded on the idea of selecting solid companies in industries certain to grow over the medium to long term because of demographic change and holding on to them. Such an investment strategy is ill suited to frequent buying and selling of stocks. The investor basing his moves on demographics would be better off with an investment adviser who is rewarded on a fee basis rather than by commissions.

With those caveats in mind, let's look briefly at some of the industries that can't help but grow as the average age of Canadians increases. The following is the demographic big picture that points the way to areas of the economy that will grow as the age structure of the population changes. The actual stock picking is up to individual investors and their financial advisers.

FINANCIAL SERVICES

As they age, people's financial priorities change. They move from debt management to asset management. When you are young, you are a borrower. In your 30s, you are earning income to pay off the money you borrowed in your 20s and early 30s. In your 40s and 50s, you are trying to build a nest egg for retirement. Except for Generation X, all of the baby boom will be over 40 by 2000. This means the financial services industry has a huge new customer base. Not only have these people reached the stage where they can let some of their earnings accumulate, but many of them will be coming into inheritances as their parents die.

It's estimated that $1 trillion will pass from Canadians now over 55 to younger generations. But the economic impact of these inheritances should not be exaggerated. For one thing, the total may not reach $1 trillion; many people spend large sums on health care in their last few years, and older Canadians may be spending more because of cutbacks to the health care system. And this transfer of assets, large though it may be, may do little for the economy if the bulk of the inheritances goes to the boomers. Money willed from an

85-year-old to a 55-year-old merely passes from one saver to another. The money is already in the economy, and it won't stimulate much new economic activity beyond fees for lawyers and brokers. Moreover, these legacies will be split up into several pieces and so into relatively small amounts. After all, the reason Canada had a baby boom was that, for a 20-year period, Canadian couples were producing three and four children each. On the other hand, money that passes from grandparents to grandchildren, from people born before 1940 to people born after 1967, *will* give a boost to the economy. This money will flow to baby-busters or to members of the echo generation, who will spend it on cars, houses, and other necessities of life. Money that is willed to charities will also tend to stimulate new economic activity because much of it will fall into the hands of poor people, who are spenders.

People acquiring large sums of money in one lump sum need advice to help them invest it wisely. Some money will be moving out of real estate owned by parents and into mutual funds and other investment vehicles sold by the financial services industry. As a result, investment dealers, law firms, mutual fund companies, financial planners, and banks are poised for major growth over the next two decades. Finally, insurance will also benefit from demographic trends. An older population has accumulated a lot of valuables that need insuring. An older population also produces a large number of travellers, who need travel insurance.

The stocks of well-managed players in the financial services industry will grow in this climate. But investors should remember that while the financial services industry holds great promise over the long term, it will continue to be subject to short-term volatility. The AIC Advantage Fund, which invests in money management companies, lost a whopping 15% of its value in 1994 when the stock market was in the dumps. But because 1993 was so good, its average return for the two years was 20%. Has the average 35-year-old bought all the mutual funds he is ever going to buy, or has he just started? The investor's answer to that question will determine whether she decides to invest in the financial services industry.

HEALTH CARE SERVICES

As people get older, their bodies start to wear out. That is why an older population needs more health care services than a younger population. Canadians' bodies are starting to wear out just as governments are putting a lid on health care expenditures. The confluence of these two events creates an opening that private industry is sure to exploit. This health industries sector will blossom in the years ahead, bringing with it new opportunities for investors sharp enough to spot them.

Many of these opportunities will arise from the restructuring of the health care delivery system. Partly to cut costs and partly in response to changes in medical practice, hospital stays are being shortened. This means that care formerly delivered in publicly funded hospitals is being transferred to the home. Some of this care will be delivered free by relatives of the patient — that's why the move to home care is such a popular cost-cutting device for provincial governments. But there is a gap between the services that hospitals used to provide and the services that families of sick people are capable of providing. These missing services could include follow-up treatments, health maintenance, or physiotherapy as well as delivery of meals, doing laundry, and housecleaning. Health care entrepreneurs are going to develop systems to deliver these services profitably in ways that will allow new companies to grow to meet the surging demand for home care. These new businesses will employ health care consultants, doctors, nurses, pharmacists, chefs, and housecleaners. Where will the demand come from? In the mid-1990s, these services are already needed for people in the fast-growing over-80 population, the parents of the front-end baby-boomers. But the big growth, as always, will come from the boomers themselves. They won't fall apart all at once, but a person's need for health care increases after the age of 50. So 1997 will be the beginning of an extended period of growth for the home health care delivery business. At first, the greatest demand will be for the services of doctors and other caregivers. Later, it will be for services previously provided in hospitals.

Population aging will also create opportunities for real estate developers, although the big growth won't commence until after 2010, when the early boomers are entering their 60s. Only a minority of seniors live in retirement homes; most live on their own or with their children. The boomers, who see themselves as perennially young, are not likely to embrace conventional retirement villages. The winners among real estate companies will therefore be the innovators who figure out how to provide for the baby-boomers' changing needs without making them feel old. A successful housing community for aging boomers will grow and develop along with its residents. It might start as a village of houses with a golf course and other recreational facilities. Later, hostel-type accommodation could be built for widows and widowers who need a greater level of service. Later still, nursing homes could be constructed as they are required.

The drug business is a subsector of the health care industry whose products will be in increasing demand as the population ages. Patent protection and the inevitability of rising sales make drug companies a promising investment for long-term growth. Prozac owes much of its success to stressed-out front-end boomers having a first career crisis and coming to terms with the reality that they are never going to reach the top of the corporate ladder. Other new anti-depressants will be developed to fill this need, and the aging baby boom will have many other health needs to fill as well. Investors interested in this market should ask themselves what afflictions most affect older people. No disease has received more publicity in recent years than AIDS, and any drug company that develops an effective treatment or vaccine for AIDS will reap well-deserved rewards. But AIDS affects only a minuscule proportion of the population, and its victims tend to come from younger, smaller population cohorts. In contrast, virtually every man over the age of 45 has some degree of enlargement of the prostate gland. After the age of 60, one in ten men suffers serious urinary problems as a result of this disorder. Drugs and medical devices that can reduce the need for surgery to correct these problems will find a huge market.

Research on therapies to mitigate the effects of menopause (see Chapter 9) will be a growth industry in the years to come. Health care companies will spend large amounts on research into hormone replacement therapy, which can ease the effects of menopause and may reduce heart disease and osteoporosis, a degenerative bone disease. One hundred per cent of the female population experiences menopause. That's why Germaine Greer's book about it was a best-seller. As menopause sweeps through the baby-boom population in the coming years, other publishers will attempt to satisfy people's thirst for information. Books on this and other health subjects will be a major growth industry in the years ahead.

LEISURE AND RECREATION

Gambling, one of the fastest-growing leisure activities in North America, is a relatively easy industry for the investor to follow. Both serious and recreational gamblers tend to be people in their 50s and 60s who have enough discretionary income to afford this pastime. The baby-boomers are about to move into their gambling years. (See Chapter 6.) Several major casino companies as well as hotel chains deeply involved in gambling are listed on the New York Stock Exchange.

Other parts of the leisure and recreation sector require more research on the part of the investor. Gardening, for example, is already blossoming spectacularly and will continue to do so. This is the classic case of an activity that the 20-year-old has no time for and the 50-year-old loves. Gardening is an excellent business because gardeners need a constant supply of things, bulbs and seeds and fertilizers and tools and books. Someone is going to do such a good job of supplying these things that her operation will become the Body Shop of the gardening business.

Upmarket travel will be yet another major growth area as the baby boom ages (see Chapter 6). But this is a complex, risky, and highly competitive business, and only the most capable players will be able to exploit that growth for steady profits. Innovative niche marketers who can deliver quality and service will probably show stronger growth rates than volume merchandisers. While a 30-year-old buys a plane ticket on a charter to Cuba, a 55-year-old is ready for something at once more exclusive and exciting, like a cruise for twenty people down the coast of Antarctica with naturalists on board to explain the sights.

Home fitness will continue to enjoy growth but the heyday of the fitness club is over. Younger people frequent fitness clubs, which is why this business grew rapidly during the 1980s. Older people can save time by buying their own equipment, and they can afford it. That's the reason for the growth of the home fitness industry over the 1990s. This industry will enjoy solid growth through the turn of the century.

RETAILING

The retailing giants of the future won't necessarily be the stores with the lowest prices. As Chapter 5 explains, quality and service, not price, are the retail watchwords for an older population. This is because a larger segment of the population will want and will be prepared to pay for quality and service. Meanwhile, younger people are entering the marketplace at a relatively slow rate. That means retailers will increasingly have to rely on margin, rather than volume, to find their profits. Customers will accept high margins only if the retailer is delivering added value. They will look for that added value in a smaller store, either independent or franchised. The big store is likely to become increasingly alienating to the older customer who prefers careful service in a calm atmosphere.

Shares in some of these added-value stores will be available and they will afford an excellent opportunity for the observant investor. We are all retail analysts, because we all inspect retail stores on a regular basis. Investors will have plenty of opportunity to decide which ones have what it takes to grow in an aging society.

FUNERALS AND CEMETERIES

Everybody uses this service eventually, which is why the bereavement industry has long been a favourite of some investors. But one has to be careful. In the mid-1990s, the fastest-growing segment of the Canadian population is the over-80s, which means funeral services are temporarily a growth industry. But a much smaller cohort will enter that age group over the next 20 years, resulting in slower growth. The real boom in this business is three decades in the future, when large numbers of boomers begin to expire. Post-boomers who time their investments well should be able to profit.

COLLECTIBLES

There's one other asset category that is a lot more fun to own than stocks or bonds. Collectibles, which include a wide array of items from classic cars to postage stamps, are likely to increase in value as the percentage of the population with discretionary income increases. Only a small portion of an individual's wealth should be invested in collectibles, and no one should make a major investment without first acquiring expertise in an area of interest. The disadvantage of collectibles is that they must be insured and protected from theft or damage. The advantage is that they add valuable diversification to an investment portfolio. Best of all, such things as fine art, antique books, or jewellery can be used and enjoyed while they appreciate in value.

Chapter 4

Jobs and the Corporation

I n the mid-1980s, something terrible happened to thousands of hard-working Canadians on their way up the corporate ladder: they got stuck. These weren't nine-to-fivers only putting in time to draw a weekly salary. They were people whose jobs were central to their lives and to their definitions of themselves. They were good at what they did and were making important contributions to the companies they worked for. They had fully expected to progress steadily upwards, at the very least into the ranks of middle management. But as the 1980s progressed, it gradually dawned on them that they weren't going to get even that far. They had plateaued.

By the mid-1980s, steady progress up a corporate ladder was no longer possible for many people who could have aspired to it in previous decades. Nor was a tall corporate ladder with dozens of rungs any longer necessary or desirable for most companies. The phenomenon of plateauing, or career blocking, was an early sign that the corporation as we had known it was about to undergo a major transformation. Plateauing was a result of demographic change intensified by the rapid development of labour-saving technology. In the mid-1990s, corporations are still engaged in the painful process of remaking themselves to adjust to these profound changes. At the same time, the nature of work, both within and outside the corporate world, is being redefined.

In the mid-1990s, small business, not large corporations, is where much of the action is in Canadian business. Small businesses are inventing new innovative technologies, developing new services, and creating new jobs. One important reason for this development is the changes, partly driven by demographics, that have been transforming the large corporations. Some of the best talent in these corporations has either left in frustration or been downsized out of a job, thereby making a priceless new pool of talent available to small business.

Corporations don't grow and develop in isolation from the rest of society. They are social organisms and as such reflect the demographic structure of the country in which they operate. Because Canadian couples had always produced more than enough offspring to replace themselves, Canadian corporations evolved over the 20th century to accommodate a rapidly growing workforce. But after 1960, the Canadian fertility rate dropped and by the late 1960s Canadian couples were averaging fewer than two children each. Canadians were no longer replacing themselves. Consequently, 20 years later, workforce growth slowed down. At the same time, computer technology was reducing the need for labour, especially the kind of labour needed to do the routine tasks typical of entry-level jobs.

The baby boom resembles a rectangle while the corporate structure looks like a triangle or pyramid (see Figure 2). We have been trying to promote a rectangle up a triangle, and it can't be done. The rectangle is there because a huge number of baby-boomers entered the workforce in the 1960s and 1970s. By the mid-1980s, they were clogging up the corporate hierarchy. There weren't enough openings for them at the top, nor were there enough people for them to manage at the bottom. So they were stuck in the same old jobs.

A triangular corporate structure works when there is a large and continuing flow of new workers at the entry level, constantly maintaining the large base of the triangle. In such a context, there is a close association between age and level in an organization. The 60-year-olds at the top direct the 40-year-olds in the middle and they manage the 20-year-olds at the bottom. This system works when there are more younger than older employees, which was exactly the case over most of the 20th century in North America as the modern corporation took shape. Even during the 1930s, a period of relatively few

FIGURE 2: CANADA'S WORKING-AGE POPULATION, 1981

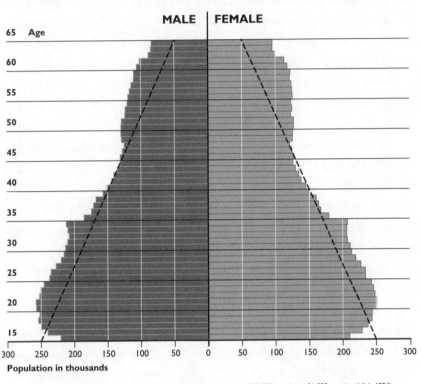

Source: Statistics Canada, *Revised Intercensal Population and Family Estimates, July 1, 1971-1991*, catalogue 91-537 occasional (July 1994)

births, the fertility rate stayed above replacement, at about 2.5 children per family. At the peak of the baby boom, it was four children per family. When the boomers grew up and went out to work, labour force growth took off in Canada, maintaining a pace of more than 3% a year, faster than any other country in the developed world. By comparison, European countries during the same period had annual labour force growth of around 1%.

Canada's economic policies in the 1960s and 1970s focussed on job creation, and these policies were successful. Canada created jobs faster than all other developed countries. Then, during the 1980s, it was the turn of the baby bust, the smaller generation that followed the baby boom, to enter the labour market. Labour force growth fell to 1.5% a year, half what it was during the 1960s and 1970s.

What do you do when there are too many people in their 40s looking for management jobs and too few in their teens and 20s to fill out the bottom of the organizational structure? Some companies tried to get older people to do younger people's work. But a 29-year-old doesn't want to do a 19-year-old's job. He thinks he's beyond that. And a 39-year-old certainly doesn't want to do a 29-year-old's job. The result was an increasingly frustrated workforce. Mid-management people were telling employees below them that they couldn't progress in their careers as quickly as they, the middle managers, had done. The implication was that the less senior workers weren't as good, when in fact their only major flaw was that there were too many of them. At the same time, information technology was enabling companies to dispense with middle managers whose major function was seen as channelling information between the upper and lower echelons. This function could now be done more directly and more quickly, but not necessarily more effectively, without human intermediaries.

During the 1980s, senior management perceived that the old organizational structure wasn't working and articles started to appear about the need for re-engineering the corporation. In most cases, this meant flattening the corporate structure. In the private sector, this was called delayering. In public sector, it was called broad-banding, meaning putting more jobs in the same salary category or level.

Companies such as IBM Canada that took the need for change seriously went from about ten levels on the corporate hierarchy to four or five. This was the right response to the new demographic reality, because the only way to promote a rectangle up a triangle is to flatten the triangle. Today the companies that haven't flattened as much are getting rid of experienced employees, laying them off or offer-ing them early retirement or severance packages. These organizations also reduced hiring during the 1980s and 1990s, and in the mid-1990s they are having to tell 35-year-olds to do jobs that 25-year-olds used to do. Is it surprising that these employees are increasingly difficult to work with and increasingly disloyal to their employers?

The difference between these two responses to demographic and economic change is the difference between delayering and downsizing. The latter is just reducing the workforce, and it can be done whether the corporate structure has been flattened or remains hierarchical. It is not necessary to downsize in order to delayer. A downsized employee doesn't just disappear. She may stay unemployed, or she may launch a new career as an independent contract worker. Or she may become one of the thousands of Canadians who have started new small businesses in recent years. As either a contractor or an entrepreneur, she has more independence than she enjoyed before, but she now lacks the security and fringe benefits associated with full-time employment in a large corporation.

The re-engineering of the corporation in response to demographic shifts has dramatic implications for careers. Let's take a look at the four basic career paths — linear, spiral, steady-state, and transitory — and examine how each has been affected by the re-engineering of the corporation.

The linear career path is one of upward mobility towards the top. A typical case would be an engineer in a large hydro company who moves through a succession of jobs, each carrying more responsibility and a higher salary, and eventually winds up in a senior management position. This career path is associated with tall corporate pyramids. These companies, with lots of levels, are the ones we are most familiar with. Their reward system is based on promotion up a career ladder. Sometimes they add a few rungs to the top of the ladder, allowing them, in effect, to demote people while pretending to promote them.

In the spiral career path, an employee spirals up the corporate structure. In other words, lateral moves are mixed with promotions. Each lateral move involves some change of occupation: for example, a move from sales to marketing or from nursing to computer programming. Typically, an employee would have four or five of these lateral moves over a working lifetime. Some of them would be within the same organization and some would be between different organizations. In organizing a corporation to make this kind of career possible, the triangle is retained for promotions, but it must be flattened out, resulting in a much broader base and more opportunity for lateral moves. In contrast to a company using linear career paths, a corporation like this has only a few levels in its hierarchy. Its reward system is focussed less on promotions and more on the satisfaction that employees get from mastering new challenges through re-education and lifelong training. Education becomes a lifelong process (see Chapter 8).

The steady-state career path is one occupation for a lifetime: the doctor, professor, or member of the clergy. To the extent that such people work in an organization, it is one with a largely rectangular structure: the Roman Catholic church, for example, with one pope at the top, a sprinkling of archbishops and other senior clergy, and a massive rectangle of priests below. A university has a similar structure, with a president, a few vice-presidents and deans, and many professors. In these organizations, the reward system is based on autonomy, fringe benefits, and tenure. Disputes frequently occur over such things as autonomy, a larger office, or attending a conference overseas.

A worker who follows a transitory career path adopts whatever occupation is necessary to get a job. He could be a receptionist, a bicycle courier, a film editor, a management consultant, or a computer programmer. This worker might be hired by a company to work on a temporary project, be part of a temporary team brought together to solve a particular problem, or be a member of a "virtual organization" consisting of various specialists operating under a coordinator, who calls on particular members of the organization whenever their special skills or expertise are needed.

In the future, the fastest-growing career paths will be the spiral and the transitory, although the steady-state career path will always be with us. These two paths best fit the new economy being shaped in the mid-1990s and beyond by demographic and technological change. Transitory workers will be freelancers. Spiral workers will work in companies with flattened corporate structures. Because of demographics, the flat structure will replace the vertical organization as the norm in North America.

The growth in spiral career paths is driven by corporations deciding to flatten. The growth in transitory career paths is driven, in part, by corporations deciding to downsize. Many corporations are deciding they can no longer afford to keep a public relations specialist or an engineer on staff. But they need the services that only those specialists can provide, so they purchase them from freelancers, many of whom are are former corporate employees who have become transitory workers either by choice or of necessity. Some of these former employees start out working alone and end up forming a larger business and hiring staff of their own. Both the spiral employees and the transitory freelancers are generalists more than specialists, flexible enough to adapt quickly to rapid changes in demand for their services. This does not mean that specialization is obsolete. Specialization is still important, but it has to be part of a broader context. The person who can offer a range of services within a broad specialty is the one most likely to prosper in the organization and economy of the future.

THE LATERAL ORGANIZATION

Smart corporations know they have to flatten the organizational pyramid, but that's not all. To make the new system work, a company has to install a new reward system based on providing challenging opportunities that require re-education and retraining instead of promotions up a ladder that no longer exists. This in turn requires a commitment by both employer and employee. It is futile for a company to flatten its structure and at the same time cut its retraining budget — yet that is exactly what many organizations have done in the 1990s. Moreover, it is also insufficient merely to send employees on courses. The best-managed companies understand that much retraining must take place on the job, whether through apprenticeship programs, mentoring, or other kinds of training.

In a flattened organization, the employee has to move from a linear to a spiral career path. That means new duties and new responsibilities. How can people take on new work they have never done before without education and training? Unless management increases the re-education and retraining budget, the flattened corporate structure will not work.

Companies that abandoned the vertical structure also need to abandon vertical thinking. A lateral company doesn't need a database listing people's academic degrees. That's appropriate for a tall corporate structure where people are going to stay in the same occupations until they go into management. Instead, a lateral organization needs to know people's job preferences, help them plan their career paths, and give them the training they need. Of course, this approach to employee management is a caring one that differs from the fashionable lean-and-mean approach, in which employees are regarded as interchangeable units of production needing no motivation other than fear of losing their jobs.

The mean approach is self-defeating, because companies that invest in worker training are more profitable than those that don't. That was the conclusion of a major study conducted in 1995 for the United States Department of Labor by researchers at the Harvard and Wharton business schools and the Center for Business Innovation, a Boston research organization. "It's a landmark study demonstrating that a company's surest way to profits is to treat employees as assets," said Robert Reich, an economist and the U.S. secretary of labour. Matthew Barrett, chairman of a hugely profitable Canadian company, the Bank of Montreal, has revived not only the bottom line but the morale of the bank by following that philosophy. "I always find myself a bit uncomfortable when I read about some CEO who says, 'Look how macho I am, I've just laid off 10,000 people,'" he told the *Financial Post*. "My view is that when you see massive amounts of restructuring happening quickly and suddenly, that's a reflection of management asleep at the switch."

If employees are assets, it makes more sense to keep them than to get rid of them. That's why delayering is a better strategy than downsizing. In fact, as Gerald Greenwald, CEO of United Airlines, has pointed out, the dogma claiming great virtue for downsizing is more a matter of faith than fact. A study of 1,000 downsized businesses showed that only 20% had gained any competitive advantage because of downsizing. The big risk, Greenwald cautions, is that instead of becoming leaner and meaner, a company will merely wind up "smaller and angrier" or, worse still, with employees who are "weaker and frightened."

Companies that flatten must make horizontal mobility possible. Suppose a member of the legal department wants to work on health and safety within the human resources department. She needs some courses to make that career switch. In a vertical organization, there is no incentive for the vice-president of legal affairs to pay for these courses in order to lose an employee to another department. Once you flatten a corporate structure, major changes in human resource policies and procedures must follow. This is one area where the conventional wisdom in favour of pushing decision-making down the line is inappropriate. Since lateral moves are made for the well-being of the organization as a whole, the decision to make them must come from those at the top of the hierarchy charged with looking after the interests of the organization as a whole. Most companies that have started out on this path have much work to do to make the new system work.

Another area in need of reform is compensation. Employees should get paid more for lateral moves when those moves improve corporate and individual productivity. In this corporate world, salary should bear little relationship to one's place in the hierarchy. Someone who has moved laterally a few times may end up earning more than the person who has just moved up one level. But one shouldn't expect automatic raises for lateral moves — raises should go to those who have earned them.

The flat organization with a spiralling workforce confers benefits on company and workers alike. Employees motivated by new challenges and new learning opportunities are more productive than employees who feel themselves stuck in a rut with no prospect of change or promotion. As well, people who move laterally to another department seldom carry any occupational burdens or past obligations with them. All of a sudden, new ideas come rushing up to the surface. In one company, an MBA became head of the engineering division because of a lateral move. One of his first tasks was to improve the traffic situation in the loading area where, for 40 years, trucks loading and unloading had crossed one another through two gates. He said, "I know nothing about this. I'm willing to take any advice." An hourly paid worker who was directing traffic said, "If you moved one of those gates, the trucks wouldn't have to cross and we'd save several minutes a day."

That simple change saved a lot more than several minutes; over a week, it added up to several hours. It happened because the new MBA at the top had no commitment to the past policies of the division and was a lateral thinker, willing to admit that the person directing traffic knew more about the problem than he did. At the same time, the previous head of the department, with his knowledge of the division's history, remained in the company directing another division and was available for consultation when necessary. Because of their own positive experiences, both managers encouraged other lateral moves throughout the organization. Employee bragging rights in this company now focus on how many assignments one has had rather than one's level in the flattened hierarchy.

This kind of organizational structure puts a greater premium on such intangible employee characteristics as flexibility and motivation — qualities that are required if companies are to respond successfully to rapid changes in their business environments — and places less value on more tangible assets such as experience and qualifications. Rigid job descriptions are inappropriate in such a workplace. At Intel Corp., for example, employees speak of "owning problems" rather than occupying specific jobs.

EDUCATION AND THE CHANGING CORPORATION

The changes being forced on corporations are at once a challenge and an opportunity for the educational system. Universities and colleges are logical candidates to provide the continuing education and retraining that spiral and transitory workers need, but offering a course every Monday afternoon for eight months is not going to help people who have to be retrained in a month. They need a course that is offered in concentrated form over three weeks. And it has to be delivered so that the knowledge can be applied immediately in the workplace. Spiral workers will need such courses in a huge variety of subject areas, from industrial relations to insurance law to ethics to plumbing.

A huge new adult clientele can be attracted to educational institutions, some of which are experiencing falling enrolments in the mid-1990s. But to win this business, these institutions will have to change some of their ways. Their new students will be there not to get a degree but to learn. The educational institution should not put bureaucratic roadblocks in their way. It should not tell a 40-year-old that he will be admitted only if he has a B+ in his undergraduate transcript. After 20 years of work experience, that 20-year-old transcript is irrelevant today, and because of grade inflation, his C could have been the equivalent of a B+ anyway. Decisions to admit should be based on the work record, experience, needs, and goals of the student. Educational institutions should also adapt their offerings to the changing needs of these mature students. If corporations, because of demographic and technological change, are placing more emphasis on teamwork and less on leadership, then courses on teamwork should be substituted for courses on leadership.

To succeed in adapting to the new world of lifelong education, educational institutions will have to understand that their new clientele is not the same as the youthful full-time students they are used to. The full-time student has plenty of time; the adult in a full-time job doesn't. The old ways of doing things are not where the marketplace is in the 1990s, and the marketplace for re-education and training is no different from any other marketplace — it demands quality and service. (See Chapter 5.) That means a course compacted into a short time period that is easily accessible (where numbers warrant, it could be delivered right in the workplace), provides a mixture of theory and application, and is of the highest quality. One of the biggest issues as lifelong learning becomes essential to the functioning of the Canadian economy is whether traditional educational institutions can meet these challenges.

THE FUTURE OF JOBS

In the mid-1990s, young people are entering a volatile, uncertain, and unsettled job market. These new entrants are the baby-bust generation.

Because they are members of a smaller cohort, demographic theory says their job prospects should be better than those of their predecessors in Generation X. And, in fact, unemployment among youth was lower throughout the deep and prolonged recession of the early 1990s than it was during the milder recession of the early 1980s. To that extent, being members of a small cohort has helped the baby-busters. The Generation-Xers were the new labour market entrants in the early 1980s, and they had a tougher time.

But knowing it was worse in the early 1980s doesn't do much to cheer up an unsuccessful job-seeker in the mid-1990s. Canada is in its fourth consecutive decade of rising unemployment. During the 1950s, unemployment averaged 4.2%, rising to 5% in the 1960s, 6.7% in the 1970s, 9.5% in the 1980s, and 11% in the early 1990s. In the mid-1990s, job-seekers of all generations find themselves marooned in what has become known as the "jobless recovery."

The reasons for this situation are well known. Shoes and fridges and tires and countless other things that once were made by Canadians for other Canadians are now imported from whichever country can make them cheapest. Canadian employers trying to survive in this world of global trade must cut costs wherever and whenever possible to be more competitive. Cutting costs often means cutting jobs.

Labour-saving technology was first embraced for demographic reasons in the 1960s and 1970s by Japan, when it was trying to compensate for labour shortages caused by falling birth rates in the 1940s. Since then, technology has taken on a life of its own. Computerized machines are used everywhere in the economy, from the checkout counter of the supermarket to a mine shaft deep below the earth. Technology continues to develop at a staggering pace, getting better and cheaper as each month goes by. The power of computers to store information and speed operations doubles every 18 months, and the cost of computing is cut in half every three years.

What does this mean for jobs? As recently as the early 1980s, it was cheaper to add workers than to add machines. But by the 1990s, the cost of labour in Canada was twice the cost of machines, according to a report published by the Conference Board of Canada in 1995. So today's companies are adding machines instead of labour. The result is improved productivity but increased unemployment. The convention- al wisdom in the 1980s was that technology would eventually create as many jobs as it took. Although the jury is still out on this question, the optimistic view is increasingly being called into question. Tech- nology continues, at a relentless pace, to destroy far more jobs than it creates. This is happening not only in Canada but right across the developed world. In a recent book, *The End of Work: The Decline of the Global Labor Force and the Dawn of the Post-Market Era*, Jeremy Rivkin estimates that 90 million jobs in the United States out of a potential labour force of 124 million are vulnerable to elimination by machines. The Nobel Prize–winning economist Wassily Leontief says, "Sophisticated computers will likely displace humans in the same way that work-horses were eliminated by the introduction of tractors."

The first jobs to go were the ones requiring minimal skills, such as routine recordkeeping or data transfer or repetitive assembly- line tasks that can be done quicker, better, and cheaper by robots. Yet these were the sorts of jobs that young boomers in the 1960s and 1970s were able to occupy with high school educations or less. The ambi- tious among them had plenty of opportunity to increase their skills while working their way up to better-paying, more responsible jobs.

Those unskilled entry-level jobs leading to middle-class secu- rity no longer exist. That is why the labour force participation rate for people between 15 and 24 fell to a 19-year low in 1995. Rather than jump into a labour market that has only dead-end jobs to offer the unskilled and undereducated, young Canadians are staying in school or going back to school. This is a wise decision. In 1994, 145,000 jobs in Canada disappeared for people with high school education or less, while 422,000 jobs were created for workers with postsecondary edu- cation. Virtually everybody with a postsecondary degree who entered the job market in 1994 got a job, although not always in their area of expertise. (See Figure 3.) Employers' preference for educated workers is entirely understandable. One of the impacts of the advance of tech- nology is that many jobs that once required only manual skills now require the ability to read, write, and calculate. A person with a post-

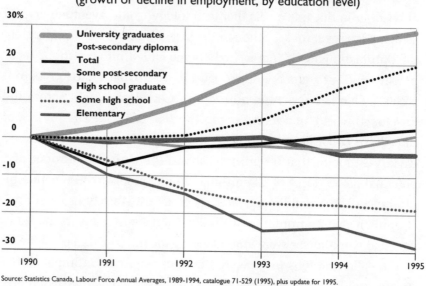

FIGURE 3: EMPLOYMENT AND EDUCATION
(growth or decline in employment, by education level)

Legend:
- University graduates
- Post-secondary diploma
- Total
- Some post-secondary
- High school graduate
- Some high school
- Elementary

Source: Statistics Canada, Labour Force Annual Averages, 1989-1994, catalogue 71-529 (1995), plus update for 1995.

secondary diploma is less likely to be illiterate or innumerate than someone with only a high school degree.

What will it take to succeed in the job market of the future? For transitory and spiralling workers, the only constant will be change. In fact, the very notion of "jobs" will come to seem an anachronism during the working lives of many young Canadians. Jobs were developed during the 19th century, when factories required units of labour to do the same tasks over and over again. In the information age, workers will apply a wide range of skills to an ever-changing series of tasks, rather than occupying a particular job. While routine tasks are being taken over by machines, non-routine ones still need people to do them. These people will need strong generic skills that can be applied to the many different challenges they will face during their careers.

One of the most important skills is communication, both oral and written. The decline in literacy has enhanced the value of those who can write clearly, concisely, and grammatically while also possessing the ability to make effective oral presentations. Interpersonal skills, including the ability to work effectively as part of a team, are

also essential. So are computer skills, which have to be upgraded continually as technology advances. Finally, the successful worker of the
future needs the kinds of skills that an old-fashioned liberal arts education still provides very well: the ability to assemble information, analyze it, and think about it. People with these skills are what Robert
Reich calls "symbolic analysts," workers who manipulate symbols
such as mathematical data and words and who identify and solve
problems. A large number of occupations fall into this category, from
research scientists to movie directors.

But a continued demand will exist for skilled people who can
work well with their hands as well as their brains. It is a paradox of
Canada's labour market that with 10% of Canadian workers unemployed, many employers still can't find the workers they need. For
example, many manufacturing firms in southern Ontario are having
trouble finding skilled machinists and other tradespeople. Partly, this
is because the demarcation line between white-collar and blue-collar
work has faded as information technology has invaded the shop floor.
The machinist in the mid-1990s is a "symbolic analyst" with a voca-
tional college degree, a knowledge of computers, and an ability to
work in a team. Larry Zepf, of Zepf Technologies Inc. in Waterloo,
Ontario, needs people like that to make the automated packaging lines
he sells to manufacturers around the world. "We want value-added
people," he says. "The skilled tradesperson we would have employed
ten years ago is much more multi-talented today. It's not uncommon
for a guy to have a machinist's paper and a millwright's paper and to
have CAD [computer-aided design] expertise and to also be a service-
man who is willing to fly to Europe on short notice. He's got to be able
to analyze and make decisions."

Throughout this book, there are clues to where the jobs of the
future will be found. The chapters on real estate, investing, retailing,
leisure and recreation, cities, and health care all point to growth areas
of the economy that will need trained people in the future. For example, the flat real estate market, resulting from the changed demographic structure of Canadian society in the mid-1990s, means that many
people will find it difficult to sell their homes for enough money to

trade up to the better houses they want. Instead, they are going to renovate, and the renovation business will boom as a result. That means work for the architects, interior designers, carpenters, cabinet-makers, painters, electricians, and plumbers who are able to create the kitchens and bathrooms of their customers' dreams. Although the architect might practise his craft on a computer rather than a drafting board, most of what these skilled workers do will never be done by computers and will always be in demand. But the key word here is *skilled*. In an aging population, shoddy work will be neither tolerated nor rewarded.

Provincial governments are closing hospitals and putting a new emphasis on home health care just as the front end of the massive baby-boom generation is about to turn 50 and start needing more health care services. That means home health care will be a growth business in the years and decades to come, bringing with it employment for a wide range of health care and personal service workers.

A demographic approach to career planning always involves analyzing the needs of the largest segments of the population. A front-end boomer has parents in their 70s and 80s. These parents need health care services that, in some cases, will be managed by their children. But those children are not health care experts, are extremely busy, and may live far away from their parents. They might eagerly employ the services of an experienced individual — perhaps a nurse laid off from a management position in a hospital — to monitor their parents' health, arrange for care as required, and report to them on a regular basis. As the health care system is restructured, many opportunities like this will open up for health care workers ready to seize them. Many of these health care workers will be former employees in vertical organizations creating new transitory career paths for themselves.

Young people planning their careers need to determine which subspecialties of their areas of interest will be most in demand. Interested in medicine? Then consider that the baby-boom echo is coming to an end in the mid-1990s. The babies in the coming years will be those born to the baby-busters, a smaller generation. That means fewer babies and less demand for obstetricians and pediatricians. On the other hand, the services of many other specialists will enjoy stable or increasing demand. For example, cosmetic surgery is used by all generations but most especially by the huge baby-boom generation, which is rapidly losing the youthful appearance many of its members value so highly. Research in this field, driven by demographics, is making rapid strides. New techniques of laser surgery, for example, have been successfully employed to remove wrinkles and other marks of aging from the faces of people as old as 86. Today about 1.5 million cosmetic surgery procedures a year are performed in North America, double the number of a decade earlier. Tracking the aging of the baby boom, cosmetic surgery will continue to grow rapidly in the years ahead. Another booming business will be cosmetic dentistry, to whiten and otherwise improve aging teeth.

This demographic approach can be applied to a wide array of occupations. Perhaps accounting appeals to you. In that case, it's worth considering that, in an aging population, white-collar crime inevitably increases (see Chapter 7). This means that forensic accounting — a term that until recently was largely unknown — will be a growth industry. The services of forensic accountants will be increasingly required by all organizations, both public and private, profit and non-profit, to detect fraud.

A young person typically has more time than money, while a middle-aged person has more money than time (see Chapter 5). Increasingly, imaginative transitory workers are finding ways to sell some of that valuable commodity time to harried, hurried, front-end boomers. Jim Davidson of Toronto is a classic example of an entrepreneur exploiting the opportunities created by demographic change. In 1993, Davidson, a former car salesman, set up on his own as an agent for people wanting to buy a used car. He had two things to offer: knowledge and time. He knew which models made good used cars and which ones didn't, he could spot cars whose provenance was dubious and whose speedometers showed less mileage than the car actually had, and he knew what cars were worth and how not to get taken by a dealer. Even with that store of knowledge, finding a good late-model used car took him time. But he had the time, and his customers, most of them busy front-end boomers in their 40s, didn't. Davidson found the car, negotiated the deal, and arranged delivery.

Davidson's business has evolved with his customers. Good used cars are getting rarer, and his customers now want new cars anyway. So Davidson has begun acting as agent for buyers of new cars, advising them on which vehicles best suit their needs, arranging test drives, and working out deals with the fleet managers of major dealerships. Davidson operates the way life insurance agents have always operated: he visits his clients at their homes at their convenience. This mode of doing business will become increasingly common in the years to come as more people become more pressed for time. Service providers such as travel agents and accountants will find themselves making house calls. Even doctors will make house calls.

Japan, because it is a much older society than Canada, provides useful clues to our future. "In Japan, you don't go to a car dealer," says Davidson. "The Nissan, Honda, or Toyota representative comes over with his laptop and CD-ROM and shows all the cars, and he has a printer so that he can leave you a printout with all the options and prices."

Davidson was born in 1967, immediately after the baby boom. Some people in his age group resent the relative success of the front-end boomers, but Davidson happily exploits that success as he builds his business. His own contemporaries have plenty of time to shop for a car on their own and they can't afford his $500 fee. "But if I get a lawyer who's off to the opera on Tuesday, and the baseball game on Wednesday, and he's having business guests over on Thursday, what's $500 to him? That's one billable hour of work."

In 1995 Davidson was still the only person he knew of operating a car-buying service in Canada, but his idea makes so much sense that he probably won't be without competition for long. In fact, he has earned fees training people from Connecticut and New Jersey who plan to start similar businesses there.

Growth in demand for manufactured goods is slow today because the largest part of the population already has most of what it needs. As Canada becomes more of a service economy, resourceful young people will continue to invent new services. In a north Toronto neighbourhood, for example, one woman advertises herself as a professional grocery shopper. Others are in the business of picking other people's children up at daycare centres or walking their dogs. As Davidson points out, the baby-boomers took most of the traditional jobs. Younger people like him "have to make our own."

More than ever, people are willing to pay to get the knowledge and expertise they want when they want it. They will pay an expert to help choose a school for their child or to solve a computer problem or to advise them on their physical or financial health. These consultants, like Jim Davidson, offer expertise and time-saving. The future will bring growing demand for the services of people who know how to deliver these precious commodities.

TOWARDS A FLEXIBLE WORKFORCE

In Canada, we go to school full-time, work full-time, and then go into retirement full-time. In an aging society, characterized by job shortages, rapid technological change, a need for continuous upgrading of skills, and underfunded public pension plans, this system no longer makes any sense. Some people are working more hours a week than they would like, while many more can't find any work at all. Some people work full-time although they would prefer semi-retirement, while others, still full of health, energy, and talent, are forced to retire at 65.

The time has come to take seriously the need for a flexible workforce in Canada. A flexible workforce would not only be happier and healthier, it would be more productive because it would make better use of the talents of all Canadians. A flexible workforce is one whose participants, rather than staying in one occupation with one employer for life, move easily between jobs, employers, and industries. It's also a workforce that allows its participants both to begin and to end their working careers gradually, and that provides plentiful opportunities for retraining.

Elements of a flexible workforce already exist. Some high schools, colleges, and universities, for example, offer cooperative programs in which periods of study are interspersed with periods of employment in the student's field of interest. This is precisely as it should be. People should ease into the workforce, combining work and study, at the start of their careers, and then gradually ease out of the workforce towards the end of their careers, by cutting down to four days a week, then three, and so on down to zero.

Senior managers don't like this idea much because they don't really want their workers to have flexibility. Management can't quite accept that a part-time worker is a committed worker. Then there are the complications of working out pension and other fringe benefits for part-timers. But these complications are minor compared with the benefits that a flexible workforce would bring. Many overworked people in their late 40s and 50s, who have paid off their mortgages and educated their children, would willingly work four days a week for 80% of their salary or nine months a year for 75%. This would save their employers large amounts of money because they are the highest-paid people on the payroll. And half a senior manager's salary pays the full salary of an entry-level employee.

Such a system should be voluntary. A mandatory flexible work arrangement puts an unfair burden on those who can least afford to work reduced hours, such as young people burdened by large mortgages or the most poorly paid workers. And those who volunteer have to be committed — for example, by signing a three-year contract promising to accept nine months, and nine months only, of work per year. That gives management a chance to plan and ensures that no one takes the program frivolously. This system benefits both the company and the employee. The company saves on the salary of a high-priced employee and, in many cases, gets a more productive employee; it also gets a chance to revitalize its workforce by hiring some younger workers. Part-time workers get time off for other things, such as establishing new businesses or careers and enjoying leisure and recreational pursuits. This system also allows workers to ease into retirement gradually. A final advantage is that the part-time senior worker is available to train and act as a mentor to the newcomer.

It's in the interest of all employees to become more versatile. If diversifying risk makes sense in personal financial planning, it makes just as much sense in career planning. Most of us would not put every penny we had into one type of investment. But we do just that when managing our own human capital: we become completely dependent on one occupation and one employer. We are therefore just as vulnerable as investors with all their money in real estate — if the market takes a tumble, they are in big trouble. The transitory worker, or freelancer, is diversified and thus not dependent on the good will or good fortune of any one employer. A salaried worker can't duplicate the independence of a freelancer, but she can be alert to possibilities for expanding and improving her skills. A salaried worker could have two part-time jobs instead of one full-time job, each in a different occupation. In that situation, the disappearance of one job would be much less of a disaster.

THE FUTURE OF RETIREMENT

Like the idea of jobs, retirement was a 19th-century invention that is becoming outmoded as the 20th century draws to a close. It was invented in the 1880s by German chancellor Otto von Bismarck to help quell revolutionary fervour among German workers. Now it has become a system in which the state pays people not to work, including quite a few who don't need the money and would rather keep working.

Just as young workers should be able to ease their way into the workforce while being trained in their chosen occupations, so older workers should be able to ease their way out while retaining the dignity and sense of self-worth that comes with productive activity. A good worker doesn't suddenly lose his skill and knowledge at the age of 65. As recent challenges to mandatory retirement at 65 by doctors at the Vancouver General Hospital and others demonstrate, many older workers see no good reason to succumb to enforced idleness when they still have the energy and ability to work.

Sooner or later, demographics will impose a system of gradual retirement as an integral part of a flexible workforce. In an increasingly competitive world, the most knowledgeable and experienced workers are too valuable to be put out to pasture before they are ready. Moreover, as has been well publicized, the ranks of Canadian seniors will begin a period of rapid growth in 2012 when the first baby-boomers turn 65. At that time, compulsory retirement for 65-year-olds will come under increasing attack. In a period of rising life expectancies and in the context of a flexible workforce, it won't make much sense. The Canada Pension Plan already allows for flexible retirement. But it doesn't allow a partial pension to be paid to a person who is only partially retired. It should.

The western Europeans, it is worth noting, already have the older society we are going to get. They are supporting it through increased productivity. As has been explained above, demographics and technology are creating a more productive Canadian economy in the mid-1990s. Companies are adding machines because they are cheaper than workers, with the result that output per worker — productivity — is rising. But if we are to support our seniors through productivity gains, tax reform will be essential. It can't be done through payroll taxes alone because of the shortage of workers to pay the pensions of all the retired baby-boomers. We have to tax capital income, which will mean higher taxes on corporate earnings and capital gains as well as the introduction of inheritance taxes.

The solution is not to do away with mandatory retirement, which is still necessary to open up room at the top for plateaued boomers and create new opportunities for younger workers. Instead, we should permit partial retirement in the context of a flexible workforce. Those in their late 50s could be working four days a week, after which they would gradually shorten their work week until they are working only one day a week by their early 70s. They could start drawing a partial pension at 55 but would not reach full pension eligibility until 75. In this way, they could remain productive members of the workforce into their 70s, gradually retire with dignity, be present to mentor younger workers, and help reduce the pressure on the Canada Pension Plan.

Because of demographics, there is no better time to reform Canada's retirement system than the mid-1990s. The cohort arriving at senior citizenship during this period is the Depression kids, the people born in the 1930s who are the wealthiest people in the country. They, more than any other group, have reaped the rewards of the rise in real estate values and stock prices in the later years of their adulthood. These seniors can afford to adapt to the changes that would be necessary as part of a move towards a more flexible workplace, including delaying full pensions until after age 65. The time for reform is now. The longer we wait, the harder it will be.

Chapter 5

The Rules of Retail

A young person has little money and lots of time. If she wants to buy a new stereo, she checks out every store in town because every dollar saved is important and, what's more, she has plenty of time to hunt for bargains. Once she's made the purchase, she takes the system home and puts it together. It doesn't matter how long it takes.

A middle-aged person has more money but less time. He's got heavy responsibilities at work and at home. He is not going to spend his precious leisure hours doing comparison shopping to try to save $50 on a pair of speakers. This person wants a top-quality stereo system from a store with a good reputation, and he wants it with a maximum of speed and a minimum of fuss. He may even pay extra to have it delivered and assembled, because the time saved is worth more than the additional cost.

In recent years, Canada has begun to undergo a major transformation, from a predominantly young to a predominantly middle-aged society. For that reason, retailing in Canada has entered a new era of quality and service. In the years to come, stores that compete on the basis of quality and service will have a much better chance of success than stores that compete solely on the basis of price. Since stores sell goods obtained from manufacturers, the makers of goods must also place renewed emphasis on quality if they wish to maintain their market share in an aging population.

As the average age of the population increases, not only do

quality and service assume ever greater importance, but product preferences change. The shrewdest retailers know how to forecast these changes and prepare for new market demands. They know that the best way to predict which way the market is headed is to look at where the early baby-boomers are now. These front-end boomers aren't a big group, but the massive boomer population of 9.8 million people always catches up with them. If you need to know which products and services will be in greatest demand in Canada in the future, take a close look at the products and services that the key group born in the last three years of the 1940s is buying today.

For example, the streets of Canada are now crowded with minivans. In the mid-1980s, minivans were comparatively rare. But who was driving them? Front-end boomers born in the late 1940s. They had young children and had to trade in their Volkswagen bugs and sports cars for something bigger. Detroit, in a rare example of timely marketing, came up with the minivan, and the rest is automotive history. As the younger baby-boomers caught up with the front-enders, the minivan's share of the Canadian car market rose steadily, from less than 1% in 1983 to 15% in 1994. Next time you see a minivan coming down the street, see who's behind the wheel. Chances are it won't be someone under 30 or over 50. The minivan is the vehicle of the baby boom.

A major market shift like that is propelled by demographics, not by marketing decisions. It was because Canada was a young country in the 1960s and 1970s that its streets were filled with cheap, small cars. This phenomenon occurred in spite of the Big Three automakers, not because of them. They would have preferred to continue selling the larger and more profitable vehicles that ruled the North American car market until the arrival of cheap European and Japanese cars forced them to deliver what the consumer wanted.

A country filled with young people is one whose retailers compete predominantly on price. In such a country, anything that can lower the average cost of production and reduce the price to the consumer is important. A young Canada during the 1960s and 1970s enabled the big retail mall to be born and to thrive, making it possible for stores to lower costs and pass the savings on to customers. The malls won't disappear but their glory days are over. In the 20 years to come, the demographic shift will favour a revival of neighbourhood specialty stores supported by loyal customers for whom price is no longer the most important factor in a purchase decision.

Stores that can deliver good products and good service will dominate this new marketplace, while stores that waste customers' time and treat them rudely will disappear. The art of customer service is something at which Canadian retailers are notoriously incompetent because, until the late 1980s, they were operating in a marketplace that didn't require it. It's no accident that countries such as Japan and Germany discovered quality and service before we did. Their populations are much older than ours, and their retailers had to respond to the demands of a changing marketplace a decade or more earlier than ours did. The Canadian retailers that prosper in the changing marketplace of the coming years will be those that succeed in adopting customer service as a way of life.

To better comprehend what is happening in the mid-1990s and what's in store in the years ahead, let's review the past quarter-century of Canadian retailing. (See Figure 4.) Between 1971 and 1981, the front end of the baby boom moved into adulthood. At the same time Canada's obstetricians were doing a good imitation of the Maytag repairman, because the baby bust reduced the demand for their services. The result was a children's market that declined by 14% during the 1970s. Inevitably, the toy and baby food businesses suffered steep declines in sales. A toy company that was good enough to beat this declining market by five percentage points still suffered a whopping 9% plunge in sales; the marketers in such a company deserved a bonus but, unless their bosses were exceptionally sophisticated about demographics, they probably got fired instead. Meanwhile, the youth (15-to-24-year-old) market was growing by 17% over the 1970s. Someone selling a product that this age group wanted — recorded music, for example — and who increased sales by 10% probably thought he was hot stuff, and yet he wasn't even keeping up with the natural growth of the market. Meanwhile, the growth of the boomers into adulthood resulted

FIGURE 4: CANADIAN POPULATION GROWTH BY AGE

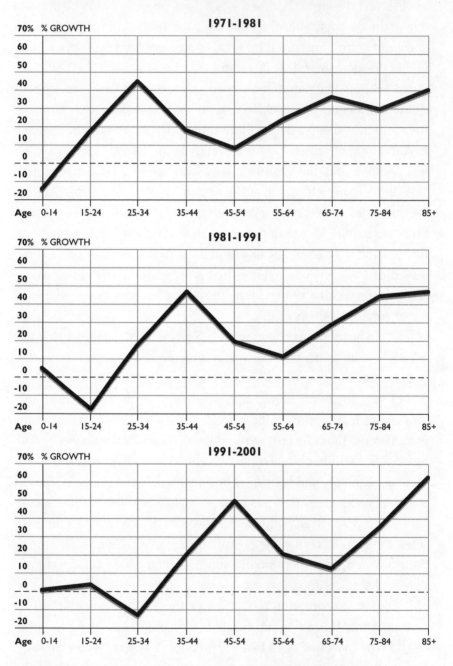

Source: Statistics Canada, Revised Intercensal Population Estimates (1971-1991) and Population Projections, No.1 (1991-2001)

in boom times for makers and sellers of all the things people need when they set up a new household: furniture, appliances, and cars, especially used cars.

The 1980s showed how dramatically markets can change from one decade to the next because of demographic shifts. The baby-boom echo began in 1980, with the result that the under-14 age group grew by 5% over the 1980s — a turnaround of 19% compared with the 1970s. That's how toy companies on the verge of bankruptcy in the 1970s became profitable in the 1980s.

But entrants into the youth market (aged 15 to 24) during the 1980s were the products of the smaller baby-bust generation; as a result, that market declined by 17%. That's why the beer industry got into trouble. It couldn't blame foreign competition for its problems because foreign brewers were effectively excluded from the Canadian market by provincial listing, pricing, and distribution systems. But government could not protect the beer giants from a 17% drop in their key group of customers. Rather than seek to expand the appeal of their products to older people, the big beer producers tried to boost their shares of the shrinking youth market. But even a company whose sales team was good enough to beat the market by a couple of percentage points still had a 15% drop, which looked pretty awful compared with the 17% growth obtained almost automatically in the 1970s.

It wasn't only the beer industry that suffered in the 1980s, of course. Performers and producers of music appealing to a youth audience found their material pushed off the air as radio stations switched to oldies formats that appealed to a target audience that was swelling by 47% during the 1980s. The stations did this not because their managers were too staid to appreciate modern music; they did it to survive. Who, after all, would want to target a market declining by 17%? Some expert opinion had it that the reason for the decline of new music was that it was worse than the music of the 1960s and 1970s. This argument does not make sense. If young people couldn't fill Olympic Stadium or B.C. Place during the 1980s, it was because there were fewer young people. No band, no matter how talented, can continually fill stadiums when the size of its target audience is in steep decline.

The biggest growth during the 1980s was in the 25-to-34 age group. Industries that understood this and were able to exploit it did well. The pet food industry in the U.S., for example, knew that people acquire their first dogs or cats at about age 28. This industry did a good job of targeting its market and enjoyed excellent growth through-out the decade. In the same years, the front-end boomers were moving out of rented apartments and into their first homes, with the result that demand for consumer durables such as appliances was strong. The consumer spent us out of the recession of the early 1980s. The arrival in the retail marketplace of this huge generation with wants greater than its cash flow triggered the growth of the credit card as a medium of payment for the masses. Annual spending charged on Visa and MasterCards grew from $4 billion in 1977 to $61 billion in 1994.

The boomers, because they are the largest group, dominate today's retail marketplace. Suppose you are a successful 45-year-old executive or professional working 60 hours a week in a high-pressure job. Your spouse also has a job with important responsibilities. Your kids are into their teen years, going through the wrenching transition to adulthood that so often makes life trying for their parents. Your own parents are in their 70s, and their declining health is increasingly a cause of concern. Meanwhile, you are running a house in the city and perhaps another in the country. You have an active social calendar. Moreover, you continue to value the leisure activities that are so important to a balanced life — recreation, travel, reading, and cultural events. A charitable organization that you've supported for many years has come to rely on your energy and expertise.

This is your life in the mid-1990s. Do you really have time to take a defective product back? Do you have time to make three tele-phone calls to find out if something you need is in stock? Of course you don't, and that's why you are no longer prepared to support mer-chants who waste your time. During the 1970s, when the front end of the baby boom was in its 20s, Consumers Distributing sometimes used the slogan "Suffer a Little, Save a Lot." In other words, even if you have to wait 20 minutes for whatever it is you are trying to buy, it's worth it because the price is lower. That approach was fine in a marketplace where people had time and little money, but it can't work in the 1990s when the situation is the reverse. That's why Consumers has long since ditched the slogan. "Today's customers don't want to suffer," says Gordon Wallin, supervisor of sales promotions for Consumers. "They want value and convenience."

There is, of course, nothing new about this. Busy people with responsible jobs have always made demanding customers. What's new is that, as the baby boom moves into its 40s and 50s, a much larger percentage of the population than before will be of the age group that insists on quality and service. That means stores that seemed invincible in the early part of the 1990s — stores like Wal-Mart, Price Club, and Home Depot — are heading into turbulent waters. These American megastores entered Canada at a time when a large segment of the Canadian population was in its early to middle 30s. At that age, many families have two small kids and a pile of debt, including a mortgage on a recently acquired house. Price is extremely important to such people, so they are prepared to invest a large chunk of their spare time in the pursuit of bargains.

But as we approach the new century, these people are in their 40s and their financial situation is growing more secure. Will they still be willing to drive 10 kilometres in search of a bargain? Will they be prepared to roam the aisles of a Price Club to save a few dollars on products they could have found closer to home? Will they be prepared to drive to an Ikea or an Idomo, wander around looking for the new table they need, go to the warehouse section to find the right package, wait in line to pay for it, tie it to the roof of the car, and then take it home to assemble it themselves? Probably not.

One way the 40-year-old discovers he's well and truly grown up is that suddenly people he used to think of as authority figures — policemen and doctors, for example — are younger than he is. Another moment of truth comes when he walks into the Ikea store he avidly patronized as a student and young adult and realizes that he's in the wrong place. He says to himself, "Hold it. I'm a grownup now. I don't have to put up with this any more." The management of Ikea understands that the demographic shift is changing the way they must do business. They know Ikea has to adapt to the changing needs of aging consumers while at the same time guarding its valuable franchise of price-conscious shoppers in their 20s and 30s. They are doing this by offering delivery and, more recently, assembly for an extra charge. This is a way of appealing at the same time with the same products to younger shoppers for whom price is primary and to older ones who are prepared to pay for extra service.

Stores whose only attraction is cheap prices face a dismal future in Canada because of coming changes in the age composition of the population. These stores won't survive unless they upgrade the quality of their service, their products, or both. A middle-aged person might continue shopping at a Wal-Mart or Price Club for commodity items such as paper towels and brand-name breakfast cereals. After all, these things are the same no matter where you get them, so quality is not an issue. Price is the main concern with such products, and the megastores win on price. But service, more specifically convenience, is also an important consideration. The busy 45-year-old will shop for basic household supplies at Wal-Mart only if the inconvenience is not so great that it cancels out the price advantage. She might, for example, like to call the store from her office and place an order that she can pick up on her way home from work. She might also eagerly patronize the first hardware store in her area that offers to assemble unassembled products at a small extra charge. Retailers are going to have to work hard to come up with ways like these to adapt to the changing marketplace if they wish to make the transition successfully.

Let's take a closer look at the needs of the different cohorts in the retail marketplace of the late 1990s.

THE CHILDREN AND YOUTH MARKET

The biggest single batch of baby-boomers — those born in 1961 — reached age 35 in 1996. That was a significant turning point, because it meant that the majority of the 9.8 million boomers were past their prime reproductive years. As a result, growth in the children's market is over until the echo kids start reproducing around 2005.

While the children's market is in decline, the youth group (15 to 24) is growing by 4% during the 1990s. This is a big rebound for an age group that declined 17% during the 1980s. As these children of the baby-boomers enter their teen years through the rest of the decade, we will see the impact in several areas. Obviously, music appealing to young people will make a comeback. Radio stations that switched out of teenybopper music into formats geared to an older audience might want to reconsider that decision.

THE BOOMER MARKET

During the 1990s, the front end of the baby boom will cause the 45-to-54 age category to explode by 50% while the back end, aged 35 to 44, will increase by 20%. This surge in the population of these age groups is the fundamental underlying cause of the transformation of retailing in Canada. Let's look at what's happening in some of the most important retail segments.

Food

As they get older, people eat less and they eat better. People in their 40s and 50s don't need as many calories as people in their 20s and 30s, and they have less of a sweet tooth. Because they are older, they are more aware of mortality and thus more likely to consider the health implications of what they eat. Moreover, they usually have more money than they did when they were young. These inevitable repercussions of aging have profound significance for Canada's $82-billion-a-year food industry.

Jim White, a food writer turned marketer and product developer, was a driving force behind the President's Choice brand of quality food products that has been so successful over the last decade for the Loblaws supermarket chain. White, as an independent consultant, now spends his time travelling all over North America creating similar high-quality house brands for major supermarket chains. He says President's Choice succeeded because it satisfied consumer demands for better food. Satisfying these needs was a complex process. In some cases, better meant more exotic. In others, it meant healthier foods low in calories and fat. In still others, it meant more indulgent foods, such as the Decadent chocolate-chip cookie that was higher in calories than an ordinary cookie. Different people with different tastes responded to these various offerings, but what they had in common was a willingness to spend more for better. "It's all driven by age," says White. "The market has gone from bulk products of inferior quality to products of better quality, either real or perceived. These products have fewer chemicals in them and they cost more. But the baby boom is willing to pay."

Lettuce is a good example, not only of what has happened to the Canadian supermarket as the boomers have aged, but of the broad shift in the entire retail marketplace from one dominated by price to one dominated by quality and service. Twenty years ago, most Canadian supermarkets carried only one kind of lettuce, iceberg. Today, they have several varieties, including lettuces most Canadians had never heard of in the 1970s. But that's not all. If she's willing to pay for the convenience, the time-pressed consumer doesn't even have to mix her own salad any more. Instead, she can buy a bagged salad containing a mixture of such exotic leafy vegetables as radicchio, red oak, curly endive, and tat soi. These are washed and stored in a special plastic bag that keeps them fresh for 14 days. White has been working with one supermarket chain to provide bags within the bags containing low-fat salad dressing and croutons. This salad not only is ready to eat, it also has more nutritional content than a salad based on an iceberg lettuce. But whereas a head of lettuce for less than a dollar will provide several days' worth of salads, the bagged salad provides only two servings and costs about $3. Such a product would not even be dreamt of in a marketplace governed by price. But in a quality and service market, it's a winner.

Natural foods and low-fat foods will be other winners in the years to come. "When you get to be a certain age, you realize you are not going to be here forever and you'd better do something to sustain the quality of life that you have," says White. "That involves a reversal of your diet. And so you drop the butter and cream — or save them for special occasions — and eat more healthily." This does not mean that middle-aged Canadians will be lining up at conventional health food stores with their sombre collections of whole grains and overpriced vitamin supplements. But they will patronize a large, elegant food store like Capers in Vancouver that combines natural foods with gourmet items or an O-Tooz Energie Bar, also a West Coast phenomenon, that serves filling, tasty, and healthy fast food in a bright, cheerful atmosphere.

As they switch to healthier diets, Canadians want more than brown rice and herbal tea. Rather than giving up chocolate entirely, they will cut down on standard chocolate bars but indulge occasionally in a superior truffle at an outrageous price. They will switch from restaurants that serve large portions of mediocre food to ones that offer small portions of beautifully prepared food. And they'll switch from Coke to Diet Coke.

Coca-Cola is a good example of a company making a successful, if occasionally painful, accommodation to marketplace transitions caused by demographics. Soft drinks are traditionally a young person's drink, so Coke seemed to be headed for trouble when the baby bust reduced the supply of its traditional consumers during the 1980s. Coca-Cola thought it was responding to changing tastes when it invented "new Coke." It didn't fully appreciate that it already had what an aging marketplace wanted: Diet Coke. This product, which is consumed by females of all ages and men over 30, is now the second most popular soft drink in Canada after regular Coke.

Meanwhile, Coke has rediscovered its pop-swilling youth market — in the developing world, which has a much younger population than the industrialized world. (See Chapter 11.) Coca-Cola, a truly global company, now earns 80% of its revenues outside the United States. Back in North America, it is busy unveiling new brands for the growing teen market of the echo. And to maintain the loyalty of the baby-boomers, Coke continues to expand its various lines of juices and bottled waters. These drinks, besides being healthier, have an advantage over soft drinks that all players in the food industry are going to need as the population ages: higher margins.

"When people start to eat less, the industry has to get as many dollars from less food," observes White. "We have to move people up from hot dogs at 99 cents a pound, because they are not going to be eating hot dogs. So how does a sausage maker stay in business? By inventing chicken or rabbit sausage and figuring out how to bead olive oil into it so it has the right kind of fat. You will have chicken sausages stuffed with dried tomato or something that's healthy. You will still be eating things that look like breakfast sausages, but they will have healthy ingredients so that you will want to eat them."

That's how demographics drives technological advances in the food industry, and that's how Coca-Cola and the sausage companies can beat the demographic odds and stay in business.

Alcohol

Two legal drugs that are major industries in our society, tobacco and alcohol, are losers in an aging population. People start using both as teenagers. Usage then begins to flatten during the 20s, stays flat during the 30s, and drops sharply during the 40s and 50s. Moderate use of alcohol is, according to many recent studies, good for the health, whereas tobacco is always hazardous. Canadians, in their collective wisdom, understand this. That is why alcohol is used by 80% of the population in their 20s and 30s while tobacco captures only 40%. Men drink more than women. Their use of alcohol declines a bit in the 30s and flattens in the 40s, while female use drops dramatically in the 40s.

The last of the baby-boomers turn 30 in 1996. That means the entire generation is now past its prime alcohol and tobacco consumption years, with only 18% of Canadians left in the age groups associated with increasing consumption. These products will continue to suffer declining volumes until the turn of the century, when the arrival of the baby-boom echo in the alcohol market will boost sales of cheaper wine and beer.

Growing awareness of the health implications of excessive use of tobacco and alcohol coupled with high taxation accounts for some of the drop in consumption, but even with less negative publicity and lower taxes, population aging alone would still result in a substantial decline. In Ontario, for example, sales of beer were 7% lower in 1995 than in 1991. Sales of wine, which is preferred by older people, declined by 4% in the same period, while those of spirits plunged 18%. In an attempt to counteract declining sales, and in response to the demands of an aging population for a decent shopping environment, provincial liquor monopolies across Canada made major improvements through the 1980s and 1990s to the level of quality and service they provided.

Cigarette smokers tend to be loyal to one brand, so tobacco companies have little opportunity to boost profit margins by winning older, more affluent customers over to better and more expensive versions of the same product. But taste in alcohol varies widely depending on age, and people do tend to move up to more expensive products. Over their lifetimes, people who enjoy alcohol proceed from beer to wine to spirits. But of course, this is not an all-or-nothing proposition. The person who casually consumed a six-pack of beer at a party in his late teens might sip one bottle a week as a 40-year-old on the night the family sends out for pizza. And the 50-year-old who has come to enjoy a shot of whiskey before dinner doesn't stop drinking a glass or two of wine with dinner. But he drinks less wine because he is now drinking spirits as well.

What does all this mean for alcohol consumption over the coming decade? The echo will be entering its beer-swilling years, bringing the beer industry's flat years to an end. It should enjoy rising sales for the rest of the 1990s and into the next decade. Wine sales will stabilize while demand for rye, Scotch, and other spirits, which has been falling for many years, will at least stabilize and may even rebound a little. This is the first good news the spirits business has heard in a long time.

The Canadian wine industry, centred in Ontario and British Columbia, moved from plonk to quality wines during the 1980s. The industry's timing was perfect, because these were the years when the baby boom was switching from beer to wine and gradually learning to tell good wine from bad. Interestingly, although Australia's vineyards started producing good wine about a decade before Canada's, its industry's sales didn't take off until the Australian boomers, like their Canadian counterparts, were in their late 20s and 30s and ready to appreciate wine.

The movement from quantity to quality is seen as much in alcoholic beverages as in the food industry. Even if Ontario icewine had existed in 1970, there weren't enough consumers ready and able to part with $40 for a half-bottle to make developing such a fabulously expensive product worthwhile. At the same time, we are seeing rapidly growing interest in exotic and very expensive single-malt Scotch whiskies and other spirits as well as a vast array of specialty beers, both Canadian and imported. Growing old isn't always enjoyable but it does have its compensations.

Clothing

"I used to take an 8, then I took a 6, now I take a 4, pretty soon I'll take a 2, and then I'm going to be 0. But I'm not shrinking. I'm the same size." That's Bernadette Morra, fashion editor of the *Toronto Star*, voicing a common complaint of that minority of the Canadian population who have grown older and wiser instead of older and wider. Not only have women's dress sizes been redefined to accommodate baby-boom bulge, even men's waist sizes have been relaxed by some manufacturers who are putting 32-inch labels on pants that fit comfortably around spongy 34-inch waists.

This kind of fantasy marketing is the industry's response to population aging. Older people don't spend as freely on clothes as younger ones, and the industry has to do whatever it can to get them to part with their cash. That's why women's apparel sizes have dropped twice over the past decade, so that a size 8 in the mid-1990s is equivalent to a size 12 a decade earlier. This infuriates slim women who find themselves hunting for clothes in children's stores. But, so the theory goes, staying the same size makes the majority feel good, and if you feel good, chances are better that you will open your wallet.

The people who spend more on clothes than anybody else are 25-to-30-year-olds. During the 1990s, this group is composed of a relatively small cohort, the baby-busters. That's the reason for the devastating shakeout that has seen hundreds of stores catering to big-spending young women fall by the wayside. These are the same stores that flourished when the mass of boomers were passing through their 20s. Dylex Ltd., the clothing retailer whose empire included Fairweather, Big Steel Man, and Town & Country, made large profits dressing clothes-hungry young boomers in the 1970s. The empire came crashing down in the 1990s when insolvent Dylex had to seek court protection from its creditors. Management errors and over-ambitious expansion in the U.S. were part of the problem. But the basic reason for the fall of Dylex was its failure to adapt its business strategy to the demographic reality that, because of population aging, the market for many of its products had shrunk.

The success of The Gap and other retailers shows that the youth market can still be an excellent source of profits despite being a smaller percentage of the total population than it was in the 1970s. But The Gap doesn't rely entirely on scarce twenty-something baby-busters. Some of its customers are affluent boomer mothers going shopping with their teenage daughters. Dylex's problem was that it continued to devote too many stores to a declining youth market with-out finding a successful way to address its former customers, whose tastes and needs had changed.

While Dylex was flourishing in the 1970s, stores selling bras and girdles were going out of business. Some people thought this hap-pened because of relaxed new attitudes about dressing spawned by the hippie movement. Actually, it was because a marketplace dominated by 20-year-olds with firm bodies has little need for bras and girdles. In the 1990s and beyond, these foundation garments will be making a big comeback. But, in general, most of Canada's $17-billion apparel indus-try seems clueless about how to respond to the demographic challenge. "Nobody's marketing to older people and I can't understand why," says Bernadette Morra. "Someone is going to come along and make a for-tune by aiming at that group."

One manufacturer who knows how to prosper in an older mar-ketplace is Armani, whose clothes for both men and women feature a loose silhouette that is kind to aging figures. Armani understands that the magic words quality and service apply just as much to clothes as to any other product in the retail world of the 1990s. The good news for the industry is that spending on clothes, especially by women, rebounds after the age of 50. Just as they do in the supermarket, these knowledgeable shoppers will buy less but better. "It's easier to manipulate a younger market into buying what's fashionable because they're insecure," explains John Winter, one of Canada's top retail consultants. "By the time you're in your 50s you've seen trends come and go for 30 years. You know what looks good on you, and that's what you buy. Women will spend more on a single item of clothing, but it's likely to be a classic like a Chanel jacket. They'll shop at stores they couldn't afford when they were younger."

One last fashion item, the running shoe, deserves a mention. The case of running shoes illustrates the danger of an overly simplistic approach to using demographics to forecast behaviour. It might have been logical to assume that companies such as Nike that rose to prominence during the aerobics boom of the 1970s would be in trouble in the 1990s, when some older boomers started slowing down. Such a prediction would have been wrong. The sports shoe business is doing fine, as a sophisticated use of demographics would have predicted. First of all, companies that started out making shoes for runners have expanded their product lines to include shoes for walkers and golfers. They also produce the basketball shoes that are so popular with the large echo generation. Moreover, just because somebody decides to give up running doesn't mean she gives up running shoes. As people get older, they need and can afford better shoes. They are more interested in arch and ankle support than younger people. A well-made running or walking shoe offers these qualities better than most other kinds of shoes. Because of demographics, it was predictable in the 1970s that a large market for shoes offering support and comfort would exist in the 1990s, as would a growing market for orthotics designed to fit the individual foot. And it should not be surprising that companies that learned how to make comfortable shoes for young runners in the 1970s would be able to adapt that know-how to the needs of older consumers in the 1990s.

Cars

A young person drives a small, cheap car. A person in his 30s or 40s moves up to a minivan. In his mid-40s or 50s, the consumer moves up again. That's why the Japanese, who understand the North American baby boom as well as anyone, introduced the Lexus, Acura, and Infiniti during the 1980s and why these and other luxury sedans have been successful. Upmarket consumers who prefer a more versatile vehicle than a sedan trade in their minivans for a sport utility vehicle such as a Jeep or Land Rover instead.

"Demographics is the whole secret," says Dennis DesRosiers, of DesRosiers Automotive Consultants, Canada's leading expert on the auto industry. "All the major trends in the automotive industry have been shaped by the baby-boomers coming through the system."

The problem for the North American auto industry is that it has never been able to figure the boomers out. Detroit was surprised in the 1960s and 1970s when first-time buyers in their 20s bought Japanese cars. In the mid-1990s, the affluent boomer in his late 40s has thrown the Big Three for a loop once again by not spending as much on cars as was anticipated. "Consumers have moved away from the habits of their fathers, who bought a new car every year if they could afford it. The market has moved to a new car every seven years, if that," says DesRosiers.

If it had a better grasp of demographic realities, the auto industry would not waste so much energy being surprised. Japanese cars flew out of showrooms in the 1970s because they offered good value to people for whom price was by far the most important purchasing criterion. And although minivans as such weren't predictable, it was obvious that people raising young families in the 1980s would gravitate towards more spacious vehicles and that any company that could create something more flexible and convenient than the conventional station wagon would do well. In the 1990s, a self-confident, knowledgeable buyer in his 40s doesn't have to impress the neighbours by buying a new car every couple of years.

But by emphasizing antilock brakes and other safety features, the automakers are on the right track. The front-end boomer is health-conscious in his decision-making in the supermarket, and he is equally health-conscious in the car showroom. Young people think they're immortal, which is why Ralph Nader was ahead of his time in the

1960s with his warnings to a youthful North American population about unsafe cars. But older people are well aware of their mortality, and in choosing a car they place a high priority on safety. That explains why Volvo, with its reputation for building cars as strong as tanks, is the most successful European manufacturer in the North American market in the 1990s.

The North American manufacturers need to work harder to win equivalent reputations for safety. They must also think more about passenger comfort. As the population ages, back problems become more common; the lumbar seat will be a symbol of the aging boomer. Eyesight also diminishes with age but the carmakers haven't yet responded adequately with improved instrument panels and radio dials. The manufacturers have the technology to produce "heads-up displays," which reflect fuel levels and other information from a semi-transparent screen coated onto the front windshield. But this technology is rarely seen in cars although thousands of over-40 consumers would welcome it.

The auto industry, as always, is behind the demographic times. The result is that the car business in Canada marked its seventh consecutive year of slumping sales in 1995, the longest downturn since World War II. People don't buy cars because the industry hasn't given them enough reasons for trading up and because they don't enjoy buying cars. The consumer in the 1990s is time-starved and despises the haggling most dealers still insist on putting him through before they will let him have a good deal. It is ludicrous to make a 45-year-old sit in an office twiddling his thumbs while the sales manager decides whether he will release one of his cars for a reasonable mark-up or whether he will force the customer to go to another dealer to play the same game all over again. Dealers insist on subjecting customers to this nonsense, and then they complain when buyers come to their showroom, test-drive a vehicle, and proceed to buy the same car from a leasing company or broker for a 3% mark-up above dealer cost without having to haggle. When this happens, dealers have only themselves to blame. Although not all attempts at a fixed-price policy have been successful, the industry is beginning to understand that the consumer has

lost interest in the haggling game. General Motors has been so successful with its no-haggle policy on the Saturn that it is moving to a similar policy for the Oldsmobile. Significantly, many Saturns are bought
for their young adult offspring by middle-aged parents who don't have
time to haggle. In Canada, GM moved in 1992 to a simplified pricing
policy with no advertised rebates and wound up gaining market share.

Car dealers must understand that the kind of customers some
of them describe as "laydowns" — gullible first-time buyers who will
accept bad deals without protest — are going to be harder to find in the
coming years. People in their 40s and 50s have bought several cars,
and they know what a vehicle is worth before they enter the showroom. What they want is a good deal without haggling. After that, they
want the service manager to respect their time. Picking up a car at the
customer's home would be one way of doing that. Performing an oil
change in ten minutes while the customer waits would be another.
Keeping the service bays open on weekends would be still another. A
one-stop service centre — mechanical and body work, while-you-wait
oil changes, car washing, plus rentals with special deals for customers
having their cars fixed — is what time-pressed consumers want. The
dealer who figures out how to give it to them will prosper in the new
retail world of quality and service.

What kind of cars will be popular in the years to come? The
era of the minivan is coming to an end. Once the kids are out of the
house, you don't need a minivan any more than you need a five-
bedroom house. That means luxury sedans and sport utility vehicles
will be the big sellers in the decade ahead. But there's one other market niche that could be a winner for those manufacturers who know
how to exploit it. People in their late 40s often use their second car as
a way to relive their youth. That's why we will see more vehicles such
as the Plymouth Prowler, a hot rod with a retro exterior but the latest
technology under the hood, which is due in the showrooms in 1997.
Another way to cash in on the boomer penchant for reliving the old
days would be to reproduce some classic big cars like the 1965 Mus-
tang. Under the hood and inside it would be a 1990s vehicle complete
with antilock brakes and CD player. But the exterior of the car should

be identical to the original. A car like that would give an aging boomer everything he wants in one package: comfort, safety, and nostalgia. Is someone in Detroit smart enough to do it? It's an open question, but DesRosiers says the Big Three's big brains are finally thinking about such issues. "The whole industry is focussed on what boomers are going to do next," he says. "The company that figures it out is going to be a big, big winner."

Consumer Electronics

Not long ago, a major electronics manufacturer brought out a line of VCRs with the stripped-down model going for the lowest price and the full-featured model going for the highest. These VCRs didn't sell very well. Then an executive had the bright idea of reversing course, redesigning the best-built and most expensive model to reduce the number of features on it and make it the simplest of all to operate. Sales turned around immediately.

In the world of high technology in the 1990s, less is more. Fewer features are better if the result is a machine that is easier to use. People over 30 did not grow up in the company of computers. As a result, they are less at home with technology than children, teenagers, and people in their 20s. A 10-year-old can load a computer game for the first time and be enjoying herself in a matter of minutes without even glancing at the manual. Her 45-year-old father could study the manual and practise for hours and still be unable to match the child's proficiency. But older people *will* embrace technology when the learning process is easy. In that sense, demographics is the driving force behind such new products as Windows 95, the Microsoft operating system whose graphical interface finally makes the PC as easy to use as a Macintosh.

Windows 95 is a response to an aging marketplace. Older people can't spend hours learning an operating system because they don't have hours to spend. Moreover, the 45-year-old came to technology relatively late in life and so learning a new software program is likely to be more challenging for him than it would be for a 25-year-old. But there are more older people than younger ones and they have more money. That is why companies are prepared to invest millions to make everything from VCRs to computer software as simple to use as possible.

Creators of new technologies tend to resist this argument. They like to think that brilliant people invent new technologies without worrying about whether anyone will want them. In doing so, they create new markets for new needs that did not previously exist. Although it is true that technological innovation creates new needs, thousands of products could be invented but aren't, because the research isn't applied to produce them. The research isn't applied because the companies that could afford to pay for it don't think they could recoup their investment. Companies hate investing money in technologies that fail to find a market. That's why they prefer to fill existing needs. By paying close attention to demographics, they can fill those needs more successfully.

To succeed in the future, a new product must offer quality and service. In the case of technology, service translates as convenience, meaning that the product must be easy to understand and easy to use. Two of the most successful product introductions were the cellular phone and the cordless phone, because they were natural extensions of previously existing technology. Everyone knows how to press buttons on a phone and anyone can learn how to push a few more. Similarly, the fax machine was an extension of the photocopier that everyone already knew. That's why even technophobes adopted the fax quickly and enthusiastically.

THE SENIORS' MARKET

In the 1990s, we have both an aging population and a slow-growing seniors' market. The reasons for this apparent paradox are simple — and important for retailers to understand. The seniors' market is growing slowly because the new entrants in the middle and late 1990s will be those born during the 1930s, a decade when few people were born in Canada. Yet we have an aging population because the largest single group, the 9.8 million baby-boomers, are entering their middle years.

An aging population and an old population are two different things, however, and when we use such phrases as "the greying of society," we have to be careful what we mean. It's true that baby-boomers are exhibiting grey hair and other signs of age. Even more will be grey by 1997 when the first boomer turns 50. But the peak of the boom, those born in 1961, won't be 65 years old until 2026. That's a long way off, and the baby-boomers as a group are a long way from being old. Marketers have to approach these people in ways that recognize that they are no longer youthful but without annoying them by making them out to be senior citizens before their time.

For the first time in our history (see Figure 4), the senior population is bifurcating into two very different marketplaces: the slow-growing, affluent group of young seniors, and the rapidly growing, much less prosperous market composed of people over 75. As a result, a single marketing strategy no longer works for all seniors. Because of the wide variations in the taste, needs, and circumstances of the senior population, it's more useful to break them down into young seniors (65 to 74), mid-seniors (75 to 84), and senior seniors (85 and up). These three groups have three distinct lifestyles. The young seniors are still healthy and spend a lot of time and money travelling. The mid-seniors are still at home but health problems are rendering them less mobile. Many senior seniors are in nursing homes.

The young seniors' market grew by 37% in the 1970s and by 29% in the 1980s. But growth has slowed to less than 13% in the 1990s. These people have done far better than they ever imagined they would when they formed their expectations in the grim days of the Depression of the 1930s. Because they did so well, they went out and acquired more of everything, including kids. That, along with immigration, is what triggered the baby boom. Today, the parents of the boomers are the richest group in Canada. They are part of the reason the cruise ship industry is expanding at a furious rate. (See Chapter 6.) Quality and service are the only way to sell to these people. They don't need much, but they can afford what they need. That's the good news for retailers. The bad news is that when young seniors have to replace refrigerators or cars, they are very tough customers because they have had plenty of experience buying refrigerators and cars.

Many young seniors will be ready to move out of empty nests

with more rooms than they need. This group is not a market for retirement homes, but many of them will be interested in new real estate developments that feature luxurious small houses fronting a golf course.

Towards the end of the next decade, the affluent Depression cohort will be entering its mid-senior years. The arrival of a wealthy group of retirees will mean an expanded market for upscale retirement homes that have more in common with luxury hotels than with the typical old folks' home. This trend is already well under way. An example is Le Wellesley in Pointe-Claire, Quebec, which has a licensed dining room, afternoon tea served daily in a lounge, a variety of recreation facilities, and a beauty salon. Luxury retirement homes charge from $950 to $7,000 a month. "These are places where seniors can be pampered and spoiled in nearly resort-style surroundings," says Samir Manji, whose company, Omega Capital Corp., owned four retirement homes in the fall of 1995 and was trying to acquire more. "This is one of the great undiscovered areas of real estate." It won't go undiscovered for long.

The fastest-growing segment of the seniors' market in the 1990s is the over-85 group. It is mainly female because women live six years longer than men, on average. It is also poor because the husbands of these women did not have transferable pensions. Few of the women had careers of their own and so they were unable to accumulate much savings. These people don't buy much. What they do buy tends to be merchandise such as incontinence pads and other health and personal care needs. Their major need is affordable nursing homes.

THE REVIVAL OF MAIN STREET

As the 1990s roll on, we will see a resurgence of the small local specialty store. An older, affluent consumer wants to shop at the neighbourhood bakery, butcher shop, or clothing boutique where the staff knows her name, her likes, and dislikes. This is good news for the quality of urban life. After two decades in which malls, megastores, and franchise operations have dominated the market, the idiosyncratic specialty retailer is poised to make a comeback. Because of favourable demographics, Canada's retail landscape is going to become more interesting.

There are a couple of qualifications to this happy prospect. Many people would never think of going shopping without a car, and so neighbourhood shopping districts that make parking available have the best chance of success. Initiatives to improve traffic flow by restricting on-street parking are therefore a threat to local shops. The other qualification is that only neighbourhoods with a substantial population of people over 40, who have more money than time, will be able to support these stores. Small towns and younger communities can't do it. For example, the oldest city in Canada historically, St. John's, Newfoundland, is one of the youngest demographically, with a higher proportion of people in the 15-to-24 age group than most other urban areas. That makes St. John's more fertile ground for suburban malls than for small neighbourhood shops.

The revival of Main Street Canada won't be the only throwback to the past as retailing embraces quality and service. Home delivery could also make a comeback. Dairyland, one of Canada's oldest milk companies, is on the leading edge of this trend. Not only does Dairyland still deliver milk, it also delivers a wide range of other groceries, from meat to detergent, to its Vancouver customers' doors. Senior seniors, a growing market neglected by most retailers, get their groceries delivered right to the fridge; the drivers also check up to see that these customers, most of whom are elderly widows, are all right. As an additional service, they take away empty containers. Prices are competitive with grocery stores and payment, by cheque, is required only once a month. This kind of service is attractive not only to seniors but also to stay-at-home parents and the growing ranks of professionals in their 40s and 50s working in home offices. It's a good example of how demographic change can take us back to the future.

By 2000, the front end of the baby-boom echo will be 20 years old. They will be entering the labour market for the first time, setting up a household for the first time, buying used cars and the cheapest fridges and stoves they can find. If they want some salad, they'll make their own rather than blow $3 on fancy greens in a bag. Retailing based on low prices is heading for a comeback in Canada. Businesses based on low prices that manage to survive the 1990s will have a new lease on life after 2000. But at the same time as the young echo generation is entering the marketplace, the 45-to-54 age group will grow by 20%, while the 55-to-64 group explodes by 50%.

This will be a confusing marketplace for many retailers. One strategy will be to address both the young and older segments at the same time. This can be done successfully if the merchant remembers that the younger consumer is interested primarily in price while the older shopper places a high value on quality and service. Car mufflers are a good example. A muffler is a muffler no matter who buys it; the difference is in the service. Offer the busy middle-aged customer pick-up and delivery and a guaranteed work schedule. Offer the younger one a 20% discount if she is willing to show up at a less busy time and wait for service. That way you satisfy the needs of both customers and keep them both happy.

Other retailers will decide to specialize in one market or the other and some will succeed. The baby boom is the largest single demographic cohort but it is only one-third of the population, and the other two-thirds also has needs to fill and money to spend. However, it's always easier to succeed in a growing market than in a smaller one, and in Canada the growth is always where the boom is. Because the boom is about to move into its 50s, Canada will have more older consumers than young ones for many years to come. The age of quality and service has a long future ahead of it.

Chapter 6

Tennis, Anyone?

"Jackrabbit" Johannsen, the legendary pioneer of cross-country skiing in Canada, was still skiing five kilometres during a weekend on the trails of Quebec's Laurentian Mountains at the age of 104. The heart-attack patients of Toronto's Dr. Terry Kavanagh, many in their 50s and 60s, recuperate by taking up vigorous exercise, and some of them go on to compete in marathons. Countless other feats of strength and endurance by older folks in Canada and all over the world attest to the truth that aging and decrepitude need not go together. In fact, experts say it's never too late to get fit, and that a fit person of 70 has the same oxygen-carrying capacity as an unfit person of 30.

But what people could do and what they actually do are different things. If Jackrabbit Johannsen were typical, he wouldn't have become famous. Most people, as they get older, become less active and less inclined to engage in strenuous activities. As a result, their leisure and recreation habits change. The impacts of these changes, on every recreational pursuit from badminton to birding, are dramatic. Moreover, these impacts are predictable.

Anyone involved in leisure and recreation can be prepared for these changes well in advance. There is no excuse for a community to spend money on hockey rinks in the mid-1990s that are likely to be empty in 2005, while neglecting to provide the parks and walking trails that an aging population needs. Canada can't afford mistakes like those; if we pay attention to demographics, we can avoid them.

The outlook isn't promising. People in the recreation field and those who earn their living as sports commentators are remarkably obtuse when it comes to the impact of demographics. Tennis in the United States has plummeted from 30 million players in the mid-1970s to 16 million in the mid-1990s. Why? The *Wall Street Journal* declared that people have been turned off tennis because "unshaven brats and grungewear fashion plates" are dominating the pro tennis tour. It apparently didn't occur to this serious, fact-filled newspaper to acknowledge the powerful demographic factor at work: the average age of Americans is increasing, and in general, older people don't play tennis as much as younger ones do.

The same imperviousness to reality is evident in the world of spectator sports. As the 1990s progress, it appears that the era of growth in professional sports might be coming to an end. Some franchises are experiencing declines in attendance. Sports commentators are quick to come up with reasons: labour unrest, obnoxious behaviour by over-paid players, declining quality of play, ineptitude on the part of some teams, increased competition from other forms of entertainment. These factors are undoubtedly relevant. In the case of baseball, for example, attendance plunged in 1995 in the wake of a disastrous strike that resulted in cancellation of the 1994 World Series and widespread resentment among fans. Yet, because of population aging, baseball attendance was going to drop anyway, if not in 1995 then in the years to come, because older people attend fewer sports events than younger ones. An important reason is that once the kids are old enough to go to a ballgame on their own, Dad no longer has to take them. That doesn't mean he will never again set foot in Olympic Stadium or SkyDome, but instead of a dozen games a season, he might take in only two or three. That's why demographics will continue to have a powerful negative impact on baseball attendance long after fans have forgotten the 1994 strike.

Of the 18-to-24 age group, 50% attend sports events. Of the 45-to-64 age group, only 30% attend. Can these numbers be changed by better teams, more comfortable stadiums, better promotion? Perhaps, but only a little: from 1965 to 1982, attendance at sports events by people aged 45 to 64 increased by all of 1%. By 2012, all of the baby boom will be in this age group. This is not good news for owners of professional sports franchises.

It doesn't necessarily mean that all of Canada's professional franchises are in danger of imminent demise. Our population continues to increase, raising the overall market for sports as for all other products. And professional franchises are located in major cities, which have a younger population than the country as a whole (see Chapter 7). As well, a franchise in a major centre like Toronto draws on a vast market, including residents of cities and towns within a two-hour drive who make the trip to one or two games a year. This means that the future of the Blue Jays, Canadiens, Grizzlies, and most — although certainly not all — of the other professional franchises in Canada is reasonably secure. Nevertheless, the days of rapid growth, sold-out seasons, and ever more lucrative television contracts are coming to an end.

A nation of young people is a society of hockey and tennis players. A nation of older people is a society of gardeners and walkers. These gentler, more individualistic pursuits replace the more vigorous activities of youth partly because the human body (even the well-trained human body) becomes less flexible and less responsive as the years take their toll. Another important reason is that middle-aged people have busier schedules, both at the office and at home, than young ones and naturally gravitate away from activities that require more time and more than one participant. If it's tough to get two time-pressed 40-year-olds together for a tennis match, it's that much tougher to get a dozen of them in the same place at the same time to play hockey. It may be possible only once a week instead of every day, as when they were younger.

The data on the impact of aging on leisure pursuits is clear and remarkably stable over time. As with all human behaviour, two key factors determine the growth of various leisure activities: the size of the population and the rate of participation. The latter undergoes dramatic changes as the population ages. For example, 16% of Canadians between the ages of 18 and 24 are waterskiers. But members of the

45-to-64 age group restrict their waterskiing activities to piloting the boat; only 2% actually put on skis and take to the water.

Of course, aging isn't the only demographic variable. Immigration is another, and high levels of immigration mean more younger people, which in turn means faster growth for active sports. An upward movement in the fertility rate would also boost participation in active sports 10 to 15 years later. But neither of these variables is powerful enough to offset the massive effects of the aging of the baby-boom generation in Canada.

As a result, projections show that resting will be one of Canada's most popular leisure "activities" in the years to come. So will TV watching, reading, hobbies, and attendance at museums, theatres, and places of worship. In contrast, participation in sports as well as attendance at sports events will become less popular. These facts have important public policy implications. Even with the impact of the youthful echo generation, Canada probably has all the football fields, squash courts, and volleyball courts it needs. If funds are available for new facilities, they should be devoted to walking trails, curling rinks, and swimming pools for recreational swimming, because an older population continues to engage in these activities.

The impact of demographics on leisure and recreation has significance for the labour market as well. If your daughter wants a career in recreation, she would be better off teaching dancing than teaching tennis, because aging boomers are more likely to take up the tango than pick up a racquet.

This sort of analysis rubs a lot of baby-boomers the wrong way. "We're different," they say. "We're fitter than our parents were, and we're going to stay young a lot longer." But if that's so, why are the ranks of symphony-goers increasing at a faster rate than those of skiers in the mid-1990s? The only apparent answer is that boomers in their 40s are behaving as people in their 40s have always behaved.

But let's take the boomers at their word and assume that they really are, both mentally and physically, younger than their parents. That's been done in Figure 5 for the eight most popular sports in Canada as identified by Statistics Canada's 1992 General Social Survey.

FIGURE 5: GROWTH IN SPORTS PARTICIPATION, 1996-2001

	AT CURRENT RATES		UNDER "YOUTHFUL" RATES	
	% Growth	Rank	% Growth	Rank
Hockey	2.36	8	3.88	7
Downhill Skiing	5.05	5	4.99	5
Swimming	5.55	3	6.33	3
Golf	7.01	2	7.56	1
Baseball	2.67	7	4.34	6
Cross-Country	7.34	1	7.35	2
Volleyball	3.33	6	3.62	8
Tennis	5.21	4	5.39	4

Source: Calculations by David K. Foot, based on Statistics Canada, *General Social Survey, 1992* and *Population Projections, 1993-2016*

These sports are hockey (a participation rate of 6.4%), downhill skiing (6.3%), swimming (6.2%), golf (5.9%), baseball (5.6%), cross-country skiing (4%), volleyball (3.8%), and tennis (3.5%). In the chart, the first two columns show the projected growth in participation from 1996 to 2001, based on historical behaviour of different age groups. Under this scenario, six of the eight sports grow more slowly than the over-15 population.

The second two columns in the chart show a participation pattern that has been altered on the assumption that in future people might behave in a more youthful manner their predecessors. As you can see, it doesn't much change the outlook for active sports; it just slows down their decline a bit. Whether or not the boomers prove to be more robust than their parents as they get older, making or selling binoculars for birdwatchers and concertgoers will be a faster-growing business in the years to come than making or selling most kinds of sporting equipment.

Let's take a more detailed look at what the future holds for some of Canada's favourite leisure activities.

HOCKEY

This is the most popular sport in Canada, played by 1.4 million people over the age of 15, according to Statistics Canada. By comparison, the second most popular sport is downhill skiing, with 1.3 million adherents, closely followed by swimming, golf, and baseball. Hockey is also one of the most popular activities among boys under 15. Minor hockey boomed right through the 1960s and into the 1970s, until the impact of the baby bust caused growth to subside in the late 1970s. One impact of the decline was that suddenly older players could get rink time at convenient hours. Some suggested that this showed hockey was gaining popularity among older players. In fact, more older people *were* playing, but only because there were more older people and because rink time was available.

Today the echo kids are in their prime hockey-playing years, so the rinks have filled up again. But the echo peaked in 1990, which means that demand on hockey facilities will peak around 2002 and decline thereafter. Because of the impact of the echo as well as ongoing demand from busters and boomers still playing hockey, Canada does need some new hockey rinks in the 1990s. But we should be careful not to overbuild. Just as no community can afford to build enough roads to ensure that rush-hour traffic moves as quickly as midnight traffic, so Canadian communities can't afford to build enough rinks to easily accommodate a decade-long hockey "rush hour." New rinks should be built sparingly and selectively, and they should be easily adaptable to curling, which grows in popularity with aging.

SKIING AND TENNIS

More than 58% of downhill skiers are under 35. Forty-four per cent of skiers take up the sport when they are under 17; only 12% start skiing when they are over 35. Skiers 24 years old and younger ski 12.3 days a season, while skiers aged 35 to 44 get to the slopes only 8.5 days per season.

Statistics like these paint a picture of a sport that inevitably declines in popularity in an aging society. The 1990s will be a reasonably good decade for skiing because the sizeable echo generation is moving through its teenage skiing and snowboarding years. That's why skiing will grow by a projected 5% from the mid-1990s through to 2001. But skiing doesn't have the growth potential of activities that appeal to older age groups — activities like bird-watching, which will grow two and a half times as much as skiing over that same period.

Some say you can't judge the future by the past. New equipment has revolutionized the sport, they point out, making it more attractive to older skiers. It's true that step-in boots and high-tech skis have made skiing easier and safer than it was. Instruction techniques have been improved and standardized. And the new detachable, high-speed chair lifts are a major advance — they are much easier to board and dismount from than the old lifts, and they allow skiers to spend more time skiing down the mountain and less time riding up. Yet another argument in favour of a bright future for downhill skiing in an aging society is that, except in deep powder snow, it isn't a particularly strenuous activity. If it were, fewer overweight, unfit people would be seen cruising expertly down the trails of Canada's ski resorts.

But the best that skiing can hope for is that all of these positive factors will add up to a small increase in the skiing participation rate for middle-aged and older people. That won't be enough to offset the abrupt decline that historically takes place in skiing with age. In 1982, for example, the participation rate for the 45-to-64 age group was a measly 3%, compared with 15% for the 18-to-24 group. In 1982, that ski-happy 18-to-24 group included a large part of the huge baby-boom generation. But in the mid-1990s, all the boomers are past their prime skiing years and beginning to enter the 3% marketplace.

Obviously, participation varies depending on the availability and quality of skiing. Statistics Canada reports that the overall skiing participation rate in British Columbia, Alberta, and Quebec, the provinces that have the biggest mountains, is as much as three times as high as in the provinces that don't have big mountains. Montreal and Vancouver both have good skiing close to the city centre. As an alternative to taking in a movie for an evening's entertainment, a Vancouverite can spend a couple of hours under the lights on one of the North Shore mountains. Toronto is not so blessed. And because Ontario has no mountains and therefore no skiing comparable to what can be found in B.C., Alberta, and Quebec, fewer Torontonians would be attracted to the sport in the first place. As a result, a higher percentage of older Vancouverites will continue skiing than older Torontonians. But more younger Vancouverites will also be skiing. The percentage fall-off in participation remains the same. Older people, wherever they live, just don't ski as much as young people.

Tennis, like skiing, has been improved by technological advances. The modern graphite frames absorb all the shock of hitting the ball so that it is not transferred to the arm and elbow, as was the case with wooden and older metal frames. Because of the new equipment, tennis players are less susceptible to tennis elbow and tennis shoulder, and the sport is more accessible to older people. But they still don't do it. Tennis participation falls from 33% in the 18-to-24 age group down to 7% in the 45-to-64 age group. That's why tennis clubs that had waiting lists in the 1980s have billboards pleading for new members in the 1990s.

For both these sports, the outlook is one of retrenchment. To maintain the loyalty of those older people who do continue to participate, tennis clubs and ski operators will have to adopt the new credo of all product and service providers: quality and service. To their credit, the managers of such ski resorts as Blue Mountain in Ontario and Mont Tremblant in Quebec have already done that. The service they offer, from the quality of food to availability of babysitting, is markedly improved from the days when they were in a seller's market. Tennis clubs are responding in the same way. One reason tennis participation falls off is that older people are pressed for time and it's difficult to get two people, or four for doubles, on the same tennis court at the same time. "I'm 49 years old and I've got a very busy schedule," says Robert Moffatt, executive director of Tennis Canada. "I can't be bothered phoning up three people to arrange a doubles. The club I belong to now does that, which helps me play three times a week rather than once."

Local ski operations that depend on day-trippers from nearby urban areas face an uncertain future. Only the very best operators among these businesses will survive into the next century. Some local hills, competing for market share among a smaller cohort of young people, may see snowboarding replace skiing as their main attraction. Those resorts that have sufficient land and snow will be able to expand their market by laying out new cross-country trails. Cross-country appeals to older skiers more than downhill.

The handful of elite destination resorts that attract holidayers from afar have better prospects than the local resorts, because they have a much bigger market to draw on. Whistler-Blackcomb, in the Coast Mountains north of Vancouver, has a secure future because it is a magnet for affluent skiers from all over North America and, increasingly, from Asia, Latin America, and Britain. Whistler has the good fortune of being the closest world-class resort to ski-happy Japan. As a destination resort, Whistler is competing not with the local Vancouver mountains but with the ski meccas of Colorado and Europe. To hold its own — and to compensate for the often soggy and unpleasant weather in the valley between Whistler and Blackcomb mountains — it will have to continue to improve the quality of its product. In future, because of aging, more skiers will choose to spend fewer hours on the slopes during their ski vacations. They will need things to do the rest of the time or they won't come, and Whistler village will have to offer more varied and better shopping and cultural activities than it currently has if it is to maintain its position.

PERFORMING ARTS

In the 1980s, the future seemed grim for high culture in Canada. Audiences were dwindling, younger people weren't coming, and the financial picture was shaky. The Vancouver Symphony almost folded and other arts companies faced an uncertain future. But music aficionados were more pessimistic than they needed to be. They fretted that, as the oldest members of the audience died, no younger people would come along to replace them because the baby-boom generation, raised on the Beatles and the Rolling Stones, would never tune in to Mozart and Verdi.

Culture lovers should relax and enjoy the music. Baby-boomers are human beings, not a new species. Previous generations also had their own popular music, and they too eventually learned to appreciate classical music. Middle-aged and older people have always been more interested in the classics than young people, and the ranks of the middle-aged and seniors will grow explosively in the decades ahead. The future of classical music in Canada has never been brighter.

When a new hockey rink was constructed in 1994 at Acadia University in Wolfville, Nova Scotia, the old one was remodelled into a centre for Shakespearean theatre. That transformation perfectly symbolizes what will happen in Canada because of population aging: attendance at hockey and other spectator sports is likely to grow at rates well below population growth, while growth in attendance at plays and other cultural events will probably exceed population growth. As a result, we will need more theatres and fewer arenas.

In the mid-1990s, the turnaround is already becoming evident, despite a lingering recession and cutbacks in government support for the arts. The Toronto Symphony, the Canadian Opera Company, the National Ballet, and the Vancouver Opera Association all report growing audiences after years of falling attendance. In 1995 the Shaw Festival at Niagara-on-the-Lake, Ontario, enjoyed record paid attendance and revenues. Other theatre companies as well as art galleries are also savouring new-found popularity.

Where have the new recruits to the arts come from? From the same people who caused sales of recorded classical music to double in the first part of the 1990s. These front-end boomers are in their 40s, the age when most people start paying attention to serious music and theatre. (It's also the age when their children are old enough to be left home alone, so that parents, liberated from dependence on babysitters, start going out again.) It was because of the front-end boomers that the Vancouver Opera Association was able to report in 1995 that 64% of its new subscribers were under 50.

These trends illustrate that the notion of "cocooning" as a permanent new lifestyle has been greatly exaggerated. Cocooning (see

Chapter 10) never was a new value system; it was merely the normal behaviour of people in their 30s with a couple of kids and a mortgage. Because so many people found themselves in that state at the same time, people unacquainted with demographics mistook cocooning for a new mode of behaviour rather than the passing phase that it was. In 1992, the Canadian Arts Consumer Profile, a national survey of arts consumption in Canada, rediscovered the obvious: most people love going out. A large majority of respondents — 66% — said they wanted to attend concerts more often. Moreover, the report dispelled the idea that fans of popular and serious culture occupy two solitudes. In fact, 25% of rock audiences reported also attending the ballet, and 25% of opera-goers paid to see stand-up comedians at work.

One other art form deserves mention: the musical. In the 1990s, with the front of the baby-boom generation in its 40s, musicals have become a multimillion-dollar business. Audiences flock to new shows such as *The Phantom of the Opera* and to old ones like *Show Boat.* People in their 20s generally don't like this kind of entertainment. People in their 40s are much more receptive to it, and they can afford the extravagant ticket prices. Andrew Lloyd Webber's timing, therefore, has been demographically perfect. He started in Britain, which has an older population, and moved to North America when North America's demographics were ready for him. Had Webber come on the scene with the same music a decade earlier, he would probably not have had the same degree of success.

The future of musicals is bright. The perfect product holds the interest of older people and is suitable for young ones as well. When you pull this trick off in the 1990s, you capture two large cohorts, the baby boom and the baby-boom echo, at the same time. That's why a show like *Beauty and the Beast* has the potential to be going strong in North American theatres when the millennium arrives.

BIRDWATCHING AND WALKING

Fans of *The Beverly Hillbillies* loved to laugh at prissy Miss Hathaway, the birdwatcher. Now many of the same people who considered Miss Hathaway's pastime so absurd can be found stomping rural trails on chilly mornings, with guidebooks, binoculars, and birding scopes in hand. At Point Pelee, a southern Ontario park renowned for its bird show during the spring migration, watchers often appear to outnumber birds.

We don't read much about this activity. That's why it comes as a shock to learn that in the United States today, 65 million birdwatchers are spending $5.2 billion annually on bird-related products. That's almost as much as the $5.9 billion Americans spend to attend all professional sports. The 65 million includes anyone who has a birdfeeder and watches birds out the kitchen window. About half that many people in the U.S. and Canada are serious enough to take excursions specifically to view birds.

It's not surprising that birdwatching has become big business. It combines gentle exercise, travel, and intellectual challenge (identifying birds) with the joy of collecting: serious birders keep detailed accounts of their sightings and compete to add rare species to their records. These factors help explain why, in a projection of growth rates of outdoor activities between 1996 and 2011, birdwatching was predicted to be the fastest-growing of all: 6% growth, compared with 3% for golf and 4.5% for fishing. Birdwatching, gardening, and walking are among the few activities that people do more of as they get older. That's why Canada will have some of the world's most closely watched birds over the coming decades.

Although birdwatching is the most peaceful and innocuous of activities, it is capable of provoking intergenerational conflict between the boomers and the busters. In Toronto and elsewhere, naturalists, including birders, have clashed with mountain bikers and in-line skaters in their teens and 20s, accusing them of severely damaging the few bits of nature that have escaped urbanization. "Recently my wife and I went birding on Toronto's Lower Don Trail," recounted a correspondent in the *Globe and Mail*'s letters column in 1995. "[We] were subjected to continual verbal abuse from both the skaters and bicyclists who considered that they and they alone had the right of passage." Another correspondent promptly replied on behalf of bikers and skaters. "The real source of danger in our parks is pedestrians who walk two or three abreast...deaf to oncoming bikers and skaters who need to pass if they are to enjoy the parks," he wrote.

In Ontario, the Bruce Trail Association has had to set up a committee to mediate the conflict between bikers and walkers. "We're hoping for a resolution, but it may be like the conflict between cross-country skiers and snowmobilers. Eventually they set up their own separate trails," says Jacqueline Winters, executive director of the organization responsible for the 775-kilometre Bruce Trail, the longest continuous footpath in Canada. "Mountain biking is more a sport of the young. Walkers tend to be over 35, very many of them professional people. The conflict will be between these two groups."

As a majority of the population moves from activities like tennis and spectator sports to ones like walking and birding, the movement to make the countryside more accessible will intensify. The most spectacular example is the Trans-Canada Trail, which is scheduled to open on July 1, 2000, as the longest recreational trail in the world. It will cover 15,000 kilometres from the east coast of Newfoundland all the way to the west coast of Vancouver Island, with a branch stretching from Calgary to Tuktoyaktuk on the Beaufort Sea. It will be suitable for hiking, cycling, horseback riding, skiing, and snowmobiling. Another example of the demographics-driven movement to make use of the great Canadian outdoors is the Canadian Rails to Greenways Network, which promotes the rehabilitation of abandoned rail corridors for recreational purposes. Similar movements exist in the United Kingdom, the United States, Australia, and New Zealand, where population aging is also occurring.

GOLF

Golf is one of the most time-consuming of all sports. A round of 18 holes typically takes four hours or more to play. In addition, golfers need to warm up at the practice tee and green before a round, place and record their bets, and replay the day's events in the clubhouse lounge afterwards. Throw in travel time to and from the course, and you've extracted six hours from a day. This is what makes golf the perfect sport for retired people; it gives a focus and purpose to their day as well as the companionship of friends and some beneficial yet not strenuous exercise. For those who aren't up to a four-hour walk in the park, electric golf carts are available. The presence of paunchy golfers on the professional tour attests that one can play this game at the highest level even without a high level of fitness.

Given all that, it's not surprising that golf is one sport in which participation increases with age, from 5% in the 19-to-24 age group to 10.2% in the 35-to-54 group, before dropping off to 8.7% in the over-55 group. And while the total percentage of older Canadians playing golf is not high, those who do play spend a large part of their lives on the course. In an aging population, therefore, golf is a growth industry.

"There's definitely a shift among the baby-boomers from tennis to golf," says Sam Gaudet, recreation director at the Algonquin Resort in St. Andrews, New Brunswick. "We used to offer tennis packages, but there's not the demand now." Evidence of golf's powerful appeal to older people is that, in contrast to most other sports, golfers play more as they get older. According to a 1990 study by Canada's National Golf Foundation, golfers aged 12 to 17 average 8.3 rounds a year, while those over 65 average 35 rounds a year.

Yet for those considering investing in the golf industry, numbers like these can be deceptive. Yes, golf is growing, but that doesn't mean any investment in golf will automatically succeed. Both the product and the timing have to be right. During the economic boom times of the 1980s, for example, many new courses opened in Canada, including some offering equity memberships for amounts as large as $50,000. Some of these courses did not attract enough members to survive as private clubs and were forced to open up to the general public. These clubs failed for two reasons. One was that, with the economic recession, many companies could no longer afford corporate memberships for their executives. But more important, the front-end boomers who were increasingly taking up golf weren't yet ready to part with a big chunk of cash for a club membership. In the late 1980s, they were just beginning to turn 40. At that age, people still have kids at home and a mortgage. In the late 1990s, as the boomers start turning 50, the kids will be on their own, the mortgage will be history, golfers will have more discretionary income at their disposal, and the courses built in the 1980s will be able to go private as originally planned. Because their developers did not pay enough attention to demographics, these courses were ten years ahead of their time.

TRAVEL

The upmarket travel business recruits its customers from affluent individuals in their late 40s and older. As this group expands in the years to come, the travel industry will reap the benefits. These front-end boomers have paid off their houses, their kids are starting to leave home, and they are at the peak of their earning power. This adds up to more discretionary income than they have ever had before. They are ready for something a bit more adventurous and unusual than the standard package tour to Mexico, Hawaii, or the Caribbean. Perhaps a walking tour of Nepal (providing it includes comfortable accommodation) or an excursion to view wildlife in Costa Rica or a trip to Irkutsk on the Trans-Siberian Railway.

Eco-tourism will be a growth industry. People in their late 40s and 50s seek out peace and quiet. They appreciate nature, they have some discretionary income, they are well travelled, and they're in the market for something new, like digging for dinosaur bones in Alberta, visiting archeological sites in Turkey, or snorkelling off a small island in the Pacific.

It is because these pioneer boomers are verging on 50 that the cruise industry will launch a dozen new megaships during the late 1990s. The first of these, the *Sun Princess*, will temporarily be the largest cruiser in the world, at 77,000 gross tons of displacement. But before the decade is out, it will be overtaken by ships that displace 100,000 tons, even bigger than such giants of the glory days of transatlantic voyages as the *Queen Mary* and the *Queen Elizabeth*. The cruise industry hopes to benefit not only from the vast new baby-boom market, but also from what has been called "three-generational bonding" — affluent baby-boomers taking both their parents and their children on an ocean voyage.

While these big ships will appeal to some, others will avoid them. Many baby-boomers pride themselves on their individualism and may balk at being part of the huge crowds these megaships will need to attract to stay afloat. Smaller ships offering trips to unusual destinations for much smaller groups of travellers will have much more appeal to this group. High-quality tours to such places as the Galapagos and Antarctica are likely to grow in popularity.

The young seniors, the most affluent group of senior citizens this country has ever seen, are another lucrative market for sellers of upmarket travel. The winners in catering to this market will be those who can offer adventurous and challenging travel in a package that recognizes the health concerns of young seniors without insulting them by making them out to be a lot more feeble than they are. Young seniors who sign up for a tour of the Himalayas are likely to be vigorous and robust people, quite capable of climbing and hiking on a wilderness trail. But they do expect a comfortable place to stay at night and good food. And if the brochure mentions that, in addition to a naturalist, a doctor will be along for the tour, the adventurous senior traveller probably won't protest too loudly.

GAMBLING

An Italian politician once argued that lotteries were bad public policy because they encouraged people to gamble away money that was needed to feed, house, and clothe their families. Nonsense, replied Amintore Fanfani, the Italian prime minister at the time. Lotteries, he declared, were perfectly justifiable because they were a "tax on idiots." What he meant was that, because the odds of winning a major lottery prize are infinitesimal, only an idiot would waste money in the attempt.

Canada, it seems, has a plentiful supply of apparent idiots. Quebec launched the first provincial lottery in 1970 and the rest of the country soon followed. By 1992, lottery sales nationwide were $1.7 billion. And lotteries, of course, are only one of many ways available for people to lose — and occasionally win — money in games of chance. Horse racing is well established in Canada, as are casinos run for charitable causes. Recently, Montreal and Windsor established permanent Las Vegas–style casinos. All told, Canadians spend $11 billion a year on legal gambling.

Still more is spent on illegal gambling in its many forms, including betting on professional sports. Finally, large sums of money change hands in private gambling, whether on the golf course or at kitchen-table card games. The latter, from a consumer standpoint, is the best kind of gambling. Unlike a lottery, which returns less than half the money wagered to bettors, all of the money bet in a private poker game winds up in the hands of the winners. But lotteries have one big attraction that a poker game doesn't: the chance, however remote, of winning a huge, life-changing prize worth millions of dollars.

Who gambles? Theory suggests that young people would have a big incentive to try to win a lottery, because if you can obtain a lot of money early in your life you won't have to work for the rest of it. Furthermore, theory also suggests that people between the ages of 25 and 50 are too busy raising children to participate in gambling. But the actual demographic profile of gamblers is different from what economic and sociological theory would predict.

Fanfani was wrong: most lottery players aren't idiots. To them, a lottery ticket is less an investment for financial return than an investment in fun and risk. Gambling, in other words, is recreation or entertainment, which is why it is discussed in this chapter rather than the one on investment. People are most likely to afford recreation in their 40s and 50s. And that is when they start buying lottery tickets and visiting casinos.

Lottery sales rose over the 1980s. The marketers maintained that happened because they developed better games and better distribution systems. Actually, it happened because the front half of the baby boom reached 40, the beginning of its gambling years. An aging population is good news for the future of lotteries. In the mid-1990s, only the front end of the boom has reached its 40s. Starting in 1997, the front end will begin moving into its 50s, which are also big lottery years, while the huge back end attains its gambling 40s.

That doesn't mean all forms of gambling will prosper. The retail credo of the 1990s, quality and service, applies as much to gambling as to any other product. The 50-year-old is a knowledgeable consumer. If she is going to buy a lottery ticket, it has to be readily available, and the game has to be sophisticated enough to interest her.

Amid growing competition for the gambling dollar, will lotteries continue to get away with offering the poorest odds of any form of gambling? Maybe not, if horse racing can make itself more accessible through off-track betting and if casino gambling continues to expand. Both pay back a much higher percentage of money wagered than lotteries do. On the other hand, public lotteries target their profits for worthy causes such as hospitals and recreation facilities; the consumer is thus prepared to be short-changed as a gambler, knowing that his losses are being used for the common good. In the face of growing competition, however, lottery marketers will have to make the social case for their product more strongly than ever before.

In the 1990s, casinos, previously allowed only in the state of Nevada and Atlantic City, have begun sprouting in other parts of North America. Some view this as a sign of declining moral standards in North America. At the same time, and in complete contradiction, arguments are voiced that the increasing acceptance of "family values" and the decline in popularity of pot smoking are signs of resurgent moral conservatism.

In fact, these changes had little to do with morality and much to do with demographics. Pot smoking declined because pot is smoked by people in their teens and 20s, and the numbers of such people fell during the 1980s. Family values came to the fore because the number of people in their 30s and 40s raising families increased. And casino gambling is on the verge of a boom because millions of baby-boomers right across North America are pushing 50. Casino gambling is an activity that appeals to people around 50 and over. The regulations that outlawed casinos are being overturned because a massive wave of 50-year-olds is about to wash over North America. Thus, the arrival of casinos in localities that once shunned them is largely a normal market response to surging demand.

In fact, gambling in general will be a major growth industry for the foreseeable future. It is already one of the fastest-growing recreational activities in North America because it offers heart-pounding excitement without the physical exertion associated with mountain climbing or whitewater rafting. In 1993, Americans spent $27 billion on legal gambling, as much as they spent on airline tickets. In 1995, Las Vegas had 89,000 hotel rooms, more than any other city in the United States, and was in the midst of a massive building boom.

But the concerns of those who regret the spread of gambling should not be dismissed lightly. Gambling is often associated with criminal activity. Just as an aging population is more interested than a younger population in gambling, so it has more criminals adept at money-laundering and other forms of fraud. These are crimes that require more knowledge and skill than most young people have yet had time to acquire. In the decades ahead, as gambling becomes ever more prevalent, our law enforcement agencies will need to develop greater expertise in combatting gambling-related crime. (See Chapter 7.)

VOLUNTEERING

A huge difference exists between leisure activities such as listening to music, rolling dice, or playing basketball and philanthropic ones such as raising money for cancer research or being a Big Brother to a child in need of adult companionship. But both are done outside the hours reserved for gainful employment, which is why the future of volunteering is in this chapter. It's not really inappropriate: leisure and recreation pursuits are fun, and volunteering is one of the most richly satisfying activities one can undertake.

The volunteer sector, which spends $51 billion a year, is an important part of the Canadian economy that is about to become even more important. Volunteering is one of those rare activities that people do more of as they get older. Young people do it too, but we call that parenting. As their kids grow up and leave home, older people have more time to offer free to worthy causes other than their immediate family. Because of population aging, volunteering, like classical music, is a pastime that will grow in the years to come.

This augurs well for the future of non-profit organizations. Non-profits deliver a variety of services — low-cost housing and rehabilitation of criminals are just a couple of examples — for which there is not always an open market. They also have lobbying and educational functions. All these activities are performed by a staff that is a mix of paid employees and volunteers. This sets non-profits such as the John Howard Society or the Heart and Stroke Foundation apart from both for-profit companies, which have only paid workers, and community groups — local residents' associations, for example — that have only volunteers. A non-profit also has a mixture of funding: it is paid, either by the recipients or the government, to deliver some programs but it also relies on grants and donations. Its management is forever trying to bolster the funding to pursue the vision of the organization.

These are complicated organizations to run, and they are likely to become even more complicated as governments back out of the delivery of services, leaving us all more dependent than ever on non-profit organizations for many of these services. The result will be rapid growth in the non-profit sector and tremendous pressure on these organizations to respond to society's new demands. Intensifying this pressure is the fact that some governments have cut their financial support for non-profit organizations just when we need these organizations more than ever. There is no demographic justification for withdrawing public funds from non-profit organizations in the mid-1990s. The peak of the baby boom is still in its 30s; these boomers are at least ten years away from having time and money to donate to volunteer organizations. These organizations need continued government support to get them through the transition period of the 1990s to an era when the demographic shift will result in increased financial support from non-government sources.

Fortunately, because of population aging, a new source of highly skilled professional managers is becoming available to guide these organizations through this difficult and challenging period. The front end of the baby boom is in its middle or late 40s. That's mid-life crisis time, when you ask what you are going to do with the rest of your life. If you are a junior vice-president in a large corporation, you realize you are never going to be president because too many other people are in the way. You're also fed up with working for someone else. This is when you seek career counselling, start your own company, and go back to church. This is also when, after years in the corporate world, you rediscover the idealistic side of your personality.

As the 1990s progress, more and more older members of the baby-boom generation will discover they have plateaued in their careers. They are going to want a more meaningful life, and some of them are going to go for it even if it costs $50,000 a year in salary. As a result, many talented and able executives, stalled and bored in the corporate world, will be available to work for non-profit organizations. Some will quit their jobs; others will be downsized out of a job. Their compensation for accepting a lower salary will be huge: the satisfaction of working for a worthy, perhaps even urgent, social cause along with more responsibility and more authority than they have ever enjoyed before.

The new professionalism that these people will bring with them may require a difficult adjustment for the old guard who have been running these organizations, and who may lack MBAs and corporate experience. But the old guard has a wealth of knowledge that the non-profit sector is going to need, and part of the challenge for the new managers will be to avoid alienating them.

Population aging means more than just a new source of paid talent for the non-profit organizations. It also means a boost to fundraising efforts, as the ranks of people in their 40s and 50s swell. These front-end boomers will be in their prime savings years; they will have more discretionary income and therefore be more likely to support organizations that serve society and that they themselves may one day have to draw on. As Figure 6 shows clearly, donating money to charity increases steadily with age until retirement, from an average of $235 by taxpayers under 35 to $481 by taxpayers over 65.

With their children grown, baby-boomers will be able to donate more of their time on an unpaid basis. But many will still be working

FIGURE 6: CHARITABLE CONTRIBUTIONS BY AGE

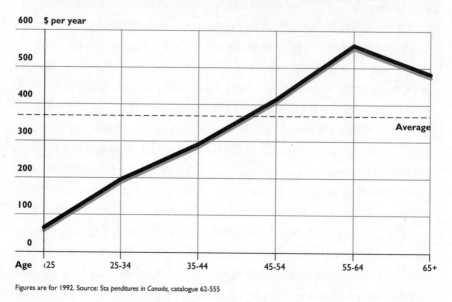

Figures are for 1992. Source: Sta penditures in Canada, catalogue 62-555

and, as a result, will still be under severe time constraints. They may be available for volunteer work, say, Tuesday nights for three hours. The organizations that are most adept at accommodating this valuable talent when it's available will reap the rewards. Since the boom, because of its size, is such a powerful element in our society, we will see renewed pressure for the Canadian government to do what the American government has done for more than 60 years: allow expenses incurred in the course of doing charitable work to be deducted from income taxes. It is up to government to find innovative ways to encourage people to get involved in volunteer organizations. If it does, all the ingredients are in place for a renaissance in the non-profit sector as the turn of the century approaches.

Chapter 7

The Future of Cities

People get emotional about the cities they live in. That's why debates about urban planning, architecture, and transportation are often so heated. More than just a difference of opinion is involved in these discussions. Those who consider themselves on the right side of controversial urban issues often assume that those on the other side are not only misguided but also guilty of bad taste, selfishness, or some other moral failing.

The emotionalism is understandable because a lot of poor planning and bad city-building took place during the 20-year growth spurt triggered by the entry of the baby boom into the labour and housing markets. Historic buildings were lost, scenic views were blocked, rapid transit lines were built in the wrong places, and the needs of pedestrians and cyclists were neglected. Almost everyone agrees that cities with lively downtowns that are welcoming to pedestrians are better places to live than cities given over entirely to the car. And good planners and developers know that, while the growth of suburbs is inevitable, sprawl isn't. But debates on urban issues too often neglect a crucial element: demographics. Planning and development decisions have less impact on the way our cities develop than changes in the composition and needs of the population.

The 20-year-old single person who lives downtown and rides the subway is not morally superior to the 40-year-old parent who drives a car. The young person rides the subway because, living downtown, he doesn't need a car and, being young, he can't afford one. The parent, on the other hand, needs to deliver her son to the hockey rink, her daughter to skating class, and the dog to the vet, and she'll pick up a few bags of groceries on the way back. Whether she lives in the inner city or the suburbs, she can't easily accomplish this trip by public transit. Twenty years in the future, the same young person who today happily zips around town by bike, bus, or subway will be at the wheel of a minivan or something similar, hauling kids, dog, and groceries. It won't happen because he has changed his views on urban planning. It will happen because he is 20 years older.

The last two decades have witnessed growth of the suburbs and decline in transit ridership. These things happened not because of planning mistakes but because Canada has an aging population. The baby-boom generation, one-third of the population, got older and bought bigger houses and bigger cars. They got busier. They had longer trips to make because they were living farther from work, and more people to carry because they were raising families. The suburbs and the automobile suited their needs more than the inner city and public transit.

DOWNTOWN AND SUBURBS

Canada has every right to be proud of its cities. When Corporate Resources Group, an international personnel consulting company based in Geneva, ranked 118 cities according to 42 measures of quality of life in 1995, Canada was the only country with more than three cities in the top 20: Vancouver (second after Geneva), Toronto (fourth), Montreal (seventh), and Calgary (12th). The highest-ranked American city was Boston, which placed 30th. Other international rankings of cities have come to similar conclusions.

Why do Canadian cities rank so high? Because they are small big cities rather than big big cities. All the cities near the top of the liveability list are small big cities like Montreal, Vienna, and Auckland. Big big cities like New York, Tokyo, and Mexico City are near the bottom. The main reason Canada's major cities do so well, and their great strength, is that they are big enough to be lively and interesting and yet small enough to avoid the severe congestion, pollution, and general unmanageability associated with the world's biggest urban centres. A second reason is that Canada's biggest cities still have healthy downtowns. It is not the suburbs that distinguish Toronto from Detroit, a once-great American city that became a symbol of urban decay. Detroit's suburbs are as handsome and liveable as those of Toronto or any other Canadian city. But, despite recent improvements, Detroit no longer has a central core that is pleasant and safe to live in and walk in, that is home to residents of a variety of income levels, and that has a good transportation system as well as a full array of entertainment, cultural, educational, and shopping facilities. Canada's best cities have all these things.

How have we done it? Through a combination of luck, good planning, and demographics. Perhaps the best example of pure good luck was Vancouver's failure to implement various schemes to slice up its downtown with freeways during the 1960s. Local politicians were eager to build, but Vancouver was saved from their folly by the Social Credit premier of British Columbia, W.A.C. Bennett, who refused to contribute any money. Bennett's power base was in the interior of the province, so he didn't need to support megaprojects in Vancouver to get re-elected. Had Toronto been blessed with similar benign neglect by the Ontario government, its downtown would not have been permanently disfigured by the Gardiner Expressway, built between 1955 and 1966, which walls off the lakefront from the city.

Toronto's great success has been in protecting vast tracts of single-family housing in and around downtown from highrise redevelopment. These neighbourhoods of red-brick houses on quiet, leafy streets have given Toronto one of the healthiest central cores of the major cities of the world. Wise political decisions to protect the stability of old established neighbourhoods were the basis for this success but demographics played a big part. During the 1970s, the front end of the baby boom flooded the market for rental accommodation (see Chapter 2). Like all young people, they wanted to be in the centre of the action: downtown. In Toronto, the policy of protecting old neighbourhoods encouraged renovation of existing structures rather than tearing them down and developing new ones. In the 1980s, when they were ready

to own homes of their own, the front-end boomers supported this policy enthusiastically and spent millions of dollars to restore and mod-
ernize old houses, ensuring the long-term viability of the downtown
neighbourhoods.

Meanwhile, in all major Canadian cities, billions of dollars
were invested in new commercial and residential buildings to meet
the demands of the huge generation flooding the labour and housing
markets. Although many uninspired developments were built, there
were also good ones, including two of the most innovative and attractive new inner-city housing projects anywhere: the south side of False
Creek in Vancouver, and the St. Lawrence project in Toronto. Immigration was another demographic factor that added lustre to Canada's
cities. Immigrants tend to be in their 20s, an age when people find
downtown living attractive. Their talents, particularly in the field of
gastronomy, further enhanced the attractiveness of Canada's major
cities.

Downtown Canada is alive and well, but there is no reason for
complacency. Canada's two largest cities, Toronto and Montreal, are
exhibiting serious signs of decline in the mid-1990s. Both cities have
more empty storefronts than they used to, as well as more homeless
people and panhandlers. The lingering recession in eastern Canada has
had a lot to do with both cities' problems, while political instability
caused by separatism has exacerbated Montreal's problems. But powerful demographic trends have been working against downtown and in
favour of the suburbs since the beginning of the 1980s. In fact, it is a
measure of just how strong Canada's downtowns are that they have
remained comparatively healthy after almost two decades during
which demographics have favoured the suburbs. In contrast, the cores
of many large U.S. cities have suffered much more severely from the
flight of affluent boomers to the suburbs.

The early boomers pushed house prices in the inner city so
high that many late boomers couldn't afford to live there. Many of
those who could afford it preferred to switch to a suburban lifestyle
when the kids came along. As a result, the arrival of the baby boom in
its childbearing years coincided with a massive growth spurt in the

suburbs. In Toronto, for example, the population of the central city increased only slightly between 1981 and 1996, going from 599,000 to 656,000, while that of the Greater Toronto Area (GTA) grew from 3.4 million to almost 4.7 million. Almost all the population growth occurred in new suburbs of new houses in new subdivisions. These houses lacked the charm of the Victorian residences of the central city but they were affordable, they were big, they had yards, and they had garages big enough for two cars or even three.

Canadians are now coming to the realization that they cannot afford this type of development any longer. In a 1995 report called *Economics of the Urban Form*, Pamela Blais, a Toronto economist, said roads, utilities, and other public services used in suburbs are paid for with billions of dollars in subsidies from provincial governments and urban taxpayers. Developers take advantage of these invisible subsidies to build inefficient communities, raising taxes and service costs throughout the area and driving away businesses. Blais's study concluded that huge savings would be available if a more compact form of development were adopted in future. In the Toronto area, taxpayers could save up to $4 billion in operating and maintenance costs over the next 25 years if more compact neighbourhoods were built, while the capital costs for roads, transit, and utilities would be as much as $16 billion less. On the west coast, the Greater Vancouver Regional District has concluded that $2.2 billion could be saved on transportation costs if new growth were more concentrated. A study showed that private cars in the Vancouver area enjoy public subsidies of $2,700 a year each, seven times the subsidy for public transit. As a result, Vancouver has developed a growth management strategy, including zoning changes and new charges for utilities such as sewers, aimed at discouraging sprawl.

Because of the demographic shift, the pressure for suburban growth should subside in the years to come, which may make such reforms easier to implement. With all the baby-boomers past their prime childbearing years and the baby-bust generation 45% smaller, new family formation will continue to slow down as will births and the pace of growth of bedroom suburbs. Moreover, an aging society with more discretionary income will be prepared to pay the user fees that analysts such as Blais are recommending, providing they get good service in return. For example, with most of the baby boom driving cars, the late 1990s will be an excellent time to build new roads paid for by user tolls.

Meanwhile, as the front-end boomers move through their 50s and 60s in the two decades ahead, the demographic shift will lead to strong growth in the ranks of "penturbanists" in Canada. That's a term invented by Jack Lessinger of the University of Washington, who believes increasing numbers of people will flee the big cities in search of a quieter and less expensive way of life. The suburbs aren't far enough from the big cities for these people — they will want to settle in small towns and small cities (see Chapter 2). This tendency will be particularly pronounced in Canada, because many urban Canadians grew up in small towns and rural districts and may want to move back home, or to a place that reminds them of home, when they retire.

TRANSPORTATION

Buses, streetcars, and subways were invented to serve densely popu-lated inner cities. They were not invented to serve sparsely populated suburbs. Public transit makes money in the core; it loses money in the suburbs. Unfortunately for public transit, the aging of the baby-boom generation has resulted in rapid growth of sprawling suburbs and stag-nation in the inner cities. The aging of the baby boom has been a dis-aster for many of Canada's public transit systems.

Canada's largest public transit system, the Toronto Transit Commission (TTC) — which serves the city of Toronto and its five inner suburbs but not the fast-growing outer suburbs — recorded 432 million passenger trips in 1985. In 1994, the system was used for only 388 million trips. Montreal's transit system also lost riders, but not as many. The Société de Transport de la Communauté Urbaine de Mont-réal carried 340 million passengers in 1994, down from 350 million in 1985.

Economic recession had a lot to do with the decline in rider-ship, as did bad decisions about transit service. As the suburbs grew, transit systems expanded to serve them. This involved shifting resources from the centre, where transit is viable, to the suburbs, where it isn't. Transit needs 4,000 people per square kilometre to pay for itself. In Toronto, the inner city has 6,540 people per square kilometre; the suburb of Etobicoke, for example, has only 2,500. Richard Gilbert, a Toronto urban consultant, says the TTC's policy of reducing inner-city service to pay for suburban service is crazy because it involves "taking away services where there is ridership to put on service where there is no ridership."

It makes no sense to build expensive subway systems or even to run conventional buses in most suburban areas because, no matter how good the service, not enough people will use it. This fact can be seen by anyone who drives down a suburban Toronto freeway unofficially called the Spadina Expressway, which connects a northern suburb to the city. The expressway has a subway line running above ground down its centre median. Except for brief periods during the weekday rush hours, these subway cars are almost empty. The people who are supposed to be riding in them are sitting in traffic jams on the expressway, watching the empty trains roll by.

Obviously, this was no place to put a subway, because the population density along its route is insufficient to support it. Demographics made such an unwise decision possible. The rapid growth of the suburbs, triggered by the movement of the baby-boomers out to the new subdivisions, gave the outlying municipalities increased political power. The suburban representatives on Metropolitan Toronto Council, a federation of municipalities that runs police, transit, and other regional services for Toronto and its five suburbs, outvoted the inner-city councillors who wanted to tunnel a subway under a densely developed street instead. Another decision that badly weakened the TTC in the early 1970s was to equalize all fares regardless of the length of the trip; going one stop on the subway downtown costs the same as a 40-kilometre trip from one side of the metropolitan area to the other. This was a way to make the profitable inner-city routes subsidize the suburban routes, in a futile effort to get suburbanites to ride the transit system. The only result of such policies is to reduce service on the successful routes, which then lose riders, a loss that is not compensated by a corresponding gain in the suburbs.

Let's take a closer look at the demographics of public transit. A person's use of the transit system rises over the teenage years and peaks at the age of 19 (see Figure 7). The 19-year-old has little money and plenty of time to wait at bus stops. Transit therefore suits his needs perfectly. The front-end baby-boomers were in their teens during the 1960s, with the first boomers turning 20 in 1967. That's why Canada's major transit systems enjoyed booming growth during the 1960s and 1970s. In those heady days of ever-increasing demand, the TTC paid its bus drivers a $50 bonus to recruit new drivers.

But the peak of the baby boom turned 20 in 1981. It was predictable that average transit use would decline after that date. A more dense form of development in the suburbs and better management of the transit system could have reduced the decline, but some decline was inevitable, as Figure 7 makes clear. Even in a hypothetical scenario in which no suburban development has been allowed, with a growing population housed instead in a much more intensively developed inner city, transit use would decline because of aging. The decline in transit use that starts at 20 continues for 45 years, right up until retirement age. By age 45, a person is one-third as likely to ride the bus as at 15. After retirement, most people have less money and more time. Predictably, they then begin to use the transit system more, but they don't make nearly as many trips as young transit riders do.

Car use starts when a teenager reaches the legal driving age, and peaks in the early 40s. This is the typical middle-aged consumer described in Chapter 5, for whom time is valuable because it is scarce. The car costs him more than a transit pass would, but it saves so much time that it's more than worth it. This is especially so for the person who lives in the suburbs. In most cases, he has no subway or other rapid transit near his home, the nearest bus stop is several blocks away, and once he gets there, the wait is often long. His workplace may well be located in some other suburb, also not well served by transit. And then there are the kids to be picked up and the shopping to be done. In this situation, the car is not just an option, it's a necessity. The advent

FIGURE 7: AVERAGE DAILY TRIPS PER PERSON, GREATER TORONTO AREA

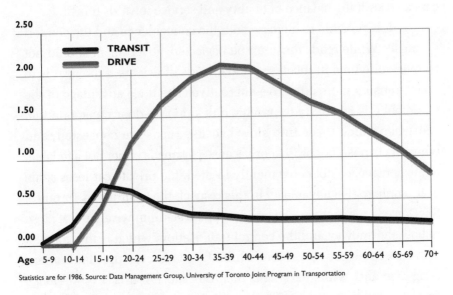

Statistics are for 1986. Source: Data Management Group, University of Toronto Joint Program in Transportation

of the cellular phone has further increased the attractiveness of the car, because it allows the suburban commuter to make good use of his time even when stuck in a traffic jam. The average suburbanite needs his car so badly that he gets in the habit of using it all the time, even for short trips that could be better achieved by some other form of transportation, such as his own feet or a bicycle.

This is where all of North America is at in the mid-1990s. The baby boom has moved off transit and into private cars. That is why transit ridership is down and the roads are crowded.

Demographics explain two-thirds of everything. This does not mean that the other one-third isn't important. In the case of transit, the other one-third is extremely important, because if ways could be found to move more people back to transit, the quality of life in our cities would benefit greatly. Older consumers are motivated more by quality and service and less by price in making product choices. Quality is a matter of taste that varies from individual to individual. For some, riding a well-made bicycle while enjoying exercise and open air is an experience of far greater quality than sitting behind the wheel of a car.

But for most, the private car is the most comfortable and fastest means of transportation. The only way to get some of these people out of their cars is to shift the balance of quality and service towards transit.

It is possible to increase both the convenience and the comfort of transit. While roads must not be neglected, government should not be over-solicitous in meeting the demands of drivers if the goal is to make transit a more attractive alternative. The huge advantage of the automobile is its ability to provide quick door-to-door transportation. But when quick turns into slow because roads are congested, and when the trip isn't door to door because parking is either not available, too expensive, or not conveniently located, the private car loses some of its comparative advantage. In this respect, the example of Toronto's SkyDome is instructive. The builders of the stadium wisely put it close to both the subway and the central train station, which is the hub of a commuter rail network. Meanwhile the roads near the stadium are congested and, while parking is plentiful, most of it is several blocks from the stadium entrance. The result? Some 36% of people attending Toronto Blue Jays games travel by public transit, compared with only 14% using transit for all trips in Metro Toronto.

Recent experience in Britain and elsewhere shows that public transit, freed from the constraints of monopoly and overly bureaucratic management, can make sufficient improvements in quality and service to win new riders at the expense of the automobile. By introducing competition into transit, the British also introduced new ideas. For example, since conventional large buses don't work in suburbs because the population densities are insufficient to support them, why not use more cost-efficient smaller buses? Since many people won't walk several blocks to a major street to find a bus stop, why not let the little buses circulate into the side streets to get them? And why not let customers hail a bus instead of having to walk to a stop? Where these and other commonsensical innovations have been introduced in Britain, service has improved, ridership has grown, and private bus companies have made money.

These innovations are successful because they fulfil the needs of a time-conscious, aging population. This population will be prepared to pay for better service, and some of these special bus routes could charge a fare between that of a regular bus and that of a taxi.

Improvements in the transit system don't depend on privatization. Recently the London Underground, still publicly owned, has improved service, regained customers, and become profitable. Canadian transit systems, heirs to a strong tradition of innovative public enterprise, should be capable of no less. But that will happen only if politicians allow the public transit systems to stop subsidizing hopelessly unprofitable routes with the revenues from profitable ones. It will happen only if politicians and transit managers recognize the demographic changes that have taken place in our cities over the past two decades and design a transit system to accommodate those changes. Transit providers should be allowed to concentrate on what they do best: operating subways, streetcars, and buses along densely populated corridors. Let private or public entrepreneurs develop new kinds of services suitable to the suburbs. The result would be better service in both the city and the suburbs, and profits for both private and public transit companies.

The large echo generation is just now moving into its prime transit-using years. For its benefit, and that of society as a whole, we must maintain safe, convenient public transit systems.

CRIME IN THE CITY

Something surprising happened in Canada during the first part of the 1990s: the crime rate fell. It was surprising because it didn't fit the reality most people knew, or thought they knew. Anyone who reads newspapers learns about gruesome, violent crimes. Most city dwellers know of someone whose house has been burglarized or whose car has been stolen. Many parents are reluctant to allow their children to wander about the neighbourhood, even if the neighbourhood is generally considered safe. Those who ride bicycles in the big city would not dream of leaving them unlocked.

This is life in Canada in the 1990s, and yet Statistics Canada's numbers say things have been getting better. In 1994, the overall crime rate, based on the number of incidents reported to police forces across

Canada, fell by 5%. It was the third year in a row that the crime rate dropped. In the same year, the rate of violent crimes fell by 3%, while the murder rate fell to just over 2 per 100,000 people, the lowest in 25 years. And youth crime was down 6%.

Why would the statistics be so much at odds with popular perception? The demographic explanation is that the crime rate is down for the simple reason that, temporarily, we have a small number of people in the crime-prone youth age groups. As for perception, we have an aging population, and older people generally are more fearful than younger people. An aging population also has more potential crime victims because it has more people who own something worth stealing. Moreover, as people get older, the likelihood increases that they, or someone they know, will have been on the receiving end of crime. And of course some older people, because they are frail, really are more vulnerable to muggers and other criminals. Thus the misconception gradually takes hold that crime is more rampant than it actually is.

But there's more to the story than that. For one thing, the recent decline comes after a period when the crime rate rose sharply. Metro Toronto had a 30% increase in Criminal Code offences between 1984 and 1994, much greater than the increase in population. For Canada as a whole, the crime rate in 1994 was 8% higher than it was in 1984, and the rate of violent crime was 49% higher. Moreover, gun use in crimes has increased because aging criminals are more prone to use guns.

At the same time, an apparent increase in violent crime by young people points to the possibility of a new trend developing that would not have been predicted by past demographic patterns. Some analysts have drawn a connection between increasing violence by youth and the disintegration of the family (see Chapter 10). "As a clinician, clearly I'm seeing that adolescents now are a lot more violent than they were," Dr. Louis Morisette, a Montreal psychiatrist, told the *Globe and Mail*. "They don't see people as whole persons — they see only a wallet that they can steal, a dress they can touch. That makes them a lot more dangerous." If youth are getting more violent, we are in for a lot of trouble as the millennium approaches, because the large echo generation is about to enter its crime-prone years.

Let's look more closely at the demographics of crime. Historically, the 13-to-24 age group has been less violent than the group just ahead of it in age. The typical 19-year-old's crime is one in which he doesn't come into contact with his victim. He knocks on the front door, and if no one answers, he goes around to the back, levers off the sliding glass door, goes upstairs to the bedroom, checks out the drawers, grabs any jewellery and money he can find, and picks up the VCR on his way out. This is your basic teenage break-and-enter.

But just as a person can expect to get promoted in the regular workforce once he accumulates some experience, so there are "promotions" in the crime workforce. A person in his late 20s, if he stays in the crime field, will move into bigger and better things. He'll graduate from breaking into homes to robbing banks. The 29-year-old's crime is more violent than the 19-year-old's. He may have a gun, and the chances that he will hurt people as well as property are greater.

Demographics explain the different growth rates in types of crime over the past three decades. We saw major growth in property crime during the 1960s and 1970s, when large numbers of baby-boomers were passing through their break-and-enter years. A shift in growth from property crime to violent crime occurred over the 1980s and into the 1990s, as the last of the boomers moved out of their teen years into their 20s and early 30s.

Different kinds of criminal behaviour by different age groups are more important than slight shifts in the overall crime rate. Violent crime rose by a worrisome 49% between 1984 and 1994, largely because boomer criminals were reaching an age when criminals are more likely to commit violence. The slight dip in the overall crime rate in the mid-1990s has not made our cities significantly safer. The public perception is right: our cities in the mid-1990s are much more dangerous places than they were in the mid-1980s.

The violent crime rate in Canada declined in 1993 and 1994 following 15 years of annual increases. This trend should continue as the large wave of baby-boom criminals moves out of its violent years and into its fraud years. After armed hold-ups, the next step up the career ladder for a criminal is into fraud: telemarketing scams, forged credit cards, and bogus investment schemes to dupe naive people, often seniors, out of their life savings. These crimes victimize not only their immediate victims but all of society; the banks don't pay for the losses incurred through bad cheques and credit card fraud — we all do, through higher fees and higher interest rates. White-collar crime is associated with older criminals because success in this type of work requires a degree of knowledge and sophistication that only age and experience can provide. And the older criminal, if he wants to stay in business, needs to find less strenuous work. He is less able than his younger colleague to hold up banks and convenience stores because he's not as strong or as fast as he used to be.

One of the biggest and least-publicized areas of fraud is theft by employees from their employers. This costs Canadian companies more than $20 billion a year. It's hard to detect because most of it is done in small amounts. For example, a manager in one Toronto organization investigated by forensic accountants at Peat Marwick Thorne had control over large amounts of cash received as payments. She regularly stole small sums ranging from $50 to $200. Over five years, these petty thefts added up to $500,000. Companies engaged in downsizing are particularly vulnerable to this type of theft, because they have fewer managers in place to watch for it and because their efforts at restructuring may have left them with demoralized and disloyal employees. White-collar crime was going to increase dramatically anyway because of population aging. That the aging phenomenon is happening at the same time as a wave of corporate downsizing makes the outlook even worse. Canada is facing an epidemic of fraud over the next decade. This presents a challenge to our police forces, because they are not well prepared for what is going to happen. The police should be making a major effort to prepare for the coming crime wave by giving police officers the training and knowledge they will need to understand and investigate complex white-collar crimes.

The lull in the growth of youth and violent crime will be short-lived because the baby-boom echo, a larger cohort, is about to replace the baby bust in the crime-prone youth age groups. Even with more effective law enforcement and a better economy, the crime rate will start to rise again. Typical teenage crimes — breaking and entering, bicycle theft, mindless vandalism — will probably become more common in the last half of the 1990s than they were in the first half.

Most worrisome of all is the possibility, noted above, that teenagers are becoming more violent. One of North America's leading criminologists, James Allen Fox, dean of the College of Criminal Justice at Northeastern University in Boston, discerns an alarming absence of morality among some echo children in the United States, which he fears could lead to a plague of serious teenage crime by members of the echo generation. A Canadian example was the murder in 1995 of a retired couple in Montreal; they were beaten to death with a baseball bat. Three echo kids were charged. One police officer said it was the first murder he had seen in 31 years that was done just for the pleasure of killing. We don't know whether this sort of crime will become more common or will remain an aberration. We do know that demographics offer no reason for anyone to feel complacent about crime in Canada. Our police forces are going to be busy as the turn of the century approaches.

THE FUTURE OF CANADA'S CITIES

Crime isn't going to go away, and neither are traffic jams and noise and litter and all the other things Canadians love to hate about cities. But demographics offer reasons to hope for the best. The departure from the parental nest of the baby boom in the 1970s gave a burst of youthful energy to our cities. Downtown streets became livelier, new theatres and night clubs opened, restaurants flourished. By 2000, the boomers' children, the baby-boom echo, will be leaving the nest in large numbers. They, like their parents before them, will give the downtown cores of our cities a shot in the arm, although not as powerful a shot because the echo kids are fewer than the boomers. Nevertheless, there will be more riders for Canada's beleaguered transit systems, more people in the clubs and bars, and more renters for apartments.

Meanwhile, the flat real estate market caused by demographic change has its positive side. Many homeowners will settle for renovating and adding on to existing homes rather than moving up to bigger, more expensive ones. Renovation is always healthy for cities because it stabilizes and improves neighbourhoods. Another result of demographic change is the advent of the age of quality and service. An aging population is more likely to support small neighbourhood stores offering good products and friendly service, and less likely to drive long distances looking for bargains at discount megastores in the suburbs. The result will be increased business for local shopping areas that maintain adequate parking.

The reason that small stores offer a more pleasant shopping experience is personal contact between the shopper and a merchant who understands the shopper's needs and might even know him by name. Personal contact is a fundamental human need, and it is the reason we will continue to have large cities even after technology has made it at least theoretically possible to dispense with them. By the mid-1990s, we have lived with phone, fax, and e-mail long enough to realize that they can't replace face-to-face contact. That is why the computer industry itself, which created the technology that some people claimed would enable us to do without personal contact, operates in clusters of companies in close geographical proximity. So do companies in such other high-tech industries as financial services, telecommunications, and biotechnology. It is no accident that many financial services companies are clustered around Bay and King streets in central Toronto, or that many companies in the computer industry are clustered in the Ottawa suburb of Kanata. In the new economy, ideas are the generators of growth and wealth creation. The best way to produce new ideas is to have like-minded people working close to one another. The best place to do that is in large urban areas, and that's the main reason Canada's big cities have a bright future.

Chapter 8

Rethinking Education

Most Canadians think Canada has a first-rate health care system and a second-rate education system. Although both the excellence of the health care system and the problems of the education system are often overstated, this piece of popular wisdom is essentially true. Health care standards in Canada are the equal of those in other advanced countries, and Canada ranks near the top on the key population health indicators of life expectancy and infant mortality. On the other hand, Canada does poorly in international rankings of scholastic achievement because the skills of our students have been steadily declining. The Canadian Test of Basic Skills has been given to a representative sample of Grade 8 students since 1966. It measures performance in language skills and mathematics. From 1966 to 1991, a period in which spending per student more than doubled, the composite score of those taking the test dropped by 6.3%, according to a study by the Economic Council of Canada. Little wonder that employers and university instructors increasingly complain that a Canadian high school diploma no longer certifies literacy and numeracy. And Canada's high school dropout rate of 30% is one of the highest in the industrialized world.

But the Canadian health care and education systems have one important thing in common: both are expensive by international standards. The health care system is the second costliest per capita in the world after that of the United States. And our spending on education, at more than 7% of gross national product, is the highest per capita among the G-7 leading industrialized countries, according to the Organization for Economic Co-operation and Development.

We are spending more on education than other countries and getting less in return. In a world economy in which success is based more on knowledge than on natural resources, Canada's relatively poor performance in education threatens our international competitiveness. Our social cohesion is also at risk. As more middle-class parents give up on the public system and enrol their children in private schools, in search of academic excellence, society becomes fragmented. The high dropout rate increases that fragmentation, creating an underclass of unskilled workers, widening the gap between rich and poor, and increasing the demands on the social safety net just when the net is being shredded by cash-starved governments.

The failure of those responsible for managing the education system to pay attention to demographics is the root cause of the system's inflated cost. Because Canada had the world's loudest baby boom, we experienced dramatic increases in school enrolments during the 1950s and 1960s. We had to expand the elementary schools, then the high schools, and finally the colleges and universities to accommodate hordes of new arrivals. As the population bulge passed through the different levels, to be replaced by a smaller demographic cohort, one school board after another made the same disastrous blunder: they failed to remove funds from the level with shrinking enrolment and pass the funds on to the next level, where enrolment was expanding. As a result, permanent inefficiencies were built into the system.

Today school boards continue to make the same mistakes and Canadian taxpayers continue to pay for them. Let's look at the impact of demographic change on the four educational levels — preschool, elementary, secondary, and postsecondary.

DAYCARE AND PRESCHOOL

The Canadian fertility rate tumbled during the 1960s, with the result that the demand for kindergarten places declined shortly thereafter. In the late 1970s, the number of births started to increase, rising still more in the 1980s with the arrival of the baby-boom echo. Preschool education was once again much in demand and, with the entry of large numbers of women into the workforce, so was daycare for the youngest Canadians. The demand was so strong that a proposal for a national daycare plan was an important issue in the federal election of 1988. Daycare had its time in the political sun only because of passing demographic conditions. In the first half of the 1980s, the combination of large numbers of preschool children, growing numbers of working women, and an active women's movement made daycare an issue the political parties had to contend with. But in the mid-1990s, with most of the echo generation beyond preschool, the politicians can put it on the back burner again. Given the importance of early childhood education and nutrition to the intellectual and physical development of all human beings, a national effort to provide high-quality daycare for every child who needs it would be one of the wisest investments Canada could make in its future. But the decrease in the numbers of parents with very young children makes it increasingly difficult to force politicians to pay attention.

The number of births has declined during the 1990s as large numbers of baby-boomers pass their prime child-producing years. The inevitable result is that daycare won't be a growth industry. Because of demographic variations from place to place, some towns and cities will be short of daycare places while others might have too many. (See Figure 8.) But in general, the outlook across Canada is for a steady, stable demand for daycare. That means a national daycare program, which should be considered a necessity in an advanced industrialized economy, is now much more affordable than it was.

ELEMENTARY AND SECONDARY SCHOOL

Going to elementary school is the only activity that is compulsory in Canada. For that reason, elementary school enrolments are the one area where demographics can predict the future with tremendous accuracy. If 1,000 children are born in a school district in 1996, it's certain that around 1,000 kids will enter Grade 1 in that school district in

FIGURE 8: PRESCHOOL-AGE CHILDREN IN 25 CITIES, 1996

	% of population	Rank
St. John's	6.1	22
Halifax	6.9	9
Saint John	6.2	19
Chicoutimi-Jonquière	6.1	23
Quebec City	6.1	21
Sherbrooke	6.3	17
Trois-Rivières	5.8	25
Montreal	6.4	15
Ottawa-Hull	6.9	8
Oshawa	7.3	6
Toronto	6.8	10
Hamilton	6.5	13
St. Catharines-Niagara	6.2	20
Kitchener	6.9	7
London	6.8	11
Windsor	6.4	14
Sudbury	6.3	16
Thunder Bay	6.3	18
Winnipeg	7.3	5
Regina	7.7	2
Saskatoon	8.1	1
Calgary	7.5	3
Edmonton	7.4	4
Vancouver	6.5	12
Victoria	6.0	24

Cities listed are the top 25 Census Metropolitan Areas. Source: Strategic Projections, Inc.

2002. The only impediment to perfect predictability is the movement of children into and out of school districts.

The big growth in elementary schools began in 1953, when the first baby-boomers turned their attention to the adventures of Dick and Jane. Increasing demands on the elementary school system, and steady expansion, continued through the 1950s and 1960s. In 1960, the first boomers reached 13 and entered junior high. That was the beginning of the expansion of high school enrolments. With constantly rising numbers of students at both the elementary and secondary school levels, the 1960s were the golden age for the growth of education in Canada.

To measure the total demand for elementary education by a particular cohort, a demographer looks at the midpoint between age 6, when children start school, and age 13, when they go on to Grade 7. That midpoint is age 9. When the peak of a cohort turns 9, demand for elementary education has peaked. After that, enrolment has only one place to go — down. The peak of the baby boom, which at that point consisted of those born in 1960, was 9 in 1969. After that, elementary school enrolments started to drop.

Until age 16, high school, like elementary school, is compulsory in most provinces, which means that, once again, demographics can predict enrolments — although with slightly less accuracy because those over 16 can drop out if they wish. The midpoint of high school attendance is age 16. Predictably, therefore, by the mid-1970s — seven years after the elementary school peak — high school enrolments started to go down.

When this happened in Ontario, the provincial government was surprised. After 30 years of school expansion, growth seemed the natural state of affairs. Neither school boards nor provincial officials were prepared for a downturn, and they weren't sure how to respond. The reason for the decline was simple: because fewer children had been born, fewer children were signing up for school. But the government decided it needed a group of experts to study the matter, so it set up the Commission on Declining School Enrolments in Ontario. Its job was to try to figure out why enrolments were down and what to do about it. The government was especially worried about what to do with excess elementary teachers and new ones fresh out of the province's education faculties who couldn't find jobs. What it should have done was send them back to university to learn how to be high school teachers over the 1970s. It also should have cut elementary school budgets in proportion to the declining enrolments and passed the savings on to the junior and high school levels, where enrolments would continue growing for some time. Instead, following the advice of the commission, the Ontario government ignored demographics and left the elementary budgets largely intact. Rather than recognizing the need to push funding forward in tandem with the largest cohort of the school population, the commission urged instead that declining enrolments be seen as an opportunity to improve education by reducing class sizes, introducing special education classes, and otherwise enriching the school system. That's how overspending gets permanently built into an education system: by leaving the same resources in the schools at a time when enrolment is dropping by up to 20%. This experience was repeated all over Canada during the 1970s and 1980s. Only the handful of school districts that experienced high immigration had full classrooms.

A Statistics Canada study in 1994 confirmed that our failure to adapt to demographic change is the reason we have one of the world's most expensive education systems. The study found that the education workforce, comprising teachers and administrators, grew by 20% between 1971 and 1991, while the school-age population was dropping by nearly that much, from 5.9 million to 4.9 million. In 1991, Canada spent $33.6 billion on elementary and high school education, a staggering $7.4 billion more than would have been spent had the ratio of students to teachers and administrators stayed at the 1971 level.

The baby-boom echo began in 1980. Inevitably, Grade 1 enrolment increased in 1986 for the first time in 20 years, then increased again in 1987. Yet the managers of our school systems were caught by surprise, proving once again that, while demographic facts are obvious once pointed out, they often go unnoticed until it's too late. Statistics Canada publishes annual demographic reports showing how many people are born each year. Thus, school boards should have known that, births having increased in 1980 and elementary school being compulsory, Grade 1 enrolments would increase six years later in 1986. But many weren't prepared. School boards hadn't systematically scaled down elementary teaching staffs during the 1970s, but population growth gradually had filled up the classrooms, and by the time large numbers of echo kids arrived at school in the late 1980s, some elementary schools were short of teachers and classrooms.

For the rest of the 1980s and into the 1990s, the echo continued to push elementary school enrolment up. By the early 1990s, many schools had installed portables. Most parents don't like portables. They are paying their share of taxes and they don't think their kids should have second-class facilities. School trustees in many parts of Canada got an earful and, as elected officials, they had to listen. As a result, in the mid-1990s, Canada is building new elementary schools.

Is this decision demographically sound? The baby-boom echo began in 1980. The peak of this cohort born in 1990 will turn 9 in 1999, after which elementary school enrolments can be expected to fall again. Immigration, even at the abnormally high levels of the 1990s, can't offset the inevitable drop in enrolment, except in certain parts of urban Canada where large numbers of immigrants congregate. The impact of declining enrolments will be felt at about the same time that some of the new schools open. As a result, many new elementary schools will be underused by the next decade. By building new elementary schools in the mid-1990s, we are building more waste into the school system and adding to Canada's excessive education costs.

What about the high schools? The decline in enrolment caused by the graduation of the baby boom started in high schools in 1976 and continued until the mid-1990s when the echo children arrived. The peak of the echo boom was 1990. These kids will be 16 in 2006. That means we will have rising high school enrolments until 2006, after which enrolments will decline again.

The situation, however, will vary from community to community. If a school district is drawing new residents away from somewhere else, its school population could rise while overall enrolments fall. That's what the Carleton Board of Education in suburban Ottawa is counting on. It is opening one new elementary school in 1996, has another scheduled to open in 1997, and has approved a third for later. These schools are in areas that are slated for growth in the Ottawa-Carleton region's official plan. But the federal government is shrinking, not growing, and the echo is over, in Ottawa as in the rest of Canada. The new schools will fill up only if Ottawa's other industries prosper sufficiently to create large numbers of new jobs and draw migrants to Ottawa from other parts of Canada and abroad.

In general, it makes no sense to be building elementary schools in the last half of the 1990s because demand is likely to fall. In the 1970s, our school systems kept the same amount of money in the elementary schools after the number of pupils had declined. In the 1980s, the same happened in high schools. Now we are in danger of doing the same thing again when elementary demand drops, as the baby boom echo graduates into junior high. If we want to ensure that Canada's education system remains more expensive than those of other countries, all we have to do is maintain the policy of refusing to trim school budgets when enrolments drop.

To accommodate demographic change and avoid squandering money, our school boards need to practise flexibility. At the turn of the century, Canadian school systems will experience declining demand for elementary education and rising demand for secondary education. Any new elementary schools built in the 1990s should be designed to be convertible to high schools. And some of the high schools that were mothballed in the 1980s or switched to other uses should be switched back to high schools in the late 1990s.

School boards need to understand how demographics affect the mix of their school population, and teachers should understand the impact on them too. The demand for elementary school teachers will peak in about 1999 and then start to decline. Training to be an elementary school teacher is therefore a risky career choice in the mid-1990s. But someone who builds flexibility into his training, gradually moving from elementary school teaching to high school teaching, can grow with the echo children and enjoy the prospect of a longer teaching career. Not every elementary teacher should learn to be a high school teacher, but one in five should move up with the echo kids. School boards need policies to encourage that transition. This simply means saying to employees, "Five years from now we won't be needing as many Grade 3 teachers, but we will need more Grade 8 teachers. Will those interested come forward?" That's how an enlightened employer can use the predictability of demographics to make unavoidable change fulfilling and challenging for its workforce, rather than hurtful and stressful.

THE FUTURE OF PUBLIC SCHOOLS

Given the demands of an aging population and the debt concerns of our governments, it is hard to justify building new schools in the mid-1990s. Most school classrooms are empty 17 hours out of 24 and 150 days of the year. Instead of enriching the system with ever more expenditures, why not extract the full potential from the existing system? We could be using schools 12 months a year and 10 hours a day. For example, if classes were held from 7 a.m. to noon and from 1 p.m. to 6 p.m., we could educate twice as many people in the same physical plant. We could get even more benefit out of the existing school buildings if they stayed in operation during the summer. The reason two-month summer vacations were built into the school system was to make the whole family available to harvest crops. But most young people now live in cities where their labour is not in great demand. Our school year, therefore, is organized to serve the needs of an agrarian economy that doesn't exist. Of course, kids should have an extended holiday. But they don't all have to take it in July and August.

In the late 1990s and beyond, the baby-busters will replace the baby-boomers as producers of children. Because the busters are a 45% smaller cohort, the birth rate will fall. An ever smaller percentage of taxpayers will have children in public schools. Most taxpayers will be more concerned with maintaining a health care system that they increasingly depend upon than an education system that their families are no longer using. As good citizens, they will want to continue to support public schools as an essential part of the social infrastructure.

But they will be increasingly intolerant of waste and less likely to vote for school trustees who decide to build new schools while keeping existing ones closed at times when they could be used.

POSTSECONDARY EDUCATION

At the end of the 1970s, something remarkable happened in Canada. Government agencies issued reports saying it was time to prepare for an inevitable decline in college and university enrolments. This prediction seemed to be based on sound reasoning. Enrolment had dropped in elementary schools in the early 1970s and in high schools in the late 1970s, so it was logical to assume that colleges and universities would be next. That these predictions were issued was in itself significant, because it was one of the first times demographic analysis was used in the Canadian public sector for strategic planning. Obviously, these agencies had learned something from seeing first elementary schools and then high schools react too late to inevitable declines in demand for their services.

Unfortunately, these predictions were off the mark. What the strategists forgot was that university enrolments are not predictable in the same way that elementary and high school enrolments are. University is not compulsory and, while 19 to 24 is the traditional university age, in an aging population increasing numbers of older students choose to acquire higher education, perhaps after spending some time in the workforce. But governments, responding to predictions of decline based on a simplistic use of demographics, cut postsecondary funding during the 1980s only to watch enrolments fail to decline as predicted.

The predictions based solely on the 19-to-24 age group ignored an important demographic factor: people over 24. In the 1980s these people were part of the large front end of the baby boom, and their presence in the labour force had created a bottleneck (see Chapter 4). Some of them decided to go back to school rather than continue to pursue non-existent job opportunities, while others decided to quit dead-end jobs and get trained for more promising careers. An economic recession and technological change further diminished job opportunities and increased the allure of postsecondary education.

The peak of university-bound baby-boomers occurred in 1979, after which the numbers of 19-year-old new entrants declined. While this was happening, a new influx of people 25 and older was arriving. The result was that, by the mid-1990s, almost one-half of all postsecondary students, including graduate and part-time students, were 25 and over, up from one-third 20 years before. This trend will continue. With an aging population, we will see an aging of both college and university campuses. The average age of students is rising, and so is that of teaching staff. The large number of teachers hired during the 1960s and early 1970s to teach the baby-boomers who were flooding the colleges and universities are still in place, leaving few opportunities for younger scholars to obtain academic positions. In 1995, according to a Statistics Canada study, 61% of the faculty members at nine universities were born before 1945, and another 36% were born between 1945 and 1960. Only 3% were born after 1960.

In the mid-1990s, demographics have finally caught up to the colleges and universities in the form of falling enrolments. The aging of the boomers and improved economic conditions have helped reduce the number of part-time and older students. Meanwhile, the 19-year-olds are coming from the smaller baby-bust generation. At the same time, some young people are shying away from university, either because they can't afford the fees or because they doubt that a degree will help much on the job market. As a result, some universities find themselves in the unaccustomed position of having to lower entry marks and advertise for students.

If we had had flexibility in our education system and good planning based on demographics, we would have taken money out of the high schools in the 1980s and transferred it to the universities and elementary schools. Today, with university enrolment slipping and high school enrolment rising, we could be transferring some of it back from the postsecondary system to the increasingly crowded elementary and high schools.

This hasn't been done, and we are left with an expensive education system. But it's not too late to learn from past mistakes and use the power of demographics to manage the education system more effectively. We know that in the first decade of the next century the large echo generation will have finished high school and will be entering colleges and universities. We also know that the millennium kids, the children of the baby bust, will be a smaller cohort. The conclusion is inescapable. After the turn of the century, Canada's elementary and high schools will need fewer resources while the postsecondary institutions will need more. It's not too soon in the mid-1990s to start planning that transfer of resources.

THE NEW UNIVERSITIES AND COLLEGES

A society newly awake to the realization that its resources are limited will soon conclude that it can't afford the current postsecondary system. We are still shutting down most of our colleges and universities for three months every year. This is unreasonable. Universities and colleges should be used 12 hours a day for 12 months a year. Of course, this does not mean that every individual professor and student should be using them 12 months a year. In a three-semester system, everybody could get one semester off, but it doesn't have to be the summer.

As well, universities and colleges are going to have to adapt their teaching methods to the needs of an older clientele. Just as a teacher approaches a 15-year-old differently than a 5-year-old, so a 29-year-old requires a different approach than a 19-year-old. The older student is more experienced, articulate, and self-confident and will do better at classroom participation than the younger student. The latter is more likely to excel at tests, where rote memory is an advantage. This means that instructors who continue to use only exams as a basis of evaluation are penalizing their older students, while instructors who don't use exams at all are taking away some of the advantage of their younger students. The older student is more likely to have workforce experience and may well still be in the workforce. She realizes time is valuable and doesn't want it wasted. She gets annoyed if classes are cancelled or if she comes to a class for which the teacher is not fully prepared. It's not as easy to push around a 29-year-old consumer as a 19-year-old who has never worked for a living and doesn't mind — or may even enjoy — having time wasted in school. The older consumer will complain if her expectations are not met. Student evaluations of staff performance are more meaningful, and more important, when the student population is older.

The older student wants his workforce experience reflected in his education. He is less interested in theory and more interested in application. Courses that are purely theoretical, unless they lead into other courses that have application, are likely to be less appreciated. An aging population will create more demand for practical courses, of the kind offered by colleges, than for theoretical courses that are the specialty of universities. That need not necessarily mean that universities lose a lot of their business to colleges. The mature student wants an intellectual challenge but he also wants an applied approach. Because of these trends, a need exists for greater flexibility within the postsecondary system and perhaps for more integration between colleges and universities.

CONTINUING EDUCATION

The changing corporate structure (see Chapter 4) and the rapid advance of technology (see Chapter 11) offer major opportunities to Canada's universities and colleges. In a knowledge-based economy, we need people who know how to learn and who keep learning throughout their working lives. The universities and colleges will be an integral part of this new economic system because many people are going to need retraining and re-educating during their working lives.

Our postsecondary institutions will have to become more responsive and flexible to meet the changing needs of their clientele. Courses that have usually been offered only over a semester of 13 weeks can be compressed into 13 days for a different clientele. In this way, workers can come off the job and in three weeks get the latest thinking in industrial relations, international economics, computer-assisted design, or whatever other area of knowledge they need.

Growth in the traditional full-time 19-to-24-year-old university population will be slow for the rest of the 1990s. Meanwhile, the need for education of people already in the workforce will grow. Rather than sit back and wait for customers, colleges and universities should build their businesses aggressively. If the demand for continuing education is coming from the workplace, then it makes good sense to take courses to the source of the demand and present them in the workplace or close to it.

Universities such as McGill, Dalhousie, and Toronto have the good fortune to be located close to the centres of large cities and close, therefore, to the workplaces of managers and other workers requiring retraining and skills upgrading. To their credit, some universities with suburban campuses, such as York and Simon Fraser, have established downtown branches. Just as Oxford and Cambridge were built far from the hurly-burly of London, these Canadian campuses were originally cloistered away from the workaday world, in part so that scholars could think and do research in an atmosphere of serenity. Now these universities are facing sharp cutbacks in government support, a decline in the numbers of new students in the traditional 19-to-24 group, and an increase in demand from potential customers already in the workforce. They can no longer afford to be ivory towers.

As an example, York University's management training centre in the heart of Toronto's financial district offers two- and three-day courses priced at about $900. Its clients are executives needing a quick hit of information, and they are tough customers. Peter Zarry, director of executive education at York, assumed the voice of one of these students in an interview in the *Globe and Mail*: "I'm not here to waste time. I'm here to learn some damn thing and the day I leave here, two or three days from now, I'm going to use it. And if I can't use it, I want my money back."

Another university in the forefront of change is the University of Calgary. It is the first institution in the country to offer a master's degree in continuing education, training educators in how to provide education in the workplace. Recognizing that information technology frees students from congregating in the same place at the same time, most of the program is being offered by computer to students some of whom live in other provinces. The fee of more than $3,000 a year is fully paid by the students or their employers. While these students will graduate with a degree, many other Calgary students will not.

Instead they will take only the offerings they need, because their objective is to acquire specific skills or knowledge rather than a prestigious piece of paper. "I would not be surprised if the majority of our students will not be degree-getting in the near future," Howard Yeager, Calgary's associate vice-president of planning, told the *Globe and Mail* in 1995.

Continuing education for the pleasure and enlightenment of the individual is already enjoying strong growth in the mid-1990s. Elderhostel, a non-profit international organization that provides short-term educational programs for seniors and pre-seniors, is increasingly popular. Elderhostel participants study on university campuses or at such sites as marine biology stations. Originally, the program was aimed at an over-60 market but, in response to demand, the age of eligibility has been dropped to 50 in Canada. This sort of education can only get more popular, especially after the turn of the century. These mature students may not care whether they get a degree, a diploma, or even a credit. But they can afford the time and money to go on an archeological dig or a museum tour. They will pay for the chance to work all day looking for dinosaur bones. This kind of education can become an important source of funding for institutions experiencing declines in government support. The 60-year-old who has a good time on a dinosaur dig with an expert from the department of archeology or who benefits from a college course on home renovation may be favourably disposed when she makes out her will. Corporations depending on colleges and universities to help with upgrading their employees' skills should also want to ensure that postsecondary institutions remain financially healthy.

THE FUTURE OF EDUCATION

Our education system has some learning to do. It needs to learn to use demographics rather than forever being surprised by inevitable demographic change. By using demographics intelligently and being flexible, the education system could make the most of the resources it has, spend less on unnecessary buildings while using the ones it has more efficiently, and have the teachers it needs when and where they are needed. This would be an important step towards bolstering the public system at a time when it needs support.

Rightly or wrongly, the perception that public education is mediocre has become widespread. Partly, this is because small families have become the norm. Most boomer parents have only one or two kids. They want the very best for these children, and they know that the prospects will be grim for anyone entering the workforce of the future without a good education. Some of these people are making financial sacrifices to withdraw their children from the public system and send them to private schools. They are not rich, but they can afford private-school tuition for one child. As Mary Percival Maxwell, a Queen's University sociologist, told *Maclean's*, "The newest wave of parents are people with all their eggs in one basket and they can't afford to drop it."

Parents of school-age children in the mid-1990s not only have few children, they themselves are somewhat older and, for that reason, both more assertive and more quality-conscious than previous generations of parents of young children. This demographic development underlies the growing demands by parents to have more say over what happens in the schools. The ultimate example is the charter school movement, which began in the United States and has spread to Alberta and British Columbia. These schools are run by groups of parents with public funding. To qualify to run a charter school, a group must meet broad curriculum guidelines while offering a program that is distinct from that of the regular public schools. Usually, this involves a back-to-basics approach, with a concentration on core subjects and standardized testing.

Critics of charter schools worry that they will fragment the public system. Supporters reply that they are open to all, and that charter schools, by introducing an element of competition into the public system, make the system as a whole more responsive to parents' demands for high standards. A decade later, these same parents may decide that their children need private colleges and universities.

Canadians have every right to demand more of their education system. Why should Hungarian students do so much better at science or Hong Kong students so much better at mathematics than their Canadian counterparts? Canadian kids are as bright as any others. What both they, and the Canadian education system, need more than anything else is higher expectations. A country that can build a first-class health care system can also build a first-class education system. We just need to be smarter and try harder.

Chapter 9

The Health Care Crunch

We use the health care system all through our lives, starting before we are born. But once out of the hospital nursery, children don't cost the health care system very much. Nor do people in their teens and 20s. The cost of health care rises gradually over a person's 30s and 40s. It is higher for women than men because of reproduction, but by their mid-50s, men are using the system more than women. Then, in the 60s and beyond, the cost of health care soars for both sexes.

Canada's 9.8 million baby-boomers begin turning 50 in 1997. Well before that important turning point in our demographic history, the rising cost of health care was already a major public policy issue. Every provincial government has been struggling to keep a lid on costs and to find ways to rationalize a system that has become the second most expensive in the world, after that of the United States, as a percentage of gross domestic product. Yet if the cost of health care is a problem in the mid-1990s, demographics tell us that, as the saying goes, we ain't seen nothin' yet.

By the second decade of the new century, when the baby boom enters its senior years, our health care system will be confronted with sharply increased demand. We need to find ways to satisfy that demand while keeping spending under control. Maintaining an excellent health care system is going to require a great deal of ingenuity and careful planning based on an understanding of demographic reality.

To understand the size of the challenge, it's necessary to understand the demographics of health care. The baby-boomers, born between 1947 and 1966, are in their 30s and 40s today. During those decades of a person's life, use of the health care system, while rising, is still below the lifetime average. Seniors, whose use of the health care system is above average, are a comparatively small percentage of the Canadian population. In 1994, only 12% of Canadians were over 65, compared with 18% of Swedes and 16% of people in the United Kingdom. What these numbers mean is that, when it comes to health costs, Canada in the mid-1990s is in a relatively favourable position.

Despite that demographic good fortune, our health care system is more expensive than those of western European countries and Japan. Britain, for example, has life expectancy and infant mortality only slightly worse than Canada and yet spends only 6% of its gross domestic product (GDP) on health care, compared with Canada's 9.2%. Japan has lower infant mortality and higher life expectancy and yet spends only 6.5% of GDP on health care, despite having a much older population than Canada. (The situation in the United States, which spends 12.1% of GDP on health care, is even worse.) The message is inescapable: Canada is spending more on health care than most other advanced countries and not getting better health in return. Either our procedures and programs are very costly on a per-capita basis, or a large amount of waste is built into our system. The challenge is to maintain an excellent medicare program as our population ages without increasing spending. But we can do that only if we allocate our resources more wisely than we have been doing.

Efforts at health care reform are well under way. Four of the biggest issues are hospital closings, the desirability of allowing a second tier of private health care to provide speedier service for those who can afford it, the future of the fee-for-service system of compensating doctors, and drug use. All of these issues are intimately linked to the demographic changes currently reshaping Canadian society. Let's look at each in turn.

HOSPITALS

The issue of hospital closings illustrates the complexity of health care reform. It is often argued that to preserve medicare and avoid the emergence of a parallel private system, health care delivery has to be made more efficient, and that means reducing our reliance on hospitals, which are the most expensive part of the system. And yet closing hospitals during an era of population aging makes expansion of the private tier inevitable, because someone has to deliver services no longer being offered by publicly financed hospitals.

Reliance on doctors increases in a person's 40s, but above-average use of hospitals doesn't occur until the mid-50s. Then it takes off. By the time you are in your late 70s, you will use hospitals five times more than your lifetime average rate of use. If you survive until your late 80s, you will use hospitals 12 times more than your lifetime average. As for doctors, by your late 70s you will call on them twice as much as your lifetime average, and in your late 80s, 2.5 times as much. In short, utilization of hospitals rises far more dramatically with age than utilization of doctors. As we struggle to reorganize health care delivery, it's important to keep these facts in mind.

Because most of our population is still in its below-average hospital utilization years, health care policymakers think that now is the time for closing hospitals. Yet when they make this case, they never mention that a massive wave of Canadians — the baby-boom generation — is on the brink of entering that period of life when reliance on hospitals begins to rise.

This is a complex issue that requires careful consideration. Health care delivery has undergone dramatic changes in recent years. New diagnostic technologies, new drugs, new surgical methods, and new ideas about treatment have all contributed to shorter hospital stays for many patients. This has made it possible to use hospital beds more efficiently and has facilitated the closing of thousands of hospital beds. In some situations, a strong case exists for rationalization to reduce administrative costs. Why operate two hospitals with closed beds in the same area when the same number of patients could be served by only one?

One reason our health care system is so expensive is that we have a large number of hospital beds. Another is that we have a high ratio of doctors to patients. The World Bank considers the optimal ratio of doctors to population as one to 650 people. Canada's ratio is one to 490 and even higher in some cities. An oversupply of doctors can drive up health care costs as a result of unnecessary consultations, procedures, and prescriptions. Moreover, some doctors are much more likely than others to put patients into hospital. The more hospital beds that are available, the more patients will be admitted to fill them. Yet research shows no correlation between hospitalization and good health. In fact, a patient is at greater risk of acquiring infections in hospital than at home.

In planning the future of Canada's health care delivery system, we should give all of these factors the weight they deserve. That having been done, it is still open to doubt whether closing large numbers of hospitals is the right thing to do just when millions of Canadians are about to start needing them. Are the provincial politicians making the decisions to close hospitals even aware of the basic demographic facts that one-third of the Canadian population will begin turning 50 in 1997, and that people over 50 need hospitals more than people under 50? If we close too many hospitals now, we may find we are going to have to reopen them ten years from now. If they have been taken out of service in the interim, that may prove to be extremely costly or impractical.

Nor is the new medical wisdom that patients should be evicted from their hospital beds as soon as possible universally accepted. In fact, it is likely to be increasingly challenged as the population ages. "Seniors are slower to recover, and the drive to shorten lengths of stay in hospital hurts them more than anybody else," says Ethel Meade, convenor of health issues for the Older Women's Network in Toronto. "When people are sent home after an acute episode, they're scared of using the equipment they still need but don't know how to handle — catheters or IV feeds, for example. Home care isn't 24 hours, and unless there's an able-bodied, live-in caregiver staying with you, you're in deep trouble. People need around-the-clock care for the first few days. That's why we're calling for 24-hour home care or for convalescent care in hospitals."

Releasing recovering people from hospitals shifts the cost

and responsibility of patient care elsewhere. Some of this care will be provided free by relatives and friends of the patient. Some will be purchased from private providers of home health care services (see Chapter 3). While these costs have been removed from the public budget, someone must pay for them, either out of pocket or in the form of unpaid labour. Many people will take time off work to care for family members who would previously have been in hospital. In this way, the cost of care will be partially shifted to employers, eroding their productivity and competitiveness. David Naylor of the Institute for Clinical Evaluative Sciences at the University of Toronto has called this cost-shifting "indirect and unfair hidden sickness taxes."

But governments, in their current budget-cutting mode, are going to continue shifting the cost of health care onto private individuals. If this is to be done successfully, we will have to develop a whole new set of housing, social service, and health care arrangements for older people. It's fine to have people stay in their own homes as long as possible, but who is going to do their laundry, cook their meals, purchase their food and drugs, and monitor their condition with a view to moving them swiftly into hospital should that become necessary? And who is going to deliver and pay for it all? In some cases, the older people themselves will be able to pay, and in others their children will. But many people will not be able to afford these labour-intensive services, and government, having closed hospitals, will be under considerable pressure to provide or subsidize them. As a society, we haven't even started to work all this out yet. It's time we did.

Health care planners seem especially eager to close hospitals in outlying areas whose populations are currently too small to support them. These planners are oblivious to the fact that in their 50s and 60s, many people choose to move back to the country. This phenomenon has already been seen in European countries that have older populations than Canada. Over the next two decades, as 9.8 million baby-boomers turn 50, we will witness a significant exodus from big-city Canada to small-town Canada. The participants in this exodus are going to need the same hospitals that provincial governments want to close in the mid-1990s.

Governments should view small-town hospitals not as a burden on the health care budget but as a powerful tool for the economic development of rural regions. In the years to come, the reassuring presence of a good local hospital will act as a magnet for relatively prosperous new retirees, whose arrival will create new demand for goods and services. These people will bring new wealth with them rather than drawing their incomes from the local economy in competition with the original residents. It is already happening in the Okanagan and other parts of the B.C. interior, where people from Vancouver and other major cities have settled after deciding to trade their city homes for some small-town tranquillity. This is one scenario where increased population really does lead to increased prosperity — something that many parts of Canada haven't seen much of in recent times. A region that loses its local hospital may be losing its best chance for economic rebirth.

THE TWO-TIER HEALTH CARE SYSTEM

"Our technological ingenuity in inventing things to do to people, in the cause of health care, has long since outstripped our communal ability to pay for them," wrote H.E. Emson of Saskatoon, a professor of pathology and medical bioethicist, in the *Globe and Mail* in 1995. His comment helps explain why, like it or not, Canada already has the beginnings of a two-tier health care system. The practice of medicine is constantly evolving, producing new treatments and procedures that create new wants and needs. No publicly financed medicare system can possibly fulfil all these demands. No one would claim that the public system should pay, for example, for laser wrinkle removal for everyone who wants it. But what of medically necessary procedures such as heart bypass surgery and dialysis? Even with the second most expensive health care system in the world, Canada finds itself increasingly unable to provide these and other required procedures immediately to everyone who needs them.

Health care by its very nature involves rationing. The Americans ration it by continuing to use a complex system of private and public insurance that leaves out 40 million people. Canada's universal public system rations health care by ensuring that when a particular treatment is in short supply, those who need it urgently get it immediately, while others wait their turn. This system worked reasonably well until the 1990s, when it started to meet resistance. The reason for that resistance is that the baby boom reached its late 40s, and ever more people of that age are impatient with delays. Because of demographics, Canada has entered a period in which quality and service are becoming more important than price. (See Chapter 5.) An older population is more demanding and more knowledgeable about the products and services it needs and is less willing to tolerate poor service. Moreover, older people have more disposable income than younger people, and they are willing to pay to get what they want, when they want it. The huge wave of aging baby-boomers will be at least as demanding when it comes to health care as they are when they buy any other product or service.

Meanwhile, the companies and institutions that conduct medical research, spurred on by demographics, are delivering a wide array of new medical technologies and techniques to mitigate the ravages that time exacts on the human body. Because of demographics, the pressure to enlarge the second tier of our health care system is sure to intensify in the years to come. Health care delivered for profit will be a growth industry. In this environment, how are we going to maintain a medicare system that delivers a high standard of essential health care to everyone, rich and poor alike? That is one of the most important public policy issues before Canadians as the millennium approaches.

Two-tier health care is often discussed as if it were an option to be considered rather than something that already exists. Yet Canada has many private clinics offering such services as eye surgery, cosmetic surgery, and in-vitro fertilization. One example is London Place Eye Centre Inc. in New Westminster, B.C., where patients undergo a procedure called photorefractive keratectomy (PRK). It uses lasers to correct a variety of vision problems caused by imperfections in the cornea. The clinic is a commercial business; the procedure is not covered by the B.C. Medical Services Plan, and patients pay about $2,500 per eye.

This is reasonable: why should Canadians be denied a treatment that many of them want if they are willing to pay for it?

Such private clinics do not threaten medicare because PRK is not an essential medical service and no public money is being diverted to pay for something that is available only to a few. However, a basic principle of medicare — equality of access — is threatened by private clinics in some provinces that charge user fees to patients and then ask the provincial health plan to pay for the medical service performed. This is queue-jumping for those who probably can afford to pay extra, and the federal government has rightly objected to it as a violation of the Canada Health Act. People should be able to buy non-essential medical services on the private market, but not if they expect the public insurance plan to help pay for them.

The big debate in the years ahead is going to be over expanding the private tier to cover essential services paid in full by the user, either out of pocket or through a private insurance plan. This issue moved onto the public agenda in 1995 when the Canadian Medical Association debated it at its annual convention. It is noteworthy that the fight over private health care was already under way before a single baby-boomer had turned 50 and entered the years of increasing need for medical services. As a huge wave of people move into and through their 50s, becoming increasingly unwilling to wait for the medical services they want for themselves and their parents, this debate is going to become red hot.

The proponents of two-tier health care have a case. They point out that we already employ crude methods to ration health care in Canada: closing hospitals, laying off nurses, and watching doctors move to the United States. Some Canadians, unwilling to wait for elective surgery, go to the United States and buy it there. But Canada also has excellent doctors and hospitals. Why not let both Canadians and foreigners buy any health service they want in Canada, thereby giving highly trained doctors an incentive to stay and generating export wealth for the economy, while taking pressure off the public system and reducing delays? Proponents of a two-tier system point out that we allow so-called non-essential services to be bought privately. Yet deciding what's essential and what's not is a difficult task that will become more difficult as medical science advances. Why not stop making arbitrary distinctions and simply allow all medical services to be purchased privately by those willing to spend their own money?

The answer is that it is unjust for the wealthy to have better health care than those who are not wealthy. The best way to ensure that Canada maintains a good public health care system is to give the rich and powerful a good reason to support it. Having their lives depend on it is a good reason. But as demographic pressures intensify, we can't cling to the status quo if we want our health care system to stay healthy. Decisions will have to be made as to what is essential and what isn't. Some expansion of the second tier will be both unavoidable and desirable. And our public tier can learn some valuable lessons from other countries, including the United States, where private insurance companies and health maintenance organizations are finding innovative ways to bring costs down. But we should never give up on the medicare system that Thomas Courchene, of Queen's University, has called the "symbolic railway of the 21st century." Canadians value medicare not just because they need it, but because it brings them together as a national community.

DOCTORS' FEES

The oldest members of the baby-boom generation are now moving into their years of above-average use of doctors' services. As 9.8 million people reach 50 over the next 20 years, the pressure can only increase. Unfortunately, Canada's health care system contains a built-in incentive for doctors to do unnecessary procedures and consultations. It is called the fee-for-service system of paying doctors, and it is especially wasteful in a country like Canada that, according to the World Bank, has too many doctors. More doctors mean more services, and more services mean more money paid out by provincial health plans. The result is rapid increases in spending — health care spending in Canada has doubled between the mid-1980s and the mid-1990s — with no evidence that Canadians are healthier as a result. In fact, some analysts claim 30% of medical procedures are unnecessary.

But if we are to dispense with fee-for-service, something has to replace it. One promising alternative is capitation, also known as rostering or population-based payment. This is the system used by health maintenance organizations in the United States and in the British national health system. Under this system, a doctor is paid for taking responsibility for the health care of a group of people; whether the doctor sees a particular individual 20 times in a year or only once has no impact on her income. This system can give the physician a powerful incentive to keep her patients healthy, through such means as counselling on fitness and nutrition, and a powerful disincentive to encourage unnecessary visits or to perform unnecessary procedures. In 1995, a national working group headed by Miles Kelshaw, a B.C. government medical consultant, prepared a report on physicians' compensation for Canada's health ministers. The report proposed that Canada switch to a capitation system in which family doctors would work in group practices called primary care organizations (PCOs). These would have rosters of patients, with annual budgets based on the number of patients and the characteristics of the population being served. All the staff members, including doctors, would draw an income out of the annual budget.

This kind of system promotes continuous care whereas fee-for-service medicine tends to treat each complaint as an isolated phenomenon. The disadvantage of a capitation system is that doctors working under it might be less responsive to the needs of a patient who needs a lot of attention. The working group addressed this problem by building competition into its proposal. Patients would get the right to choose which PCO they joined and which doctor they saw within the PCO, and they would also have the right to quit. PCOs that provided bad service would thus lose customers and see their budgets shrink, with the reverse being true for good PCOs. Capitation can be designed with incentives for doctors who wish to work harder for higher incomes. And of course the system would not be acceptable if doctors had the right to send patients away; if they did, some of the sickest patients might not be able to get medical attention.

In the United States, 50 million people get their health care under capitation systems. A study done over ten years and published in 1995 in the *Journal of the American Medical Association* found that the care these patients received was just as good as that given to patients treated by fee-for-service doctors, at 40 per cent of the cost. The main difference was that clients of capitation practices were hospitalized less and got fewer drugs.

This is one area where demographic trends and the need for governments to restrain health care spending point to the same conclusion. Not only can we no longer afford the fee-for-service system, it is inappropriate for a society with an aging population. Fee-for-service rewards doctors who maximize the number of patients they see and penalizes those who take the time to explain and discuss health problems with their patients. Yet the latter approach is exactly what a more mature, knowledgeable, and demanding consumer of health care needs and expects. A patient in her 50s, who may well be older than her doctor, is not going to tolerate patronizing, authoritarian, assembly-line medicine.

If fee-for-service is inappropriate for the middle-aged, it is even more remote from the needs of the elderly. Fee-for-service discriminates against doctors who specialize in geriatrics, according to Michael Gordon, vice-president of medical services at Baycrest Centre for Geriatric Care in Toronto. "As geriatricians, we get paid the same as a general internist for a consultation — about $100," Gordon said in a 1995 interview in the *Toronto Star*. "But a geriatric consultation can take an hour and a half whereas a general medicine consultation may take 45 minutes. We put in two or three years after our internal medicine training and often our incomes go down. In care for the aged, fee-for-service is counterproductive."

Chapter 5 argued that demographics will propel retailing back to a future of neighbourhood shops offering personalized service to loyal customers. Demographics coupled with the de-emphasis on hospitalization could push medical practice back to the future. Doctors with an aging clientele will have to get out of their offices and see patients in their homes, because there is no other way to deliver high-quality care to older patients. The doctor who visits at home confers great benefit on her oldest clients. She can check on their living conditions, go into their medicine cabinets and get rid of dated drugs, and give patients an important morale boost simply by letting them know that someone cares enough to come and see them. In some cases, a paramedic, working under the direction of a doctor and trained in geriatric care, could make these visits. If we want people to remain independent as long as possible, and if we are serious about reducing reliance on hospitals at the same time as our population is aging, then this old-fashioned kind of medical practice has to be the wave of the future.

A medical practice that is appropriate to a mature population involves a partnership between patient and physician aimed at maintaining good health through a healthy lifestyle. It also requires the contributions of other specialists, including pharmacists, nutritionists, physiotherapists, nurses, and home care specialists. This sort of approach goes by different names: health promotion, preventive medicine, wellness, shared decision-making. It is more likely to occur under the capitation system than under fee-for-service.

The evidence is strong that shared decision-making results in better medical practice. In this regard, the work of Dr. Jack Wennberg of Dartmouth Medical School in Dartmouth, New Hampshire, is particularly instructive. He investigated the phenomenon, also well known in Canada, of wide variations in practice patterns from location to location. Why, for example, were tonsillectomies performed nine times as often in one town as in another in the same state? Why were prostate operations, bypass surgeries, and hysterectomies anywhere from two to four times more likely to occur in certain localities?

Wennberg found that treatments were chosen without reference to any detailed comparative analysis of the costs and benefits of different options. Doctors often did not know which treatment was best for their patients. Wennberg advocates a system in which the patient makes major decisions on his health based on full and impartial information. To that end, he and his colleagues prepared a video on the problem of frequent urination caused by enlargement of the prostate gland. This is a medical issue that will be very much in the limelight as the baby-boom generation ages, because virtually every man over the age of 45 has some degree of enlargement, and after age 60, one in ten men suffer serious urinary problems as a result of it. The treatment options include surgery to remove the tissue that is causing the enlargement or learning to live with the discomfort. The advantage of surgery is that it relieves the symptoms; a disadvantage is that in some cases it can cause impotence. The videotape shows doctors who favour different options and includes interviews with patients who have experienced each treatment.

The results of showing this video were remarkable. At a health maintenance organization in Denver, patients educated by the video, as well as by a surgeon, chose surgery half as often as patients advised only by their surgeon. Given the other side of the story, people were prepared to accept some discomfort in return for avoiding a major operation. This case study prompted the New York Times to come to the following conclusion in a 1992 editorial: "Shared decision making, backed up by hard outcomes data, leads to better care at a fraction of the cost." The Times also noted that a health maintenance organization, with a strong incentive to avoid unnecessary surgery, is more likely to adopt shared decision-making than an individual surgeon depending on fee-for-service. The great strength of shared decision-making, the Times concluded, is that it gives patients "a sense of power and participation" and at the same time has the potential to save billions of dollars.

This is medical practice in tune with the needs of an aging society. First of all, a mature patient wants and expects to participate in key decisions affecting his life. Second, decision-making based on known facts about outcomes, and not only on physician preferences, helps ensure that the limited resources available for health care are spent wisely. In an aging society, whose population will inevitably make increasing demands on the health care system, we have no option but to spend money wisely because none will be available to waste.

DRUG USE IN AN AGING SOCIETY

Taste in drugs, as in so much else, changes with age. The average drug user sniffs glue at the age of 12, smokes pot at the age of 20, shoots crack or sniffs cocaine at the age of 30, and takes a Valium at 40. Note that all but the last of these drugs are illegal. An older person is much less likely to engage in reckless experimentation than a younger one. Partly that's because a young person who persists in heavy illegal drug use has a reduced chance of ever becoming an older person. Also, an older person is more aware of mortality and more concerned about health than a younger one. Consequently, in an aging population, illegal drug uses declines. A study by the Addiction Research Foundation in Toronto showed that the highest percentage of users of illicit narcotics were in the 30-to-39 age group, which counted 36.5% of all users. The 40-to-49 age group had only 6.7% of users. Aging, therefore, is a more effective weapon against illicit drugs than law enforcement.

Illegal drug use increases sharply among 20-year-olds, continues to rise during the 30s, and then falls off sharply in the 40s. If we haven't heard much about glue-sniffing or marijuana in recent years, it's not because these drugs are not still available and in use. It's because the young people currently using them are a smaller group.

Because the baby-boomers are the largest cohort, their drugs of choice are the ones that make the news. When the boomers were teenagers, glue sniffing was big. In the late 1960s and through the 1970s, pot smoking was rampant, and the campaign to legalize marijuana attained the status of a political movement. Why did this political movement run out of steam? Because the baby-boomers passed through their pot-smoking years, and the cohort currently smoking pot is too small to mount an effective campaign.

A serious drug user then turns to cocaine in his 20s and uses it for a while. Then either he gives it up or it kills him. The statistics tell this story clearly: 10% of 25-year-olds use cocaine, compared with 5% of 40-year-olds and 1% of 50-year-olds.

Today the front end of the baby boom is moving into the age group whose drugs of choice are legal. That is why we are seeing a surge in the use of tranquillizers, anti-depressants, and sleeping pills. One of the most popular new drugs of recent years is the anti-depressant Prozac. While that product and similar new ones are widely prescribed, the use of older anti-depressants is also increasing.

It is not necessarily a boon that a large segment of society is switching from illegal to legal drugs. The legal ones can also be dangerous to health. In 1995, the *Canadian Medical Association Journal* published a study that found that the doctors who wrote the most prescriptions also had the highest death rates among their patients. This study found that some doctors, in trying to maximize the number of patients they could process per day, did not take the time necessary to find out what was wrong with these patients. That kind of medical practice results in overmedicated and inappropriately medicated patients. It increases the risk of adverse reactions, and it is costly.

Our society is highly dependent on chemicals. With an aging population, we need to devote increased attention to the misuse of drugs, both legal and illegal. The managers of both public and private drug benefit plans along with the medical community should develop prescribing guidelines to ensure that misuse does not occur. And law enforcement agencies will need increased forensic accounting capabilities to examine hospital records and doctors' records for evidence of the abusive use of legal drugs.

Prescribing guidelines are already appearing as part of the attempt by governments to hold down rising costs of their drug plans and improve patient care at one and the same time. The increasing need for prescribing guidelines, as for the other changes in medical practice described in this chapter, comes from demographic change. In Ontario, spending by the Ontario Drug Benefit Plan, which used to provide free prescription drugs to seniors and people on social assistance, was growing by as much as 17% a year during the 1980s. Since older people tend to be sicker and need more medicine than younger people, and since the greying of Canadian society had barely started, it was obvious that such growth rates were unsustainable. Part of the problem was what Janet Hux and David Naylor of the University of Toronto have called "inappropriately expensive prescribing." Their 1994 study found that the use of expensive antibiotics increased when the patient had full drug benefit coverage but was reduced when the physician was reminded of price. Another part of the problem was that some physicians didn't know enough to make good prescribing decisions. Guidelines prepared by the top experts in each field can help physicians prescribe only those drugs that are needed and for the length of time they are needed.

In an aging society, this can be done only if patients are treated as individuals. As two Canadian experts, William McKim and Brian Mishara, point out in their 1987 book *Drugs and Aging*, wide individual variations exist among the elderly, many of whom are healthier than much younger people. Drugs are not what older people need most for their health, the authors conclude, because good eating habits and exercise are more effective ways of prolonging life. Drugs should be used where appropriate and with the understanding that they are neither good nor evil, and that all drugs can be dangerous if abused. For example, Aspirin, which many people consider harmless, is one of the leading causes of overdose deaths in Canada. On the other hand, "heroin addicts who observe certain precautions can live to a ripe old age in good health despite a lifetime of use of this illegal drug."

Although that may be so, few old people actually use heroin. In fact, the passage of the baby boom out of its pot and cocaine years means that the days of booming growth for the illegal drug industry in Canada are over. However, the outlook for the criminals who engage in this industry isn't entirely bleak because the larger echo generation is entering its drug experimentation years. While cocaine will fade into the background because of the aging of the boomers, pot may make a comeback by the turn of the century.

A legal drug, tobacco, will also attract a large number of new customers during the same period. The tobacco industry cannot survive unless it persuades children and teenagers to try its product, because few adults take up the habit that is the leading cause of death in Canada. Eighty per cent of smokers are addicted by the age of 18, and 90% are hooked by 21. In the mid-1990s, the 6.9 million Canadian echo kids are entering those gullible, reckless years when people get hooked for life on nicotine. The federal government's decision to make smoking more affordable by lowering taxes and the Supreme Court's decision in 1995 to overturn the ban on cigarette advertising could not have come at a worse time.

HEALTH CARE IN THE FUTURE

For the time being, Canada does not have a health care crisis because it still has a relatively young population. The crunch won't really come for another 20 years, when the boomers are in their late 50s and 60s. That gives us time to learn how to allocate our resources wisely and ensure the maintenance of a first-class medicare system.

During the 1990s, the fastest-growing segment of the population is the over-80 population, mostly poor older women born before World War I. They are a relatively large group, and for the rest of the decade, they will continue to put stress on their children and our chronic care facilities. But that problem will dissipate over the next decade as the oldest seniors depart and the current young senior group moves into the senior senior category. These people are wealthier, and thus better able to finance their own care; and because they were born in the 1930s, they are fewer in number than the current batch of senior seniors.

Baby-boomers have a tendency, annoying to post-boomers and pre-boomers alike, to assume that whatever phase they are going through must be of universal interest. Nothing can cure them of this and, given their dominant position in the mass media, there isn't much the rest of society can do about it. So get ready to be inundated by a flood of articles about health issues related to aging. Prostate problems, already mentioned, will be big news. Menopause, which affects the entire female population, will be even bigger.

The menopause debate will be interesting, because it highlights a conflict between two values dear to many members of the boomer generation. One is the high status given to things "natural," whether it was dispensing with bras in the 1960s or eating unadulterated food and wearing clothes made from natural rather than synthetic fibres in the 1970s and 1980s. The less one tried to improve on nature the better. The other value is the one that has made the cosmetics industry, along with cosmetic surgery and cosmetic dentistry, into a booming business; it says that just because a person is no longer young doesn't mean she can't look good and feel good. In the case of menopause, this value clash is represented by the controversy over estrogen.

After menopause, which usually occurs by the early 50s, women stop producing the hormone estrogen. Taking estrogen, in the form of pills, patches, or creams, is a way to offset the physical impacts that occur naturally as a result of this change. Estrogen relieves the hot flashes, vaginal dryness, and night sweats that occur as the ovaries reduce their estrogen production. More important, current research indicates that it dramatically reduces the risk of heart disease and of osteoporosis (thinning of the bones), which can result in severe fractures. Estrogen also improves a woman's sex life by rejuvenating the vaginal tissues and reducing dryness. And there is evidence that it improves memory. Against these significant benefits are a number of drawbacks, including increased risk of breast cancer, the possibility of weight gain, and the expense and nuisance of having to take drugs for many years.

Many doctors are in favour of estrogen, saying that the benefits far outweigh the risks. That explains why, well before the first female boomer had turned 50, estrogen was already the best-selling prescription drug in the United States. But some doctors, along with writers such as Germaine Greer, argue that it's wrong to interfere with nature's course and turn a normal event in a woman's life into a condition requiring long-term drug therapy. With the front end of the baby boom entering its menopause years, this debate will be with us for many years to come.

Finally, as our health care system evolves, Canadians will have to wake up to the close link between health and the economy. In the mid-1990s, more than 3 million Canadians receive social assistance, and 20% of all Canadians, including many senior seniors, are living below the poverty line. That is not a prescription for a healthy society. A mountain of evidence exists to prove that unemployment and poverty are the prime causes of poor health, yet this fact is rarely discussed in the context of our health care system.

"Studies in all parts of Canada consistently show that people at each step on the income scale are healthier than those on the step below," John Millar, the British Columbia health officer, wrote in a 1995 report. In Vancouver and Victoria, for example, twice as many infant deaths occurred in low-income neighbourhoods as in wealthy districts. The *British Medical Journal* said the same thing in a 1992 editorial: "Unemployment begets poverty which begets ill health and premature death."

What this means is that we can't expect our health care system to deliver miracles, no matter how well we reform it or how much money we spend on it. An effective way to keep health costs down is to make sure Canadians are working in well-paid jobs and have sufficient incomes, especially into their retirement years. Given the demands on our health care budget that an aging population will make, sensible economic development and social policies are more urgently needed than ever before.

Chapter 10

What's a Family?

Demographics are an invisible force that can affect even our most intimate relationships in surprising ways. For example, it would never occur to a 25-year-old who is popular with the opposite sex that if born 10 years earlier, he or she might not have been quite so popular. But in romance as in so much else, being born in the right year is an advantage. In some cases, what seems like a new behavioural trend — "cocooning," for instance — is in fact the inevitable result of a demographic shift. Let's take a closer look at how demographics can affect family life and other relationships among people.

BABIES

In the early 1980s, a senior official in the Ontario Ministry of Health with some knowledge of demographics had a plan. He knew that births had declined through the 1960s and 1970s. He knew that the fertility rate was way down and that the chances of modern women reverting to having three or four children each were remote. Therefore, he reasoned, Ontario's hospitals should be developing a strategy for closing maternity wards during the 1980s, since births would surely continue to decline. At the same time, in preparation for the aging of society, these facilities should be transformed into geriatric wards.

As Alexander Pope wisely said, "A little learning is a danger-ous thing." It was true that the fertility rate was down, and it was also true that society was aging. But there was more need for maternity wards than for geriatric wards at the start of the 1980s because the birth rate would inevitably go up, and seniors, just as inevitably, would remain very much a minority in Canadian society.

The birth rate did go up because the huge number of women born during the 1950s and 1960s moved into their childbearing years. Even if women have relatively few kids, as these boomer women did, a lot of people having one or two kids each at the same time means a lot of business for maternity wards. That's what happened during the 1980s as the baby-boom echo arrived. Hospitals had to give up any ideas of closing maternity wards, just as schools had to contend with a sudden rise in kindergarten enrolment, followed of course by rising elementary school enrolment. As for the seniors, the growth in their numbers slowed during the 1980s for the simple reason that not many people were born during World War I. Demographics are easy to understand, but without careful analysis, the timing of appropriate policies can be way off.

The baby-boom echo is petering out in the mid-1990s. This comes as a surprise to some who thought that because the birth rate rose during the 1980s, it would continue to rise during the 1990s. Instead, births began to fall off after 1990 because the most proficient baby producers — women in their 20s — declined in number. The 1980s, after a 20-year decline in births, was exactly the wrong time to consider closing some maternity wards. The right time is the mid-1990s, after 15 years of high births. The money saved should be shifted not only to geriatric wards, but also to facilities to care for heart attack and stroke victims, as the front end of the baby boom approaches its prime heart attack and stroke years.

In the mid-1990s, the effect of the increase in marriage age combined with women delaying childbirth in order to pursue careers has resulted in more older first-time mothers than ever before; women in their 30s are giving birth to almost 20% of first-borns. But the salient fact is that 80% of first-time mothers, still an overwhelming majority, are women in their 20s. Despite the social and economic changes affecting the status of women, women are still four times as likely to give birth in their early 20s as in their 30s. Yet most women in the population of childbearing age have now moved into their 30s. Many of these women are having trouble getting pregnant, but they aren't ready to give up. That accounts for the significant improvements we have witnessed in recent years in techniques to treat infertility. This scientific effort is driven purely by demographics. It will run out of steam by the turn of the century when the majority of boomers will be too old to have babies.

MEN AND WOMEN

When they marry for the first time, men usually marry women about two years younger than they are. And women, obviously, tend to marry men about two years older. This simple demographic fact has important social implications. For women of marriageable age it means that, in the 1990s, they have more choice among potential partners than men do. The balance of power in male-female relationships has shifted their way. (See Figure 9.)

The number of people born in each year kept climbing until 1959, the peak of the baby boom. After 1960, the baby boom declined into the baby bust, which lasted until the late 1970s. When birth numbers are rising, there will inevitably be more 26-year-old females than 28-year-old males. That puts the 28-year-old male in the driver's seat, because he has a greater choice of females of the right age to choose from. That's what happened in the first phase of the baby boom. But if numbers are dropping from year to year, then 28-year-old males will outnumber 26-year-old females. This started to occur by the mid-1980s, when the peak of the baby boom reached its mid-20s, the age when permanent relationships are generally established. It's definitely the situation for young people contemplating partnerships in the mid-1990s. There aren't enough 26-year-old women for all the 28-year-old men who are looking for partners. The women can now pick and choose.

The average age of first marriages declined during the 1950s and 1960s, stabilized in the 1970s, and then climbed back up in the 1980s. Newlyweds were 25 and 22 in the 1950s; they are 28 and 26 in the mid-1990s. The two-year-gap has remained fairly stable over the

FIGURE 9: GENDER RATIO AT MARRIAGE
(males age 27 to females age 25)

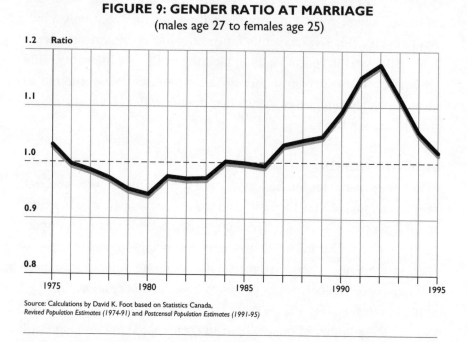

Source: Calculations by David K. Foot based on Statistics Canada,
Revised Population Estimates (1974-91) and *Postcensal Population Estimates (1991-95)*

past 25 years. This gender gap can have a big impact on social mores. Take the case of a front-end boomer, born in 1950 and reaching 28 in 1978. Fewer men were born in 1950 than women in 1952. This meant that in the potential marriage relationship, men were in short supply relative to women. This may explain the growth in cohabitation as the huge boomer generation moved into its adult years over the late 1960s and 1970s. The shortage of male partners may have contributed to a decision by more women to get on with their lives by looking for ways to fulfilment other than marriage and a family.

There were other reasons for the changes in personal morality that marked the 1960s and 1970s, including the arrival of the birth-control pill, the relaxation of the divorce law, and the movement of women into the labour force. These were events of far-reaching significance for family life. Women were now free to have multiple partners, to postpone or reject motherhood, and to pursue careers. And as they pursued those careers, they gradually evened the balance of power between men and women still further. A woman whose earning power is as great as a man's can do without one if she prefers;

or if she does choose to have a partner, she can leave him if she becomes dissatisfied.

This new fact of life has contributed to a decline in the popularity of marriage in Canada. So has the reality that many people, having lived through their own parents' divorces, have a negative opinion about marriage. Many others, whatever their attitude to marriage, tend to avoid or postpone it during rough economic times. For all these reasons, the marriage rate in Canada has been dropping steadily since 1990, and those who are getting married aren't doing very well at it; in the mid-1990s, one out of every three women in their 20s who have been married is either separated or divorced. The change in social mores is so profound that many Canadians are abandoning the concept of marriage as a prerequisite for having children; almost one in three new babies in Canada today is born to unmarried parents.

Evidence of the huge advance made towards equality of the sexes is that some men now admit without embarrassment to being "househusbands." This is the result of the simultaneous arrival of the baby-boom echo and the movement of women into high-paying jobs. If the arrival of small children requires one partner to stay at home and the wife is earning the larger salary, then it makes obvious economic sense for her to stay in her job. And of course, in many cases there is no choice in the matter: he has lost his job to the recession or downsizing, and she has been able to keep hers.

At the same time that some men are claiming househusband status, many women are reclaiming that of housewife. Demographics are the reason. During the late 1980s and early 1990s, the peak of the baby boom was passing through its family formation years, the late 20s and early 30s. Families with children under five are often easier to manage when one partner stays home. This demographic event coincided in most of Canada with a severe recession. Jobs were scarce, and that was another good reason to take a temporary break from work. As their children grow up, many of these temporary housewives and househusbands are likely to re-enter the workforce.

The redefinition of the family in Canadian society also

includes the movement to formalize and legitimize marriages of same-sex couples. Demographics again play an important role. People in their 20s are more likely than older people to engage in temporary relationships and don't concern themselves with such boring matters as health plans and pension benefits. But in the mid-1990s, with the huge baby boom moving through its 30s and 40s, these people are ready for a more permanent relationship and are becoming concerned about their future and their children's future. As part of a large cohort, boomers are not shy about asserting their rights. That's why in the 1990s, same-sex couples in permanent relationships have begun demanding the same legal and economic benefits that society confers on traditional marriages, including the right to adopt children. Some women choose to introduce children into existing lesbian relationships. In other cases, gays and lesbians who entered heterosexual marriages in their 20s have abandoned those marriages in their 30s and 40s, replacing them with openly homosexual alliances. Because children are involved in some of these situations, the issues of custody and adoption have become extremely important.

All these complex changes in the structure of the family add up to a social experiment of major proportions. The results so far are mixed. That men and women are better able to free themselves from unhappy relationships is all to the good. It is also good that women now have equal opportunity to fulfil their talents in whatever way they choose. On the other hand, the breakdown of the traditional family has brought with it a huge increase in the number of single-parent families. And the evidence is mounting that children in such families are at a disadvantage. Studies show that they are more likely than the children of two-parent families to be undernourished, to get pregnant as teenagers, and to drop out of high school, and they are less likely to go on to postsecondary education.

Because of demographics, Canadian family life will be marked by continuing turmoil for the foreseeable future. The peak of the baby boom enters its late 30s in the late 1990s. Many of these people have been married for a decade. If a couple is going to split, it will usually happen after about a decade of married life. The average Canadian marriage that ends in divorce lasts 11 years. Because a large number of couples have been passing through that stage, Canada has witnessed rising divorce rates, which are likely to continue for the rest of the 1990s. This means the trend towards more single-parent families will continue.

But despite all the change that is taking place, it is too soon to write off the traditional family. For one thing, the traditional two-parent family, with one parent working and the other at home, is still what most people say they want, according to an Angus Reid poll conducted in 1994 for the Canada Committee for the International Year of the Family. Second, the age gap favouring females in the 1990s probably favours the traditional family. Marcia Guttentag and Paul Secord of the University of Houston studied several societies where men compete for a smaller number of women. They found that in such societies, the traditional marriage flourishes. The average age of first marriage drops, marriage and birth rates climb, and females quit the workforce to become full-time homemakers. This demographic trend in favour of traditionalism will be operating in Canada until the echo generation reaches marriageable age, starting around 2005. And although it may not be powerful enough to offset the social trends working against the traditional family, it can significantly slow down the pace of change.

But while it is wrong to write off the traditional family, it would also be wrong to put too much stock in the alleged revival of "family values" during the 1980s and 1990s, because that phenomenon is likely to be transitory. When do you have family values? When you have families. Today the boomers are in their 30s and 40s, with houses and mortgages and young children to fret over. Family values didn't matter to them much as 20-year-olds in the 1970s, any more than they interested 20-year-olds during the Roaring Twenties. And when the echo generation begins leaving home, at the turn of the millennium, don't be surprised if it appears that society has once again begun to neglect family values and to rediscover sex, drugs, and new music. Social observers will herald the arrival of yet another value shift, but the real reason will be the demographic shift. Sex, drugs, and alternative music are alive and well in the mid-1990s. It's just that the baby-bust generation currently enjoying them is 55% the size of the baby boom, and so the rest of society pays less attention to its preferences.

COCOONING

Faith Popcorn, the American marketing guru, has succeeded in putting a new word into the language: cocooning. The notion of cocooning struck so strong a chord when Popcorn invented it that *le cocooning* was adopted by French-speakers as well. Cocooning means cosying up at home. Whereas in the 1970s people were dancing and drinking all night in discos, Popcorn's research revealed that in the 1980s — stressed out by overwork, noise, crime, and sundry other ills of modern life — the same people preferred to snuggle up in their living rooms, shades drawn tight, in front of their television sets and VCRs. Of this, Popcorn had ample proof: VCR sales were skyrocketing, as were sales of take-out food and microwave popcorn. And along with rising VCR sales, Popcorn noted one other result of cocooning: births in the United States in 1990 were the highest since the baby-boom year of 1960.

Popcorn confused cause and effect. In her book *The Popcorn Report,* she suggested that people first decided to stay home and then, to give themselves something to do, decided to have children. But the reality was exactly the reverse. The huge baby-boom generation, in both Canada and the United States, moved into its childrearing years and, inevitably, started spending more time at home. Call it cocooning or what you will — it was normal, predictable behaviour.

In this as in so much else, the baby boom was no different from any previous generation. Children are great consumers of their parents' time, energy, and money. Couples raising children have less time, less energy, and less money to go out on the town than they had when they were childless. So they settle for ordering take-out and renting a video instead of dinner in a restaurant followed by the theatre or a movie. But they still love going out (see Chapter 6), and once the kids are old enough to stay home without a babysitter, they will leave the cocoon more often, although they won't stay out as late at age 41 as they did at age 21. Cocooning seemed to be a popular new lifestyle only because so many boomer parents were passing through the same phase of their lives at the same time. The next cohort to enter the cocoon will be the baby-bust generation. When that happens, it will seem as if cocooning has gone out of style — and that will be true, not because of a value shift but because there are half as many baby-busters as baby-boomers.

THE OLDEST PROFESSION

Much confusion surrounds the subject of prostitution because Canadian newspapers, inexplicably, insist on subjecting their readers to a regular stream of articles discussing the pros and cons of "legalizing prostitution" as if this ancient profession actually were illegal in Canada. In fact, no law forbids prostitution although, like many other occupations, its conduct is subject to strict regulations.

The effect of these regulations is to prohibit prostitutes from soliciting clients in the street, from working for someone else, and from carrying on business in a permanent location. Of course, the regulations are often disobeyed, with the result that illegal prostitution flourishes in our major cities. But many other prostitutes operate as independents, and they are engaged in a lawful business. The courts do not interpret their advertising — through word of mouth or in explicit newspaper ads — as soliciting. They do not work for pimps. They do not operate out of a single place of business, which would be an illegal bawdy house, but instead meet clients in locations not primarily used for paid sex.

What do demographics have in store for these law-abiding prostitutes, as well as for their colleagues operating outside the law? From a business standpoint, the news is good. Most prostitutes are women or men in their late teens and 20s; most of their customers are men aged between 30 and 50. This means that changes in the age structure of society can have a major impact on both the supply of prostitutes and the demand for their services. For the remainder of the 1990s, prostitutes will be drawn from a smaller cohort, the baby bust, while their customers will come from a large one, the baby boom. In other words, the impact of the current demographic situation is to both limit the supply of prostitutes and expand the demand for them. One likely result will be rising prices for sexual services.

With the echo generation entering its teenage years, this couldn't happen at a worse time. Anything that entices more people into prostitution is not desirable, because prostitution is not a desirable occupation. It can be dangerous and degrading even for independent, law-abiding professionals. Street prostitutes suffer appalling working conditions. Most of them become drug addicts and, because of ruthless exploitation by pimps, are able to retain only a small fraction of their earnings. There is evidence that prostitution increases with unemployment. This means that the combination of rising demand and continuing high unemployment could lure people into the trade who might otherwise not have considered it.

The best way to reduce the appeal of prostitution is to build an economy that offers challenging, well-paid employment to young people. Meanwhile, since attempts to enforce the regulations against illegal prostitution have proven extremely ineffective, municipal governments and police forces in recent years have been looking for ways to protect residential neighbourhoods from the sex trade while making life less dangerous for prostitutes. Some reform is badly needed. In view of the demographic trend favouring the growth of prostitution, which will make this occupation tempting to many echo teenagers, that need will take on new urgency in the years ahead.

THE SANDWICH GENERATION

Life expectancy at birth for Canadian men is 75; for women, it's 81. Over the next decade the parents of the baby-boomers will be approaching those ages. Many of these parents will be in declining health and will need extra attention from their offspring. At the same time, front-end boomers will be engaged in the often difficult task of guiding their teenagers through the transition from childhood to adulthood. They will also have increasing responsibilities at work. These people are the meat in a generational sandwich.

Of course, this phenomenon isn't new, but a number of factors are at work that are going to make sandwiching a much bigger problem for more people than ever before. Many women are working in senior, stressful, time-consuming jobs. That's important because women are the ones who most often take on the job of caregiving. Many of these same women had children later in life than was the norm in past generations. Meanwhile, people are living longer. All these elements increase the chances of someone being responsible for both children and parents at the same time.

Because life expectancy is lower for men, chances are that a woman will be present to take care of a male partner who has a disabling health problem. But if a widow falls ill, there's no partner around to look after her needs. At that point, the responsibility falls on the children, who are in their late 40s and 50s. A 1994 Statistics Canada study found that twice as many women as men were both working full-time and caring for an elderly relative. Because women are more likely to be sandwiched than males, sandwiching is an important reason why more women haven't risen to senior positions in their careers. The woman who becomes a senior vice-president at the age of 51 may not go on to become president, because she chooses to devote more time and emotional energy to caring for a dying parent.

Here's how one family has responded to the needs of a mother in declining health. Of the three sons, the youngest still lives close to his mother, while the two older ones, who have been more successful financially in their careers, live in distant cities. The two wealthier brothers have paid for a house for their mother to live in and pay two-thirds of the cost of owning and running the house. But all three brothers share ownership of the house, the youngest paying his share by spending time caring for the mother. The mother pays the youngest son's share of the costs as rent. This arrangement works to everyone's satisfaction because all three sons are doing their part, none feels taken advantage of, and the mother is well looked after.

In the world of mobility we live in, this is an example of the kind of innovation that will be needed as families cope with the decline and death of parents. The boomers, because there are so many of them, grew up in a world of sibling rivalry. But to help their parents complete life's journey in peace and dignity, they will have to learn to exercise sibling cooperation instead.

The inevitable decline in health of one's parents has other implications as well. It increases a person's awareness of mortality, which often leads to an increased interest in spirituality. This often coincides with the presence of teenage children whose parents would like to acquaint them with their spiritual heritage. It also results in greater health awareness, which is why 45-year-olds tend to drive more safely, smoke and drink less, and pay more attention to what they eat than 25-year-olds. These trends are likely to continue as the rest of the boomers enter their 40s during the next decade.

Chapter 11

An Older, Wiser Canada

D emographics are so fundamental a phenomenon, operating at so deep a level in human society, that most of us are not aware of them, just as we are not aware of an underground stream flowing silently beneath a big city street. Yet demographics are too useful a tool for explaining the world to remain underground. The preceding chapters have shown how they can throw light on the future of such things as school enrolments, real estate investments, and public taste in cars. Demographics also have a lot to say about such big issues as Canadian constitutional negotiations and international flows of goods and people. Demographics help us understand what was at stake when anglophone Canada sat down at the negotiating table with Quebec, just as they enable us to anticipate Canada's future place in a world of expanding global trade. Let's conclude this survey of the impact of demographics on Canada's future by looking at some of those big issues.

DEMOGRAPHICS AND THE CONSTITUTION

Canada is composed of three distinct societies, each with a different fertility rate. These societies are anglophone Canada, francophone Canada, and aboriginal Canada. (Within anglophone Canada, there is some variation from province to province. In 1993, Newfoundland had the lowest fertility rate, 1.3, while Saskatchewan, at 2.0, had the highest.) The dramatic demographic differences among anglophone, francophone, and aboriginal Canada help explain why both the

Meech Lake and Charlottetown constitutional negotiations ended in failure.

In the 1920s, the fertility rate in Canada was 3.5 children per family. This national rate included an average of 4.5 children for each Quebec family and 3 children for each family in Canada outside Quebec. Quebec's relatively high fertility, reflecting its Roman Catholic heritage, continued throughout the 1920s, 1930s, and 1940s. During this period it didn't matter whether Quebec took in as many immigrants as other parts of the country. Higher fertility allowed Quebeckers to maintain or even increase their relative share of the Canadian population.

The Quiet Revolution of the 1950s and 1960s included a demographic revolution, as Quebec women increasingly ignored the Catholic prohibition on birth control. As a result, fertility started to fall. By 1959, the fertility rate in Quebec was the same as in the rest of the country, and since then it has often been lower. Quebec's fertility reached a low of 1.4 children per family in 1986, well below the replacement rate of 2.1 and one of the lowest fertility rates in the world. Since then Quebec's fertility has recovered somewhat, reaching 1.6 in 1993. By then, Quebec no longer had the lowest fertility in Canada; its rate was the same as B.C.'s, higher than those of three Atlantic provinces, and only slightly below the overall Canadian fertility rate of 1.7.

In the mid-1990s, therefore, Quebec's fertility is low but not abnormally low: Quebec is merely exhibiting the reproductive behaviour that has become the norm in all modern industrialized societies. Nor is it remarkable that women in a predominantly Catholic society would decide to have few babies. Such strongly Catholic countries as Spain, Portugal, and Italy also have very low fertility: Spain and Italy, at 1.2 children per family in the mid-1990s, have the lowest fertility in the world.

The recent upward movement in Quebec's fertility rate wasn't enough to prevent the province's population from dropping below 25% of the Canadian population in 1994 for the first time since Confederation. This happened not only because of continuing low fertility but also because more people leave Quebec every year than move to it. Quebeckers also have somewhat lower life expectancy, adding further to the downward pressure on the population.

Quebec started as one of two founding nations of Canada, with 43% of the total population. Now it finds itself as one among ten provinces with a shrinking share of the total population. Justifiably, it fears that this trend will lead to a loss of power and political influence within Canada. It is not surprising that a cultural minority in such a situation would reach out to the majority for some assurances or guarantees. Nor is it surprising that some members of that minority would push for sovereignty in the belief that it would enhance their power and protect their culture.

This demographic crisis helps explain the Quebec position over the past 20 years of constitutional negotiations and two referendums on sovereignty. The dip in the population below 25% was disturbing to the collective psyche of Quebeckers; that is why Quebec fought during the Charlottetown negotiations for a guarantee of 25% of the seats in the federal Parliament. Quebec's demographic crisis provides much of the impetus for the sovereignty movement, but it may also be a reason why the sovereignty movement has lost two referendums. The supporters of sovereignty are drawn almost exclusively from old-stock French Canadians and, because of their low fertility, there haven't been enough of them to win a majority for their cause. Should continuing political and economic uncertainty cause an exodus of non-francophone Quebeckers, that could be enough to tip the balance in favour of secession in a future referendum, assuming that the separatists can maintain the loyalty of a large majority of francophones.

The Charlottetown constitutional process, in addition to being about the francophone-anglophone divide, was also about the relations between the native and non-native populations. While Canada as a whole has a below-replacement fertility rate, native Canadians are in the midst of a baby boom. As a result, 36% of the aboriginal population is under 15 years of age, compared with only 21% in the total population. Native Canada is much younger than anglophone or francophone Canada. Quebec's demographics stand in stark contrast to native Canada's: in 1995, it surpassed British Columbia as Canada's oldest province, with only 19% of Quebeckers under 15.

The major need of any nation with a youthful population is education and jobs for its young people. If these are not available, the inevitable results include migration (in the case of native Canadians, away from their own communities to Toronto, Winnipeg, Saskatoon, and other cities), rebellion, suicide, crime, and family breakdown, among other social pathologies. This is the context in which aboriginal leaders, understandably, are seeking greater control over land and resources in order to rebuild their communities.

The demographic divide among Canada's three distinct societies helps explain why it has been so difficult to reach agreement on a new constitutional framework for Canada. We Canadians tend to be overly self-critical in castigating ourselves for our seemingly endless constitutional bickering. But in fact, compared with many other countries facing similar situations, we have generally managed our differences peacefully, even in the absence of a fundamental agreement.

Other demographically divided societies have not fared so well. In the Pacific nation of Fiji, the fertility rate of the East Indian community is higher than that of the native Polynesians. This demographic disparity resulted in an electoral victory by a party representing the Indians, followed by a military coup by the Polynesian-dominated military. In the Middle East, the fertility rate of the Arabs in the occupied territories is much higher than that of Israel. Clearly, demographic differences are not the only reason for the revolt against Israeli military rule. But 15-year-olds are more likely to throw rocks than 50-year-olds. And when a whole generation of young people has nothing to do, resentment against an unacceptable political situation turns readily into violence.

This does not necessarily mean that Canada can't solve its problems without an escalation of the sort of violence that has erupted in some native communities in the mid-1990s. But our chances of living in harmony will be enhanced if we have a better grasp of the demographics and hence the needs of Canada's three distinct societies. Once the opposing sides in constitutional negotiations understand these crucial demographic realities, they will understand one another's positions better. And that enhanced understanding will improve our chances of coming to agreement.

DEMOGRAPHICS, TECHNOLOGY, AND EMPLOYMENT

A fundamental link has always existed between demographics, technology, and employment. In a society with a lot of young workers, labour is in abundant supply and is thus cheap. Moreover, young people are still borrowing — for an education, a car, and a house. A young person who has just struck out on his own has to spend all of his income getting established in life. If he has a job, it's an entry-level job at a relatively low salary. He has no money left over for investments. In a predominantly young country, because only a small section of the population has any savings, capital is priced high because it is in short supply. Consequently, real interest rates, which are the return on capital, are high. That is why young countries have abundant labour and scarce financial capital.

That was the situation in Canada during the two decades, from the mid-1960s to the mid-1980s, when the huge baby-boom generation was moving onto the labour market and becoming borrowers. In those economic conditions, a new technological advance has to be either extremely good or absolutely necessary for competitive reasons before a company will adopt it. In a labour-rich, capital-scarce country, there is no great incentive to borrow money in order to acquire new technology. Borrowing is further inhibited by the high interest rates that are the norm in a capital-scarce country. As a result, from 1965 to 1985 Canada trailed such older countries as Japan and Germany in adopting new technologies. It wasn't because we were Luddites, but because we were younger and had more labour and less financial capital than those countries did. What we needed to do during those years was not to instal robots in our factories but to find jobs for our young people. And that is precisely what Canada did.

This was a good strategy if what we wanted was to preserve social harmony. But it was not a strategy that would increase productivity. When the workforce receives a huge influx of young people, lacking both experience and the latest machinery, labour productivity falls. On the other hand, these young workers gain valuable experience, which contributes to future productivity. And social harmony is enhanced when they are able to get established in the workforce.

In an aging society, the growth of the workforce slows down. Meanwhile, because more people are older, they have more money to invest, and the supply of capital increases. Because of demographic change, wages ultimately rise while interest rates come down. Capital therefore becomes cheaper, and there is more incentive to use it to invest in new technology as an alternative to increasingly expensive labour. This demographic phenomenon was at the root of Japan's phenomenal transformation into an economic superpower. Japan, which had a birth dearth following its defeat in World War II just when North America was starting its baby boom, had no alternative but to be an early postwar adopter of technology. When you put lots of new machines in place and you have a slow-growing workforce to use them, productivity soars. In the automobile and consumer electronics industries it specialized in, Japan became the most efficient producer in the world over the 1960s and 1970s. As a result, it could produce cars more cheaply than the Big Three in North America. The early Japanese cars weren't always the best or most reliable, but they were the right price and the right size for a young North American population. Japan's achievement eventually forced American automakers to automate in order to compete. Strange as it seems, Detroit got robots in the 1980s because Japanese women didn't have babies in the late 1940s.

In Canada, we should have seen a similar pattern towards the end of the 1980s, when the last of the boomers became adults and the new entrants to the labour market were coming from the smaller baby-bust generation. And in fact, Canada did experience a decline in youth unemployment during the 1980s because we had fewer young people to be unemployed. At the same time wages for entry-level positions increased. But a severe recession in the first part of the 1990s drastically reduced the availability of jobs for everyone, especially the young and inexperienced. Moreover, the presence of the entire baby boom in the labour force at the same time meant that labour continued in

abundant supply, depressing wages. To make matters worse, the federal government sharply increased immigration levels to 250,000 per
year, by far the highest per-capita levels in the world, further increasing the supply of labour and adding to the downward pressure on
wages. Other forces keeping a lid on wages included the globalization
of the economy, which meant Canadian workers were now competing with workers in low-wage countries. Free trade prompted some
Canadian companies to relocate their manufacturing operations to low-
wage areas outside of Canada. Global competition also led Canadian
companies to trim their workforces as part of a desperate search for
higher productivity.

Nevertheless, there remained in Canada in the mid-1990s an
underlying demographic trend towards higher wages for entry-level
workers. Without this trend, wages for young people would be even
lower than they are. But by the end of the decade, this trend will have
run its course, because the arrival of the front end of the baby-boom
echo will unleash a new wave of young workers into the job market,
once again putting downward pressure on wages and upward pressure
on the unemployment rate.

The North American Free Trade Agreement is an experiment
in creating a trading bloc of countries with different demographic
profiles. Mexico is much younger than Canada or the United States.
For Mexico to embrace technology in the mid-1990s would be misguided, just as it would have been wrong for Canada to do so in the
1970s. The Mexicans' need is not to save labour but to create jobs for
their many young new entrants to the job market. But as Mexico's trading partner we have to accept that, because the supply of Mexican
labour is so large, the wages Mexican workers can command will be
lower than would be acceptable in Canada. This is not a malevolent
policy imposed by advocates of free trade but rather an inevitable
result of the different demographic profiles of the partner countries.

DEMOGRAPHICS AND MIGRATION

To uproot oneself and attempt to build a new life in a new location is a
difficult and challenging undertaking. If you are going to migrate, the

best time to do it is in your 20s. At that stage in your life, you have finished your education but haven't yet launched your career. You are old enough to cope with the arduous process of moving to a new country but still adaptable enough to integrate into a new culture and, perhaps, to master a new language. You have the latest skills but only entry-level salary expectations. And you have a long lifetime ahead of you to reap the benefits of the move.

These facts explain why countries with a high percentage of people in their 20s are the major sources of migrants. Even if such a country is doing well economically, it may not be able to provide enough jobs for all of its young people. Some of those who can't get good jobs will leave in search of economic opportunities elsewhere. One of the places at the top of their list will be Canada, which, with the United States and Australia, has been one of the three major immigrant-receiving countries since the end of World War II. These three, along with Israel and New Zealand, are the only countries that officially want immigrants. They are the only countries that operate immigration programs through which they set numerical targets and apply selection criteria.

A demographic perspective reveals that the changing character of immigration to Canada is determined more by the demographics of the source countries than by immigration policies made in Canada. Until our immigration regulations were revised in 1962, non-whites were systematically excluded from coming to Canada as immigrants. Not surprisingly, therefore, during the 1950s the countries of northern Europe — Britain, Germany, Scandinavia — were our major source of immigrants. But that would have been the case for demographic reasons even in the absence of a "white Canada" policy. Northern Europe, today the region with the oldest population in the world, in those years had plenty of people in their 20s who believed they could improve their economic circumstances by departing a Europe devastated by war for Canada, the United States, or Australia.

The second-oldest region of the world is southern Europe: Greece, Spain, Italy, and Portugal. But in the 1960s and 1970s, those countries had plenty of people in their 20s. That's why so many of

Canada's immigrants during those decades came from the countries of southern Europe.

The next-oldest region of the world is southeast Asia, which began sending people to other parts of the world, including Canada, in the 1970s and 1980s, decades when it had a surplus of people in their 20s. Asia remained our major source of newcomers throughout the 1980s and into the 1990s. But much of Asia got its fertility rates under control during the 1960s, which is why the stream of newcomers from that region will slow down by the turn of the century.

Latin America took longer to reduce its fertility rates. That is why it is the next region of the world with a surplus of people in their prime migrating years. Increasingly, over the late 1990s and during the first decade of the next century, more of Canada's immigrants will probably come from Latin America.

What of the more distant future? A phenomenal 46% of the population of Africa is under 15 — almost half the population. These people will reach their prime mobility years shortly after the turn of the century. At that time, all the Western industrialized countries, including Canada, will experience huge migration pressures from Africa.

What should Canada's policy be in the face of immigration pressures from Latin America, Africa, or anywhere else? To maintain a sensible immigration program that balances our own needs with humanitarian goals. There was no demographic basis for the high immigration levels of the early 1990s. As was pointed out earlier, Canada's population would have been increasing even without any immigration, because Canada has one of the highest birth rates among industrialized countries. It was this high birth rate that created the echo generation. The birth rate will decline as the baby boom ages past its childbearing years. But this does not mean, as advocates of high immigration levels sometimes claim, that Canada is in imminent danger of depopulation.

No one can predict what will happen to fertility in the future. The fertility rate fluctuates, and even a small increase can have noticeable impacts on future population size. If fertility were to rise to 1.9, for example, the number of immigrants needed to maintain the existing level of population would be half that required when fertility was 1.7.

A federal investigation of Canada's demographic future, the Demographic Review, proved that no demographic case exists for high immigration levels. In its report, issued in 1989, it made a projection of what would happen to Canada's population if we had no population growth from immigration. Assuming a fertility rate of 1.7 and net migration (immigration minus emigration) of 0, Canada's population would stop growing in 2011 and then begin a long, lingering decline that would continue until the last Canadian, unable to find a mate anywhere from Victoria to St. John's, died of loneliness in 2786. This sequence of events, of course, is purely theoretical. No modern society has ever vanished because of the failure of its people to reproduce, although it has been suggested that such civilizations as the Roman and Aztec empires declined in power as their fertility declined.

The point is that even if below-replacement fertility continues in Canada, we need only a relatively small amount of immigration to maintain a substantial population. This simple point requires emphasis because misinformation is widespread. For example, a 1995 article in the *Toronto Star* stated: "As in the rest of Canada, Quebec's low repro- duction rate requires massive infusions of immigration if the population is not to decline." Exaggerated claims like this create confusion in the public mind over the important policy issue of immigration levels. The fact is that even with net immigration of only 80,000 a year (half the level in the mid-1990s), our population, according to the Demographic Review, would continue growing until 2026 and then decline almost imperceptibly until it stabilized at 18 million eight centuries in the future. In other words, with immigration at levels well below "mas- sive," Canada's population would not decline at all until after 2026, and the decline during the rest of the 21st century would be minimal. As for the prospect of Canada arriving at a stable population in the distant future, that is not cause for alarm. Many European countries already have stable populations, and Europe remains prosperous. An absence of population growth results in increased productivity, less unemploy- ment, and reduced pressure on both urban and rural environments.

Immigration policy should not be based on an imaginary demographic crisis. Many people would like to move to Canada to work or to join their families or because they are fleeing persecution. But we should manage the policy so that both immigrants and hosts benefit from it. That requires taking demographics into account when we set both immigration levels and selection criteria. Today our immigration program, more through accident than by design, is finally in line with demographic realities, because immigrants in their 20s are coming at a time when the number of Canadians in that age group has declined. But as the echo generation enters the labour market in the first decade of the next century, Canada will need to consider curtailing immigration. It does not make sense to bring in a flood of 20-year-old immigrants to compete for scarce jobs just when large numbers of Canadian-born 20-year-olds are also entering the labour market. Doing so would be unfair both to immigrants and to resident Canadians.

Just as they influence immigration, demographics also influence emigration. People tend to return to their roots when they retire. Many Atlantic Canadians who moved to central and western Canada in search of jobs will return home when they retire. And so will many Germans, Italians, and other immigrants who came to Canada during the 1950s and 1960s. Emigration from Canada to western Europe will probably exceed immigration for the foreseeable future. We don't know how many people moved from Canada to Italy in 1994, but it's a near certainty it was more than the 600 Italians who came to Canada as immigrants in the same year. Economics has little to do with the flow of people between two countries such as Italy and Canada that have similar per-capita incomes. Demographics are the decisive factor: Italy has few people of migrating age, while Canada has many Italian-born people of retirement age ready to return home.

DEMOGRAPHICS AND TRADE

Since young people eat a lot, a country with many young people will have a high demand for food. People in their 20s and 30s are setting up new households, and they need furniture and appliances and cars. That's why a country with many people in their 20s and 30s experiences intensified demand for manufactured goods. People in their 40s and 50s don't eat as much as people in their teens and 20s, and they have already bought most of the major manufactured goods they need. They need travel, financial, and health care services. Countries with a high percentage of middle-aged people have reduced demand for agricultural and manufactured products and increased demand for services.

Canada has already lived through these transformations. First we increased our agricultural productivity. Then we developed a strong manufacturing sector. Finally, over the late 1980s and 1990s, our service sector experienced rapid growth. That is why we have seen a proliferation of small companies in Canada. A small company can't produce automobiles, but it can provide financial planning or travel services.

In international trade, older countries have an advantage. They know the marketplaces of younger countries because they have already experienced the same demographics in their own domestic market. Ikea had had plenty of experience supplying household furnishings to young Swedes assembling their first homes before it arrived in North America to exploit a huge new market of young baby-boomers.

Canada is now in a position to benefit from growing demand for manufactured goods in southeast Asia and especially Latin America, parts of the world that are younger than we are. That doesn't mean our companies can't continue to sell manufactured goods in North America, or that a Canadian company such as Magna can't continue to do well in the auto parts business in Europe. But the big growth in demand is more likely to come outside of our traditional European and North American markets. Our exporters need to be aware of the demographic basis for this opportunity and become more aggressive in exploiting these new markets.

Demographics also influence money movements. A young country needs to borrow and an older one needs to lend. That's why the lending countries are older ones such as Germany, the United Kingdom, and Japan. People in their 40s and 50s are savers and investors, and those age groups are where the largest chunk of Japan's population has been over the past two decades. But as they reach retirement age, people start to cash in their chips because they need the money to live on. That means Japan will increasingly be forced to draw on its assets to support the retirement and health care needs of a much older population, and the result will be capital flowing back to Japan. After the millennium, when demographics have gradually turned Canada and the United States into nations of savers rather than spenders, Canada and the United States will begin to take Japan's and Germany's places as lenders to the world.

THE GREY INTERLUDE

To judge by some of the articles about the greying of society you'd think Canada is on the verge of becoming a nation of doddering old folks. It's not true and it never will be.

The first baby-boomers won't turn 65 until 2012. By then, the era of grey power will truly have begun: from 2012 to 2031, all the baby-boomers who are still alive will be seniors. But it's not true that Canada in the mid-1990s is the most rapidly aging society in the world. Japan has a much more rapidly aging population than Canada, because its fertility rate dropped in the 1940s and ours did not begin to fall until the 1960s. The Europeans are also older than we are and will be for the foreseeable future. Canada starts the aging process from a much younger base than Japan and Europe. In the mid-1990s, Canada has only 12% of its population over 65 whereas Sweden, one of the world's oldest countries, has 18%. In 2020, Canada will be where Sweden is today. Even when all the baby-boomers are over 65, Canada's elderly as a percentage of its population will match, not exceed, the rest of the developed world.

People are going to keep having babies because they want babies. If they didn't, Canadian women unable to achieve pregnancy would not be combing the world for children to adopt and paying large amounts of money to fertility clinics. Meanwhile, when the last boomer turns 65, many early boomers will be dead. This isn't cause for celebration, but it is the major reason why Canada is never going to turn into a country of the aged. The baby bust, a smaller group, will replace the baby boom as Canada's young seniors when the larger baby-boom echo will just be leaving its productive middle years. And the echo, because it is a larger group than the bust, will produce a bumper crop of kids. And so it goes — Canadian society will continue to rejuvenate itself as the decades unroll.

Canada can cope, and even prosper, during the grey interlude of boomer retirement if we plan for it and make the necessary changes. How do older countries cope with an older population profile? They let younger countries do the low-wage, labour-intensive jobs while they develop a highly skilled, technology-based workforce at home. The best technology enables them to add value to the products they produce. In short, they compensate for the increase in the retired population by doing everything possible to enhance the productivity of the working population.

They also make changes to their taxation and pension policies. Because there will be relatively fewer taxpayers, government will have to move gradually from taxation of labour income to taxation of capital income. In the mid-1990s, large numbers of baby-boomers are in their prime earning and spending years. In such a society, a tax system based on income and sales taxes makes sense. It won't make as much sense in a future in which more income, of necessity, will be generated by technology and capital. A country with an aging population has to consider increased taxes on interest, dividends, capital gains, and corporate profits. It also has to consider taxes on things that currently are not taxed, including foreign exchange transactions and, in Canada's case, wealth. There is plenty of room for reform without imposing any undue hardship on the wealthiest Canadians. A study by American economist Edward Wolff in 1995 found that personal wealth is taxed at a much lower rate in Canada than in such staunchly capitalist societies as Switzerland and the United States. Among 22 countries, Canada ranked 21st in percentage of tax revenues derived from wealth taxes.

As for pension policy, it should be remembered that when Canada incorporated a retirement age of 65 into most of its legislation in the 1920s, life expectancy was about 61. Not many people were expected to collect pensions. In the mid-1990s, life expectancy is 78, so that the average Canadian can expect to collect a pension for 13 years. Life expectancy will probably rise in the years to come as medical advances lead to increased longevity. The result will be greater pressure on both public and private pension programs. That's why governments are looking closely at these programs. Reforms might include raising the age of eligibility, reducing payouts, cutting off high-income recipients, installing a mandatory, self-financing public retirement plan that would require increased contributions, and increasing taxes on corporate profits to take some of the burden of supporting the pension plan away from payroll taxes. But discussion of the future solvency of public pensions should not ignore the important role of continued economic growth and increased productivity. As Canadian industry benefits from increased availability of capital and technology, there is every reason to expect strong growth in productivity in the years to come. That, along with improved management of the pension plan, should be sufficient to ensure the incomes of our retired workers.

Other solutions involve the flexible workforce discussed in Chapter 4. Why shouldn't a senior be able to work half-time and take half a pension? The taxes the part-time worker would contribute to the public treasury would help pay for her own pension. All these options should be considered as part of a process of integrating workplace policy, tax policy, and pension policy. The sooner we act, the less painful the process of change will be.

What sort of country will the greyer Canada be? Demographics offer no reason for doom and gloom. For the next two to three decades, the baby-boomers will be workers, taxpayers, and increasingly savers. Because more Canadians will be savers, more money will be available for capital investment to make our industry more technologically advanced, more competitive, and more productive. Meanwhile, other countries will offer growing markets for the goods and services that these industries produce. And Canada will become less dependent on foreign lenders.

Fears are often expressed about how Canada will cope once

the large baby-boom generation reaches its retirement years. Before panic sets in, it should be remembered that even the oldest boomers won't reach 65 until 2012. It should also be remembered that the Canadian workforce by then will have been reinforced by the large echo generation. The combination of the echo and the baby bust is larger than the baby boom, so there is little reason to fear a shortage of working-age Canadians during the grey interlude of boomer retirement. Who knows, we might even get the Canadian unemployment rate below 10%, where it has been stuck for far too long. If we are truly successful in finding employment for all Canadians who are eager to work, the ultimate proof of that success would be labour shortages. Should those occur, jobs can be filled by young workers who wish to immigrate to Canada from countries that have a surplus of young workers. But there should be no illusions about the ability of immigration to make a grey Canada less grey: an immigration policy based on the family, as Canada's is, can never rejuvenate a society.

Some of the changes wrought by the demographic phenomenon of population aging pose difficulties to society while others are beneficial. For example, an older society requires fewer goods, which hurts those in the business of manufacturing and selling goods. But an aging society requires many more services, and that means new business opportunities for other entrepreneurs. An aging population is more knowledgeable and experienced, but it is also more prone to health problems. In the final analysis, what is the balance between these pros and cons? Is the demographic shift good or bad? The answer is that it is neither. It is simply a fact of life, and the better we understand it, the better we can prepare for the changes before they occur and adjust to them once they have taken place.

One important benefit of having an aging population is that older people traditionally have shown themselves to be more generous than younger ones. They give more, both of their money and of their time. Older people are also more knowledgable, because they've been around long enough to learn something. So while Canadians aren't about to become a nation of greybeards, they are about to become an older, wiser, and perhaps more caring people.

If we prepare for the grey interlude to come, we can both enjoy the benefits and manage the inevitable challenges. Demographics enable us to do that because they give us the power to see the future. All we have to do is use it.

Demographic Forecasting

This appendix describes the technical framework of demographic forecasting, the science that provides the foundation for the conclusions in this book. Although demographic forecasting is based on mathematical concepts, one does not need to be a mathematician to understand demographics. With a little effort, anyone can grasp the basics of demographics and appreciate its implications.

Applying demographic forecasts, as presented in Appendix II, is the next step. It is easy to develop a forecast for an individual product or activity using a calculator or a spreadsheet on a home computer.

AVAILABILITY AND USE
Demographic forecasts, or population projections as demographers prefer to call them, are available from many sources. Statistics Canada, the national data gathering agency, not only collects all the data that are needed to produce demographic forecasts but also produces such forecasts for the nation, provinces, and territories. These demographic data and forecasts are used for many purposes. Besides the numerous uses outlined in this book, they also play an important role in influencing the monetary transfers between governments in the Canadian federation. Private consulting firms use these Statistics Canada projections or, alternatively, develop and sell their own population forecasts based on their own variation of the Statistics Canada approach.

Many regional and municipal governments also produce demographic forecasts to assist them in land use and transportation planning. Population projections can reveal their future requirements for roads, schools, sewers, and parks. Not surprisingly, these forecasts can become political footballs, as each local authority attempts to attract federal or provincial funds to pay for infrastructure. You can usually get copies of forecasts for your own use from the relevant agencies, for a modest fee to cover the cost of reproduction. A good general rule to remember when using them is that they are much more likely to overstate population growth than to understate it. A small but expanding list of consulting companies and consultants also provide regional demographic data and forecasts. Once again, these must be used with a critical eye. But they tend to be more conservative on population growth unless they have been produced for developers trying to obtain zoning changes for commercial or residential construction.

An understanding of population growth and aging illuminates both the past and the future. Although the past can be measured with considerable accuracy, the future is inherently uncertain, so different agencies and consultants can come up with different forecasts. They cannot all be correct, but some will prove more accurate than others.

The ideas of the analyst who is producing the demographic forecast are called assumptions — for example, assumptions about future immigration policy. No one can be certain what political party will be in power in the next 20 years or even the next five, nor can anyone know what policy regarding immigration levels will be in effect in the future. To account for this inherent uncertainty about the future, demographers have adopted the alternative scenario approach. Since different assumptions about immigration will automatically lead to different population projections, demographic forecasts have to account for different scenarios. Different forecasts will have different numbers, but all are produced from a common understanding of the determinants of population growth.

This common foundation is called a population projection model. In practical terms, this model is a set of mathematical instructions programmed into a computer that calculates the numerical implications of the various ideas or assumptions provided by the analyst.

This is where informed judgment is crucial. Only a few assumptions are needed to produce a population forecast; anyone with access to a population projection model can produce one. What makes one population forecast better than another is the quality of judgment that has been brought to the task.

This is why demography is a social science. Demographic forecasts are scientific in the sense that the results are reproducible: the same assumptions always lead to the same results. However, their use involves judgment about human behaviour — fertility, mortality, and migration — which varies over time. That is why the future can never be predicted with certainty.

That is also why demographers prefer to call their forecasts "projections" — they project the consequences of informed judgments. Population forecasts are not predictions. The population projection model is not a crystal ball that sees the future. It enables the user to see a variety of futures depending on the assumptions that are put into the model. The projection that has, in the analyst's judgment, the most likelihood of coming to pass may be labelled the most likely or base-case scenario. This is often mislabelled the forecast by those who desire a prediction. It is this confusion that often gives demographers, economists, and anyone else who uses a model to peer into the future a dubious reputation.

Strategic planning needs alternative scenarios to be strategic, so alternative demographic forecasts can be an important component of strategic plans. Of crucial importance is whether the alternatives lead to different action plans. Fortunately, in many cases alternative population forecasts do not require dramatically different action plans. Generally they are not different enough. So for many purposes, it really does not make a big difference which population forecast is used. But it is crucial to use a population forecast in any strategic plan.

In the end, even an uninformed forecast may turn out to be an accurate prediction of reality, but this can never be known until the future has passed. Meanwhile, population forecasts can provide a powerful way to understand and anticipate the inherently uncertain future.

POPULATION PROJECTIONS

What are the essential ingredients of a population forecast or projection? Another way of asking the same question is, What makes a population change in size? Clearly, births increase a population while deaths decrease it. In-migrants increase a population and out-migrants decrease a population. Therefore, population change is defined as births minus deaths plus in-migrants minus out-migrants. This is the first foundation of all population forecasting.

What is true for the whole population is also true for any subgroup in the population, with one notable exception. Births can be added only at age zero, so in all other age groups births are not part of the formula. The number of 50-year-old males in Canada today is the number of 49-year-old males last year, minus the deaths of those in their 50th year, plus the number of any new immigrants, minus any emigrants who would have been 50 by the end of the year. This calculation is based on the unassailable fact that every year a surviving individual gets one year older. This is the second foundation of all population forecasting.

Note that the same calculation underlies all population projections whether for a nation, a province, a region, or a town. The only difference between these applications is the definition of a migrant. For a national projection, migrants include both immigrants and emigrants. For a provincial projection, they include those who arrive in the province from another country or another province and those who leave the province. For a region, those moving between regions within a province are also included as migrants. For a town, all people moving in and out of the town are considered migrants. This makes population forecasts for smaller areas somewhat less accurate because, with more elements to consider, there is more uncertainty. But the basic foundations remain the same.

The same principles that determined the past can be used to forecast the future. So the population next year is the population this year plus the expected number of births, minus the expected number of deaths, plus the expected number of in-migrants, less the expected number of out-migrants over the next year. The key to making this calculation successfully is finding the expected numbers to put in the forecast.

Where do the expectations for births, deaths, and migrants come from? Births depend on fertility in a population, which reflects a myriad of factors that determine human behaviour and procreation. Obviously health status is important for both the mother and the child if both are to survive childbirth. Beyond that, the decision to have or not to have children depends on the availability, use, and effectiveness of various birth-control techniques and the economic status of the family into which a child would be born. Finally, the likelihood of giving birth depends on the age of the mother. Younger and older women are less likely to give birth than those in their high fertility ages of the 20s and early 30s.

Since a society is a collection of individuals, collective fertility is determined by the same considerations as individual fertility, including the age distribution of women in the population. Societies with proportionately more women in the prime childbearing ages will produce comparatively more births.

To take this into consideration, demographers focus on a society's fertility rate (children per woman) rather than the birth rate (births per thousand people). The fertility rate measures the average number of children a woman will have over her lifetime if she follows the current fertility behaviour of all women. The number differs by where she lives, and it changes over time. It is a useful number that is indicative of the average family size. Since two children are necessary to replace the two parents, replacement fertility is a number around two.

The fertility rate in Canada was more than 3 in the 1920s and under 3 in the 1930s before it began to rise in the 1940s. At the peak of the postwar baby boom in 1959, fertility peaked at almost 4 children per woman. By the late 1960s, it had fallen to well below replacement. In the mid-1990s, it is around 1.7 children per woman.

What of the future? Will fertility remain below replacement, will it decline even further, or will it rebound to replacement or even higher, as it did after World War II? No one can be sure. But the demographic forecaster can explore all possibilities using alternative fertility rates of, for example, 1.5, 1.7, 2.1, and 2.5 to generate four alternative scenarios. The forecaster might label the 1.7 fertility scenario the most likely or base-case scenario given current information.

A similar approach is followed with respect to deaths. Once again, the number of deaths in a population reflects a host of factors, prime among which are the psychological, physical, and economic status of the individual in the population at large. Because older people are more likely to die than younger people, an older population is likely to have comparatively higher numbers of deaths and thus a higher death rate than a younger population. To take this into account, demographers focus on the average life expectancy (years per person) rather than the death rate (deaths per thousand people) as an indicator of longevity. It measures the average length of life for an individual of any age if that individual could live out the remainder of his or her life under current mortality conditions. Average life expectancy varies over jurisdictions and over time because mortality conditions are different. The most frequently used number is life expectancy at birth, which also means the average age of death. In most societies, women live longer than men, with the result that the average is higher for females than for males. Life expectancy at birth in Canada has been rising since the 1930s, when it was about 60 for men and 62 for women. By 1993, it had reached 75 for men and 81 for women.

Will this trend continue? Many believe it will, especially given continuing progress by medical science in combatting disease. But it is not certain, as the recent decline in life expectancy in the former Soviet bloc and the emergence of a new disease (HIV/AIDS) have indicated. Once again, the demographic forecaster can explore alternative assumptions. The most likely or base-case scenario would probably be a continuation of past trends. An optimistic scenario, perhaps based on a major breakthrough in medical research, would show acceleration of past trends, while a pessimistic alternative, perhaps based on recent experience with the impacts of rising crime and poverty in the former Soviet bloc, might forecast a reversal of past trends.

For a nation, the relevant migrants for demographic forecasting are people coming from other countries (immigrants) and people going to other countries (emigrants). Canada's annual immigration over the 20th century has been volatile, ranging from a high of 400,870 in 1913 to a low of 7,576 in 1942. More than 100,000 people came to Canada in every year between 1903 and 1914, while fewer than 30,000 people came to Canada in every year between 1931 and 1945. In the postwar period, the largest number of immigrants was 282,164 in 1957; the smallest was 71,689 in 1961. These numbers probably provide reasonable bounds for any realistic immigration assumption. The average for the postwar period is about 150,000 persons a year. Levels in the early 1990s exceeded 200,000 persons a year.

Federal legislation requires that Canada's future immigration levels be announced in October of the preceding year. These levels must be determined in consultation with the provincial governments, taking economic and demographic considerations into account. The interpretation of these "considerations" is variable even within the mandate of one government, and can be even more so if governments change. As a result, it is almost impossible to predict what the chosen level of immigration will be from one year to the next, let alone from one decade to the next.

Once again, the demographer can explore the implications of different immigration levels for population forecasts. Perhaps the postwar average (150,000 persons a year), current levels (200,000), and even the occasionally mentioned figure of 1% of the population (300,000 a year) might be considered. The middle of these three would probably be designated the most likely or base-case scenario.

The final component for a national population forecast is expected emigration. Births, deaths, and immigration can be measured through administrative registration requirements, but no direct measure of emigration exists because exit permits are not required for people leaving Canada. Estimates of emigration can be compiled from statistics that count Canadians entering other countries such as the United States, and these can be checked every five years using census counts. But it is an imprecise measure.

Most recent estimates place emigration at about 50,000 people a year. In its population projections, Statistics Canada uses an assumption that generates a forecast of rising emigration over time, starting at around 47,000 people a year. Some evidence exists that emigration is related to previous levels of immigration and, perhaps, to the state of the economy, but it is doubtful that a more precise assumption is available, given the current state of the research. Once again the demographic forecaster can choose alternative emigration levels or rates to develop alternative population scenarios.

For provincial and regional demographic forecasts, further migration assumptions are necessary to account for migration between provinces (interprovincial migration) and migration within provinces (intraprovincial migration). This is a data-intensive task. Because Canada has ten provinces and two territories, there are 132 bilateral flows to consider in the Statistics Canada provincial and territorial population projections alone. For intraprovincial migration, the data requirements can be much larger still, since there are many levels of local agglomeration (regions, counties, municipalities, cities, townships) and many jurisdictions that people can move between. In these cases, it is common to consider each unit in isolation and just look at the in-migrant and out-migrant flows combined, without considering the different sources and destinations. Although this approach requires far less data and analysis, it comes with a cost. Unlike international migrants, whose arrival changes a nation's population size, people moving within a country leave the total size unchanged and influence only the distribution of the population.

In this internal movement of people there must always be both winners and losers among the various regions. When all regions are not explicitly considered together in a population forecast, it is easy to lose sight of this basic consistency requirement. Localities wishing to show future population growth may overestimate in-migration and underestimate out-migration. Without the winners-and-losers requirement explicitly built into the population forecasts, there is no way to determine whether all the individual locality assumptions when taken as a whole are consistent. Migration assumptions that deviate substantially from past averages should, therefore, be treated with caution.

RESULTS

Statistics Canada periodically publishes *Population Projections for Canada, Provinces and Territories* (as catalogue 91-520 occasional). The December 1994 issue of this publication, which covers the period 1993 to 2016, notes that the population projections are based on a combination of component assumptions, encompassing:

- three fertility assumptions: the total fertility rate remaining constant at 1.7 children a woman or gradually changing to 1.5 or 1.9 children a woman by 2016;
- three mortality assumptions: the 1991 life expectancy at birth of 74.6 years for males and 80.9 for females, reaching 77.0 and 83.0, 78.5 and 84.0, or 81.0 and 86.0 years respectively by 2016;
- three immigration assumptions: the annual number of immigrants in 1993 of 250,000 persons remaining constant or changing to 150,000 or 330,000 by 2016;
- one emigration assumption: the 1988-93 annual average age- and sex-specific rates remaining constant over the projection period (which results in emigration levels of from 46,800 to a maximum of about 59,000 persons by 2016);
- three interprovincial migration assumptions: central, which is most favourable for Ontario, Quebec, Manitoba, and Saskatchewan; west, which is most favourable for British Columbia, Alberta, Yukon, Northwest Territories, and the Atlantic provinces; or medium, which is an average of the central and west scenarios.

Additional assumptions for non-permanent residents and for returning Canadians are also used. This set of assumptions yields a total of 27 possible national projections, with a combination of three fertility, three mortality, and three immigration assumptions, and 81 possible provincial-territorial projections with the three additional interprovincial migration assumptions. In order to keep the analysis and report within manageable limits, only four were selected for inclusion in the publication to provide plausible maximum, medium, and minimum population growth levels for each province or territory and for Canada as a whole. All projections commence in 1993.

The low-growth alternative combines the low fertility, low life expectancy, and low immigration assumptions with the central inter-provincial migration assumption. Population growth averages 0.8% a year over the projection horizon, resulting in a total Canadian population of 31.4 million in 2001 and 34.2 million in 2016.

The medium-growth alternative combines the medium fertility, medium life expectancy, and medium immigration assumptions with the medium interprovincial assumption. Population growth averages 1.1% a year over the projection horizon, resulting in a total Canadian population of 31.9 million in 2001 and 37.1 million in 2016.

The high-growth alternative combines the high fertility, high life expectancy, and high immigration assumptions. Population growth averages 1.4% a year over the projection horizon, resulting in a total Canadian population of 32.4 million in 2001 and 39.9 million in 2016. In addition, the high-growth alternative is available under both the west and central interprovincial migration assumptions.

In all population projections, the baby boom shows up as aged 35 to 54 years in 2001 and aged 50 to 69 years in 2016. By 2001, its relative size will have shrunk somewhat, to about 31.4% of the Canadian population. By 2016, the baby boom's share of the population will be declining faster, depending on the growth of the population, from 27.6% in the low-growth alternative to 26.3% and 25.3% in the medium-growth and high-growth alternatives, respectively. Births stopped augmenting the boom in 1966, and by the turn of the century immigrants will be in the younger age groups. Moreover, the boomers' influence on Canadian society will diminish in the future as increasing numbers of them die. Nonetheless, even in 2016 they will remain over a quarter of the population under the more likely scenarios.

Which of these scenarios should the informed user of demographic forecasts use? By implication, Statistics Canada suggests the medium-growth alternative. However, since the production of these population projections, immigration levels have been reduced from 250,000 a year to about 200,000 a year. Over a decade, this difference amounts to half a million people. This substantial difference is concentrated in certain age groups, so using projections based on the medium-growth alternative will probably overestimate growth. On the other hand, immigration levels in the mid-1990s are well above the postwar average and the low-growth assumption of 150,000 a year, so use of the low-growth alternative will probably underestimate future growth, especially in the 21st century. The strategic planner could use both; the pragmatic user might use an average of these two publicly available forecasts. The alternative is to purchase a custom forecast either from Statistics Canada or from any other provider in either the public or the private sector.

Product and Activity Forecasting

A ppendix I explained how demographic forecasts are created. This appendix shows you how to use one or more alternative demographic forecasts to assess the future of a particular product, service, or activity.

The procedures outlined here are equally applicable to both the private and public sectors. They can be applied to both goods and services, to both appliance sales and health care delivery. They can be applied to products sold in the marketplace, such as binoculars, and to activities for which no market exists, such as birdwatching. They can guide business plans and public policies. Every application can be viewed as an activity that involves a product. Playing tennis requires both a court and a racquet. Even walking requires walking shoes. This is why this appendix is titled "Product and Activity Forecasting."

Once again the procedures, while mathematical in nature, are not difficult to understand. Numerical examples are provided on which to base your calculations, as well as tips on the presentation of results. But before investigating these procedures it is useful to ask a few questions. These questions can help in getting the best use out of the forecasts.

DEVELOPING USEFUL FORECASTS

First, what is your catchment area? Are you primarily concerned with the town, the region, the province, the country, or even the world? It might be useful to carry out a series of forecasts based on an ever-expanding market area. If they all suggest a similar conclusion, then you can proceed with confidence. If the conclusions differ, as they might for Alberta and New Brunswick or for Canada and Japan, this would suggest the need to consider a different marketing strategy in each area or, perhaps, to abandon a particularly unattractive market for the products under consideration.

Second, what is your vision? What do you expect to learn from the forecasts? Chapter 5 outlined the base-case scenarios against which your product and activity forecasts can be compared. The North American marketplace is dominated by the baby-boomers and, to an increasing extent, by their children, the echo generation. The boomers are all in their 30s and 40s in the mid-1990s, while most of their children are preteens. These facts suggest that the most rapidly growing markets of the following decade are going to be for products and services used by, and activities participated in by, those in their 40s and 50s. At the same time the declining teenage and early-20s market of the previous decade should produce moderate growth over the next decade, at least in Halifax, Ontario, and western Canada, where the baby-boom echo is apparent.

Another growth market is seniors. The older seniors born before World War I and during the 1920s will provide a rapidly growing market for a limited range of appropriate goods, services, and activities. On the other hand, the younger seniors who will turn 65 during the late 1990s are a smaller group as a result of the birth dearth that occurred in the 1930s.

A third question is about alternative scenarios: How many should you use? More often than not, population forecasts will indicate qualitatively similar conclusions because of the dominance of one trend: the aging of the boomers. Obviously, population forecasts with faster growth will generate more rapid growth forecasts for products and activities than population forecasts with slower growth. Very often growth is essential to business success, and alternative forecasts can give the planner the information necessary to estimate the likelihood of success. Suppose it is discovered that the success of a particular venture depends on market growth that will occur only in the event of a fertility rate of 2.3 children per woman or an immigration intake of about 350,000 persons a year; the viability of such a venture will be drawn into question by alternative demographic forecasts. If a drop in fertility to 1.2 children per woman, the current rate in some European countries, would bankrupt a product line, that information may be an important advance warning of the need to diversify.

The next question concerns the level of detail required. How much information about age, gender, components of growth, and number of years is needed? An important tip is to make sure that the key population assumptions are clearly specified on every page of projection output. It is easy to mix alternatives up when the amount of detail skyrockets. For most purposes, five-year age groups will suffice. It is usually desirable to break these down by gender if there is reason to believe that men and women purchase or participate differently in the product or activity under consideration. In some applications, such as daycare and school enrolment projections, single years of age data will be necessary. As for projection horizon, it is a good idea to produce a forecast for at least 20 years into the future and perhaps for a subsequent 30 years in quinquennial (five-year) intervals. These data may not be necessary for most purposes, but they will allow you to explore and understand the longer-term trends at work. For example, with births falling and deaths rising in an aging population, constant levels of immigration inevitably imply a slower-growing Canadian marketplace. As a result, even a product that has consistently outperformed the market may experience slower growth in the years ahead.

What do you really want to find out from the forecasts? Do not hesitate to request a components-of-growth table with each population forecast, which summarizes births, deaths, in-migrants, and out-migrants in each year. This can often be a useful diagnostic tool that can refine your understanding of the numbers and can sometimes lead to refining the assumptions. It is a good idea to obtain birth, death, and migration rates and any other convenient indicators over the forecast horizon. Growth rates for age groupings can be particularly useful in product and activity forecasting. You may even wish to keep track of certain generations (see Chapter 1) and their shares in the population over the forecast. These are all relatively easy programming add-ons that can be done by the forecast provider or by the user once the forecast has been completed.

How will the data be presented? Remember that pictorial representations of data have a greater impact than tabular representations, especially in an aging population, where increasing numbers of users are suffering from deteriorating eyesight. Always make sure that printers are producing clear copy in large print. Colour also adds to a document's impact. All these requirements should be considered before embarking on a forecasting project and signing a contract.

Probably the most important question is "How can I make population forecasts work for me?" Customization is the essential ingredient of product and activity forecasting. But do not forget to give thought to the questions outlined above as you work through the following procedure.

CUSTOMER FORECASTING

Population forecasts are the first component of product and activity forecasts. The second component is who makes use of the product or activity in question. This could apply equally well to toothpaste, beer, automobiles, cocaine, insurance, symphonies, or hospital beds. Although this section focusses on product forecasting, the procedure would be the same if the focus were on a service such as dry cleaning or an activity such as theatre-going. Moreover, the procedure is not limited to privately produced products sold in the marketplace. It can also be applied to services supplied by the public sector.

Who are your customers, demographically? Some organizations, such as hospitals, have excellent records of their customers. Good marketing departments usually have a solid understanding of a company's customers, developed either from customer files and direct contacts or from market surveys. Beer companies have a pretty good idea of who consumes their products. Trade associations frequently assemble information on an industry's or sector's customer base and make it available to all members. The Canadian Direct Marketing Association has information on how its members can reach their clients for different products. And Statistics Canada often collects information on sectors of the economy and their customers. From these data it is possible to find out, for example, who reads books and magazines. Finally, you may have only a rough idea of your customer from fragmentary files, direct contacts, or anecdotal evidence. Even this can be used if no better data are available.

One useful and often overlooked source for demographic information on customers is Statistics Canada's Family Expenditure Survey. This survey has been conducted periodically since the early 1960s at approximately three-year intervals. It shows expenditures on more than 400 individual items in the consumer budget that can be classified by the age of the head of the household. This source can be especially useful to small and medium-sized firms that do not have marketing departments with research capabilities.

In short, there are many different potential sources for demographic information on the customers of your products or product lines. As many as possible should be consulted because — compared with the population forecast, which is based on census information — all product information is based on a much smaller sample. It is simply not possible to consult every possible consumer on the likelihood of their purchasing your product. So customer information must be estimated from sample surveys and other sources, and estimates need to be checked as often as possible.

Usually there are noticeable variations in the likelihood that a customer will purchase a product over his or her life cycle. Young people eat lots of food, whereas older people tend to eat less. Young people play sports, while older people tend to seek out less active pursuits. Young criminals are more likely to commit a break-and-enter, while older criminals are more likely to be involved in fraud. Expenditures on video rentals decline with age, while spending on prescribed medicine increases. Sometimes the age profile differs noticeably by gender. Women, for example, are less likely to hunt and fish than men but more likely to attend the opera or ballet.

The likelihood that an individual in any age category purchases a product (or participates in an activity) can be measured in one of two ways. Surveys can ask respondents whether they have purchased or intend to purchase a certain item. The proportion responding in the affirmative in each age group then provides a measure of the likelihood of purchase. Alternatively, the number of customers can be measured by selling tickets, memberships, or products, and the ratio of the total customers to the population in each age group gives a measure of the likelihood of purchase by any individual customer. Usually it is only possible to do this for the population at large. Other methods must be used to break it down by age group.

If you know the likelihood that any individual will purchase your product and you know the number of individuals in the population, you can count your customers by multiplying one by the other. The same calculation can be done in each age group as well. In this way, you can build up a demographic profile of your customers or customer base. Note that this separates the task into two parts: human behaviour, represented by the likelihoods or probabilities of purchase, and numbers of potential customers, represented by the population. This separation is the foundation of product and activity forecasting.

An example can illustrate the calculations. Figure 10 represents the customer base of an unidentified product in 1991. Many real-world data are presented in this way, but the use of an unidentified product enables us to focus on the calculations without speculating on the accuracy of the data. This is a product that is not used by children, so the data commence with 12-year-olds. These data may have been obtained from a customer database, an industry survey, or a representative sample compiled by a marketing department or market research firm commissioned to construct a profile of a company's or industry's customers. The customers are allocated into various age categories (column 1), which may or may not be equal in size and probably have no relationship to any of the generations outlined in Chapter 1. In this example, the various age groupings cover 6 to 15 years, and maybe 35 years for seniors; the baby boom aged 25 to 44 in 1991 is spread out over three age categories. The estimated or actual number of consumers in each age category is shown in column 2. This is followed by a percentage distribution over the age groups (column 3). This column may

FIGURE 10: SAMPLE CUSTOMER BASE

Age Group (1)	Customers ('000) (2)	**Distribution** (3)	Population ('000) (4)	**Distribution** (5)	Rate (%) (6)=(2)÷(4)
12-17	215	**5.1**	2283.6	**9.7**	9.4
18-29	780	**18.7**	5415.7	**23.1**	14.4
30-39	982	**23.5**	4942.6	**21.1**	19.9
40-54	1331	**31.9**	5152.7	**22.0**	25.8
55-64	486	**11.6**	2428.6	**10.4**	20.0
65+	385	**9.2**	3211.0	**13.7**	12.0
TOTAL	4179	**100.0**	28434.2	**100.0**	17.8

Population data from 1991 census. Source: Calculations by David K. Foot

be referred to as the market share column, and these numbers often form the basis for the marketing strategy.

There are two limitations to the numbers in columns 2 and 3. First, they inevitably reflect the size of the chosen age categories, which are usually arbitrary and chosen for convenience. It would be surprising if there were not more consumers in the 15-year 40-to-54 category than in the 6-year 12-to-17 category or the 10-year 30-to-39 category. The second limitation of these data is that they inevitably reflect the age structure of the population. They may indicate more about the age distribution of consumers in the marketplace than anything about the market penetration of the product, even though they represent the product's customers. Note that, by definition, market shares must add up to 100%, and no product has a 100% market share.

To understand product market penetration, it is necessary to combine the customer data with data on the overall marketplace — that is, with demographic data. If these customer data are nationwide, the relevant demographic data are Canadian population data from 1991. These can be broken into age groups and presented opposite the customer data (column 4) and also presented in share or distribution format (column 5). Note that the total population of 23.434 million is the population 12 years and older, and that the shares are relevant to this total. Thus, for example, the 65-plus group is 13.5% of this population, whereas it was 11.4% of the total Canadian population in 1991.

Seldom does the share distribution of the marketplace (column 5) match the share distribution of the customer base (column 3). This is good news for demographic forecasting of products, because it implies that product market penetration differs by age. If this is true, then the changing age distribution in the marketplace will have an impact on the fortunes of the product. The more the distributions differ, the more important demographic analysis is.

Reviewing these data yields some interesting puzzles. There were more actual customers in the 40-to-54 age category, yet there were more people or potential customers in the 18-to-29 category. The average number of customers in any age group is highest in the 30-to-39 category (at 98.2 in each year), even though there were more customers in the 40-to-54 category. The challenge is to make sense out of these numbers.

With 4.2 million customers in a target population of 23.4 million, the average market penetration of this product is 17.8%. The same calculation can be carried out for each of the age categories (column 6). These numbers reveal that above-average market penetration occurs in the middle ages (30 to 64) and below-market penetration occurs for the younger and older members of the population. Consequently, the higher number of customers in the middle ages reflects both the higher number of boomers in these ages and a higher likelihood that they will purchase the product.

It is the age-specific penetration rates (or, in other applications, participation rates) in column 6 that are particularly important for product forecasting with demographics. They provide the likelihoods that each member in any age category will be an actual customer. They capture the purchasing behaviour of the population. They may be broken down by gender or other demographic descriptors, but these are nòt considered in this example to keep the calculations as simple as possible.

These market penetration data are often a closely guarded corporate secret. Sometimes, for confidentiality or other reasons, the only data that are released to the public are the percentage distribution of customers (column 3) and the overall market penetration rate (17.8% in this example). However, this information is sufficient to calculate market penetration by age (column 6). Note that if the customer distribution (column 3) is divided by the relevant population distribution (column 5) for each age category and then multiplied by the overall market penetration rate (17.8%) the result is the market penetration by age (column 6). For example, if 23.1% of the population (aged 15 to 29) accounts for only 18.7% of the customers, then there must be below-average market penetration in this group.

Now look at the figure from right to left. Note that the penetration (or participation) rate (column 6) multiplied by the population (column 4) produces the number of customers (column 2). This calculation is the basis of demographic product forecasting. Different population numbers will produce a new column of customer numbers. This is where the results of demographic forecasting enter the calculation. Note that this calculation effectively holds customer behaviour in each of the age categories (column 6) constant. This is exactly what is needed if the impact of demographics on product performance is to be isolated. Moreover, it provides a solid first estimate of the customer base of the future. As has been noted elsewhere in this book, this calculation alone can explain at least two-thirds of the future.

Population forecasts enable this calculation to be done for every year into the future, which produces a projected stream of future customers. Alternative demographic forecasts will produce alternative customer streams. The faster growing the population, the faster growing will be the customer base, although because of the subtle influence of age structure there will not be a one-to-one connection. This simple multiplication can be done by hand or by using a calculator or a computer spreadsheet package. Anyone can become proficient in demographics-based product forecasting.

Applying these participation rates to Statistics Canada population projections for the years 2001 and 2011 results in customer forecasts that indicate a product that experiences market growth of 17% over the 1990s (1991-2001) followed by slower growth of 10% over the subsequent decade (2001-2011). These figures correspond to average annual growth of 1.6% and 0.9% a year, respectively.

How can these forecasts be evaluated? First, they can be compared with total population growth over the forecast period. The easiest way to do this is to calculate the overall market penetration rate in each year. If this is rising, then the product is performing better than the market; if it is falling, the product is not keeping up with market growth. In this example, market penetration rises to 18.3% in 2001 because the boomers are moving through their maximum penetration ages. It then remains unchanged in 2011 as the boomer children start entering the high penetration ages and compensate for the boomer departures into the lower-penetration older ages. However, the distribution of customers has changed dramatically. In 1991, 53% were 40 and over; by 2011, 64% will be 40 and over.

These forecasts can also be placed in a historical context. Of course they can be compared with recent history for the product. But probably a fairer comparison is to re-estimate the past under the same procedures. This is called backcasting. It helps answer the following question: If current age-specific penetration rates had applied in the past, what would have happened to customer growth and to the overall market penetration rate? Applying this procedure to the 1971 and 1981 population data reveals a product whose customer base just kept up with population growth in the market, resulting in overall market penetration rates of 17.2% and 17.3% respectively. This means that for this product line, it was more difficult to raise market share in the 1970s than it was in the 1980s or 1990s. The aging of the boomers will result in an increase of one percentage point in overall market penetration between 1981 and 2001. This may not seem like a large increase, but many companies fight over numbers like this and such an increase can make all the difference to the bottom line. Of course, it is predictable that the management of this product line will probably receive good bonuses for these good results — results that have almost nothing to do with their performance.

SALES FORECASTING

Often the number of customers does not tell the whole story of a product's performance. That a person is a customer is useful information but it tells little about the strength of his loyalty. A golf course, for example, is interested not only in the size of its membership but also in the number of times each member plays over the season.

This type of information can also be incorporated into product projections. Here the focus moves from market penetration rates to the average customer purchases (or use) over a year. This could refer to the average number of tubes of toothpaste or the number of rounds of golf. Now the numbers of customers in Figure 10 (column 2) are replaced by product sales by weight, volume, or some other physical measure in each age category. Then, as before, these total sales figures (column 2) are divided by population (column 4) to obtain sales per capita in each age category (column 6). Where company data do not permit total sales to be broken down by age of customer, there may be other sources that can be used to accomplish the task. Often industry averages can provide one means of disaggregating company sales by age category. Another potential source is Statistics Canada's Family Expenditure Survey, which shows average expenditures by Canadian families on over 400 consumer items including food, clothing, household, transportation and recreation, personal care, and health care product lines. These expenditures can be categorized by the age of the head of the household. Although this may not be a perfect indicator for sales by weight or volume for any particular product, it can provide a useful approximation on which to base a product forecast.

It is also easy to extend the procedure to accommodate revenue from sales. Revenues reflect not only the number of customers and their loyalty in terms of volume of sales, but also the price of the product. Moreover, it is revenues that directly affect profits. In this application, customers or sales are now replaced by revenues in each age category (column 2), and the same procedure is followed to obtain average per-capita revenues (that is, customer expenditures) in each age category for the product. Once again, if relevant company data are not available, other sources can be used to provide an estimated age distribution of revenues. The Family Expenditure Survey is a particularly attractive source because it refers directly to average family expenditures in dollars. Its major limitation is that it may not be available in the desired year, especially if the year is recent.

The procedure is the same in sales forecasting as in customer forecasting. The task is separated into two components: the population forecasts component described in Appendix I, and the human behaviour component represented by per-capita sales information described in this appendix. Multiplication of these two components in each age category then produces a sales forecast for each year over the forecast period. Alternative population forecasts will generate alternative sales forecasts, which can be especially useful for use in strategic plans. Growth rates can be calculated and product viability assessed. It is even possible to examine the numerical implications of product price changes and of age-targeted marketing strategies by modifying the per-capita sales figures and recalculating the results.

STABILITY

Human behaviour is remarkably stable over the life cycle, at least when it comes to market purchases and participation in many activities. We go to school, leave home, rent apartments, start families, buy homes, and make intensive use of hospitals at similar ages.

Of course, we do not all get our first pet at 28, our first house at 34, and our bifocals at 48. Nonetheless, enough people do experience these events around these ages that the likelihood of the average person experiencing them is both high and stable over time. In fact, the likelihood or probability of doing all kinds of things often varies quite predictably over the life cycle. It is this stability in human behaviour that makes demographic forecasting such a powerful tool.

Increasing longevity may mean that each generation is healthier at each age than its predecessor. But this may only mean that on average the tennis racquet gets put on the shelf four or five years later in life over a generation of perhaps 25 years. Even these changes occur very slowly and predictably. Of course no one wants to be average; we all want to be individuals. But each of us is average over a broad range of human behaviour. That we like to emphasize the things we do that are not average, such as going to the symphony at 17 or rock climbing at 70, verifies the proposition. Our non-average behaviours make us individuals. But for the majority of product purchases in the market-place or other activities, we act much like the average.

This stability is not universal. Pollsters have demonstrated that our attitudes on a variety of issues often change, and our voting preferences have certainly been volatile in recent years. That is why many topics that interest sociologists and political scientists cannot be satisfactorily explained using demographic forecasting. But these are not the subjects of this book.

The introduction of new products into the marketplace cannot be anticipated by demographic forecasts. But once they are established in the marketplace, demographic forecasting can be a useful predictor of future trends.

But even in these cases the procedures outlined in this appendix can be used to examine the implications of changing human behaviour or new products. If a company believes that it has a successful new marketing program or a new product that can change behaviour in the market, or in a segment of the market such as the youth segment, the product forecaster can modify the market penetration (or participation) rate to reflect the anticipated impacts and use the same procedure to trace out the implications for the future customer base or sales. Similarly, if a government believes that promotion of healthier lifestyles results in the population being more active, appropriate activity participation rates can be modified to reflect these anticipated changes and the implications traced out for the future. It is even possible to simulate the impacts of everyone in the population acting as if they were five or ten years younger by moving the entire participation profile back one age category. This is called sensitivity analysis. How sensitive are the numerical results to the introductions of new behaviours? The procedures outlined in this appendix provide a way to answer this question.

Such changes in practice usually occur slowly and so have little impact on product forecasts over the next five or ten years, which is where demographic forecasting has its greatest power. Moreover, the numerical implications of quite noticeable changes in behaviour are not nearly as dramatic as is often believed. In Canada, the aging of the baby-boom generation tends to dominate all product and activity forecasts based on the Canadian marketplace. It is this feature of the demographic profile that solidifies the stability of most product and activity forecasts in Canada.

Obviously, the further one looks into the future, the more uncertain the results. New behaviours and products have more time to get established, and there is more time for changes in the assumptions underlying the demographic forecasts. For this reason, long-term projections of more than, say, 20 years are not the focus of this book. But assuming that a 40-year-old today will behave like a 45-year-old of today in five years' time and like a 50-year-old of today in ten years' time is a solid foundation on which to build a vision of the medium-term future.

Demographic forecasts provide an excellent foundation for planning over the next three to 15 years. But they are not useful in explaining volatile movements in the stock market or the economy that are short-term in nature. And they are not crystal balls that permit us to gaze accurately over a lifetime of almost 80 years, although they may work better than many other crystal balls.

Index

The text of this book is set in Melior,
which was designed by Hermann Zapf in 1952.
The headlines, subheads, running heads, and folios are set in Gill Sans,
designed by Eric Gill and issued by Monotype in 1927.

Book design by James Ireland and Sara Tyson

Figures by Rose Zgodzinski

① Demographics – Boom
                 Bust
                 Echo

② Immigration — 20's — <u>late</u> early to 30's

early affecting late – boomers making way for bust
  "   "   "   bust   "   "   " echo

Japan example of an economy later applied in Canada

Praise for Catherine Mann's Elite Force series

Under Fire

"Absolutely wonderful, a thrilling ride of ups and downs that will have readers hanging onto the edge of their seats."

—*RT Book Reviews* Top Pick of the Month, 4.5 Stars

"Wild rides, pulse-pounding danger, gripping suspense, and simmering, sizzling, spiraling passion… Mann once again gives the reader a spellbinding story with special super heroes."

—*Long and Short Reviews*

"Catherine Mann does it again, delivering a fast-paced, edge-of-your-seat tale."

—*BookLoons.com*

"I was glued to the page—read the whole thing from start to finish in one sitting. It's just that good."

—*The Book Binge*

"Packed with fast-paced action and passion that will burn you up! Thumbs up."

—*Seriously Reviewed*

"A solid romance thriller… Hunky, honorable heroes…"

—*Bookaholics Romance Book Club*

"If you enjoy a steamy, action-packed romance, pick up the Elite Force series."

—That's What I'm Talking About

"Witty, sexy, and can kick your ass with just a look."

—Books-n-Kisses

"A solid read with great characters who have awesome chemistry… Taut with suspense."

—One Good Book Deserves Another

"I am loving this Elite Force series… Military mysteries with sexy heroes and intelligent and equally sexy heroines, these stories keep you turning the pages, keep you guessing, and keep your emotional upheaval on uneven ground until the very last page. Get ready for a wild ride!"

—The Good, the Bad and the Unread

"Catherine hooked me in right at the very beginning and over the course of each chapter, she slowly reeled me in until I was fully hooked and sad to see that the story was over."

—Love Romance Passion

"I was glued to the page—read the whole thing from start to finish in one sitting… A delightful and sensuous book."

—The Book Binge

"Mann continues to be one of the strongest romantic suspense writers I read and enjoy."

—Smexy Books

Hot Zone

"Fast paced and filled with intriguing characters… The many twists in this story keep the tension running high right to the last page."

—*RT Book Reviews*, 4 Stars

"Mann's tender yet heart-pounding story vividly creates the chaos of both disasters and love."

—*Booklist*

"Mann steals romance readers away for a second steamy, suspenseful adventure with her doughty team of Air Force pararescuemen."

—*Publishers Weekly*

"Catherine Mann's powerful writing sweeps the reader into pulse-pounding dangers, gripping suspense, and spine-tingling passion. She creates super heroes that send the heart racing… *Hot Zone* assails the senses, offers up an offbeat sort of humor, and stirs emotions from the very depths of one's being—a transporting read."

—*Long and Short Reviews*

"Catherine Mann wins again with a novel of the pararescuemen… This is not one to miss!"

—*Night Owl Romance*, 4 Stars

"A complex, exciting thriller with a strong cast. Catherine Mann provides a superb action-packed tale."

—*The Mystery Gazette*

Cover Me

"This summer sizzler is one cool romantic read... For romantic suspense readers who love tough-as-nails women partnered with military heroes, Mann's Elite Force series is for you."

—*RT Book Reviews* Top Pick of the Month, 4.5 Stars

"Mann delivers plenty of thrills and charged erotic situations with this first in a new series featuring pararescuemen, elite U.S. Air Force heroes ready for tense 'land, sea, or mountain, military missions or civilian rescue' around the globe... Fans of military romantic suspense will welcome this bracing thriller with a strong-willed heroine and sensitive, hard-bodied hero."

—*Publishers Weekly*

"Catherine Mann writes an amazing combination of keen suspense, unique characters, and heart-stopping romance. I'm a fan!"

—Lori Foster, *New York Times* bestselling author of *Bewitched*

"Catherine Mann takes military romance to the next level... Mann as always writes a riveting military romance, but *Cover Me* had a fresh boost and drive that will keep readers engaged throughout. Discovering the mastermind and the reason behind it will stun you."

—*Night Owl Romance* Reviewer Top Pick, 4.5 Stars

"Enthralling… Whenever I read a book by Catherine Mann, I know every scene will be conveyed with a genuineness rarely depicted by any other author. The tension is gripping… while the romance will touch your heart."

—*Single Titles*

"I couldn't put it down if I wanted to, and trust me, I didn't want to… The scenes are vivid and the characters unforgettable."

—*Long and Short Reviews*

"Gripping… the characters are vibrant and captivating… the story is as unique as it is charming. Catherine Mann does not overstuff with her knowledge of the military, but compliments the book with it and lends credibility to the story."

—*Romance Fiction on Suite101.com*

"Nonstop action and strong characters make this book one you don't want to miss. From the intense opening scene to the romantic final page, I was captivated. Catherine Mann is an auto-buy for me!"

—*The Romance Studio*

"Ms. Mann is one of my all-time favorite romantic suspense authors and I'm always ready to get my brain revving in one more of her sexy, hot reads."

—*Dark Diva Reviews*

"So well-written… so much heart… Catherine Mann is an excellent weaver of a story."

—*Once Upon a Romance*

FREE
FALL

CATHERINE
MANN

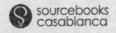

sourcebooks
casablanca

Published by Sourcebooks Casablanca, an imprint of Sourcebooks, Inc.
P.O. Box 4410, Naperville, Illinois 60567-4410
(630) 961-3900
FAX: (630) 961-2168
www.sourcebooks.com

Printed and bound in Canada
WC 10 9 8 7 6 5 4 3 2 1

To Maggie

I am so proud to be your mother!

"The meeting of two personalities is like the contact of two chemical substances; if there is any reaction, both are transformed."

—Carl Jung

Prologue

Horn of Africa

WHEN STELLA CARSON WAS EIGHT YEARS OLD, HER mother rented the movie *Out of Africa* so Stella could envision where her mom lived when she left Tallahassee for Peace Corps trips. Those images had helped through the first night alone saying her prayers. And through a summer with her brothers as babysitters while their father drove his UPS route.

In the fall, a photo of her mother went in her backpack, helping Stella hold strong during a rocky start of third grade when she landed in the principal's office for a playground fight. Nobody would make fun of her daddy's efforts to send his baby girl off to school, even if her braids were lopsided with mismatched bows. Stella knew how to punch like a boy, thanks to her three older brothers.

Her siblings had failed to mention the importance of saving the infamous Carson left hook for the walk home, off school grounds.

But she'd survived the principal's punishment, as well as her father's disappointment, by envisioning her mom dispensing medicine and mosquito nets to needy kids. The school wouldn't suspend her anyway because they needed Stella's perfect scores on standardized tests. Tuning out the principal's lecture, she'd stroked one of the mismatched ribbons between her fingers, tabulated the number of pinholes in the ceiling tiles, and pretended she didn't need her mother.

When Stella was fifteen her mom died on one of those annual aide trips. She had a tough time understanding why Melanie Carson chose to leave her family to help other families in a foreign country. It didn't make sense to a grieving teenager, and Stella craved answers. Understanding. Order.

By college, she'd realized if she didn't decipher what really happened the day her mother died and find peace for the restlessness inside her, there would be no building a family of her own. Something she desperately wanted. So she'd changed her major to criminal justice, landed a job in Interpol's American office as a code breaker, and poured all her energies into wrangling an assignment in Africa.

Here. Now. In a country every bit as magnificent as in the movie *Out of Africa* and as tumultuous as her feelings about the place that stole her mother.

Finally, she could piece together her mom's last days. Find answers about her mother's mysterious death. And if not answers, at least gain closure.

Although her whole quest would be moot if she didn't squeeze more life out of the sleek boat she was steering at breakneck speed along the Arabian Sea into the Gulf of Aden.

Stella thumped the already maxed throttle, the metal so hot to the touch it damn near blistered her palm. Logic told her the engine didn't have anything more to give. Still, she calculated angles to take the choppy sea faster. She stayed well clear of the other vessels just as they stayed away from her. Everyone kept their distance in these lawless waters.

The hull's nose popped over a wave and slammed back onto the churning surface. She bit her tongue. The metallic taste of blood filled her mouth. The motor revved and muffled, catching hold of the water and shooting forward again. Seconds counted. Timing was everything.

A team of Navy SEALs and a pair of Air Force pararescuemen were counting on her to be in place for the pickup if things went wrong with their helicopter rendezvous. Sure, those special operations dudes could swim for miles, but even the most elite of the elite warriors didn't relish hanging out in shark-infested, pirate-riddled waters.

Sea spray stung her overheated face as the sun melted downward in the sky. She gripped the steering wheel tighter, her eyes on the sonar and radar screens feeding images of the SEALs and pararescuemen—also known as parajumpers or PJs. Six SEALs and two PJs were diving, about to "count coup" on a suspected pirate frigate, a stealthy tap-and-go.

The mother vessel was towing four faster skiffs for overtaking their targets once they reached the open sea. Except today the U.S. forces were under water disabling the smaller crafts, something the Somali pirates wouldn't discover until they were out in the middle of the sea ready to prey on others. Those four malfunctioning boats, clearly dismantled right under their very noses, would screw with their heads.

Never underestimate the power of psychological warfare.

As a field operative for Interpol, she'd been sent

to assist with the investigation into stolen artifacts by pirates off the Horn of Africa, to decipher the codes and patterns to their movements. Local government officials in the region had requested international help. Those stolen treasures brought major bucks on the black market, money then used to fund separatist groups and local warlords that increased criminal chaos. Groups responsible for instigating ruthless uprisings. Rampant looting where women were brutalized. Young males, barely teenagers, were being pressed into service. At least one of those child soldiers was on that main vessel today.

Another reason the PJs had been tapped to participate was for the safety of the kid as well as the SEALs if things went to hell. PJs received the same SEAL training needed to carry out the mission, but with additional medic skills to make a house call behind enemy lines. PJs were like Supermen with EMT bonus powers.

There hadn't been any PJs around for her mom. Melanie Carson died here and her family had been given sketchy details along with her body to bury. Authorities had written off the injuries as results of a car accident. Stella hadn't believed them then any more than she believed them now. She'd worked her entire career with Interpol with one goal: to find the truth about her mother's death. Finally, she had her chance and she wouldn't allow anything to derail her plans.

Today's launch of her mission was everything.

A helicopter had dropped the SEALs and PJs in the water five miles out from the pirates. Afterward they were supposed to swim five back where the chopper should be able to pick them up. But as a fail-safe, she and four heavily armed CIA operatives stayed nearby in the speedboat.

She'd plotted contingencies, and more contingencies for the contingencies, because logic was her strength, her secret weapon even. It was all about backup plans.

Pop, pop, pop.

The unmistakable sound of gunfire carried across the water. Stella braced, sweat chilling under her bulletproof vest. She looked over her shoulders at her four CIA teammates aiming MP5 submachine guns.

"Is it pirates?" she shouted over her shoulder, wind tearing strands of hair loose from her braid.

"Don't think so," an operative known only as Mr. Smith barked back, scanning the distant horizon where two fishing boats bobbed. Of course, CIA agents were always Smith or Brown. Or if working in a pack like today, Jones and Johnson joined in. "They seem to be shooting in the air, partying maybe."

His buddy Mr. Brown squinted into the scope on his gun. "The place is littered with these bastards. I'm not trusting that party spirit."

Mr. Jones hitched his weapon higher. "We can outgun them."

Stella eyed the horizon. A whale arched just ahead, then slapped its tale in a majestic display so at odds with the turmoil playing out on the water's surface above them. "Or we can stay cool and keep moving closer in case the chopper needs to bail out."

An explosion in the sky sent shock waves across the water. The CIA dudes dropped to their knees. So much for keeping cool.

Stella steadied the boat and studied the radar. Her

heart punched into her throat. Had the pirate ship blown up? Had the PJs and SEALs been injured in the raining debris and flames?

No.

The radar offered plenty of details.

But the news?

Bad.

As bad as it got.

"The chopper exploded," she announced, forcing her voice to stay flat, calm. Professional.

Now that she knew where to look, debris rained in the distant sky, a splash spewing on the horizon. The crew she'd briefed this morning was almost certainly dead, and if not, a different contingency was in place to search for them—a second PJ pair. Just the thought delivered a sock in the gut as she thought about another child hearing the news that her mom or dad wasn't coming home.

But she had to push through the feelings threatening to suck her under. Her role now? Crystal clear.

"We have to get our guys out now rather than waiting for them to swim closer. Those look like dolphin fins out there, but if I'm wrong... We need to move."

Nailing the throttle again, she compartmentalized. Later, she would climb up onto the embassy roof alone and mourn the aircrew. At this moment, her focus had to be on extracting the men in the water.

How far had the special ops men swum from the vessel? How close would she have to sweep by the known pirate frigate? And the unknown bad guys in these waters? Who had launched that rocket at the chopper?

She took a read off the sonar beside the radar,

homing in on the blips. Beacons sent signals from her pickup targets. Men. Swimming. Closer. She eased back on the horsepower. Searching the surface for the slightest… ripple.

"Got 'em," Mr. Smith announced with conviction an instant before she saw what snagged his eagle eyes.

The barest perceptible cuts through the water. The pirate vessel was a surprisingly distant shadow in the sunset. Good God, how had the men made it so far so fast? Even if the other boat was speeding away.

She cut the engine back to idle. Her four CIA field agents went into action while she kept the boat as steady as possible. They didn't talk much—but dudes from the agency rarely spoke. One at a time they hauled sleek bodies in wet suits onto the deck. Her muscles burned as she gripped the wheel straining to spin free.

Man after man rolled onto the deck. Six, seven… eight.

The final guy whipped off his face mask and pinned her with piercing brown eyes and an intense focus that kept people alive beyond the odds. The air snapped in an indefinable way that defied the logic she embraced.

Adrenaline.

Had to be.

Right?

He nodded once, giving her a thumbs-up. "Go, go, go!"

Done.

Shaking off the momentary distraction, she revved the engine to life again. Her brain cycled to contingency twenty-freaking-two, a cave cut into the mountainous shoreline. Minutes passed in a blur as she drove and watched the screen, monitoring traffic. Pathetically few officials policed the area. A boat racing across at a reckless speed wouldn't appear at all out of the ordinary around this place.

Even as the yawning entrance to the cave came into sight, she refused to relax her guard. She pulled back on the throttle. Entering slowly, she scanned while her quiet companions held their MP5s at the ready. Would an Interpol operative, four CIA agents, six SEALs, and two PJs be enough to face anything that waited inside? The low hum of the motor echoed like a growling beast in the cavern, one light strobing forward into the darkness.

Illuminating a waiting U.S. fishing boat.

Her final contingency.

Her plan had to work; otherwise, she would screw up her hard-earned chance of working in Africa before the mission barely got off the ground. She flung open the door to the small forward cabin of her speedboat. The clang of metal hitting metal echoed in her mind like the closing of her mother's coffin. Melanie Carson's daughter would not give up on day one.

Digging around in the hull, Stella pulled out small duffel bags, one after the other, tossing them to each of the men in wet suits.

"Change, gentlemen. We're about to become American tourists on a sightseeing excursion. Mr. Jones," who could blend in best with the locals and even spoke a regional dialect thanks to his mother, "will be our guide. We're swapping boats, then splitting up at the dock. Blend into the crowds. Report at the embassy. You've got a duress code if you need to call in. Any questions?"

Only the sound of oxygen tanks and gear hitting the deck answered her.

"Good." Her heart rate started to return to something close to normal again.

The sound of zippers sent her spinning on her heels to take care of her own transformation. She unrolled a colorful rectangular cloth, an East African kanga, complete with the standard intricate border and message woven into the red and orange pattern.

It would be hot as hell over her black pants, top, and bulletproof vest. But a little dehydration was a small price to pay for an extra layer of anonymity.

"Need help?"

She turned and there were those coffee dark eyes again. Static-like awareness snapped when she looked back at the intense gaze that had held hers earlier as he'd lifted his face mask. Except now he was more than eyes and a wet suit. He was a lean, honed man in a pair of fitted swim trunks he must have worn under the diving gear. He was glistening bronze with a body trained for survival anyplace, anytime.

The boat rocked under her feet from a rogue wave. At least she thought it was a wave.

"Uh, no, I'm good. Thanks. You should get dressed. We need to haul butt out of here." And his current state of undress definitely didn't qualify as "low profile."

"I meant, do you need help with the cut on your temple?" He gestured to the left side of her face, almost touching. "You brought along two PJs for a reason, ma'am."

Her skin hummed with a sting that her brain must have pushed aside earlier for survival's sake. She tapped the side of her forehead gingerly.

"Ouch!" Her fingertips were stained with blood as murky red as her hair.

"A bullet must have grazed you," he said with a flat Midwestern accent. A no-accent really, just pure masculine rumble. "Could have been much worse. This was your lucky day, ma'am."

"Stella." For right now she could be more than Miss Lucky Smith.

"They call me Cuervo."

Call him.

Call signs.

No real name from him for now. Understandable and a reality check to get her professional groove back on. "Do I need stitches?"

He tugged a small kit from his gear, a waterproof pack of some sort. "Antiseptic and butterfly bandages should hold you until we can get someplace where I'll have time to treat you more fully."

We.

Her brain hitched on the word, the answer to who she would be partnering with as they escaped into the crowd. She wasn't saying good-bye to him—to Cuervo—at the dock. Irrational relief flooded her, followed by a bolt of excitement.

"Thanks, Cuervo. Blood dripping down my face would definitely draw undue attention at an inopportune time." She forced a smile.

Still, his face, those eyes, they held her, and while she wasn't a mystical person, she couldn't miss the connection. Attraction? Sure, but she understood how to compartmentalize on the job. This was something that felt elemental. Before she could stop the thought, the words *soul mate* flashed through her head.

And God, that was crazy and irrational when she was

always, always logical. Her brothers called her a female version of Spock from *Star Trek*.

Still, as those fingers cleaned her wound, smoothed ointment over her temple, and stretched butterfly bandages along her skin, she couldn't stop thinking about spending the rest of the day with him as they melded into the port city and made their way back to the embassy.

Damn it, she could not waste the time or emotional energy on romance or even a fling. Right now, she could only focus on working with the Mr. Smiths and Mr. Browns of her profession. She needed to make peace with her past, *then* move on with her life. Then, and only then, she would find Mr. *Right* and shift from the field to a desk job so she could settle down into that real family dream she'd missed out on.

Yet those brown eyes drew her into a molten heat and she had the inescapable sense that Mr. Right had arrived ahead of schedule.

Chapter 1

East Africa: Six Months Later

FIVE YEARS, EIGHT MONTHS, AND TWENTY-NINE days sober.

Staff Sergeant Jose "Cuervo" James flipped his sobriety coin over and over between his fingers as he reviewed the satellite feed on the six screens in front of him. If he and the multi-force rescue team around him didn't save Stella Carson in the next twenty-four hours, odds were his coin would end up in the trash.

The cavernous airplane hangar echoed with the buzz of personnel calling directives into headsets and the low hum from each image on the dozen screens. Techies gathered information for the eight-man rescue team— two Air Force pararescuemen, eight Navy SEALs, and five CIA operatives. The volume on the speakers increased whenever something of specific interest captured their attention about Stella and the eleven college students who'd been kidnapped with her during a foreign exchange trip.

Only one screen interested him. The one showing Stella being held hostage by separatists in some concrete hellhole south of the Horn of Africa. His eyes ate up the image of her—alive—for now.

She wore jeans and a black tank top with gym shoes, looking five years younger than her twenty-nine years and just like the exchange student she was pretending to be. Her titan red hair was half in, half out of a ponytail. A long strand stuck to blood on her cheek from an oozing gash in her eyebrow that made him think of the scratch on her head from the bullet that grazed her the day they'd met. The day she'd saved *his* ass.

Right now, she was dusty, strained, and bruised. But still keen-eyed, pacing around her cell, nothing more than concrete walls with a pallet and bucket in the corner. A table filled another corner with a scattering of artifacts and relics. Frustration knotted his fists as he held back the urge to reach through the screen and haul her out. To hell with the objectivity and the logic she worshiped.

Usually his job as a pararescueman gave his life focus and stability. But today's assignment was more than just a mission. Stella Carson was more than an Interpol agent to pluck out of a sticky situation. She was the only woman he'd ever loved.

She was also the woman who'd dumped him four weeks ago.

He prayed to every saint he'd memorized in parochial school that the captors bought her cover story of being an over-privileged student studying overseas on Mommy and Daddy's nickel. He couldn't even let himself think about all the atrocities committed against women in this region. He could only focus on willing her to stay alive. God help her if they figured out she was a top-notch intelligence operative with an uncanny aptitude for code breaking.

God help them both if he failed to get her out.

He'd been told little when he'd boarded the plane

at his home base in Georgia, only knowing they were being tasked to rescue a kidnapped group of students. Not unusual to keep him in the dark until deeper into the mission. He'd understood the op was covert and their slide into the country would be off the books. Their aircraft looked more like a large civilian charter jet than a military transport.

He damn well hadn't guessed Stella was one of the captives until he was airborne. He'd almost lost his shit right then and there. Only the burning need to be damn sure they didn't have any excuse to kick him off this operation kept him from going postal.

At least he'd gotten his rage under control by the time they'd flown into Camp Lemmonier, a U.S. base in Africa, and pulled into the waiting empty airplane hangar. They'd slipped in by pretending to be part of the advance security team for the U.S. vice president's wife's upcoming visit. Once inside the hangar, they'd off-loaded their gear—shipping containers emptied and flipped over to be used as tables. The other four CIA agents—techies—monitored two fifteen-inch computer screens each with a massive flat screen above all to feed images from the smaller units.

A Predator unmanned surveillance drone sent pictures from outside the compound and relayed thermal imaging of individuals inside. The craft, flown by remote control, had also released a smaller reconnaissance craft—the ultimate "bug."

Nanotechnology made it possible to fly in a miniscule spy vehicle that looked like a fly or spider, a nano air vehicle or NAV. The miniature drone didn't have the distance capability of the Predator, but the maneuverability was unbeatable. The minute size provided the ultimate disguise, sending back visual and audio feed via satellite. Even though other countries knew of the existence of the technology, it wasn't like they could swat every fly and stomp every spider.

The lead CIA agent on their extraction team—a craggy-faced dude calling himself "Mr. Smith," surprise, surprise—clicked the controller in his hands and shifted one of the smaller screen images to feed into the larger wide-screen above the rest.

"This footage was made yesterday at zero-eight-hundred when the Predator spy drone successfully deployed NAVs for an inside peek." Smith hitched the dusty leather belt, his dark shirt and pants well-worn and generic looking as his four identical workmates. "We were lucky enough to make contact with Agent Carson."

The screen captured her eyes narrowing briefly as she stepped closer to the minute surveillance device. She nodded, just a tiny dip of her head that she knew she was being watched and somehow she'd decided the eyes were friendly. Yet, she didn't give anything away to the pair of scared students huddled in the corner with an unconscious third on the floor in front of them.

Mr. Smith zoomed in so close Stella's freckles came into focus. "Once she knew we had eyes in the room, she fed us information like a pro."

Jose leaned forward, elbows on his knees as his eyes zeroed in on his favorite freckle, the one just below her ear where he'd discovered she liked to be kissed the day they'd flown to Queen Elizabeth National Park. He could almost taste her skin even now, watching her on screen.

She walked to a corner and stared up at what appeared to be a regular surveillance camera to keep watch over prisoners. "We need medical supplies in here," she shouted, her husky voice reaching through the airwaves to grip him right around his heart. "Do you hear me, people?"

The operative fast forwarded through her pointing out two injured students and three more devices in her dank concrete room; each step took her past piles of ancient pottery and stacks of other stolen pieces of art. "She alerted us to the location of the cameras in the room and the students throughout the building—as best she could."

Her pacing slowed beside a stack of ancient tribal masks. "You can't just lock all of us away." Her fingers skimmed along a gold gilded antiquity. Drawing their attention to the room's storehouse of stolen historic treasures? "I'm no good to you if I die before you even get to torture me for answers."

Torture.

Rape was rampant here.

Mutilation of women was commonplace.

Bile burned the back of his throat as a hole threatened to crack open his chest. What had she been through during her three days of captivity? Jamming the fear to the back of his brain, he focused on using his training to help her. He wouldn't be any good to her if he didn't hold it together.

His eyes flicked to other screens, images of the rest of the rooms, one in particular. Chains hung from the ceiling. Knives glinted in a line on a nearby table. A battery with cables lay too damn close on the floor. The semiconscious man being carried between two guards appeared alive.

Jose forced himself to assess the young man medically. Pararescue training included extensive schooling as a medic and no doubt those skills were needed for this mission. The wide screen filled again with Stella's image, the time stamp at the bottom showing the footage had come in late yesterday afternoon.

"Hello?" She waved her hand in front of one of the bad guy surveillance cameras. "Your guards are due back in a half hour anyway to bring that watery soup you call supper… Oh yeah, and you call it breakfast, but no actual lunch because we shouldn't eat enough to have any energy. Instead of your sunrise/sunset buffet, I'd rather have a bucket of water and antibiotics."

Mr. Smith froze that frame, leaving the smaller images running in both past and real time now, offering two Stellas to watch in addition to the full screen close-up of her pale face with keen green eyes. "Notice, she told us the guard's schedule—or at least the part we can expect. Sunrise and sunset. We can infiltrate at that moment, when we know where the guards will be. It's better to face the certainty. You'll be going in just before dusk as they take her supper tonight."

Screens flickered and shifted with feeds of everything from jungle perimeter to the rusted chain-link fence. Jose imprinted every detail in his brain. Nothing could be tossed aside as inconsequential.

"Gentlemen," Mr. Smith continued, scratching his jaw along the beard they all grew when undercover in-country for any length of time, "I trust I don't need to stress how important it is that this rescue goes off without major incident. With the vice president's wife coming for a goodwill visit at the end of the week, security is crucial."

If there weren't civilian students involved in the kidnapping would they have left Stella there to die in the interest of preserving "security"? His fist clenched around his sobriety coin in his pocket. He was the first person in a long line of family alcoholics to make it this far in AA.

"Sergeant James." Mr. Smith turned his attention to Jose. The frozen image of Stella fast forwarded. "Here's the part that brought you here today."

Stella hitched her hands on her hips, her face directed right at the nano bug. "I really could use some Jose Cuervo."

The CIA agent clicked the remote again and again, skipping to different frames where she repeated over time… "Jose Cuervo… Jose Cuervo… Jose Cuervo…"

Cuervo. An ironic reminder of a bad encounter with a bottle of the tequila, and due to his name Jose, the call sign stuck. *Jose "Cuervo" James.* He forced himself to concentrate on the deceptively bland CIA operative in charge of the whole operation.

"We looked into her file and your name—or rather your call sign—caught our attention. We realized the two of you worked a mission together six months ago. Our files indicate you became more than friends."

So much for their attempts to keep the relationship secret. Apparently big brother really was watching.

"Yes, sir," he answered simply, catching a look from his fellow teammate out of the corner of his eye.

He'd been paired with Tech Sergeant Gavin

"Bubbles" Novak, the least chatty PJ in their squadron, but the best medic. Bubbles had also been there the day Stella had pulled them out of the Gulf of Aden.

A wave from one of the techies drew their attention back. The main screen filled with Stella in "real time." His mouth dried at the thought of seeing her now, so vibrant he ached to step into the image with her. The screen showed a door opening in Stella's cell.

Shit. Why did they have to sit around here with their thumbs up their asses reviewing footage? They needed to get to her. Now.

A guard tossed another limp body on the floor, the resulting groan from the guy the only sign that their latest inquisition had left the student alive. The guard's shaved bald head gleamed from the bare lightbulb swinging from the ceiling. He wore camouflage pants and a T-shirt with the sleeves cut, no military rank visible. Ammo straps crisscrossed his chest. A rifle hung over his shoulder.

A blade was sheathed at his waist in a belt holding more bullets.

Stella's eyes went wide with perfectly played innocence and horror. "I don't know what you want from me. I'll tell you everything I know. Can I just have some water first, please?"

The guard hooked his hand on the strap of his automatic rifle slung over his shoulder. "We want to know who you are." His accent was clearly local, Somali most likely. "Why were you and your fellow spies on our property?"

"I've told you already. My name is Stella. I'm a foreign exchange student. These are my friends in the same program, but we're all from different schools. We were on a day trip when you found us, a study on ways to improve distribution of food during a famine. We only wanted to help." She backed step by step until she bumped a table of ancient pottery. "I'm begging you, can I just go home?"

"You must think we are very stupid." The bald guard blocked the doorway out. "I do not like to be insulted."

"I don't like being taken captive." Her hand slid to the table, her fingers closing over a broken handle off a cup. She tucked the remnant into the back of her waistband. "I want to call my embassy."

She tugged her T-shirt as if for emphasis, effectively hiding her makeshift weapon. Pride filled him. Damn, she was amazing.

His mind raced back to the first time he'd seen her when he'd hauled himself out of the sea and into the rescue boat. She'd been at the wheel, holding the boat steady against the hammering waves, unbending with the wind tearing at her fiery red braid. There'd been bullets, a blown up chopper, and blood streaking down her face.

Not a romantic meeting by any stretch.

Their sprint through the marketplace to the embassy had left them both weary as hell, wrung dry by the job. Afterward, he'd found her on the embassy roof, grieving for the aircrew of the downed chopper. That explosion had shaken him more than a little too.

He'd been planning to have his one cigar a month to decompress. He'd taken up smoking when he kicked the booze, then had to kick nicotine as best he could. One cigar a month when stress got to be too much wasn't the best option, but it didn't drag him back under the way one drink would. So he carried a Cuban smoke in his pocket at all times. He'd had it half out when he stepped onto the roof… and then he'd found Stella.

He hadn't smoked a cigar since.

Their attraction had been immediate. Explosive. Their five-month affair had been frenetic as they "dated" wherever their paths crossed on missions and assignments throughout the Horn of Africa and farther along the Eastern region, even over as far as Uganda. They'd lived on the edge, drunk on an edgy attraction that provided a greater high than could be found in any bottle.

Until they'd crashed. Broken up. Ripped each other's heart out.

A quick elbow jab to his side brought him back to the present. He looked sharply at his team bud—Tech Sergeant Gavin "Bubbles" Novak—nodding toward the images again. Screen three filled with a male stretched out on the floor, a student beaten to a pulp for information who appeared to be hanging on by a thread.

Stella knelt beside the pummeled student, her hands going to each wound as if to make sure to document every injury for the rescue team watching. Her gaze was so intense.

Something tugged at him, but he couldn't pinpoint what. From her position, her back to the enemy's camera, she clearly meant to hide something from her captors watching. She stared up into the bug, her blinking strange, erratic. Was she drugged? He watched closer, searching, slowly realizing…

Holy crap, there was a pattern.

Jose held up a hand, snapping his fingers for attention.

"Agent Smith, get a close-up on her face there. Do you see? She's blinking."

"Yeah, and your point, Sergeant?"

"She's blinking Morse code." The longer he looked, the more certain he became. "Like the Navy pilot captured during the Vietnam War. He blinked 'torture' in a televised interview."

"And you think she's doing that now."

"Stella's a code breaker. You know that from her file. But you wouldn't know she talked about stuff like that all the time."

They had talked about it. And that had to be why she'd hedged her bets in trying to get him here to watch the footage. A long shot? Maybe. But her situation called for extreme measures.

Jose sat up straighter. "And there. She's tapping her fingers, but always away from the bad guy cameras."

"Tap code? Like the language the Vietnam prisoners used to talk to each other from cell to cell?"

"Right. She's trying to communicate, to give us as much information as possible." Damn it. If they'd seen this earlier, the information would already be decoded. Now… "Who knows what else she may have uncovered?"

Mr. Smith scratched his bristly chin. "Weighing the risk of waiting against missing some info she may be sharing, we can't afford to delay. You'll go in and we'll feed her messages to you as we unlock them," he said with surety, but his forehead creased with concern. "Is your personal baggage with Agent Carson going to present a problem?"

How much did Smith know? The breakup last month had been bad. It had hurt like hell—still did. But it had been quiet as well as permanent. He'd come to grips with the fact he would spend his life without her.

But he could not, would not, accept a world without Stella Carson in it. "I'm as focused as I've ever been. I know my job and I've been tasked to get *all* the hostages out alive."

"That's what I needed to hear." Smith turned from the image of Stella on the main screen. "Gentlemen, time to roll."

Jose stole one last look at the only woman he'd ever loved, soaking in what could be his final glimpse of her alive. The door behind her opened again. She pressed her back to the wall. Fast. Her eyes alert.

A captor with hard muscles and harder eyes walked inside, tossing another unconscious student in a heap in the corner. He paused in front of Stella, one lip lifting in a sneer.

"Once we finish with the last of your friends, you are next."

Jose's fist closed around the coin. *Bloody hell.*

She was next.

Next to be tortured.

Next to be killed?

Time was running out for a Hail Mary rescue. That didn't mean she intended to go down without kicking in some teeth on her way out of this world. Sure, the local government had asked for international help in dealing with the warlords, but that wouldn't guarantee her presence would be actively acknowledged. Field operatives disappeared sometimes. It was a hazard of the job. Would these stone walls become her funeral crypt, entombing her here with other dead bodies and priceless artifacts?

The door closed, giving her a temporary reprieve to search the room, to prepare herself and hopefully launch more warnings. When she'd identified the nanotechnology surveillance equipment, she'd allowed herself to hope her messages would get through in time. And if not? She'd relayed as much information as possible. Some might not have noticed her blinking and tap codes, but she'd bargained on Jose remembering their conversations. She'd scrambled for every idea possible to leave clues that she needed him brought in to watch the surveillance feed.

Had he seen her?

Regret chewed her gut over the way she'd ended things, and she couldn't help but wonder if he felt the same. Even if they weren't meant to be together, she'd hurled horrible words at him and those could be the last she spoke to him. Was there a chance to tell him if he was on the other end of that video feed? Would he recall the good times between them, their exotic dates over to Queen Elizabeth National Park and up into Egypt? Heaven knew she would never forget the sound of his laugh. His easygoing approach to life, the way he cared for the people around him had drawn her to him from the start.

She pressed her hands to her eyes, dizzy from lack of sleep and minimal food. What if she was hallucinating about the whole mini spy drone? Charlotte's Web up there could be wondering what the hell was going on. And damn, she really was crazy if she focused on anything other than doing everything possible to get out of here. It wasn't just her life on the line.

She blinked a final Morse code in the direction of "Charlotte." Details about the guards and discussions she'd overheard, everything possible to protect the rescue team coming in. Would it be enough to help an extraction team before her turn at the inquisition?

She'd taken her fair share of knocks from her three big brothers while playing basketball, football, and pretty much any other sport, because if she didn't join them, she got left behind. She'd always punched right back. She'd held her own with her fists, fingernails, and whatever else she could lay her hands on. She would do the same here.

Searching for any other possible tools among the stolen artifacts, she continued her rambling litany in hopes good guys were on the other side of that nano spy bug. "If somebody doesn't send some antibiotics back here we won't last long enough for you to ransom us off to our country in exchange for whatever the going rate is for students."

Rambling on for whoever might be listening, she pocketed the preserved jaw of some small animal to use like spiked brass knuckles. The tip of a tusk went in her sock.

Too bad they hadn't stashed her in the ancient war tools room. Just as she'd expected from the beginning, they were gathering artifacts to sell on the black market to fund their separatist group, headed by a radical warlord. The same group that had recently blown up the American ambassador's private residence, hell-bent on stirring unrest.

But they were planning something more here, something big. Maybe for when the vice president's wife came to visit to bring national attention to the plight of women in the region? Stella had made progress with one of the guards by pretending to be a student sympathetic to their cause. But somehow, they'd grown suspicious or been tipped off.

Years ago her mother had tried to help the same people who now held her hostage. Talk about irony. And she was still no closer to figuring out missing details from the day her mother died.

The door opened again. Her stomach plunged. She tucked her ankle behind her other leg, just in case they caught sight of the bulge in her sock. The scariest of her captors—not the sneering bastard, but the man who showed no expression at all, a short lean man who should have appeared harmless but reminded her of a cheetah rather than a lion. Just as fast, strong, and lethal.

Wordlessly, he grabbed her arm in a vise grip and hauled her from the room. Would the surveillance bug follow her? Was she on her own now? How close was help? She had to operate on the assumption she was being watched and that help was on the way.

If she could just stay alive long enough.

"Where are we going?" Down a dank hallway, past the two dead Americans tossed in the corner like sacks of garbage, not even a hint of dignity given to the lifeless hulls that once housed a human soul. She vowed to do everything in her power to make sure their families got their bodies back. "You really don't have to do this. I'll tell you whatever you want to know."

She looked up at the camera in the hall. The enemy's

camera. She'd been left alone so far. The captors had gone for the older ones first, assuming she was a junior agent, low-level status, which meant less intel. They'd gone for the big fish first.

Or maybe they hoped the sounds of torture would soften her up, make her break faster.

She couldn't weaken. Too many people in the field depended on her silence. Names. Lives.

Guilt weighed her down. She'd been selfish to come to this region of the world with her own agenda. She'd accepted the assignment in hopes of uncovering more about her mother's death in the region fourteen years ago—distracting enough. Then she'd met Jose and her focus drifted even further.

Her eyes shot back to the dead bodies—an innocent student and a CIA operative. Had a lapse on her part cost them their lives? She'd been so damn sure their cover was rock solid. Even when the separatists had taken the group of students hostage, she'd prayed that was their only agenda. That they didn't know they'd also landed four undercover operatives as well.

And there was still hope they didn't know about her. How ironic that she'd come here to retrace her mother's last days and now she was walking in her footsteps in a more literal way. Her mother's battered body sent home in a box, the cause of death labeled a car accident. And Stella never had the chance to say good-bye, to apologize for sending her mother off that last time by screaming how much she hated her for leaving them again.

So many regrets.

And her most current regret? One of her biggest? The

way she'd broken things off with Jose, the man she'd been so certain was her soul mate.

If she thought about him, she would cry, but then maybe that would seem more natural. She'd tried it at first—no luck. But if it bought her time now, then hell, she would try anything.

She envisioned Jose's shoulders sagging when he realized she was serious about ending their relationship.

Tears filled her eyes in a flash. Using the emotion to her advantage, she looked up at the cold, detached guard. She let the tears roll down her cheeks, allowed all her anguish to show for once.

"Please, call my mom and dad. They'll pay you anything you want to get me back."

Her cover story would hold under scrutiny. Her passport traced back to a concocted profile of her life as a pampered rich kid from Florida who lived off of a hefty trust fund, continuing to enroll in college to avoid getting a job. She'd slid right into the group of students. For them, she'd risked bringing Jose into harm's way, something she never would have done had she been the only one taken. But for the students and for whatever plan these ruthless bastards were cooking up, she had to think like an agent.

Not like a woman whose heart still ached for a man she couldn't have.

Her captor jerked her to a stop at the end of the hall. The doorway loomed in front of her. And landing on the corner of the frame, a buzzing little fly.

She stared up into what she prayed was help and one last time she blinked…

Warning: Land mines at the camp gates.

—◦◦◦—

Stella's voice echoed in the earpiece of Jose's comm set as he stood in the open hatch of a C-130 cargo plane. Wind roared through the open portal. Parched earth and thirsty frankincense trees sprawled far, far below. The rebel camp waited.

With Stella inside.

All he needed was the signal to go and he would jump with Bubbles and the SEALs, parachuting into the compound in the twilight, HALO style—high altitude, low opening. The best way to slip in unnoticed. No tipping anyone off by bringing a helicopter too close. The cargo plane would drop them off at thirty thousand feet with an oxygen mask into a free fall. He would wait until the very last possible second to pop the parachute.

Then they would charge the camp on foot.

"Go, go, go!" the loadmaster shouted the command into the mic.

His boots pounded along the metal ramp as he ran to the edge and…

Jumped.

Arms and legs extended, his body split the air, speeding downward. He hurtled through the dusky sky, into utter silence other than the sounds from his headset… more feed from Stella's surveillance and a low hum of radio chatter from the aircrew. But he only heard the echoes of Stella from the satellite feed.

The command center still ran the feed in the background in a way he could hear her faintly. Listening to her sob tore him apart, even knowing she was acting her role as a terrified student. But the slaps by her interrogator weren't fake. The punch was followed by a stifled groan.

Then more questions. They didn't believe her or her friends. Someone was here spying.

And God help her, they were right.

How long could she hold out? He wanted to send her a sign to hang on, to let her know he was on his way at top speed. Wind whipped over him.

Hearing her tortured was a hellish abyss that could suck him in faster than any free fall. Damn it all to hell. He had to think of something, anything else, or he would lose his shit. His mind latched onto an image of her at a squadron party. People hadn't known they were dating. They'd both been hepped up on accidental brushes and hot glances.

But those times he'd watched her when she thought no one was looking… those times hit him hardest. Such as at that picnic when her eagle eye picked up his teammate Bubbles's one vulnerability. Hulking big, badass Gavin Novak didn't like fuzzy things… like the inside of a jacket or texture of certain foods. She'd grabbed a peach and chased Bubbles around the bonfire, threatening to rub it on his arm. Her laughter, her playfulness, all bundled up with her insightfulness made for a compelling, irresistible woman.

Stella was also a complex woman he couldn't begin to understand. He'd just watched her, her every move turning him on and inside out as he'd fallen for her. Falling as hard as he was going to land if he didn't pay attention. He needed to count down the seconds to deploy his parachute.

Another slap echoed through the sound waves along

with her cry. "I don't know anything except you're going to kill us for nothing. Why not ransom us for money? Anything other than this…"

"Shut. Up," her inquisitor shouted. "I am going to ask you again, what were you and your friends doing on our property? Which government agency are you spying for?"

"You can't torture information out of people if they don't know it," she answered with just the right amount of quiver in her voice.

"You play the innocent act well, but I do not believe you."

Jose eyed the perimeter of the compound, growing closer and closer. He clutched the ripcord to his parachute. Counting down. Waiting as long as possible to deploy the chute, to minimize the chance of being seen in the sky. *Three. Two. One.*

Yank.

The silky nylon filled with air. Lines went taut. Straps jerked, jacking his nuts up somewhere around his ears. He pulled the guide ropes toward the ground. Very little reaction time for a HALO. The landing would come hard and fast. He kept his eyes up. Staring straight down at the ground for landing was actually counterproductive and would send him on his ass. Instead, he monitored the compound, noting positions of guards. Lights began to flicker on in the isolated compound.

He scanned the horizon, picking out the specks of the others slipping through the night sky. Through the trees. To the gritty earth. Wham. He felt the shock clean through. He tucked into a controlled landing…

Heels. Knees. Roll to his side. Shake off the stunned-stupid feel and get to work.

He cut free his chute lines and launched into a crouch, ready. His headset crackled to life again with Mr. Smith's gravelly voice, not Stella's smooth tones.

"One of our techies is working through Agent Carson's messages. Tap code indicates at least twenty rebels in the compound. Two guards in the front, three in back. Even the cook carries a gun."

Each piece of information that filtered through brought images of Stella, keeping her cool as she blinked or tapped out the information. Darting, he zigzagged toward the compound, staying low, submachine gun aimed, 9 mm holstered for backup. He made eye contact with Bubbles about ten feet away. The SEALs faded from sight as they surrounded all sides of the secured building.

A spotlight popped on, sweeping toward him. Jose dropped to his belly, flat into prickly dhirindhir brush. Beads of sweat tracked through the camo paint on his face.

"Shit," Mr. Jones's voice hissed through the earpiece, obviously deciphering bad news. "She said there are land mines at the gates. True entrances are hidden within the fence. Avoid the gates. I repeat, do not use the gates. Locate the camouflaged entrances, or as a last resort, climb over."

"Roger," he whispered, blinking his eyes clear of sweat.

The SEALs around back would deactivate the electric fence. Then they would have to move faster than fast. Flat to the ground, he waited, waited... And go.

He shot to his feet and tossed pebbles at the fence. No sparks. He risked a touch, found it cool, but didn't see any secret entrances on this side. Launching up, he scaled the fence, chain-link rattling in his hands. Bubbles kept pace beside him until they both vaulted over. He landed with a puff of dirt spurting from under his boots. His headset echoed with sounds of engagement on the other side.

As Stella had warned, he found the first of the east side guards. Bubbles raised his MP5. Aimed. Two barely perceptible *pop, pops* hissed, muffled by a silencer.

Bubbles lowered his submachine gun and tapped his headset. "Guards in front cleared."

Affirmatives echoed over the headsets. Finally, Smith's. Thank God. "Roger. Update on captives. Of the twelve taken captive, two dead, four wounded. Images show at least one is critical."

Not Stella, damn it.

Even as his instincts screamed at him to go after her now, his brain went on autopilot, training imprinted so deeply in his muscle memory his body reacted without thought. He flattened himself to walls, whipped around corners. The steady *slug, slug, slug* of his heart stayed even, in control. Reports echoed low in his headset, students secured. Both bodies retrieved. Four wounded, located, and loaded.

Only Stella remained, deep inside, in the interrogation room. Guarded. He reached for his weapon.

Bubbles was the first to shoot again.

Jose didn't have time to worry his reaction time might be off. He had to move, step over the downed guard, and pray when he and Bubbles opened the door and stormed the room that muscle memory training would be spot-on.

He plowed through and found… Stella. She sat tied to a chair in the middle of the room. Her wiry interrogator stood behind her with his fist in her hair, a knife at her throat.

Chapter 2

STELLA FOUGHT BACK THE URGE TO LAUNCH TOWARD JOSE.

The knife at her throat pressed an icy reminder of the need to hold very still. Her senses went on hyper-alert to the stench of her captor's garlic breath, the stickiness of his sweat, the steely press of ammo strapped to his chest.

Focus, damn it. She was a trained professional. That should be what carried her through. Instead she drew strength from the conviction in Jose's eyes. Somehow he'd found a detached professionalism that was deserting her. She ached to call out to him, even knowing she couldn't afford the least movement, not even the tremble of her lips as her mouth watered.

But she could soak up the sight of him.

Jose. Here, decked out in camo, survival gear, and pointing an MP5 directly at her captor. She'd expected him to be brought in to break her code, not participate in the actual rescue operation.

But he'd more than heard her. He'd come for her. For a split second the adrenaline poured from her toes. Every ache in her body throbbed to the surface. Every bruise. Scratch. Fear. And yes, even an aching vulnerability when it came to this man. All of it bundled together, firing inside her, then doused, pushed aside as she focused on survival. If he'd infiltrated the compound without setting off land mines, without a sound of alert, someone must have picked up on her codes.

Her codes.

She needed them now. She could blink without moving her throat, without alerting her captor behind her.

Simple Morse code. Something easy to understand.

She held Jose's deep chocolate eyes but found none of her former lover in those depths. He was still one hundred percent focused on the mission. As he should be. As *she* should be.

She blinked. *On three. One. Two. Three.*

Stella inched left, the slice of the blade cutting into her throat, but God, if Jose could just take the—

Shot.

Bullets whistled past her ear.

The hold around her eased, thank God. She pushed back into her guard's stomach and his arm fell away altogether. She toppled her chair in case Jose needed her clear to continue shooting. Her shoulder slammed the ground and she bit back a scream.

Still, a groan slipped between her gritted teeth. Jose charged over to her, yanked some kind of cloth from his pocket, and knotted it gently around her throat. It was okay. She was okay. He was alive and so was she. She gulped in air, breathing deeply for the first time since her captor had pressed that blade to her throat.

"I'm fine," she gasped while he untied her, the familiar scent of him settling her nerves with each shaky inhale.

"You will be."

"And the others?"

"Taken care of." He grabbed her elbow and eased her to her feet. "Let's go."

His touch seared her skin, his strength so welcome after the past three days—an eternity. She tucked closer to Jose's side for balance as spots danced in front of her eyes.

His burly pal Bubbles filled the doorway. He pivoted hard and took the lead. Jose looped an arm around her waist and hauled her with him.

So much for a heartfelt reunion. But then she had often accused Jose of being illogical. Now she couldn't complain when he did everything right to save her life. They didn't have time for a huggy, feel-good moment. She needed to think, to be sure everyone had been accounted for.

"Did you get everybody?" Stella pressed for details. "Even the two that are dead?"

The failure of their lost lives threatened to send her to her knees again.

"Two dead. Four injured," Bubbles clipped out. "The SEALs got 'em all."

"No, *five* injured. Thirteen hostages total. It was twelve plus me." She forced her mind to cycle through the events of the past three days, praying she wasn't confusing things in her exhaustion. "Did you clear the room where I was held? It's…"

"We know where it is. We saw your message."

She'd guessed right about the robotic fly. She hadn't been hallucinating. "Then let's go. Maybe the room beside it? But there were definitely at least five injured."

Bubbles raced from room to room, cell to cell, and appeared again so fast and silent they could have renamed him Ghost. Just when she'd given up hope, Bubbles came out with his arm hitched around the injured fella—Sutton Harper—steadying him. The tortured student dragged his leg behind, clutching his arm to his stomach. His blond curly hair was plastered to his head with grime, his hiking clothes damp with perspiration. But he was alive.

Jose pressed his finger to his headset, listening, then nodded. "All accounted for. No more waiting. We've got to roll if we're going to make the chopper pickup."

Sutton limped slower, groaning. "Go without me. Seriously, dude. I'm holding you back and that's a risk to Stella. You can send someone for me later."

"No can do." Bubbles powered on, hauling his patient.

Sutton nodded to Jose and Stella. "Then you two go. Take her and leave."

Stella shook her head. "We stay together."

Of course Sutton, an honest to God twenty-two-year-old student, an innocent in all of this, didn't know her role here and she sure as hell didn't intend to tell him. Knowing would only put him further at risk if they were unable to escape now. She was able to protect herself. In fact, her job included protecting him.

She turned to Jose. "Help him so we can move faster. I'll keep up." She willed herself to stand steely strong in spite of her aching ribs and throbbing shoulder. Exhaustion and hunger gnawed at her. "We don't have time to argue."

Hesitating for only a second, a second where his eyes flashed with frustration and urgency, Jose moved forward and hitched his shoulder under Sutton's other arm. "Let's roll out."

Stella ignored her own aches and focused on one foot in front of the other as Jose and his PJ teammate hauled Sutton through the narrow cinder block corridors, stepping over dead guards, ducking out into the courtyard.

Even the weak, last rays of the sun stung her eyes after three days inside in captivity. She blinked away spots. Her foot caught on a root protruding from the cracked earth. She flung out her arms to brace her fall. Her palms slapped the rough bark of a gnarled galool tree.

"Stella?" Jose called back over his shoulder, shooting an arm out.

"I'm good. The light blinded me for a second. Keep going."

Steady on her feet again, she dashed forward, catching up and keeping pace, running toward the oh-so-distant sound of helicopter blades slicing the air. How far to the helicopter pickup? Asking would only waste precious breath, and even if the chopper was miles away, she wouldn't slow down. This was an all-out race for their lives. Sure, the guards had been taken down, but reinforcements would be on their way soon. This particular separatist group was large, organized with the support of a powerful warlord.

And damn it, Jose was in the line of fire because of *her*. Fighting for professionalism was tougher than ever for her now, leaving her edgy, angry.

Scared.

The most dangerous emotion of all as it made them all vulnerable.

She'd selfishly begun this journey seeking information about her mother. Now she knew it was about lots of mothers and children, just as the VP's wife hoped to highlight in her visit. And while Stella wouldn't look away from facts about her mother if they came her way, she had a mission to complete.

Was the frenzy and the separatists' big "plan" all tied into the upcoming visit of the VP's wife? Her visit here, the causes she stood for, didn't sit well with many in the region.

And Jose had been drawn into the middle of this hell.

He stopped shy of the gate, adjusting his hold on Sutton. "Bubbles, you crawl over and I'll hoist him up to you."

The land mines. Of course. God, how horrifically ironic if she'd lost focus now when she was so close to escape.

Jose looked back at her. "We're almost home free. Once we're past the fence, it's only a couple of minutes to the helicopter pickup." He cupped her shoulder and squeezed. "Hold tight, Stel, okay?"

For that moment, he was her Jose again, the feel of his hand so familiar her body reacted by instinct, swaying toward him. God, she'd missed him. Even if they weren't a couple anymore, at least she would have the chance to take back some of the horrible things she'd said to him. And the faster they got away from this place, the sooner she could start on that.

"I'm not even close to giving out. Lead. I'll follow." As if to bolster her, the wind carried the sound of the approaching helicopter. No doubt searching for a barren spot of sandy earth to land. This place was such a mix of rain forests and desert with dying trees. Contradictions of lush history and cruel corruption. She'd hoped to help tip the scales in favor of the good. Now she just wanted to stay alive.

The echo of helicopter blades cutting the air *whomp, whomp, whomped* closer.

Sutton went wild-eyed for a second. From delirium or hope? He broke away from Jose and charged toward the gate.

Right toward the section she'd overheard a guard say was booby-trapped.

Panicking, Stella screamed, "No! Land mines!"

Jose catapulted toward Sutton, whose frenzy had somehow overcome his pain. Jose held the guy's legs, pinning him as Bubbles climbed back over the fence to help.

Sutton thrashed with a frenetic energy. "Get off me. Get off me now!"

Was he suffering from combat trauma because of their time here in the compound? The student cycled with his feet, hiking boots sending pebbles and rocks spewing across the path.

Onto the land mines.

Ah hell.

She covered her head a second before…

The explosion shook the ground. Ripples concussed the air, slamming her back to the rocky earth. Bubbles flew through the air and landed on his back with an "oof."

And Jose? Oh God, where was he? She squinted, peering through the dust poofing upward. A shape took form a hand's reach away, familiar, rangy, and masculine. Alive and already rolling to his feet again. The downed fenced lay just at their feet, only inches shy of crushing them.

Relief sang through her as loud as the ringing in her ears. She cradled her head in her hands and fought vertigo. She swallowed hard, trying to clear the pressure crackling, popping.

Damn it. She sat up straighter, pushing through the pain to listen.

Gunfire echoed in the distance—backup for them or the separatists?

Jose pressed his hand to his headset. Listening? "No more time. The chopper has to bail—and so do we." His face went dark as he tapped the earpiece. "I'm losing contact. Damn it."

Sutton sat holding his head. "What do you mean?"

"Chopper's gone. They're taking fire. They can't wait any longer and risk everyone else on board. That's all I got before the headset shorted out." Jose hauled Sutton to his feet. "We run and evade until they can come back."

The chopper was gone? Her stomach lurched, her heart *rat-tat-tatting* like the gunfire.

Sutton swayed, his knees buckling as his eyes rolled back in his head. Jose tucked his shoulder into the injured student's gut and hefted him into a fireman's carry. Sutton's arms hung limp, his whole body slack with unconsciousness.

Jose turned to his teammate. "Bubbles, lead the way."

"Roger that, Cuervo."

Not even wincing at the extra hundred and sixty pounds of unconscious student, Jose picked his way around the rubble toward the gaping hole in the fence—the only blessing from the explosion.

Gunfire grew louder, closer. The outer realm of security was engaging. Jose was right. They needed to bail. How ironic that she'd always been the one pointing out the logic, the reasons they were perfect together, and how their future fit. He was the wildly impulsive one. The romantic.

Yet here and now, he was keeping his cool, completely in the moment. *She* wanted to lose it, to scream over the danger she'd put him in.

And yet she'd done what she had to in order to get the innocent students out. She would do the same again.

If only she'd had time to learn more about the group's agenda.

Local government officials had pleaded with the UN for help. Intel on the warlord indicated he wanted control of an already unstable region. They had pirates on their side operating as rogue mercenaries, funding their operations and splitting the profits. If they gained control, the area would be at the mercy of a brutal totalitarian regime where the rights of children and women would become nonexistent… There were so many horrific scenarios for what they could have in mind and she'd only begun to scratch the surface.

But if she'd been there longer, she would be dead. She had to focus on one thing only now: keeping her head on straight and staying alive.

———

Jose resisted the urge to rub his five-year sobriety coin again.

Hyenas seemed to mock him in the distance as he trekked farther and farther from the compound, deeper into the night to keep Stella safe. Everything he'd bottled up steamrolled him. This day had been—hell. And it wasn't over.

The weight of the student didn't drag him down. He'd trained with heavier, once carrying hulking Bubbles for ten miles. But the burden of how close he'd come to

losing Stella back there? That threatened to send him
to his knees.

Damn it all, he should be celebrating getting her out.
If things had gone according to plan, she would be in a
doctor's care being checked over and eating real food
rather than a prepackaged protein bar. She should be in a
safe compound, rather than in the wilds of Africa with the
guttural growl of lions echoing in the distance. She should
be heading off to sleep in a bed with fresh sheets—

He stopped those thoughts short. He would be better
off not thinking about Stella and sheets.

She was alive. He needed to concentrate on keeping
her that way until he could load her onto a rescue chopper. She had to be maxed out after her time in captivity.
Shifting the student more securely over his shoulder,
Jose shot a quick glance left to check on Stella. She
marched alongside him, pale but steady as she swacked
a stick ahead of her to check for warthogs and other
African jungle beasties. To clear for scorpions and
snakes. Vermin as lethal as her captors.

What exactly had she been through? What had she
endured in the days before the surveillance cameras had
been flown into her cell?

Bile rose in his throat again, and he pushed down the
lurking question that threatened to drown him. Stella was
a survivor. She had pocketed a small arsenal of weapons
out of the artifacts. He had to focus on the survivor part
of her, the professional part, because allowing himself
to dwell on the personal… on the essence of Stella…

Hell. Back to the work side of her, the part that had
carried her through this nightmare and whatever shook
down. He'd always admired her dedication to her job.

When they'd been dating he'd thought he found the perfect woman. One as tied to work as he was. She would understand his call to serve and he understood hers. But it turned out she wanted the one thing from him he couldn't give.

So many regrets slammed over him, yet he couldn't ignore the fact that today he could have lost even the comfort of knowing she was alive. Sure, it tore him up thinking about her building a future with someone else, but that pain was nothing compared to the hell of envisioning her dead. The crushing hell he would have lived with if he'd arrived too late.

Shit.

Bubbles slowed as they neared a muddy stream and stopped under the umbrella of a leafy higlo tree. "Time for a breather."

"I'm good," Jose insisted and he was—physically. It was his brain that was about to explode. "Stella?"

"I'm all right," she insisted, then swayed on her feet.

"Damn it." Jose shifted the student over to Bubbles in a flash.

His teammate assumed the burden without hesitation and settled the dude against the tree trunk. "We're safe here for now. I'll check over the student. You take care of Stella."

"Jose?" Her whisper carried on the night air with the distant chirrup of a cheetah. Stella jolted. "We shouldn't stop. I can do this. I don't want to hold you back or make us a target."

Dark circles stained under her eyes, but sharp attention sparked as she scanned past the tree to the wild dogs lapping from the shallow stream.

Even now, she was worried about him. Regardless of

what she'd been through, the lack of food and sleep, she was ready to kick ass again with the help of a protein bar. She was every bit as incredible as he remembered, indomitable. And alive.

To hell with objectivity.

He gripped her shoulders, and without another thought, he hauled her to his chest. He held her vibrant and whole body against his. He buried his face in her hair that still held the barest hint of her eucalyptus shampoo in spite of the hellish few days.

"God, Stella, I didn't think you were going to make it out of there." His voice rasped in his throat, each word, every emotion grating through him like broken glass. Each word sliced him so tangibly he could have sworn he saw the starlight glinting off the shards.

"You made it in time." She pressed her forehead to his chest, her fists gripping his survival vest.

"You called."

"I can't believe you're here." She trembled in his arms.

His body zeroed into just the feel of her against him and for a few seconds he allowed himself to forget she needed him to be a different kind of man. To forget they were in the middle of nowhere. To forget he still had tough questions to ask her.

A cleared throat had him pulling back. Even keeping a steadying palm on her waist, his arms already felt empty without her.

The injured student—now clearly awake—whistled lowly in the dark. His back against the trunk, Sutton Harper half grinned, despite his injuries. "I take it you two already know each other? Because if not, I'm feeling shortchanged on the post-rescue TLC."

Jose shot a scowl at Bubbles for failing to alert him that their extra passenger was back in the land of consciousness. Bubbles shrugged. The trumpet of elephants blasted in the distance. The wild dogs twitched their satellite large ears before sprinting off in a streak of mottled fur.

Stella pressed a hand to her chest. "You're awake. Thank God you're all right, Sutton."

"Anybody got food?"

Bubbles leaned over him, checking the cut above his eyebrow. "This isn't a 7-Eleven, dude."

Jose gathered his scrambled thoughts and elaborated for his not-too-chatty friend. "What he means to say is that he needs to check you over first. You were unconscious for a long time. We can take a few more minutes, but then we need to find somewhere to hunker down for the night."

Stella handed Sutton a canteen. "Maybe some water would help?"

"Yeah, that would be good." Sutton took a swallow and passed it back. "Tell your boyfriend thanks."

Her hand shook as she swept stray hairs back from her face. "Old friend."

The guy held out his uninjured hand. "Well color me lucky. I'm Sutton Harper, and to whom do I owe my life and my firstborn child? She called you Jose, right?"

He simply grunted, easing back from Stella, keeping an arm around her waist. Names weren't passed around in his or Stella's professions and he would prefer the less known about her life, the better.

Harper lifted an eyebrow at his curt response. "How cool to have an on-call military boyfriend if you happen to be kidnapped by warlords in a foreign country. Kinda coincidental for a simple student, don't you think?"

Unease iced up his spine.

Stella stepped aside. "I guess I'm just a really lucky lady. Your good fortune too, to be kidnapped with me, don't you think?"

Bubbles passed the student a protein bar. Damn good distraction and a reminder they had practical concerns.

Jose studied Harper, noting his pale face and twisted ankle. A few superficial bruises and some scratches, but no stitches needed after all. Butterfly bandages would take care of what he could see. Granted, not all torture left visible marks and there could be more injuries under his clothes. But right now he was wondering if the student had flipped, giving over information... Except what did he know?

He damn well didn't need to learn anything more. "I think we need to stop chitchatting and find somewhere to park ourselves until our next ride rolls around."

"Next ride?" Harper sat up straighter and scrubbed his sleeve over his sweaty brow. "So you dudes really do have a plan B. That's a relief. Preferably something that doesn't bail on us when it gets a little hot."

What the hell? Saving this fella's ass had cost them those precious seconds. If the student hadn't panicked and set off the land mine, they could have made it to the rendezvous point, and they wouldn't have brought a slew of forces charging right at them.

Jose forced a smile. "You sure are picky for someone who just got rescued."

"Chalk it up to nerves. Makes me mouthy. Sorry to be an ingrate. Thanks for the Rambo moment." The student's voice rang with sincerity, easing some of the tension. "What can I do to help now since I've been a total slug so far?"

"Can you walk on your own or do you still need to be carried?" Jose turned to Stella. "And you? Are you sure there aren't any medical issues I need to know about?"

She tucked a strand of hair behind her ear with a shaky hand. He sensed a brittleness in her from her efforts to hang on to professionalism to the end. And pride, he saw that too in her eyes, a defensive wall she'd erected between them because of how they'd ended things. He scratched the ache lodged in his chest—not that he expected any relief from the pain of losing her, from the teeth-grinding frustration of knowing he wasn't the right man to give her what she needed.

Sutton cricked his neck from side to side. "Isn't there a boyfriend/girlfriend conflict of interest in you treating her?" He held up his hands. "What? I'm standing, ready to walk."

Bubbles coughed once, flicking a fuzzy caterpillar off his arm in disgust. "Quiet's a beautiful thing."

"Fair enough." Sutton raised his hands again. "I'm embracing the chi of quiet."

Jose slid an arm around Stella's waist for support, nothing more. She'd made that clear enough when she broke things off with him. There could never be anything more.

—◆—

Stella wasn't sure she could take much more.

She understood they needed to get far away from the

compound. The place would undoubtedly be crawling with bad guys. She prayed they assumed everyone had flown out in the chopper, but they couldn't count on that.

Still, Jose was making damn sure their tracks were covered. Now Bubbles had Sutton over his shoulder, the student's ankle having given out after five minutes of hobbling.

They were all business—and her brain was still locked on that impulsive hug from Jose. For that moment, she'd forgotten all about their fight and the fact that he didn't want to build a real life with her. She could only lose herself in the undeniable connection they shared, a chemistry that could too easily make her lose her objectivity when she needed it most.

Stella stepped alongside him as they trekked through the scrub brush, around acacia trees, the thorny branches reaching out like gnarled witch's fingers. "Is it safe to talk?"

"For now," Jose said, jabbing a stick at the high grasses for snakes, keeping his eyes on the horizon. "Just keep it low. Stay on the lookout. If we're lucky, they don't even know we're out here. They'll think we all got away in the helicopter."

"That's what I'm hoping." She leaped over another protruding root. "I can hardly believe you're really here."

"You sent for me," Jose answered, eyes ahead, searching through the night.

That she had. Guilt scuttled around inside her again, like the lizard scrabbling up a tree trunk, but she knew she would do the same again.

"I wasn't sure the message would be picked up." She was careful to keep her voice low so Sutton wouldn't hear the details. "I wasn't even sure they would understand the message if it did go through."

"They didn't understand."

"But you did." She'd suspected and now she knew for sure. "Because of that time we slipped away to a hotel along the Nile River, and in the restaurant I blinked Morse code to get you to…"

"Proposition me. Yeah. Pretty much."

She stumbled and he caught her elbow. She forced a smile. "Keep going. I'm okay."

Not really. Three days of limited food and sleep deprivation was taking its toll, but she couldn't give in. She couldn't let her guard down for a second when even a racing ostrich could be dangerous.

"You can do it." He slid his arm around her waist with the familiar ease of a lover. "One foot in front of the other, like the snowman in that kiddy movie."

"With legs like melting snow." She laughed on a gasp.

His arm went tighter, pulling her more firmly against his side, muscles moving against her in perfect synch. So familiar. So sensuous. "Do you need me to carry you?"

"No." The pain of remembering how good it was with Jose was almost more than her exhaustion-stretched body could withstand. If he took her in his arms, she could well say something she would regret. "No need. I. Can. Hold. On."

"You're amazing, woman. Now let's get the hell out of here."

Had he brushed a kiss over the top of her head or was that just the heat of his breath, of his words? She was likely starting to hallucinate as her body gave out after all she'd been through.

Her side hurt from the pace. How far had they gone? A mile at least and she wasn't carrying another human as Jose had done earlier and like Bubbles was doing now. Even as Jose helped her, he wasn't even breathing heavy as perspiration sealed their clothes to their skin. His buddy Bubbles—the PJ with a fuzzy phobia— cleared the path ahead, Sutton bobbing unconscious again over his shoulder.

They pushed through more scrub brush, past a fat buffalo thorn tree that jutted at awkward angles as if desperately searching for a drop of rain. Deeper and farther they trekked. No sound of the helicopter. No sound of gunfire, just the faraway snort of animals—a rhino or buffalo maybe. And the sound of her labored breathing, the crunch of their footsteps.

Okay, *her* footsteps.

The two superhumans barely made a noise even as they charged ahead full steam. Their hard-muscled bodies moved in sleek stealth mode into nigh wrapping around them all like a humid blanket. Or was she losing consciousness? She gripped Jose's vest tighter to anchor herself to his side, use him like a crutch.

One more step, she told herself time and time again.

Finally, they stopped.

She almost missed the fact she wasn't walking anymore since the world seemed to be spinning. They were standing in a small clump of Acacia trees with twisted trunks. Branches spoked like an umbrella, creating a shadowy cave of sorts.

Bubbles slid his burden to the ground, then sagged

back against a gnarled trunk, gasping for a second before he dropped to his knees beside Sutton. He shrugged out of his pack and pulled out medic gear.

The student was in good hands.

Stella pried her numb fingers from Jose's vest and slid to the dusty ground. Sitting cross-legged, too tired to move, she allowed herself to look her fill at the man she'd thought she would never see again. With smooth efficiency, Jose gathered broken branches, snapping off longer ones to make shelter. He showed no signs of slowing, only his bloodied uniform and the streaks of sweat through his camo paint, testified to all they'd been through this evening.

Lean, with a whipcord strength, he had a runner's body—a by-product of marathons he ran in addition to his special operations military training. He'd told her once he used intense running regimes to help him fight a drinking problem. While he'd been sober for five years, he still attended AA meetings and ran. And ran.

His body shouted health and vitality and pure sensuality. She'd wanted him the second she'd seen his angular good looks. She wanted to stroke her hands over his sleek black hair and test the texture between her fingertips.

Her eyelids grew heavy, and so easily she could envision just falling asleep, knowing he would keep her safe. But damn it, she had to pull her weight for as long as she could. She had a job to do and she'd already asked too much of Jose today.

She struggled to stay conscious a few minutes longer. "We're camping here? What can I do?"

"Nothing for now. We'll only be here for tonight. The beacon on my tracker will bring help as soon as it's safe—hopefully by morning. Meanwhile, we evade." He dug into his survival vest, plucked out another protein bar, and pitched it to her. "The best way you can help is get your strength back up."

Her mouth watered. She didn't have to think twice about the wisdom of this. She tore open the wrapper with her teeth and bit into the nutty chocolate bar. Forcing herself to chew slowly, she swallowed down the first bite and resisted the urge to gobble the thing whole.

Even with the protein bar earlier, she had a long way to go before she felt full again. "What about your headset? Is it working at all?"

"It cut out completely just after the explosion." He used fishing twine from his vest to tie three limbs together into a tripod tall enough for a small lean-to.

"But you touched your ear and said we needed to run. I thought you got instructions…" She shook her head, trying to piece together those crazy few minutes after the land mine blew, how he'd said something about the headset shorting out. "Bubbles? Is yours working?"

"Nope."

Stella gripped her head in frustration. "Would you care to elaborate?"

"Nope," Bubbles answered.

Sutton propped up on one elbow, scrubbing a hand over his groggy face. "I would hate to be stranded on a deserted island with him."

Still, it was beyond incredible they'd gotten out of there at all. She looked into Jose's deep brown eyes, the shade even darker chocolate in the night. He reached to clean the nick on her neck from the guard's knife earlier. She'd forgotten in the harried drive to escape.

The glide of Jose's fingers along her skin was bittersweet pleasure. Even the antiseptic sting couldn't dull the pleasure. Her mind was too weary to put up boundaries, and her thoughts raced back to another time she'd seen him fresh from the field—a mission rescuing two fishermen captured by pirates and held hostage. Sweat plastered his coal black hair to his head. He'd hauled on camo, but it was clear he hadn't showered since the swim. His rangy body had been taut with residual tension from the mission. He was intense and mesmerizing and hot as hell. They'd had great sex...

Still, in the end they'd broken up in a heartrending argument that left her shattered. So much so, she feared she'd let her emotions cloud her professional judgment. That somehow she'd been off her game because of the breakup. That she was responsible for the kidnapping and loss of life.

Even now, they'd missed the chopper. Sure, Sutton's freak-out had slowed them down, but had her exhaustion been a factor as well? Damn it, she had to keep her emotional distance.

And that included keeping her hands to herself.

She clenched her fingers together as Jose repacked his medic gear. She scanned their little makeshift camp. Bubbles cleaned up a scrape on Sutton's head. Jose draped a whisper thin camouflage tarp over the stick tripod he'd built earlier, his movements and the shelter barely perceptible in the shifting night shadows.

He looked up sharply. She bit her lip, a flush burning her face at being caught staring at him so openly. "Uhm, I was thinking..."

"Stella?" he interrupted, whispering, stalking

toward her with a leopard-like grace. "Don't. Move. Truck's approaching."

Before she processed the words, he'd stretched over her, melding their bodies together as he pushed her to the ground.

Chapter 3

JOSE'S HARD MUSCLED BODY PRESSED HER INTO THE DUST.

Stella froze while a Land Rover jostled along a rugged path nearby, shocks squeaking. A jagged rock dug into her cheek, but she barely dared breathe much less inch away. Jose had sent up the alert about the vehicle mere seconds before the headlights peeked through the brush. If he'd heard the truck any later, they could have been discovered.

Adrenaline seared her veins again, different from earlier when they'd hugged. Edgier. That was about tender relief. This was about survival. Raw feelings. Instincts. Her body responded to his on a primal level.

And neither of them had so much as moved a muscle.

The 4x4 drove closer, the sound of grinding gears overpowering all other night sounds. Each slow, shallow breath mingled with the scent of baked earth and musky man. Her heart pulsed so hard, Jose had to feel it just as she felt the steady beat of his pounding against her shoulder. Was it her imagination, or had their hearts synced up in this elemental moment? Or was it only that they were both so in tune because of their training?

Except right now, her feelings for him were nowhere near detached and professional.

The light swept over them... and past. Still, she didn't dare move. Not yet. Seconds blended into minutes and even longer. Relief tingled over her like a sunburn, sending every nerve hyper aware. The urge to flip over and wrap her arms around Jose was damn near impossible to resist. But if she held him, she knew it would lead to a kiss this time, a line neither of them could afford to cross.

And if she wasn't mistaken, he was every bit as aware, every bit as *aroused*, as she was.

Then the heavy night air swept over her as he rolled aside and into a crouch. The taillights faded along with the sound of the misfiring engine. The danger had passed. For now. The truck could have been a threat or it could have been anyone. Regardless, it served as a reminder she couldn't let her guard down for even a second. It wasn't fair to rely on the guys. They had enough on their plates keeping everyone alive. Bubbles had already gone back to treating Sutton, leaving Stella and Jose paired off.

She searched for something benign to say, anything other than the too personal and vulnerable thoughts plaguing her. "How were you able to talk and run so easily all that time? Even for a marathon racer, this was intense."

"Bubbles and I have been pulling overtime on Wii Fit."

He delivered his answer with such a deadpan face, she almost missed his attempt to lighten the mood of a hellish day. A laugh burst free, then another until her laughter verged on hysteria. But she couldn't stop. It was as if someone had pulled the plug holding in all her emotions, and now they flowed out, the fear, the pain, the relief, all mingling together and pouring free. She sat back on her butt and held her aching ribs.

And God bless him, Jose seemed to understand. He

didn't say a word to stop her. He didn't even look at her like she was nuts—the way Sutton was eyeing her as Bubbles disinfected cuts and assessed bruises. But then Jose knew her, he understood her, even if he didn't want a future with her.

A month into her relationship with Jose, she'd confessed she loved him, that she'd fallen for him the first time she saw him and wanted to spend forever together. He'd said he felt the same—but she fast realized their ideas of settling down were vastly different. At first, she'd deluded herself into believing he simply wasn't ready for the white picket fence and a couple of kids because he was two years younger than she was. She wanted to believe with time he would come around to her way of thinking. Building a family someday was everything to her.

Apparently he didn't really feel the same, not in the ways that counted. Could he really expect to stay in this high-octane sort of rescue environment until the day he died? She couldn't and she'd told him so.

Her daddy had always said not to make ultimatums unless you could live with either answer.

She scrubbed her wrist over her cheeks, swiping away grimy tears. "Sorry about that."

"You're okay," Jose said simply, keeping that wall between them.

"Thanks to you I'm okay." She wished there could be some kind of middle ground between them, a way to—what? Stay friends? That wasn't possible and she knew it. Being around him reminded her of those lost dreams, and that simply hurt too much.

"Not just me." He brushed aside her thanks. "We all worked together."

Sutton snapped his fingers, leaning back against a fat tree trunk. "Uhm, hello? I don't mean to sound ungrateful. Where I'm sitting we're stuck out in the middle of nowhere so the rescue thing still feels iffy."

Bubbles looked up from spreading out medical supplies to stitch a gash in Sutton's arm. "Wanna go back?"

"You're a comedian." Sutton winced at the press of an antiseptic wipe.

"Not really," Bubbles said.

"Then why the hell do they call you Bubbles?"

Jose tossed smaller branches and leaves along the tarp to add to the camo effect. "Ever heard of irony?"

Needing to put space between herself and Jose, Stella pushed to her feet and gathered Sutton's gear Bubbles had haphazardly tossed aside during treatment. She folded his shirt sleeve that had been cut away to expose the torn flesh—a by-product of flying debris from the land mine explosion. Sure, the fabric was nothing more than a rag now, but nothing could be wasted, not as long as they were on the run. She hefted up Sutton's backpack.

"Uhm, hello again?" Sutton started to lean forward only to stop short when Jose held him in place for stitching. "That's mine."

"Sorry, buddy, but we need to pool supplies." She unzipped the bag—and found a pile of artifacts inside.

Had he been gathering tools as she had? She eyed a pottery shard, a hammered steel amulet. And a folded cotton kanga cloth, with the traditional script along the border. She smoothed her hand along the finely woven fabric, rubbing it like a talisman, as if she could somehow absorb whatever inspirational message had been traditionally included.

"Hey," Sutton called out. "Can I have my bag?"

Jose looked up sharply. "Keep your voice down. Evading isn't evading if you forget to whisper."

Suspicions nipped at Stella as she thought of the student's stash and his quick assessment of her earlier as a possible spy. Her fingers gripped the fabric for a final second before she set aside the backpack. She needed to help Jose set up camp so she could eat and sleep. Store strength in case their time waiting out in the wilds lasted longer than a few hours.

And as she stared at Jose, she couldn't escape the notion they were both running away from the massive emotional fallout simmering just beneath the surface. That could be deadly for both of them, especially when they couldn't be certain how long they would be stuck out here together. She would have to find time to talk to him tonight, later when the others were asleep, and clear the air once and for all.

~~~

Back pressed to the tree trunk, Jose sat watch while the others slept. He monitored his charges for the millionth time.

The student was curled up under the lean-to clutching his backpack. Bubbles dozed sitting up against the other side of the tree. No doubt, he could be fully awake, weapon drawn in a millisecond.

And Stella.

She curled at the front of the shelter, unofficially adding a layer of protection for the student. Once Sutton had drifted off, she'd slipped the rectangular kanga cloth out from under her shirt—the same embroidered cloth she'd found in the student's pack earlier. She shook it out over herself, adding another layer of camo to her creamy skin. Her red ponytail splashed over her face, hairs lifting with each exhale.

Yeah, he'd volunteered to take the first shift.

He couldn't have even catnapped anyway. His body was too hepped up from touching Stella again. The unplanned hug was one thing. But that moment when he'd stretched over her, protecting her even though it was clear she could protect herself… The texture of her hair over his hands and her familiar curves stirred him all over again.

Shit.

He rested his submachine gun on his knee, eyes scanning the landscape of trees and shadows. Night sounds echoed around them, birds and insects. An occasional growl of something wilder.

His gaze slid back to Stella—and he found her staring at him. Her green eyes glinted in the dark like a magnificent cat. He'd protected her as best he could today. Now he had one last role to fill, being certain, absolutely certain, she wasn't hiding anything from him about her capture, hiding an injury, toughing things out rather than asking for help.

He set his MP5 aside and touched the ground next to him.

She didn't even hesitate. The cotton kanga cloth slithered from her body and she scooped it up, before sliding over to sit by him. She shook out the woven fabric in her hands, the rusty red and gold coloring blending into the landscape as they settled over her legs. Smart woman, always thinking.

Jose angled his head to hers. "Don't let Harper Sutton see you with his…"

"Sutton Harper," she corrected, nodding toward the snoring twenty-two-year-old.

"Right. Don't let him see you playing with his stuff."

"It's not his. It was part of the stash at the compound." She toyed with the fringe along the edges of the kanga that reminded him too much of their last weekend together when he'd bought a similar cloth for her. "But it would be a shame to waste its camouflaging potential."

"True that." He couldn't avoid the question any longer. He had to ask, "You would tell me, right?"

She looked up sharply. "Tell you what?"

"If they hurt you back there. If you're injured in ways that aren't readily visible… Or if you were assaulted." The last word brought more shards of glass up his throat.

She clasped his hand. "Jose, I would tell you. But I wasn't assaulted. They had a very specific purpose in their questioning. I don't know what they would have done to try and intimidate me, and I don't know specifics on what they did to the others. But they believed me to be a low threat, so I was left for last. You got there in time."

Thank God.

His head fell and his eyes squeezed shut tight with relief. She squeezed his hand hard again as more of that relief racked his body.

Once he trusted himself to speak again, he asked, "And what about other injuries? Noticing anything new now that the adrenaline's gone?"

"I'm sore, and I'm exhausted. We weren't fed well. But I'm telling the truth. None of the injuries are life threatening. Lying about that could only hold you back later."

"We're not out of the woods—so to speak."

"As far as I'm concerned this is a serious improvement." She laughed softly.

He touched her cheek. Just her cheek, nothing anywhere near as intimate as that impulsive hug earlier or the thousands of other caresses they'd exchanged. She eased away self-consciously and tugged at her hair band. Shaking her hair free, she threaded her fingers through and swept it back again.

His hands ached with the need to do that for her. His body throbbed with an even greater need to settle her in his lap and hold her through the night.

A crackle in the distance had him on his feet in a low crouch before he'd even fully registered the sound. His hand went to his gun. More of that muscle memory from training taking over, sending his body on autopilot.

Do whatever it took to keep Stella alive. Never had his pararescue motto been so blazingly in the forefront of his mind. *These things we do, that others may live.*

The fat moon sent light streaming through the branches. The tall grasses and scrub brush rustled... A cheetah darted past. Stella went steely still, the best reaction. A shot could bring worse than a jungle cat already disappearing from sight.

Exhaling hard, she shrugged. "My nerves are a little ragged."

"You're incredibly composed considering all you've been through." He offered her the opening to share more if she needed, to speak at her own pace rather than him asking.

She leaned back against the tree, shoulder to shoulder with him. "I'd damn well better be able to keep myself together."

"You're not a machine." And neither was he. It took all his self-control not to pull her onto his lap and rub her back until she slept in his arms. "You've held your own the past few days and tonight. Remind me never to piss you off."

"You already did," she said wryly, before looking away. "I wondered if I would ever see you again. I wanted the chance to tell you... Well, doesn't matter now."

"What doesn't matter?" he pressed. "We have all night."

"It's best we don't go there, not now." Her face closed up fast. "I had thought we could use this time to talk some things through, but I'm realizing this isn't the time or the place to go into that after all. I just can't afford to risk losing it. Not now. I have to focus everything on keeping myself together until we're out of here."

He pulled back, raising his hands. "Okay, okay."

"I apologize," she deflated. "I'm just on edge. I was really starting to lose hope back at the compound."

He could see she was about to crumble now. She needed an outlet of some sort, comfort, but she wouldn't want his comfort. So he opted for something she would accept. Humor.

"Sorry if we didn't mobilize a major rescue operation quickly enough for you."

A smile tugged the sides of her cracked lips. "I'm an ingrate, aren't I?"

He passed her lip balm from his survival vest. "Olive branch?"

She touched her lips. "Are you saying I look like hell?"

"You look... alive." That one word was everything.

Slowly, she took the lip balm from his hand and slicked it over her mouth. She put the cap back on with careful precision. "Alive is definitely a bonus today, one I wasn't sure I would get."

His eyes held on her mouth, the night and frenzy of what they'd been through gathering in his gut, making him thirsty for a taste of her.

He wanted to hold onto his sobriety coin right now so damn bad. "How did they capture you?"

Shadows chased through her green eyes, like clouds over the midnight moon. "I got careless."

"I know you. You're never careless. I'm the impulsive one."

She shook her head. "It's my fault two people died. I should have done something."

"It's not all about you, babe, and trust me, you don't have a corner on the market when it comes to second-guessing yourself." He toyed with the end of her ponytail, tugging lightly. "Hey, where's the Stella I know? The tough cookie who chewed me out a few minutes ago because I didn't show up earlier?"

"That was just the hypoglycemia talking. I missed breakfast. Low blood sugar and all." She rolled the lip balm between her palms, back and forth. "Give me a glass of OJ and I'll be my normal chipper self again."

"Chipper?" He snorted softly. "Not a word I would think could be found on any of your agency psych profiles."

"Psych shmike." Her slicked lips went tight. "It's my job to pretend to be the person of the day. Maybe chipper wasn't on the menu... And speaking of menus, I could really use something more to eat. I wasn't joking about the low blood sugar."

"Another protein bar?"

"I'm so hungry I'll even eat that." She extended her palm, her fingernails cracked and torn.

He passed over a peanut butter crunch bar and not for the first time wished he had more to offer her. "You still haven't told me how you got captured."

"I'll talk in debrief." She tore open the wrapper. "You don't have a need to know."

She bit off a quarter of the bar and chewed, making it quite clear she wasn't saying a word more than she wanted. And that fast he saw her find that strength he'd been nudging her for, except she used it to put space between them. Shutters went up in her green eyes and she crab walked toward the lean-to with the rest of her protein bar.

What wasn't she telling him?

His mind churned with horrors and he had no one to blame but himself that he'd given up the right to press her for answers.

Ajaya curled up under the floor of the compound where they'd held those American students captive.

His muscles were cramping, but he didn't dare get up even though he'd stopped hearing American soldiers stomp around hours ago. Now the revolutionaries had come crawling in afterward, searching. If they found him, they would make him join up again. Shoot people. Get shot at. The punishment for disobeying…?

His throat burned with puke.

Sweat trickled down his head and into the mud, sticky from the perspiration pouring off his body from more than heat. A scorpion scrabbled past him fast and he didn't so much as flinch. He was scared to death. Not of the lethal sting. He was scared to hope he could escape today.

No more beatings. No more blood.

He'd been taken from the orphan school eight months ago, forced to join their "army." His first kill had been with a knife. Then they'd rewarded him with a gun. Every time they made him shoot, made him kill, he vowed to be the best so he could turn the weapon on them one day. He imagined what it would have been like to have this gun earlier to protect his mother, his sister, and little brother before they died, along with his father. He would have used that gun to take his family somewhere safe.

Ajaya came from a Sanskrit word, *jaya*, victorious. Unconquered.

What a joke.

He was cowering in this stinky cubby like a scared rabbit. The past eight months hadn't made him stronger. They had only made him desperate to escape this kind of life. He would do anything to make that happen. Even if that meant letting them go through with their plan to murder hundreds of people at the embassy? Right now he thought yes, he could even do that.

The American soldiers that stormed the compound speaking English and shooting guards, they didn't know what they'd taken with them. He'd watched through a crack. They'd stuffed stolen artifacts in their clothes and packs, maybe to protect themselves, maybe to sell. The

Americans had no idea what the bastards would do once they realized what the Americans had really taken. It wouldn't be long either since it would be the first thing they looked for. They were already tearing apart the compound now, searching for it, the key to their plans to set off something horrible at the American embassy.

Except it wasn't here. If he could find it, he finally would have something of value, something he could sell, a ticket out.

He was scared, but he had skills now and he had an advantage. He knew which way those four Americans had gone. If he could find them first, he could get what he needed and barter it for enough money to get away. He would leave Africa and go to India and study Sanskrit. He would be a student, not a soldier.

Although first, he had to be a soldier just a little while longer. Ajaya clutched his rifle to his chest and focused on images of his mother, his sister, and little brother. He envisioned them alive, leaving with him.

A lot more comforting than remembering their dead, bloody bodies as he'd hidden in the scrub brush, stuffing a fist in his mouth to stifle his screams.

And he realized he wasn't a scared rabbit now after all. He was a cornered lion, ready to kill.

Chapter 4

STELLA CURLED UP WITH THE WOVEN CLOTH AROUND her, determined to sleep, knowing she needed to store strength in case they had to evade for any length of time.

Her head resting on the crook of her arm, she hugged the cottony fabric tighter around her again. It seemed wrong to use something so beautiful, so carefully woven, for protection against night crawlies, but she was practical. She needed to rest, so she cocooned herself in the rectangular kanga.

Not that sleep came easy. She could have blamed it on her micronap earlier, or the fact that violent forces could stumble on them at any minute. Except she knew the real cause of her restlessness sat a few feet away. Jose. The feel of his arms around her lingered. His unexpected hug had rocked her to her toes, making her question all of her so-called resolutions to stay away from him forever. Even trying to clear the air had her heart in her throat and she'd balked.

She'd held strong against the urge to contact him for the past month because she'd known seeing him would hurt. A lot. There'd been no way to foresee how much. She needed to accept there would be no easy break-off, no way to clear regrets. She needed to move on. She wasn't fool enough to think she could change him. He said he didn't want to settle down. He absolutely did not want children because of his own messed up childhood with an alcoholic mother. Because of his fears about staying sober himself. Even though he'd been dry for five years, he was convinced he couldn't risk having kids.

Nothing she said had changed his mind, and she couldn't keep lying to herself. Whether he'd been telling the truth or concocting an excuse he knew would make her run, he'd pushed her away and he'd meant it.

She wrapped her heart up again, as tightly as she wrapped her body in the patterned fabric, tracing her fingers along the scripted border. She would keep up her guard when she was with Jose. But here, in her dreams, she could think back to those early days after they'd met, the days when she'd dared to hope there could be a future for them...

Stella had been on her fair share of dates in her life, but this first date with Jose definitely ranked as the most unique.

He'd invited her to go with him on a long distance trip to the "zoo" as casually as if they'd been home in the United States rather than in Africa. As she sat beside Jose on a rocky ledge overlooking a jungle waterfall, she had to admit Queen Elizabeth National Park was a little more than a zoo.

In the week since she'd rescued Jose from the Gulf of Aden, they'd both been tied up with work. He'd been instrumental in the final takedown of a local pirate ship. She'd worked debriefs with the CIA.

She'd been damn proud of how well she'd focused on her job even with the distraction of heated glances exchanged with the sexiest man she'd ever met. Then she'd gone to her quarters on the local base six days after they'd met and found him sitting on the floor outside her room. But rather than hit on her, he'd asked her out on a date.

An old-fashioned, so damn sweet request that she'd melted.

The next day, they'd slipped away on a helicopter to Uganda, to Queen Elizabeth National Park for the weekend. She wasn't even sure how he'd arranged for the chopper transport, and she decided she didn't need to know. For the moment, she could simply go with the flow. She was glad for the date to escape the sense of failure that she hadn't learned anything new yet about what happened to her mom.

And most of all? Finally, she could spend time with Jose "Cuervo" James, take time to discover if there was more to the attraction than just lust. Although with the hiking pace he was setting, neither of them would have energy for much of anything at the end of the day.

Four miles into their trek at the park, she'd learned the man had endless energy away from work as well. And patience. He sat with her on a rocky ledge near a waterfall, watching the wildlife. She scoured the trees with buttress roots protruding, somewhat wary of the snakes and other beasties hiding in the verdant rain forest, but the glittering view was well worth any tugging wariness. The shady spot provided relief from the heat while she went mellow, soaking in the view.

How could one man pour so much energy into sitting still? Without moving a muscle, he positively hummed with more vitality than most radiated while running a marathon. Minutes ticked by while she watched him watching the monkeys and chimpanzees swing from branch to branch.

His eyes slid over to her. "What?"

She smiled back, seeing the attraction she felt echoed in his eyes. "I'm just intrigued by how intently you're studying the monkeys."

"They're cool dudes." He pointed toward the trees growing together with linked limbs. "For me it's like how others 'people watch' at the mall. I enjoy figuring out their different personalities, their quirks, their cliques. It's always different."

A monkey stole another's banana and took off swinging from limb to limb. Stella laughed, the sound floating out, echoed by a baboon hanging from one arm.

"So, do you come to Queen Elizabeth National Park often?" she asked, loving the thrill of discovery, of learning even seemingly insignificant details about his life.

"Actually, this is my first time here." His smile reached his eyes, glinting like the sunlight refracting off the waterfall. "But I do a lot of nature hikes through national parks wherever I travel."

"Clearly you're active, given your job."

His eyes slid over her, lingering just long enough to be complimentary without turning smarmy. "You're no slouch yourself—given *your* job."

"We could compare PT scores." She tapped his chest just over the Boston Marathon logo on his T-shirt. The well-worn cotton carried the heat of him, and she ached to flatten her palm against his heartbeat. "But I would wager yours beat mine. I'm a code breaker, not a superhero."

He closed his hand over hers, holding and lowering. Not letting go. "Can we stop with the superhero stuff? I'm just a guy out with a girl on a date."

"A date in Africa, complete with a helicopter ride." And hand holding. "But hey, okay, if this is normal for you, I can't wait to see your follow-up."

He winked. "Prepare to be dazzled."

She already was—and it had nothing to do with the grand gesture of a helicopter. It had more to do with his instinctive thoughtfulness, from noticing which flavored water she preferred to remembering how her nose burned in the sun. She didn't need a keeper, but after taking care of herself since elementary school, she had to confess it felt nice to have someone who... cared.

Leaning back on her hands, she watched the way the sun dappled along the lean lines of his face. "What if I'd given out halfway to the waterfall?"

"Then we would have watched the water buffaloes instead."

"Water buffaloes are cool. Elephants and lions too."

"True, true." He nodded toward the cluster of trees. "But these little dudes? Cooler. Way cooler."

"Why is that?" she asked, realizing he had a point in bringing her here. This wasn't a random choice.

For a moment, she didn't think he would answer. He just stared out over the glistening waterfall surrounded by trees. The wind rippled his T-shirt and khakis as his booted feet hung over the edge. "Every year, my dad gave my sister and me money to buy summer passes to the zoo while he worked. My sister—Bianca—and I would pack a sack lunch and a jug of Kool-Aid. We would spend all day at the zoo hanging out."

"Sounds like fun." An idyllic image took shape in her mind. "How old were you?"

"We started when my sister turned eleven and could babysit me."

"Your mom worked?"

He shook his head, scooping up a handful of pebbles and tossing them from hand to hand. "She was… sick."

"I'm sorry," she said, waiting, but he didn't elaborate. "How many days a week did you go to the zoo?"

"Monday through Friday. We slept in late, then my sister and I headed over. It was walking distance." He tossed a small rock over the edge into the swirling waters below. "I know. Sounds bad, two kids walking alone."

"I'm not judging." Okay, that was a lie, but she wanted him to keep talking. "I'm listening."

"There were lots of things to do at the zoo that came along with that pass—movies and learning centers. Plenty of places to duck inside if it got hot." He flicked stone after stone over the edge, never still even when he was sitting. "After a while, the staff knew us, so we got lots of perks."

"Such as?" She didn't want him to stop. She wanted to know everything about him.

"Like free train rides around the zoo. I always rode up front and rang the bell. After a while, the tour guide would let me narrate parts of the ride."

"And you liked the monkeys best. Because?"

"Look at their families." He pointed. "Look at the mom. Cool, huh?"

The picture came together of a little boy spending all day at the zoo with his sister, all the time wishing his mom was there too. And what about his father? She felt small for thinking no one cared for her as a kid. Her dad had tried, and while her brothers had been obnoxious as hell, they loved her.

Who looked out for Jose? Who'd taken care of him and his sister? Her heart squeezed tight for the boy he'd been and the strong man she was just beginning to know.

Before she could think, she cupped his face in her hand and leaned in to kiss him, just a light brush of her lips to his, but wow, the total rightness of the moment melted over her like warm caramel, pure sugar and indulgence. Then he thrust his hands in her hair and brought her closer to him, his mouth sealing to hers.

She wanted to memorize the moment, but he scrambled her thoughts until she just immersed herself in the moment. The warm sweep of his tongue against hers. The peppermint taste of his toothpaste. The rasp of his afternoon stubble along her fingertips. It was a first kiss beyond anything she'd experienced, special and intense.

And she wanted more firsts with him.

His hand slid from her hair, grazing along her neck in a way that stirred a soft purr of pleasure in the back of her throat. Yes, this was physical attraction at its most elemental, but stoked by so much more.

God, no half measures here. She was all out falling for a man she'd known for only a week...

Chattering monkeys called to Jose in the night as he watched over Stella sleeping under the lean-to. It was almost morning, almost time to make their move. He and Bubbles had swapped off watches a couple of times through the night. Now his buddy catnapped against a tree and the student was taking a leak a few feet away. A baboon shouted down from a few branches up.

Jose pinched the bridge of his nose, pushing back memories of another time in the wilds with Stella on their first date. He'd wanted her to understand where he stood, where he came from. While he hadn't rolled it all out there from the start, he'd laid the groundwork for telling her. He had baggage that dogged him every day. He could never afford to be complacent. Alcoholics lived one day at a time, never taking sobriety for granted.

Honest to God, he'd thought he and Stella could have something.

Sutton zipped up his pants and pivoted back to the camp. He limped over. "Hey, dude, I'm sorry for griping earlier about the rescue operation. I realize we were only there a short time."

"Over seventy-two hours," Jose answered, understanding full well those three days would have seemed endless to a hostage.

"Right. But I get that hostages sometimes sit in captivity for months or even years. It was hell thinking of my mama seeing my picture broadcast week after week, wondering if I was still alive..." He shook his head. "I'm damn grateful to know I'll be Skyping with her by... When? Tomorrow?"

"That's the plan." If the chopper made it here. Soon, he hoped. He pulled his eyes from Stella and back to Sutton.

"Nice to hear." The student held an elephant tusk, his thumb tracing carvings along the length.

Jose glanced at the backpack, then at the tusk again. "What did you expect to do with that?"

"I didn't take this. Stella did." He set it aside and scratched through his dirty curls. "I think she was planning to use it as a knife. She was a lot smarter in her choices than I was, wasn't she? Fossil teeth and tusks. If I'd thought like her, I might have been out of there sooner."

Jose just listened, trying to get a bead on this kid. "She's a sharp girl. Her big brothers taught her to take care of herself."

A benign enough answer.

Sutton pulled a small shield out of his backpack and tapped his head lightly. "I was thinking protection, like a bulletproof vest or whacking someone on the head. Not as clever or effective as a tusk or something sharp. Hell, I don't know what I was thinking. When you're a kid, you wanna be a cop or firefighter, the hero in a crisis. Real life is a lot more complicated."

"It always is." He scooped up a handful of pebbles.

Sutton looked sideways. "I was such a fucking basket case I was pretty much useless. Not Stella though."

Of course she'd held it together. She was a highly trained Interpol operative who'd managed to send out a coded message that got everyone saved. She'd kept her head in a nightmare situation. And she'd done it all without once revealing her real identity to her captors or to the students she accompanied.

She was so damn amazing she took his breath away.

Jose funneled the pebbles through his fist into his other palm. "Sutton, you can't beat yourself up over what's in the past. You're alive."

"Not everybody made it out that way. Thing is, I don't know if I could do any better now. I'm still so scared I could piss myself."

"No shame in that." He poured the pebbles back into his other hand.

"Easy for you to say. You're a superhero."

Superhero? Crap. Stella had called him that once. Too bad nothing could be further from the truth. "We all have our kryptonite."

"What's yours?"

Alcohol. Stella. Yeah, he had two great big weaknesses. He dumped the small stones onto the ground. "Enough sharing. Get some sleep. Your chatter's distracting me from my job."

"It's Stella, isn't it? She's yours... but she's living her dream to be a student abroad?"

He stayed silent. Was the kid digging? More than once he'd hinted that he knew she had a deeper reason for being here. Had her cover been blown?

"She's smart. Pretty."

His jaw clamped tight, possessive instincts roaring. Whoa. Wait. Was this kid going somewhere else with his questions? "Do you have a point?"

Sutton shook his head. "Not really. Just wondering what kind of guy lets a woman like her get away."

Great. Now even the kid was calling him out on his idiocy. As if he didn't already know. "Prop your ankle on the log. It'll keep the swelling down."

Sutton set aside the shield. "Are you dudes SEALs or what?"

"Special Operations involves a number of different branches—SEALs, Rangers, Green Berets, pararescuemen."

"Which are you?"

"Pararescuemen—sometimes known as pararescue jumpers, PJs."

"Were you all PJs?"

Nosy little dude. "Does it matter?"

"You're not going to tell me, are you?"

"Do you really need to know?" Was the kid more than a student too? Government agencies kept secrets from each other all the time.

"Point made. Thanks to all those movies and documentaries and books, I've heard all about SEALs. Tell me more about these PJs."

Jose scanned the perimeter, monitoring every shifting branch and shadow, assessing every scratch or crackle. For now, all could be chalked up to nature. "We rescue. Let's just say we PJs thank God the SEALs are on our side and the SEALs thank God for us when they need someone to haul their asses out."

"Kinda like 'you fuck up, we pick up'?"

Sounded like the kid knew a little about the PJs after all. Kid? Sutton was around twenty-two. Jose had had four years of active duty military service under his belt by then.

Jose just stared back, silently, until a rustling from the lean-to pulled his attention off the kid. Rolling to his feet, he landed in a crouch by instinct. Weapon drawn, he scanned the dark.

Stella raised a hand. "Hold on. Just me."

Jose lowered his gun. "Sorry to have woken you."

"You didn't. I'm too wired to sleep long. Once we get out of here, though, I'll be comatose for days." Sitting up, she pulled the wrap around her shoulders like a shawl. "PJs don't like to talk about themselves."

"Then let's not," Jose said, night sounds humming in agreement.

She shoved her thick red braid over her shoulder, sweeping the escaping wisps away. "Most folks have never heard of the pararescuemen. There are only about three hundred and fifty in the world."

Sutton hooked his arm on his knees, leaning in. "That's crazy cool. Dude, you should be bragging in bars left and right. Think of the babes you could score."

Stella scrunched her nose in disdain. "So you're the kind who pretends to be an astronaut to pick up women?"

Sutton clapped a hand to his chest. "That would be very dishonorable."

Damn straight.

Stella scooted closer. "Their training takes nearly two years. They do the SEAL survival stuff, assault, protection courses, as well as becoming medics—except for the officer on the team. Anyhow, their focus is on rescue, but they need the insertion and force protection skills to make that happen."

Jose couldn't figure out why the hell she was telling all this stuff about PJs, and then it hit him. If she put the focus on his job—more of a known entity—then it took the focus off her real job. She was good. Really good.

So he let her keep talking; no hardship. He could just sit and take in the sight of her, so sexy with her hair mussed from sleep. After a month away from her, he soaked up the sound of her.

He was a sap.

Sutton held up the shield, grinning. "So I shouldn't piss off these two badasses. What else should I know about your boyfriend?"

"*Former* boyfriend," she said quickly, too quickly. "He and his buds rescue downed pilots in war zones—even jump into the ocean to assist during astronauts' landings. But their work isn't restricted to military settings; they help SWAT teams, the FBI."

Sutton whistled. "Hairy stuff."

As much as he preferred not to talk about his work, Jose reminded himself this kept the focus off Stella's job.

He clapped the kid on the shoulder. "If you call jumping into a minefield hairy, then sure, it's hairy stuff. Another of my buddies, Franco, was dropped onto a mountain in Afghanistan to rescue a Green Beret with his legs blown off in a minefield. We couldn't risk the rotor wash of a landing helicopter setting off another mine that would take out the whole aircraft and everyone in it. So Franco parachuted in alone. He used his medic training to secure the patient, then the helicopter hoisted them both up."

"Hey," Stella said, "that's the same buddy of yours who rescued the lawyer and her nephew from earthquake rubble last year. Right, Jose? You do civilian rescue work too."

"They were buried underneath layers of concrete slabs." Jose kept on talking, since sure enough, the kid wasn't focusing on Stella anymore and that was good for a lot of reasons. "Franco not only crawled through with stabilizing medical help, but also stayed with them through aftershocks until rescue teams could free them."

Sutton leaned back against the tree trunk. "That's one helluva bedtime story."

Although, the sun was rising, which meant they would either be leaving or evading. "You only have about a half hour left to catch some shut-eye."

"Then I'd better make the most of it." Sutton's eyes slid closed.

And as the student began snoring lightly, Jose realized he had no buffer between him and Stella. Nothing left but the two of them and a boatload of messy history.

———

In spite of all her intention to button up her heart tight, Stella couldn't bring herself to sleep away these last minutes with Jose, not with the dream of their first date still curling through her mind and into her heart. The sun was rising and the chopper would certainly be arriving soon. They would go their separate ways again.

So even as exhaustion tugged on her every cell, she forced her eyes to stay open. She tugged the ponytail holder free and began braiding her hair loosely.

Jose's eyes glowed coal hot in the night. "Are you seeing him?"

Surprise jolted her. "Sutton? Really? God, no. He's just a kid."

"Twenty-two, according to the briefing info we got on the hostages before rolling out. He's not that much younger than either of us. Hell, I'm a couple of years younger than you and that never seemed to matter to either of us."

She saw jealousy—and hurt. The first would have made her defensive, but the latter made her lean forward and stroke his jaw lightly.

"Well, I am not seeing him. Why would you think that?"

She was still so raw from their relationship, she didn't know when—if—she could think about commitment again. And how scary was that? She was nowhere closer to finding out anything about her mother and she'd screwed up any possibility of a relationship with Jose. She wanted a family of her own, but she couldn't think of being with anyone else.

But what about Jose? Had he already moved on? Was that why he thought she could?

She couldn't stop herself from asking, "Are *you* seeing someone new?"

"I make it a point not to be dumped more than once every six months. Since you broke it off with me four weeks ago, I have five months left to be careful and stay completely single. No risks to the heart."

Her fingers still carried the feel of his unshaven jaw. "Risks to the heart?" How the hell could he place this all at her doorstep? Anger welled inside her. "If we're laying it out there, don't forget I wanted more with you."

"Just so we're clear here." He tugged the end of her braid. "I asked you to move in with me."

The connection of his hand on her hair shimmered clear to her roots and pissed her off. "Yeah, well, call me old-fashioned but I was hoping we could have it all—house, family, rocking chair retirement with grandchildren—and you also made it clear that was never going to happen."

So much for keeping her distance.

He gave her braid a final tug. "Keep right on fighting. You can let down soon."

The way he knew just how to bolster her, how to read her, brought a lump to her throat. Spending time with him now was bittersweet, knowing how it would end.

"Stella…" He pulled his 9 mm from the holster. "For you."

He had his machine gun, so it made sense. Still, she appreciated having control of her safety again after the helplessness of the past three days.

"Damn you," she whispered, cradling the handgun in her hands.

"What did I do now?"

"You understand me," she admitted, her anger peeling away, leaving nothing but the hurt behind. "I almost hate you for that. Be horrible, okay? Be a total jerk. Make this easier for both of us."

He cupped the back of her head, his fingers massaging into her scalp. Tempting her all over again. If she could just give up her dreams, she could have him...

Then she would resent him, truly hate him in the end.

A low hum started in her brain, a buzz of frustration or doubt? Either way, it grew louder and louder until...

Jose went tense. His hand fell away and he launched to his feet. "The helicopter's here."

The CIA agent pulled out his buzzing cell phone, but he didn't recognize the number scrolling across the screen. Not unusual, since they used disposable names and identities on a regular basis.

He held up a hand to his two fellow operatives for them to carry on with their brief about the aircraft picking up the rest of the team. He would be right back. Sidling out of the small conference room, he ducked into a deserted computer cubicle in the hangar-based mobile command center and thumbed the on button.

"Yes?"

"Hello, Henry Pope." The tinny sounding words carried

over the phone, unrecognizable with a voice changer distorting the sound.

That didn't scare him. But the fact that the person had used his real name? That scared the shit out of him. Only one person would use his name on this line while he was in the middle of a top secret op in Africa.

"How did you get this number?" Damn it, their business was concluded. He'd done what they asked. The debt had been settled.

"My people can always find your number."

All those video screens and the hum of activity in the next cubicle over had his skin crawling. If a Predator unscrambled his encrypted signal… "I can't talk now."

"Then just listen," the mechanical voice continued. "There's a young man who will be on the flight with the rescued hostages."

How the hell did they know that clear across the ocean? He looked around him at the computers with workers hunched over the screens, wearing headsets and monitoring data. Who? Who was trying to sabotage his life? Was someone here talking to him or feeding information?

Maybe if he kept the person talking, he could find the bastard who'd been making him dance like a puppet for the past year. He wasn't some errand boy.

He'd paid off his debt. "What is it you want?"

"Very simple. We just want to know what he says, who he implicates."

"Who is this person?"

"Check your messages when they land. We'll send you the rest of your assignment then."

That sounded easy enough, but he didn't need their help anymore. He wasn't going to risk his ass for nothing.

"No can do," he lied. "I don't have access to what you want. Sorry, but I'm out."

"I'm disappointed to hear that. But not surprised."

A crackle sound on the other end of the line and then…

"Henry?" The voice changer had been removed. His wife spoke now, familiar, dear—terrified.

Panic twisted his gut in half. "Charlotte? Are you okay?"

Please Lord, let her be all right. His mind was already racing to a horrific conclusion.

"They haven't hurt me, but they have guns, Henry. They carjacked me." Her voice cracked on a sob. "They have Ellie too. We were in the minivan together. I'd just picked her up from preschool."

Whimpers carried over the line, his daughter in the background.

Nausea welled, and he tried like hell to swallow it back. He was going to be sick, right here in front of everyone in the hangar. His secret would be out and his family would suffer the consequences.

Sweat beaded on his brow. He had to keep his cool, for his family, for his career, for his life.

"Stay calm, Charlotte. I'll take care of everything. I promise."

"Henry, I love…"

The phone line went dead.

Chapter 5

His time with Stella was at an end.

Jose eyed the approaching aircraft with relief—and yeah, a little disappointment since he would have to say good-bye once and for all. This bizarre pocket of time together was over, reopening all the wounds that had only just started healing after Stella dumped him the first time.

There wasn't a damn thing he could do about it. Their ride had arrived, descending about fifty yards away. Not a helicopter after all, but a CV-22, the Air Force's newer tilt rotor aircraft. Engines on the wings moved, enabling it to do vertical takeoff and landings like a chopper, then point forward to fly like a regular plane. The CV-22 combined the maneuverability of a helicopter with the speed of an airplane.

The military wasn't messing around here.

Jose stood along with Bubbles, both of them sliding in place along either side of Sutton Harper, propping him as he hopped on one leg.

Jose glanced left at Stella, knowing he had to help the lame student, knowing she could take care of herself. But aching with everything inside him to toss her over his shoulder and carry her straight to the aircraft himself. "Stella? Are you good?"

"I'm fine." Her hand fell away from her ribs, the ribs he'd seen her cradling one too many times. "The sooner we get onboard, the sooner I can let you medics baby me to pieces."

The CV-22 descended, blades *whomp, whomp, whomping*, pushing the air downward. Tall grass bowed in an outward circle.

"Go," Bubbles shouted. "Go, go, go!"

Bubbles's words popped like a starter pistol through Jose's brain. He ran. His body worked on instinct from dozens of marathons, countless missions. His feet moved, legs pumping with everything inside him. Sprinting out from the cover of trees. Each step pushed the fresh scent of morning out of the ground.

As he raced closer to the helicopter, he could already almost smell the familiarity of it, a mustiness of past missions mingling with the scent of hydraulic fluid. This was his life, the military. Dreams of enlisting had been the only thing that kept him going as a teenager when his mother's drinking got worse. When his sister started drinking too.

He'd been thirteen years old then, parked in front of the television for the summer because his sister drank away their zoo pass money. He'd seen a commercial about joining the Air Force, seeing the world.

For him, anywhere sounded better than where he'd been that day—

"Jose!" Stella's scream just barely carried over the roar of the helicopter.

He jerked his head around fast and saw her. She'd stopped dead in her tracks, a gun in her hand and horror plastered across her face. His 9 mm that he'd given her, not really expecting that she would need to use it. He followed the line of her aimed weapon.

A teenage boy ran out of the tree line with a rifle slung over his shoulder. A couple of goats scattered as he plowed forward, his words carried away by the wind.

"Halt!" Stella shouted.

The boy froze, his eyes wide, but his hold on his rifle looked practiced, comfortable. Stella leveled the gun, pointing with the fluid ease of training. Jose's stomach rose up to his throat. The thunder of the lowering CV-22 echoed the roar in his head. The boy didn't seem much older than Jose had been when sitting in front of the television all those years ago, dreaming of joining the military but too young to make that dream come true yet.

Carefully, the boy tossed away the weapon and raised his arms in the air, the rising sun swelling behind him. Wind from the rotor blades whipped his too large khakis and T-shirt. His broad forehead was furrowed, his hair buzzed short. He was skinny, but it was tough to tell if that was from hunger or just teenage lankiness.

It all happened so fast, not more than five or six seconds, and in that time, any of them could have shot the boy. Or given the way the kid handled the rifle, he could have killed them in their hesitation. What the hell were they supposed to do with him now?

Stella approached him with the weapon still drawn, both equal in height. "Go back into the trees, away from the aircraft."

Jose shoved the student onto Bubbles and followed her, scanning the trees. "Stella, we need to leave."

The boy took a step toward her, hands still in the air. "Let me come with you," he said in heavily accented English. "Please, ma'am, take me with you. Do not leave me here. They will kill me."

Bubbles barked, "We gotta go."

"No!" The kid lurched forward. "I know things, important things. I will tell you."

Anyone could say that, but if what he said was true... Shit. They couldn't stand around here chitchatting. "The boy comes with us. We don't have time to sort it out now. We'll search him for explosives and weapons and if he's clean, cuff him and load him up."

The boy didn't even hesitate. He thrust out his wrists. Jose took the battered rifle, then patted him down, finding no explosives.

Bubbles stepped into the void and pulled out a set of plastic cuffs. He zipped the kid's wrists tight. "Let's bounce."

Jose escorted the kid, leaving Bubbles and Stella to haul the student the rest of the way to the waiting aircraft. The crew chief inside the CV-22 reached out to steady each passenger up the back ramp and into the belly of the craft. Webbed seating stretched along either side, metal beams and cables lining the cargo hold. Jose strapped in the kid straight off, not trusting the teen, not trusting anyone. Especially when Stella was involved.

He didn't give ten damns right now how much professional training she had. This was his rescue. His gig. And he wasn't lowering his guard for an instant until he had her safely back at base.

The back load ramp groaned as it closed, sealing them inside with the crew chief and flight engineer. Jose dropped into a seat and strapped in beside Stella just as the CV-22 lifted off. Still, she had his gun trained on the kid.

Could she do it? Shoot a teenager?

Their time together hadn't involved work, not after the initial meet-up in the Gulf of Aden. They'd just been two people dating, getting to know each other. He hadn't seen her on the job, and he sure as hell hadn't seen a woman who could draw down on a teen.

Had her nerve-wracking time as a hostage messed with her head? Maybe he shouldn't have given her the gun after all. He closed his hand over hers, slipping the weapon from her grip, and she didn't even protest. But then perhaps she was thinking like an undercover agent after all, trying not to draw attention to her training.

Although her standoff with the kid a few minutes ago had been mighty damn official.

The engines groaned as they shifted, pointing the rotors forward. The CV-22 accelerated, speeding forward at double the pace of a helicopter. They were that much closer to freedom.

Completely free for her to walk away from him.

He blinked the fog of denial clear from his eyes and scoured the hollow inside of the aircraft. Almost as hollow as he felt.

Sutton pointed at the kid, shouting over the roar of the engines. "You were with them, the ones who held us at the compound."

Jose looked fast at Stella. Had she known that too from the second she saw the kid? If so, no wonder she'd drawn a weapon. And no wonder she hadn't wanted to let the boy go.

The teen held up his cuffed hands, fingers splaying in some kind of universal pleading gesture. "They made me. I didn't have any choice. Until now. I came to you."

Sutton turned wild, scared eyes to Jose. "Are you just going to believe what he says?"

"Doesn't matter," Jose answered. "He's in custody. We'll sort it out later."

So far they'd managed to keep her real identity from Sutton, although the student had been eyeing them suspiciously since realizing they had once dated.

The way they'd worked together to get to this point had been so damn smooth, even when they'd been derailed by the land mine. Why the hell couldn't she see how good they'd been together? He'd wanted her to just accept him as he was, a great big flawed human being who was doing the best he could, one day at a time. He could already hear her answer of how he should be, what he could be—a father. God, she'd even suggested he go to medical school.

With her sitting so close, he found himself thinking about her tearful, angry request during their last fight. Really thinking, even though it made his gut knot. The engine slowed again, jerking as the engines shifted upward like a helicopter again. Landing. Time to think was over.

Before he could gather his scrambled thoughts, the back hatch opened again. The bright sun swelled inside, stinging his eyes. He blinked, seeing the hangar that held their command center, the CIA dudes and SEALs waiting. He was back where he started.

Except now the welcoming crew included more than the CIA dudes and the SEALs. His PJ team stood with them—Brick, Data, and Fang out front.

And in that moment, Jose was the thirteen-year-old kid again, sitting in front of the TV watching an Air

Force recruiting commercial. He saw what had gotten him out of his screwed-up home, away from his family. He saw what had pulled him up again after he'd surrendered to the family legacy and become an alcoholic.

And he knew without question there wasn't a middle ground for him with Stella. All he had was this rapidly closing window of time with her.

Stella watched the clock as the somewhat nerdy-looking Mr. Brown questioned the teenage boy, while hard-ass Mr. Smith observed from a corner. Of course, the geek thing was Brown's act. His specialty? Martial arts, anything from Krav Maga to a black belt in karate. His unassuming appearance—five foot seven, wiry, and wearing glasses he didn't need—had caught more than one person off guard in the field.

Would it work with the teenager?

They'd been placed in the small office in the hangar, a ten-by-ten coffee break area now being used as an interrogation room. She would be debriefed later. But for now—so far as the kid knew—she was just a freed prisoner who'd identified him as one of her captors and was listening in to verify what he said.

The second she'd seen him charging toward the CV-22, she'd recognized him. She'd noticed the kid a couple of times. Every person and every second of her captivity was catalogued in her photographic memory. The teenager had looked a helluva lot more fearsome at the compound, holding a gun and guarding his corner of the camp.

When she'd seen him running toward her, her gut had

cramped with the fear she'd barely let herself feel while she was held captive. And before she could think, her instincts as a field agent went into high gear and she had Jose's gun in her hands.

The whole ride back to base, she'd felt Jose's eyes on her, felt his questions.

Felt the draw to be with him.

But until she had a few answers of her own, she couldn't risk even talking to Jose. Sorting out the tangled mess of emotions inside of her would be tough enough on a calm day.

Sorting through them right now with an interrogation to get through was impossible. So the best thing she could do? Finish this interview with the teenager as quickly as possible so she could use what little time she had left with Jose to find some closure. She couldn't spend the rest of her life feeling like her heart was cut out of her chest every time something reminded her of him.

The teen—he called himself Ajaya—cupped a canned cola with shaking hands and looked everywhere but into anyone's eyes. "I lost my parents in an uprising when I was ten. I was sent to a school for orphans. The people who took me, they target boys like me, ones with no family."

Mr. Brown didn't even glance up from his iPad tablet as the kid poured out the heart-tugging story. "You speak English well. You must know the odds tell me that's unusual for a child in your circumstances."

"I had very good teachers at the orphan school." He took a slurp of his drink. "I had hopes of working at the embassy. Of traveling. I did not expect to travel this way. I did not go with those men by choice."

"How did they take you?" Still, the CIA agent didn't show even a hint of sympathy, just total absorption in recording the information.

Mr. Brown played the distracted academic well. Meanwhile, Mr. Smith crossed his arms and tucked himself more tightly in the corner, watching, listening for the least hint of a lie. And that was also why she'd been allowed to listen in. She'd been in there. She had access to more of what went on. The teen's eyes kept flicking to her, as if questioning why she was here, but he was wise enough not to ask.

Ajaya's throat moved with another long swallow, his coffee-dark eyes deep wells of fear. "They pretended to be maintenance people there to fix the electricity. They made me unconscious and took me away. Next I woke up in the back of their van. But they did not work alone. They had help."

Finally, Mr. Smith straightened, weathered creases in his face digging deeper as he frowned and looked directly into the young man's eyes. "Help? From who?"

"From one of my teachers at the orphan school where I lived."

Annie Johnson closed and locked the door to her classroom.

Most people lived for the end of the workday. Not her. She only came alive during those eight hours she spent at her desk and in front of the board—with her students. But today had been especially rough, with her eyes drawn back to those two empty desks, knowing more of her students had been snatched away by pirates and there wasn't a damn thing anyone could do about it.

She swept the cloth up over her head and started for the door, fighting back the frustration. The hallway here at the orphan school didn't change year after year. Not really. The same bulletin boards, just different artwork and poems, same teenage themes.

Same threats.

Dropping her keys into her pocket, Annie hitched her book satchel over her shoulder and started down the dimly lit hallway. She'd come here to teach believing that she was smarter than the rest of the people on staff. Beyond her two advanced degrees, she'd traveled the world.

How arrogant she'd been.

In over a decade at the school she'd learned so much more from these kids, children who'd seen a lifetime of loss and pain before they reached eighteen. She wanted to save them all but had come to accept no one person could carry that off.

However, for the hour or two they each spent in her class every day, she could give them an escape. She could transport them to another world when she taught literature. That's how she lived her life these days, one hour at a time. Her dreams came in smaller pockets of time rather than grandiose plans to save the world.

She stepped out into the fading sun, the dusty wind stirring her skirt around her calves. The teachers' quarters were a short walk away, a dorm-like setup where each staff member had a two-room efficiency apartment. Her dreams were definitely more scaled down these days.

She rounded the corner of the clay building—and slammed into another wall. Or rather she slammed into a person. A man, one of her fellow teachers.

"Sam," she gasped. "You startled me."

Samir Al-Shennawi had moved here from Egypt a year ago to teach history. And from day one, he hadn't hidden his interest in her.

"Annie," he answered, not budging. "I've come to walk you to your quarters. You should not be out alone."

"You're thoughtful, but the security guards are always a shout away."

"And I am their reinforcements." He smiled but still didn't budge.

Samir—Sam—was different from other men she'd known, and she hadn't led a nun's life during her exile here. While she hadn't slept with him, Samir pushed her for something far more intimate than any of those other men. Friendship.

"I will walk you home," he insisted.

"It's only three buildings away." She pretended not to notice the curious stares. Everyone knew Sam had a thing for her, but they also knew she'd kept her distance. "Your help isn't necessary."

Still, she waved for him to walk beside her.

"I do understand it is not necessary. But I will walk with you anyway." His smile fanned creases from his eyes behind his little round glasses. "My mother would be very angry with me if I forgot the manners she taught me."

She pretended not to notice the curious stares of other teachers and students as she passed the dining hall. "You're a pushy man."

"Not really."

And that was true. He had a reputation for being a mild-mannered academic, the epitome of nerdiness. Except when it came to pursuing her. He was always quietly there, waiting with those intense sexy eyes of his.

"So then, Sam…" She smiled at him, letting herself flirt a little as a relief against the horrible day. "If I told you to go on ahead, you would?"

He walked silently beside her, staying in step along the dirt path leading to the teachers' dorm.

Laughing, she hooked her thumb on the leather strap of her bag. "Like I said. Pushy."

"Ungrateful."

"Excuse me?"

He glanced down at her, reminding her he had eight extra inches of height on her. "Since we are tossing around adjectives, I will volley one back your way. Ungrateful."

Now that struck a nerve, reminding her of arguments with her husband. Her dead husband. "I'm supposed to be *grateful* for the gift of your presence? Well then how about this adjective? Egotistical."

He tapped his chest. "Protective."

That sat a little better on her prickly pride. "Oh, you're worried about me? Now don't I feel foolish? I thought you were hitting on me."

His smile flattened to a deep scowl. "I would never hit a woman."

"Sorry. That's an idiom for making a move on a woman." Still he looked confused so she continued, "A romantic move."

"That too."

She stopped. "You're making a move on me? After a year of following me around."

"Following you around? You make me sound like a puppy. I am merely a devoted man, a patient man. I have actually been *making moves* for quite some time, but apparently my *moves* were not obvious enough to capture

your attention. It could be a difference in cultural court-
ship rituals. You may add intelligent and persistent to
the adjective list. Good night."

She watched him walk silently away, tall and broad
shouldered. And persistent.

Her husband had been upset by her choices, angry
with her. He'd even asked her to come back. But he'd
never once been persistent.

Yes, Samir Al-Shennawi intrigued her. He made her
want to learn more, made her want more.

Except how persistent would he stay if he knew she
was a trained killer?

Jose planted himself in a chair outside the break room
door so he wouldn't miss Stella when she left. He was
dead on his feet, running on fumes, but sitting was the
only concession he would give himself. Sleep could
come later, once he saw her and knew she was taken
care of.

The CV-22 was parked behind him, the crew gathered
around the back hatch. On the other side of the aircraft,
the CIA command center was still in place with screens
glowing. The hangar hummed with pockets of activity.

But he could only think of Stella.

She had been in there with the boy and the head CIA
dude for over three hours. She needed to rest, eat, recharge. Even knowing he wasn't stopping either didn't
take away the driving urge to rip the door off with his
bare hands and haul her out of there.

It was as if the past four weeks apart never happened.
He was right back in those first hours after she'd dumped

him, certain she would change her mind, wondering
what he could do to change it for her.

Damn stupid.

Focus on the now. Do his job. What he did best.

The light sound of footsteps gave him a one-second
warning before his teammates pulled up alongside
him. Brick, Data, Bubbles, and Fang were more than
just a few fellas he worked with. They were fellow
PJs. They put their lives on the line together, would
die for each other.

No one knew him better. And right now that could
be a problem, gauging by the way they were grinning,
ready to razz him. Bubbles leaned back against a pallet
of stacked crates while the others advanced.

His buddy Brick propped a foot up on the chair beside him, a stubborn rock-headed dude with a marsh-
mallow heart, especially since he got married. "Wanna
play marry one, kill one, screw one? Category? Brad
Pitt's women: Jennifer Aniston, Angelina Jolie, and
Gwyneth Paltrow."

His friend *would* remind him of the way he'd picked
on his buddies for not wanting to join in the word game.
Not too long ago, he'd razzed Rocha for being all uptight and in love.

Ironic how life cycled around. "I'll pass."

Brick dropped into the seat beside him and clapped
Jose on the back. "Not as funny when you're the one in
over your head, is it?"

Fang—which actually stood for Fuck, Another New
Guy—crouched down in front of him. "So, Brick, is it
true what they say about married sex?"

Data's eyes lit with curiosity, but then the squadron

brainiac was curious about everything. "What do they say? And who is 'they'?"

Baby-faced Fang scratched his buzzed short hair. "Married dudes who say the sex dries up after the vows."

Jose cursed. Sex was so not what he wanted to talk about now with Stella so fresh in his mind he could swear the eucalyptus scent of her lingered.

Brick scowled. "Now hold on there, partner. Any man who's talking about sex with his wife is either a loser or not working hard enough."

Fang blinked once, twice. "I'm not getting what you mean, dude."

Shaking his head, Brick laughed. "Can't coach stupid."

The shared laughed knocked around inside the hangar's high ceiling, ricocheting off beams. Familiar camaraderie. Their gift to him in the middle of hell.

As the chuckles died down, Bubbles shoved away from the wall of stacked crates. "The key to married sex, single sex, any sex at all? Foreplay is the road to happiness, my friends."

Jose looked from one shocked face to the other, more than a little stunned himself.

"Whoa." Fang whistled. "Who knew he could talk?"

Some of the tension eased from Jose's shoulders. His buds knew him, knew just how to step in and defuse the moment.

Except, why were they here? "Brick, what's going on? Why the big welcoming party?"

"Long story. It's all connected to the vice president's wife's visit. Security and some exercise. Blah, blah, blah. You and Bubbles will be tied up here anyway with debriefing the kid and the rescued hostages." Brick nodded to the coffee room door as the knob turned. "And there's your lady now. Good luck."

His friends peeled away as the door opened.

Stella stepped out first, while the CIA head honcho stayed inside with the kid. She pulled the door closed after her, resting her head against the panel.

Someone had given her clean clothes even if she hadn't showered. She'd changed into fresh jeans and a simple gray T-shirt. She still kept the long kanga cloth hooked over her arms. Perhaps she kept it to wrap around her if they stepped out in public, or maybe she held it out of nervous habit. But she seemed to take comfort from the cloth. He didn't bother pondering the "why" of it any further. He'd seen enough combat stress to know everyone handled things in their own way.

And that damn Mr. Smith should know the same. Instead the hard-ass had kept her tied up in extra debriefs for three hours.

"Stella?" Jose scratched his tight throat and pushed a halfway normal voice free. "Are you okay?"

Her shoulders went tense again and she turned slowly, scanning until her eyes landed on him.

"I'm fine." She wrapped her arms tighter around her waist, the long red cloth hooking on her elbows.

He might not be able to fix whatever had messed with her head, but he could damn well monitor for any medical concerns. He looked into her eyes, checked her pupils, took her wrist, and counted her pulse. And even as he did his job he also couldn't stop thinking like the man who cared about her, the man who didn't want to play games. The man who'd loved her.

Still loved her?

He counted her racing pulse. "Did a doctor check you over when you changed clothes?"

"I don't need one." She eased her wrist from his hold. "You already cleared me."

Damn it. He should have guessed as much. "I'm not a doctor."

"You could be."

He folded his hands over his chest. "Stella…"

She put her fingers on his mouth. "Sorry. I didn't mean to travel old scripts."

Fair enough. He didn't want to waste time arguing with her either. He palmed her waist and guided her into a private corner behind the wall of crates, away from listening ears and prying eyes. The shadowy corner behind the pallet of wooden boxes created the bubble of solitude he needed to finally talk to her alone.

"Is the boy settled?" he asked. "Did you learn anything?"

"Agents Smith and Brown are still talking with him. We simply played it that they wanted me there to verify what a hostage would have seen." She sagged back against the metal wall, exhaustion stamping dark circles under her eyes. "For now, the kid's story sounds like I would expect to hear. Orphaned in a civil conflict. Kidnapped by a clan militia force. So totally innocent it's guaranteed to break your heart."

"You don't believe him?"

She chewed her bottom lip for a long second before answering, "I don't know. His story sounds too practiced. Too stock. He's going to have to offer us something more before I can believe he wasn't responsible for his actions at the compound. People died, a truly innocent student and a damn good agent."

The thought of how that could have been her nearly drove him to his knees. He flattened his hand on warm metal to keep from punching the wall, which would only draw attention to them when he finally had her completely alone for the first time since they'd escaped that compound. "Can you tell me what the hell was going on there?"

"Investigating different warlords, following the path of the stolen pirate stash." She held the cloth tighter around her waist. "Sometimes it feels like we're putting out fires without ever having access to the source."

"Maybe it's time for you to pack it in."

She frowned, staring back into his eyes. "Are you crazy? You of all people should understand dedication to the job."

She had a point. So where the hell had his comment come from? From his deeper frustration that had nothing to do with logic, the gut-twisting burn of knowing she could have died. Living without her was tough enough, but at least he'd been able to envision her alive, walking the same planet as him.

The dam broke on the wall he'd built to hold back all that fear so he could get the job done, get her out of there.

"Stella, why are you still here? Really? I don't care if your job gives you superhero status too, but someone should be looking out for you."

"I can take care of myself."

But she shouldn't have to, not all the time. The real question detonated inside him, the one that had been eating him up inside since he'd first stepped into this airplane hangar and saw surveillance images of her on those screens.

He gripped her by the shoulders. "What were you doing inside that compound where you could have fucking been murdered?"

Her brows shot upward, her chest rising and falling faster and faster. She looked away fast, her eyes darting. Avoiding? He didn't have to be a body language expert to know she was working on what to say, crafting her words.

Finally, she looked at him full-on and blurted, "I came here to find answers about how my mother died."

There was no denying the hoarse honesty in her whisper. He processed the words with the notion that he'd thought he knew everything about her. God knows he'd shared his secrets with her. He'd assumed she had done the same.

"I thought your mom was an aid worker killed in a car accident." He recalled everything Stella had told him, how Melanie Carson had spent half of every year in Africa dispensing aid in villages. "In this region, right?"

She nodded. "That's what we were told, but I think the car accident story was just to cover her injuries so we wouldn't question why her body was beaten up."

"God, Stella, I'm not sure what to say." He touched her cheek, all the comfort he expected she would accept. She had to have some kind of proof. She was too logical to say that about her mother on a hunch, which meant she'd been planning this all along, even when she was with him. "We were together for five months. Why didn't you mention this to me before?"

And yeah, that stung a little. He'd poured his guts out to her, shared his demons.

She scrubbed her hand over her face, shaking her head slowly. "It's not exactly romantic pillow talk."

He knew a cop-out answer when he heard one. "We did more than sleep together."

"Honestly, Jose." Her mouth went tight. "You didn't need to know about my mother, so I didn't tell you."

"And *you* accused *me* of holding back?"

Her shoulders slumped. "I'm sorry I hurt you and I mean that. Being together like this must really suck for you."

Straight for the jugular. He half smiled. "I'd forgotten how blunt you can be."

"I'm a factual person—and we only broke up a month ago." She touched his chest lightly.

"Feels longer than that." He cupped her face, thumbing the corner of her mouth.

She chewed her bottom lip, her teeth so close to his thumb. "How long are you here?"

"Until the morning. Then I'm out of here. Move on to the next phase."

Not much time left with her, but he didn't intend to waste a minute of it. His pulse thumped stronger, harder in his ears. Could he do it? Put his heart out there for her to crush again just for the chance to sleep with her one more time?

Hell yes.

He angled closer. He could almost taste her, just from memory.

"Jose, wait." She pressed her hand harder against his chest. "That isn't what I meant."

"Really?" He nibbled her bottom lip.

She sighed, her breath tangling with his next breath.

"Really," she said softly, her mouth moving along his. "I told you about my mom because I thought we could use this time to talk things through more fully, to get closure."

Right now this felt more like a second chance than an ending. He skimmed a kiss along her jaw. "Okay, then you talk." He kissed his way down to her neck. "I'll listen."

Her head fell back, giving him fuller access. "Because even though we broke up a month ago, it hasn't been simple to close the door on what we… shared. I've realized I need more time with you."

And just that fast, her hands went into his hair. She guided his mouth back to hers and kissed him. Full-out kissed him, and God help him, he was all in.

He slid his arms around her and hauled her closer. The familiar give of her curves against him felt so damn good. He knew they couldn't take this any further, not here, not now, and there was a certain freedom in that. And knowing he could just taste her, hold her, be with her—that drove him crazy. The past four weeks without her, thinking about never seeing her again, had damn near driven him nuts.

The touch of her tongue to his sent a possessive growl humming low in his chest. He didn't know what tomorrow would bring, although he hoped tonight would find him and Stella in a shower together, then a bed, where he would use every bit of foreplay in his arsenal.

But here, now, he needed to hold onto control for a while longer.

Stepping back, he eased his mouth from hers and slid his hands around to cup her elbows. His senses went on high alert, taking in everything about her, from the softness of her skin to the brush of the cotton cloth she still held.

"Stella, if you're through here, let's head over to the

quarters where we can be alone, talk about where you want to go next…"

The sound of the door opening again echoed up from the other side of the stacked crates. Stella blinked fast, clearing away the fog of passion from her eyes. She hurried around the corner, back into plain sight just as the teenage Ajaya stepped out, his eyes wide and panicked.

"Where are you taking me? You cannot just send me back there, not when they know I have been here." His voice cracked, his agitation increasing the longer Mr. Smith stayed silent beside him.

The agent was playing the kid, pushing him for more with psychological pressure rather than physical harm.

Ajaya tugged at the hem of his overlarge T-shirt. "I know things, more things. I know about that."

He pointed to Stella.

Jose stopped cold, his hand sliding around her waist. Mr. Smith didn't even blink.

Ajaya waved his hand toward Stella again. "The cloth, the one stolen from the compound. The writing in the border. It tells their plans."

Mr. Smith blinked.

Foreboding iced up Jose's spine, years of survival instincts shouting this was about to get bad. Really bad. He resisted the urge to thrust himself between Stella and whatever the kid was about to say.

Stella inched forward, her hands twisting in the wrap. "What plans, Ajaya?"

"To kill people when your vice president's wife visits." The teenage boy reached toward Stella, his fingers almost brushing the rippling fringe. "The details are written in a code in the fabric."

Chapter 6

STELLA UNWOUND THE CLOTH FROM AROUND HER waist, handling the fabric as carefully as crystal. Cradling the material draped over her hands, she took in the pattern scripted along the edges. The stark halogen lights high in the hangar glinted on flecks of silver thread.

Messages were commonly woven into the patterns or borders of these cloths, so that in and of itself wasn't unusual. There was no reason to beat herself up over not considering it before now. All the same, she wished somehow she'd considered the possibility that a cloth was more than a "cloth."

Could the boy be lying about a more insidious meaning? Or was he telling the truth? Either way, they had to move forward on the assumption that he was telling the truth.

A translator would have to decipher which variation of the local language was used. Even if the words seemed benign, a decoder—like her—would have to discern if a hidden meaning had been inserted.

Unless the boy was lying to buy time.

She looked up at the teenager. His dark eyes were wild with desperation. She believed he would do anything to stay safe. Was he wily enough to make up a really good lie?

A tug pulled her out of her thoughts as Mr. Smith eased the wrap from her hands. "Where did this come from?"

"Uhm…" She blinked fast to clear her blurry eyes and dulled senses. "Sutton and I both took items from their store of stolen goods for survival purposes. This was from Sutton's backpack."

Mr. Smith folded the fabric carefully. "Then I think we need to make sure Mr. Harper passes over his backpack before he leaves here today. Sergeant, could you please escort Stella to her quarters? She needs rest and medical care after her ordeal. We've asked enough of her."

She had a million questions she wanted to ask Ajaya and the enigmatic Mr. Smith, the same Mr. Smith she'd been working with since she arrived in Africa six months ago. But he couldn't relay that. Obviously. Because as far as the teenager and all the hostages knew, she was just a student getting debriefed, fed, and evaluated like all the rest of them. And even as a full-fledged operative, she didn't always get clearance on everything.

But God, she ached to be in on this.

Her gaze flicked to Jose, then back to Mr. Smith. The CIA agent was right. She needed to rest up while he finished the interrogation. Once they had a handle on what was in the border of the cloth, if there was a code to crack, she would need a much sharper mind. Right now, she felt like she was walking through peanut butter.

Jose's arm went around her waist, and she didn't bother protesting. She leaned into him and let him guide her out of the hangar.

The blinding midday rays stung her eyes as she took in her first comprehensive look at the American base here. Rows of plain tan buildings sprawled ahead, baked and cracked by the harsh African sun.

Step for step, she walked alongside Jose. The heated concrete steamed warmth through the soles of her gym shoes. "Where exactly are we going?"

His hand felt warm and right against her waist. "You're no good to yourself or anyone until you eat some real food, shower, and sleep."

"I know I need to clear my head, but walking away from work is easier said than done." A trio of jet planes split the clouds overhead, leaving contrail to fade in their wakes.

"No offense, Stella, but have you looked in the mirror today?"

His leg brushed against hers, his lean strength as familiar to her as her own skin. How strange to feel stirred in the middle of utter exhaustion. Especially when he'd just told her she looked like crap.

Ouch. "I've avoided mirrors." She stopped at a corner, waiting for a line of camouflage trucks to roll past. "It's been a rough few days."

"Exactly why you need to forget about everything for a while."

"Easier said than done right after hearing there's a group planning some kind of massacre." God, she felt like she was running in circles, a futile and exhausting endeavor.

"The kid also said the plan was tied into the vice president's wife's visit." He gave her a reassuring squeeze. "So we have a couple of days. You can take this time to recharge—really recharge—while Mr. Smith and Mr. Brown and however many more Jones and Johnson buddies of his can help out doing their jobs."

"Why have you assigned yourself to be my babysitter?"

"Honestly, I don't trust anyone else. You're mighty damn good at maneuvering people." He guided her past a long open-air building with a metal dome roof. "I care about you, and I understand you."

That's what made this all hurt so much, knowing he still cared. "Thank you for being here, for being so damn good at what you do."

For caring.

He stopped outside a two-story concrete building, steps leading up to the second floor. She stared up into his eyes, bracing herself for the inevitable jolt of awareness, the delicious shimmer that ignited her nerve endings with the promise of pleasure. An intense pleasure unique to being with Jose.

"Jose?" Was that whispery voice really hers?

"I know." He cupped her shoulder. "Not easy to just pretend everything's okay between us."

Her skin flamed to life, pushing aside the fog of exhaustion. "I'm sorry for dragging you into this, for hauling out all our past baggage again."

"You did what had to be done. You're damn good at your job too." His hand fell away. "My room's down the hall. Since your gear is all back at the hostel where you were undercover as a student, I rounded up some essentials for you while you were watching the questioning of Ajaya. I put the stuff in my room."

Her eyebrows shot up.

He raised a hand. "Before you get riled, I'm not suggesting we sleep together, and if you insist, I'll find another place to bunk. But I gotta confess the past couple of days really screwed with my head. I need to know you're okay, or I'm not going to be able to close my eyes."

"So you're saying this isn't just about making sure I sleep? It's about helping you too?" A smile tugged at her mouth as well as her heart. "That I need to stay stapled to your side like a teddy bear in order for you to get any rest."

"Yep…" He nodded. "I guess that pretty much covers it."

Not too long ago, she would have done anything to be with him. And now? She didn't know where they stood, and she was too tired to breathe, much less sort through her personal or professional tangles. Which made her answer a helluva lot easier to justify.

"I'm honest to God too exhausted to argue with you. Let's watch out for each other, and we'll deal with everything else later."

She started climbing the steps to do the one thing she'd never expected ever to do again.

Sleep with Jose.

———~~~———

Jose sat in the uncomfortable-as-hell armchair and watched Stella sleep as the clock ticked away the hours into the middle of the night.

Once they'd stepped into the small barracks room, she'd washed up while he ate, then eaten while he showered. By the time he'd joined her, she'd been passed out asleep in the double bed tucked in a corner. He should stay in this chair.

Should.

But what the fuck?

He'd slept with her before, and it wasn't like they were going to have sex again. Even though that kiss earlier had damn near sent him to his knees.

He shoved up out of the chair, his body groaning from the past twenty-four hours of surviving. He needed to recharge too if he expected to be one hundred percent for Stella. Settling onto the bed, he eased his legs up, careful not to jostle her. His head sank back into the piled pillows—he'd bought extra when he got her some clothes since he knew how she loved fat, fluffy pillows under her head and to hug. He tucked his hand behind his bed and stared at the ceiling, keeping a couple of inches between him and the woman of his dreams sleeping next to him.

Life was a bitch sometimes.

But at least Stella was safe. He would worry about the possible doomsday message woven into that cloth later. For now, he had solid military-issue walls surrounding her.

With concrete walls and industrial bedding, it wasn't much in the way of accommodations, but the mattress was decent. The halfway-functioning air conditioner unit in the window gushed air that was cooler than anything outside. He'd stayed in worse. Still he wished he could offer her better.

But he had to accept he'd done all he could for her here. Sleep would do the rest, a deep slumber. Her catnap last night out in the wilds had been far from restful. Now she slept hard. Her red hair fanned out on the pillow, dry and carrying the scent of him since apparently she'd used his shampoo. Her eyelids twitched with deep REMs. A lightweight robe covered her whole body but clung to damp curves.

Sighing, she rolled over and looped her arm over his stomach. His abs contracted at the warmth of her, her slim, toned arm so damn familiar. As if the shower fresh scent of her wasn't already driving him nuts. Damn good thing he wore camo pants and a T-shirt. Although full-out body armor wouldn't be enough of a barrier between them.

His arm rested along the dip of her waist. Her curves fit to his side, the give of her soft breasts searing him, making him ache to cradle the weight in his hands. He knew every inch of her body. They'd been good together, beyond good, better than anything he'd had with any other woman. Hell, when he was with her he couldn't think of anyone but her. Still couldn't even though they were no longer a couple.

Would she be in his system like this for the rest of his life?

He eyed the scratch along her neck from the guard's blade. A blade that had come too close to taking her life. Even a bit more pressure, a second's hesitation on either of their parts would have left her dead. He willed his heart to stay steady. Careful not to wake her, he thumbed just beside the cut, along the place he'd discovered when he'd first kissed her at Queen Elizabeth National Park. Right over the freckle on her neck where he'd kissed dozens of times during the five months they'd dated.

Every protective urge inside him flamed to life. No matter how many times his brain insisted it was over between them, his body argued otherwise. She was his. And maybe that wasn't cool or PC, but damn it, that's just how it was for him. On some primal level, a connection linked them that he didn't begin to understand. That he didn't have a clue how to sever.

Sometimes he wondered if they'd met on a regular

day in an ordinary kind of place if things might have been different. They'd played out their affair in a remote corner of the earth, in places with deep-rooted history. They'd made love for the first time with the sound of the flowing Nile waters echoing through their window.

Every minute of his time with her was branded in his brain. Not just having sex, but their whole weekend in Egypt, one of the handful of times they'd been able to sneak more than a few hours together. He'd been determined to make the most of a whole weekend with Stella, to sweep the incredibly practical woman off her feet with the most luxurious, impractical getaway he could plan.

So he'd taken her to Aswan with tropical palm trees and the Tombs of Nobles cut in the high west bank of the Nile. They'd gone on a camel ride to the Monastery of St. Simeon. She had an adventurous spirit, but that day he'd discovered a romantic heart underneath. He'd seen it when she heard the story of the Mausoleum of Aga Khan and how his wife laid a rose on his tomb every day, a tradition still carried on by the village even after her death.

Jose had made a mental note to cover Stella's bed in roses one day. He'd never had the chance to fulfill that vow. Damn, regrets were a bite in the ass.

Holding her against him, he let the sound of the whooshing air conditioner echo in his ears like the sound of the Nile during that date five months ago…

The Nile River flowed by as it had done for thousands of years for millions of couples, but for Jose, there was only this woman. Only Stella sitting across the table from him.

Parked on the restaurant terrace, he leaned on an elbow and watched her savor the Egyptian stew served in a clay pot. The road below was clogged with cars and bicyclists, horns and shouts drifting up. From inside, Nubian folk music echoed with people clapping along to the drum and lyre.

Stella swayed ever so slightly. A lock of her thick red hair slid out from under the silk scarf she'd draped over her head in keeping with local dress. He didn't have to reach across to remember the feel of her hair gliding across his fingers when he kissed her.

Which he intended to do again. Soon.

For now, though, he indulged himself by simply listening to her talk between bites. He periodically dipped his bread into his soup, the spices exploding through his senses already on hyperaware around Stella.

She reached for the pewter goblet of juice from local fruits. "My mother would have loved this place, the paintings."

"Your mom was an artist?" he asked, wanting to know everything about her.

"More of a stylist." She set down her drink, her nose flaring as a whiff of incense carried on the night breeze. "She created works of art from pieces of earth, mud smears, berry juices. Every art project was a science project too. She was the ultimate recycler even before it was in vogue."

"Sounds like my buddy Wade's wife." He reached across the tablecloth and stroked the top of her hand.

A smile flickered across her face when he touched her. "I enjoyed the time she and I spent together on projects. I sent her pictures when she traveled here—"

She paused as the waitress refilled their goblets and placed a pot of mint tea to go with a dessert of cookies and candied figs. His mouth watered and it had nothing to do with the food and everything to do with a certain lady agent.

Once the server turned away, he tapped Stella's hand. "Tell me about one of the paintings."

"The summer before she died, we vacationed at the Outer Banks in North Carolina." She looked down and away, picking up a fig with fidgety fingers. "I think my parents were trying to work on their marriage. Her absences strained their relationship."

"Like in military marriages." He'd seen more than his fair share crumble, relationships that had appeared rock solid.

Couples who didn't have the added stress of alcoholism lurking every damn day.

"My dad didn't see it quite that way at all. He couldn't find anything noble in what she did. He just wanted his wife back, an everyday normal life where he came home from driving his UPS route and had dinner with his whole family." She blinked back a hint of tears. "But he loved her, so he tried. She tried."

She shook her head.

He squeezed her hand. "You were telling me about a piece of art you made together."

A couple at the next table looked at their clasped hands with a disapproving eye. The last thing he wanted to do was draw attention to them by dissing local customs. So he let her go and poured them both a cup of tea.

She tucked the loose strand of hair back under the

scarf, her composure sliding just as neatly into place again. "My mother and I were on the beach collecting seashells, sand dollars, and bits of seaweed. I used a piece of driftwood as my canvas. I made a portrait of her, my seashell mama. I still have it, actually."

"She sounds fascinating." Like her daughter.

"I wanted to go with her. I begged her to take me with her since I was in high school. She said no."

"It probably wasn't safe for you." If he had a wife and kids... But he didn't. He wouldn't. Any thoughts of being with a woman forever ended when Stella walked away from him.

Stella spooned sugar into her tea—three spoonfuls. "She said the same thing, but I reminded her that sometimes entire families went on mission trips. I had looked it up in the library. I showed her all my research and suggested we should all go with her, or if the others didn't want to go, I would. I had it all worked out how I could take care of myself..." She stirred, clinking the spoon against the cup in time with the music. "And she still said no."

"That had to hurt." Hell, it hurt just hearing her talk about the memory.

"Tough day all the way around." She lifted her steaming tea. "Then I had to face my dad, who I'd just begged to leave."

Their moms had let them both down. He totally got the pain that went with that, for the kids and the father. He stirred a quick teaspoon of sugar into his tea to keep from reaching for her again. "What did he say?"

"Wanna go to the movies?" She laughed softly, if a bit darkly. "He let me buy all the popcorn and candy I wanted. He and I are alike. Talking about feelings and stuff—we're awkward."

Their waitress approached the table again and Stella looked more than grateful for the distraction this time. "Sir, we are one of the few local establishments that offer alcohol beverages. May I—?"

He held up a hand. "No thank you. We're fine." As the server walked away, he looked at Stella, realizing he shouldn't have spoken for both of them. "Should I call her back? Just because I don't drink doesn't mean you can't."

"No thank you. I'm good with the tea." She studied him intently, like he was a mystery to solve. "That must be difficult for you."

He looked at her watching him and realized… She knew. He hadn't told her about his alcoholism, but somehow she'd learned about it on her own. Of course, the woman was a professional agent. Apparently there wouldn't be any secrets from her.

"Who told you? Or did you figure it out?" He forced himself to sit still, really still even though he wanted to charge right over to her side and ask if this was a deal breaker. "I wasn't holding back; just waiting for the right time to bring it up."

"I guessed, actually, although I wasn't certain until now. I understand if you'd rather not talk about this." She stared back, her gaze accepting, open. Sympathetic. "Men use half as many words as a woman."

She declared it so matter-of-factly even though her green eyes glinted like dewy grass. And then he recalled what she'd said about having trouble expressing emotions, like her father.

So she rolled out studies to bolster those feelings she didn't know how to express.

Something strange tugged at his heart, something that felt like… affection? So different from lust. "Studies show that, do they?"

"You're teasing me?"

"A little." To give himself time to figure out what he wanted to say next. "I'm sober. I've been through a rehab program. And honestly, Stella, during that time I've talked about the drinking, about staying sober… and talked and talked and talked. I went to AA—I still go whenever I can make meetings."

She nudged his teacup toward him. "I'm guessing there isn't a weekly group three doors down in some of the places you've been sent by the military."

"Hey," he smiled at her, grateful for levity to ease the tension, "that was a pretty good joke."

"I was serious."

"Oh, uh, sorry?"

She smiled. "Got you that time."

He smiled back, so damn entranced by this woman who already understood him better than anyone he could remember. "You still surprise me, Stella."

"I don't know why. I'm pretty boring." Her eyes lit with more of that tenderness that poured over him like aloe on a burn. "But we were talking about your drinking. Perhaps we could begin with why you started."

She sounded so clinical. So precise. But instead of being put off by that seeming detachment, he was totally drawn in. If she had a tough time dealing with messy emotions, she could only be wading into his past crap because she genuinely wanted to know. Maybe she even cared.

"Stella, you know about statistics and studies. People can be genetically predisposed to alcoholism." Maybe she would deal better with the more practical explanation. "You see one person get wasted every Friday night and then when he needs to stop, no big deal. Then someone else drinks half as much only to learn he's totally hooked and the downward spiral starts."

"You're saying it's in your DNA?"

"My mother, her father. Every generation as far back as I can trace." What a legacy. He felt the weight of it all the more now as he told Stella, wondering if the words would send her running. "The stories people tell in AA about what triggered it for them... I don't have that story. It just happened. One day I was hanging out with the guys drinking and the next day I realized, holy shit, I couldn't quit."

"You said your mother was an alcoholic." She reached across the table and he could see her frustration at not being able to touch him. "That had to have left its marks on you as an adult."

Down on the street, a shrill horn honked right beneath the terrace, louder than the steady drone of shouts and voices from the marketplace beside the ancient, storied river. Jose peered over the balcony, the scent of spiced meat rising from a vendor's cart.

"Don't try to make excuses for me. My dad held a steady job as therapist—there's irony in that, don't you think?" The old saying about not being able to cure your own family was sure as hell true. "We never went hungry. Mom didn't drink when my sister and I were little. When things got tougher for her, Dad always brought supper home and made sure my sister had enough money to look after me while he was at work."

Except she'd eventually used that money to buy booze for herself.

Stella sat quietly, just listening, never judging even though he judged himself. He refused to blame anyone for the decisions he'd made in ignoring his family history.

"My older sister left at eighteen, enlisting in the military to get out just like I did. Except she left the Army when she went into rehab for the second time, when she had to sign over custody of her two children."

Now that part made her forehead furrow.

"How old were you when you quit drinking?"

"Twenty-two."

"So that means you've been sober for five years." Her forehead smoothed. "That's quite an accomplishment."

"See, that's one thing about being an alcoholic. I can never allow myself to grow complacent."

Did she get what he was saying here? How he was trying to tell her he couldn't risk ending up like his mother or his sister, unable to care for their children. He was scared as hell to risk failing as a parent. He was going to make damn sure to break the cycle.

The weight of it all piled on top of him, threatening to smother him. He looked around the restaurant, at the exits, needing air and space.

Stella touched his arm lightly and his gaze zeroed back in on her fast. She looked at him with an understanding, or at least he hoped so, damn it.

"Stella?"

"Do you know Morse code?"

What the hell? He blinked through his confusion. "Of course. It can be crucial in a survival situation."

"So you could understand if I blinked a message to you right now." She tapped his wrist once more before folding her hands in her lap. "Something that might be too risqué to say in such a public place."

"I believe I could."

He followed the sweep of her long eyelashes as she blinked to him a message that showed she understood him completely.

Time to leave. Together.

―⁓―

Stella kept her eyes closed, pretending to still be asleep recharging from her time as a captive. She just wanted to be close to Jose for a little while longer, because once she looked up at him, the reality of their breakup would be there between them. For a while longer, she could indulge in the feel of his lean body pressed to hers. She could draw in the scent of his shampoo with each breath.

How could everything about him be so familiar even after a month apart? She'd been trying so hard to forget him, even thought she'd made real progress. Wow, had she ever learned otherwise. All their time away from each other seemed to have faded. And as long as she kept her eyes closed, this little faraway room and the generic bed could have been their hotel room in Egypt that night they'd first made love.

They'd had dinner on the Nile after an exotic day of sightseeing. He'd delivered another wildly unique date. Nothing about Jose was ever predictable, which made him all the more intriguing to a woman who'd devoted her life to solving puzzles.

Her heart had been tugged by how hard he'd worked to build a life for himself. She'd known there was no turning away from him, from the inevitability of what her heart and body wanted.

She'd blinked Morse code at their table, then again later in the crowded elevator, enjoying making him deliciously uncomfortable. Although from the glint in his eyes, he hadn't really minded.

And then they'd been in their room together. Alone. And hungry for each other. Some things definitely never changed…

Silently, Stella did a half circle in their hotel room in Egypt. Her job had taken her around the world, but this place still struck a dreamy chord deep inside her. An archway swept over the double doors leading out to a terrace with mosaic tiles. Lights from an island shore and boats on the Nile glittered in the night, the same waters that had served as such an incredible backdrop for her romantic meal with Jose. Words failed her right now, but apparently he felt the same, so that was cool.

Turning back to the room, she took in the heavy furniture, the gold gauze draped in a swag over the carved headboard of a king-size bed. Jose stood in the middle of the space in a loose linen shirt and pants, a quietly commanding presence just by existing. He didn't have to try. He was one of those individuals born with integrity, with an earthy magnetism.

But he didn't make a move on her as she would have expected. He just tossed his wallet on the armoire by the

TV along with his room key. She thought she caught sight of a condom tucked in his wallet, but that didn't matter. She carried her own.

Nerves tapped in her stomach and she tried her best to decipher why she was scared, but apparently nerves didn't know Morse code. She knew this was right and she was absolutely certain she wanted to be with him. The scents of their date swirled in her mind so tangibly she could swear she still smelled the incense, the spices, and the light glistening of perspiration. The things they'd shared with each other about their childhoods had been intense, unifying.

While she couldn't help wishing they'd met at a less complicated time, they were here together, now, and she wasn't turning away.

"Jose," she said simply, "this night has been almost perfect."

"Almost?" A dark eyebrow angled upward.

Nerves tingled along her already sizzling skin. She'd been thinking of this since their first date, in reality probably since the moment she saw him lift that scuba mask on the boat. She knew this was right, that he was *the one*, but with expectations so high, she couldn't help fearing somehow something would go wrong.

Steeling her spine and pushing back doubts, she pulled her hand from her hobo bag and placed a condom on the bedside table. "But I bet we can make it one hundred percent perfection by morning."

He ambled toward her, one sexy step at a time. "That's a bet I'm more than happy to take."

Then he kissed her and the last thing she thought about was the room's décor or timing. All she cared about was the man in her arms. He swept back the green cloth over her hair, the silky fabric slithering down and off. His hands followed. Stroking. Tempting. Along her back and sliding down to cup her bottom. Her body melded to his. Her breasts went tingly and tight against the muscled wall of his chest. The rigid length of his erection pressed into her stomach.

Kissing him, being with him set her on fire in a way that so defied logic she was caught unaware again and again. And right now, she didn't want reason. She just wanted to feel.

He touched her with the same intuition he'd shown in how he'd known just what to say when her heart had been bare and hurting over sharing about her mom. Jose understood and that connected them. She'd recognized they were meant to be together from the first moment she'd seen him.

The way he swept off her blouse and loose fitting pants with such ease, he could have been her longtime lover. His moves synchronized with hers. His clothes fell away into a pile as entwined as their bodies. Bare flesh to flesh, his skin sealed to hers, the cut and definition of masculine hardness turning her inside out.

His lips trekked down her throat and she could swear she heard him whisper "freckles" with a low growl before his finger teased her nipples, plucking with just the right amount of pressure to make desire pulse through her. She pressed her knees together against his thick thigh. She squeezed harder against the moist ache between her legs, burning for more. With each husky word Jose whispered against her skin, he promised to deliver.

And as she was fast learning, this was a two-way

street, with her touching him and finding that every stroke brought her as much pleasure as she gave. Her fingers played over the flex of muscles along his chest. She scored her nails lower, his washboard abs twitching into deeper refinement. His skin was like warm butterscotch, tempting her to...

She flicked her tongue along his collarbone, salty sweet and all hers. He ducked to capture her mouth and the minty taste of tea remained. Was everything about him perfect? Even the way he'd handled adversity with a humble strength. God, he was making her fall deeper in love with him by the day. By the hour.

And right now, by the caress.

Backing toward the bed, her legs tangled with his until the mattress met her calves and he lowered her onto the coarse tapestry spread, her feet still hanging off the bed. Before she could think, he knelt on the floor at the foot of the bed and leaned forward to press a lingering kiss to her stomach. His intent became abundantly clear as he hooked her legs over his shoulders and nuzzled the inside of her thigh.

Being so open and vulnerable to him could have been awkward, but everything with Jose just felt natural. Right. And utterly blissful. Pleasure rippled through her with each intuitive stroke of his tongue, every caress of his talented fingers. She ached to be closer to him, to feel him on top of her, inside her, and just the thought of that alone sent her the rest of the way over the edge. Her back arched into the release, again and again, her restless hands grasping at his head, his shoulders, urging him upward.

Somewhere in a distant functioning part of her

brain she noticed how he sheathed himself before sliding upward, kneeling over her, moving with her up the bed. Every rasp against her super-sensitized skin made her shiver with aftershocks as she inched toward the piled pillows.

Her head sunk back into the downy softness as she clasped at Jose's shoulders, unrecognizable murmurs rolling from her as she urged him closer. Yet, he still held back, driving her crazy with his mouth along her breasts up to her neck, until finally, thank God, finally he kissed her with an incredible mixture of passion and tenderness. Then thrust inside her, stretched her, filled her, and she knew…

Their date, being together was absolutely perfect. So much so it scared her to think of losing him.

Chapter 7

JOSE SENSED THE CHANGE IN STELLA WHEN SHE WOKE, the way her breathing shifted in their small military quarters. He'd been with her so often, he knew the feel of her body asleep—and awake. She'd woken at least twenty minutes ago, but for whatever reason, she chose to keep her eyes closed while she rested her head on his shoulder.

At least she'd rested for more than six hours since the questioning in the hangar. He sure as hell wasn't going to argue about holding her. He just stroked his hand along her shoulder, the memory of that night in Egypt so damn real in his head right now, he went hard at the images swimming in his mind. He'd known he loved her but suspected if he said it right after sex, she would have thought he was talking with his dick rather than his heart. So he'd waited for the right moment to tell her.

Not that it all mattered in the end. He should have been smarter, should have seen the train wreck before they both crashed full-on into a massive heartache that was still kicking his ass.

Before he could stop himself—and hell, he didn't even want to stop—he kissed the top of her head. And how sappy was that? He was all choked up over nuzzling her hair. Her hair, for God's sake. He'd been with this woman dozens of times, tasted every freckle on her body. He squeezed his eyes closed, resting his forehead on her and just breathing in the unique scent of her that overrode any shampoo.

Her hand fell to rest on his shoulder, signaling she was finally ready to admit to being awake.

He eased back to look in her eyes. "How do you feel?"

"Better, rested. Thank you." Her fingers trailed down to his chest and his body twitched in reaction. "Jose, it would be horribly cliché of us to kiss right now… or more."

His body went even harder against his fly in reaction to her words. "Clichés aren't always bad."

She closed her eyes tightly, resting her head against his shoulder. "Can we just talk? Just see if we can hang out here together? I don't want to say good-bye yet, but honest to God, Jose, I can't go back."

Did she realize how her nipples beaded against the robe, making him ache to sweep open the neck and take each peak in his mouth?

He decided to take hope from the fact that she wasn't running out the door. He hugged an arm around her shoulder. "Stay put. The less you move the better it is for both of us."

She looked up quickly.

He just winked.

Stella relaxed against his side. "I've said this before, but it bears repeating. This would be much easier if you could be a jackass."

"There are a lot of things that could make this simpler, but life isn't going to pave the way for us. So for now, let me just be glad you're alive and we'll just ignore the rest." Like his raging erection. "Anything I can get for you? Food? Something to drink?"

"I'm good now. You were right. I was running on fumes before. I needed to recharge." Rolling to her back, she pushed a hank of hair off her forehead. "Have you heard anything about the teenager? Or the other hostages?"

Even as they settled into a no-sex agreement, God, how easy it was to lay in a bed together and talk with the familiarity of lovers. How easy it would be to tug the tie on her robe and make them both forget the hellish past four weeks apart.

His hands clenched. "No earth-shattering news. Just a text from Bubbles a couple of hours ago." He scooped his cell phone off the bedside table and double-checked. No new messages. He tossed it on the bed between them where it bounced once before settling. "The other hostages have been medically evaluated. Everyone was processed separately, so they think you're simply in another room. Sutton and the others should be flying out and heading home within a few hours."

"Which technically, I am." She pushed against the mattress, sitting up.

And driving him crazy with the way her knee peeked between the part in her robe.

She hugged her knees. "And the boy? The code?"

"I'm sure Mr. Smith will contact you once he has something."

"Waiting is tough."

He knew that was an understatement for her. He'd seen just how hard it had been for her to walk away from decoding whatever message lurked in that cloth. Stella might not be the most overt with her emotions, but she took her job seriously and her methodical mind had an almost obsessive need to untangle puzzles. He had the feeling she'd probably been trying to break the code from memory even while she'd slept.

"Most high-risk jobs are ninety-nine percent waiting and one percent high-octane insanity." He should roll out of bed, get dressed, and get the hell out of here. He should. But he stayed right where he was because being tempted with her was less painful than being without her. "You said you came here searching for answers about your mother, that you had unanswered questions about how she died. What do you think happened?"

He genuinely wanted to know, and the conversation seemed to be a safe passion douser. Besides, he understood that she needed a distraction before the mystery code drove her crazy. Knowing she hadn't told him her suspicions about her mother's death before now also made him question how close they'd really been before.

"I'm not sure exactly. I was fifteen when she died. The casket was closed." She pinched the bridge of her nose, the only sign of emotion as she recited the facts coolly. "They said she sustained head injuries. Supposedly, she was alone driving in the rain and that she spun out into a tree. A branch... killed her."

He didn't care how calm her voice sounded. No one could be unaffected by that. He took her hand in his, linking fingers. "Not seeing her body had to have made things more difficult."

"I only said the casket was closed. The funeral director still let us see her after he'd made her more... presentable. Her face was so puffy and distorted..." She swallowed hard. "They had to put a wig on her."

"Perhaps seeing her wasn't the best idea for a teenager

after all." He stroked his thumb back and forth along the speeding pulse in her wrist.

"I had nightmares for a long time." She cut her eyes toward him. "I still do on occasion. Ones where that puffy face with a wig morphs back into the face I remember. She whispers to me to help her…"

"God, Stella…" To hell with distance. He wrapped his arms around her shoulders and hauled her against his chest.

"Here's the thing." She gripped his T-shirt and he knew she held onto her self-control even tighter. "We were also given photos of the accident site and the crumpled vehicle being towed away."

"Something's bothering you." He loved her analytical mind as much as he loved the rest of her. And obviously things hadn't added up for her regarding how her mom had died.

"I could see the tire tracks leading up to the tree, right to the long, broken off branch. Except no matter how many times I looked at it, I came to the same conclusion." A shuddering breath shook her shoulders. "The limb had to have gone through the *passenger* side. My mother wasn't alone in that car and she wasn't driving. Why did they lie? Who hurt her? Was that car accident even the cause of her death?"

She'd been solving mysteries even as a teenager. "What did your father have to say?"

"He insisted I was in denial from grief. He offered to get me everything from a new puppy to therapy. I just wanted my mom." She touched his jaw. "But I guess you understand that. You know you tugged my heart that day monkey watching at the National Park. All those images of you as a kid hanging out at the zoo studying families… You still tug on my emotions, Jose."

The talk of families rather than just mothers steered toward dangerous territory for them. "Stella…"

Sitting up, she put her fingers over his mouth. "I know. It's not wise for us to discuss this, especially in a bed, but nothing about us has been smart or planned. I certainly didn't bargain on finding someone like you when I came to Africa. I'd expected to find my Mr. Right once I put the past to rest."

"Sorry to wreck your plans." He kissed her fingers. "I mean that. But I am who I am."

Damn it, if he could figure out a way around their different views for the future, he would. But they'd talked and talked this to death with no progress.

"For a man who's so confident in the work world, I just don't understand how you can't see your strengths in your personal realm. I believe in you."

Anger nipped at the edges of his already dissolving resolve. "Dumping me was a funny way of showing your faith in me."

"I have so much faith in you I refuse to settle for anything but your one hundred percent." She swung her legs off the edge of the bed. "I need to get dressed and go."

And here they were again, at a fucking impasse. He reined in his anger with a gritty control that had carried him through marathons and missions. "Then I guess that's my cue to get to work."

He rolled to his feet and snagged his uniform jacket off the back of a chair.

"I'm sorry to have kept you from your team. You must have a lot to prep for the vice president's wife's visit."

He buttoned up his uniform. "Actually, I'm not on call for that until tomorrow. So for now, you have a bodyguard."

The best thing for both of them right now? To lose themselves in work. Completely.

That didn't mean for a second that he was backing off. For whatever reason, she'd landed in his life again and every second with her only reinforced one glaring fact.

Walking away wasn't an option anymore.

———〰———

Ajaya shuffle-walked beside his two "guards" and tried like hell not to wet himself. He wanted to run away into the dark night and just disappear, except there was no place to hide even if he could get past the fences and captors.

He could only stick by the two agents leading him to his quarters—if that was really where they were taking him. He understood too well about prison cells and torture chambers.

He was so damn scared and tired. It had been a dangerous move climbing onto that helicopter. But at that moment he had been more afraid of the people chasing him than the aircraft he had run toward. All he had been able to think about was leaving, flying as far away as possible. He'd been terrified one of the hostages would recognize him and accuse him of horrible things. God, how he envied them being able to leave. Even now, he could see some of the hostages in the distance loading up on a plane to go.

He prayed the interrogators believed him when he

said he wanted to get away. That much was true. He had even offered up the information about the pattern in the cloth to make them trust he told the truth.

But it was so scary figuring out how much to say without getting himself in trouble if the others took him back.

Keeping pace with his silent guards into the dimly lit night, he resisted the urge to ask them where they were going. To beg them to help him escape to… Where? He had nowhere to go. He just wanted to be alone and safe for one night. Just one night to sleep with a full stomach and no fears.

"Sir, where are you taking me?" he asked the one who had been called Mr. Smith. The fact that he had not been passed over to people in uniform frightened him. He should not warrant this level of attention.

"As I told you earlier, we are escorting you to a room." Mr. Smith walked soundlessly. The guy was downright creepy with his dark suit and black hole eyes that didn't have any emotion. "There will be a guard outside your door—for your protection too—until we check out your story."

"Why would I lie?" He sounded desperate, he knew, but maybe that was good.

"Because you have been identified as one of the kidnappers."

"I am just a kid." A kid who felt a million years old.

"All the more reason for us to look out for your safety as well." Mr. Smith's jacket parted to reveal a gun.

The other man, Mr. Brown, stopped outside a concrete block building. "Let's get the kid a Happy Meal and tuck him into his race car bed. I'm beat."

Beat? Ajaya flinched back, pressing his spine against the warm wall.

That word must mean something different than he thought. Because beating... He swallowed down vomit.

If he could just go back in time. Back to the school where he'd been sent after his family died. He'd been so intent on revenge he had been willing to sign on, thinking he would be a warrior.

Instead, they'd turned him into a murderer.

If these men beside him learned the things he had done, they wouldn't be offering him Happy Meals or anything else. He wasn't innocent anymore. He couldn't go back to the school, and he certainly did not want to go back to the people who'd taken him.

But he could not stay here much longer. They would lock him up for life once they learned everything about his past.

He scraped his fingers along the rough exterior, wishing he could anchor himself to the spot. Mr. Smith unlocked the door and swung it wide. Two uniformed guards with machine guns slung over their shoulders stepped out and flanked either side of the door.

Mr. Smith swept a hand toward the open door. "Here we are. Your room."

Ajaya peeled himself off the wall and inched inside. Warily.

He looked from side to side at the clean cool space with a big bed on one side. He found his boxed "happy meal" on a small table. They were obviously trying to lull him. To win him over. It was going to take more than food and a bed. The others had tried that and he wouldn't be cheaply bought again.

Still, he smiled his thanks and prayed they would leave faster. He just wanted to be alone to eat and shower.

And plan.

He hadn't decided how to get out of here yet, but if he bided his time long enough he would come up with a plan. He still had more information to share, later, if he needed it. For now they would be busy figuring out the secrets encrypted into the pattern on the cloth. Although once they translated the writing, he suspected they would never unravel the code. That was probably the only thing keeping him alive.

Because even though he'd needed to hide here from dozens of monsters out to get him, there were monsters here too.

⁓

Stella jogged down the outdoor steps—über careful not to brush against Jose—as they made their way through the base, back to the command center in the hangar.

She'd been foolish to think she could share a room with him for even a few hours and suffer no consequences. More than just memories of making love tormented her. She may have been asleep most of the time, but being so close to him knocked the props out from under her self-control. Being with him, curled up close to his warm, familiar body, and talking to him taunted her with how well they fit in more ways than just sex. She missed him. She ached to be with him, and she didn't know how to stuff down those feelings again.

And a nighttime stroll sure as hell wasn't helping matters.

At least she was wearing more than a robe now. After

bolting off the bed to put distance between her and the memories of her first time sleeping with Jose, she'd rushed into the bathroom to change into jeans and an embroidered tunic.

The past few days of captivity must have stripped away her ability to put up walls. She needed to get back to work, to refocus her thoughts and numb her emotions. Above all, she needed to keep things light, superficial.

She wrapped her arms around herself. "The lights are off in the chow hall. I sure hope they sent some boxed meals to the hangar."

His boots thudded a steady pace beside her. "Remember when we went out to eat in Egypt?"

Gulp. Apparently he wasn't going to follow her lead on small talk. "How could I forget our dinner by the Nile? I recall every word we said, and yes, I remember staying in the hotel with you and making love with you for the first time. It would be an obvious lie to say otherwise."

She walked faster.

So did he. "Me too."

Anger fed off her simmering sexual frustration. She stopped abruptly, her gym shoes squeaking as she pivoted to face him. "Why in the world would you bring that up now?"

He clasped her elbow, pulling her closer, the deserted walkway giving an illusion of privacy—intimacy. "You want the truth? Here it is. The past month without you has been hell." His voice went raw. "Then thinking you would die in that camp took hell to a whole different level."

"Jose," emotion clogged her throat, "of course there are still residual feelings. But that doesn't mean…"

"No. Not residual or leftover or fading feelings." He

caressed her face. "I've decided I'm not sure how I can live the rest of my life without you."

His touch was so strong and tender on that star-filled night... it was all too much. She swayed closer to him, her breasts brushing the familiar hard wall of his chest. "You're not playing fair."

"None of this is fair, Stella." His dark eyes held her with a shivery intensity. Night sounds reverberated in the distance—a Jeep inside the base, a wild beast stirring outside. "How is it fair that we would fall in love with each other when we have such a fundamental difference of opinion about what constitutes the perfect life together?"

"One of us would have to compromise." She couldn't douse the whisper of hope smoking through her that they were even having this discussion.

He stroked down along her arm, just a simple caress that stirred her more than a kiss from any other man. She'd been drawn to Jose on a deep and undeniable level from the first moment she'd seen him. She just hadn't expected chemistry and kismet to have such a harsh sense of humor. Just looking at Jose now hurt so badly she fought the urge to fall to her knees.

"What if I said," he swallowed hard, "that I'm willing to do whatever you want?"

For a greedy instant, she wanted to throw her arms around his neck and hold on, to say to hell with the smart decision or the inevitable. She just wanted him and would give up anything, do anything to be with him. Until reason smothered the whisper of hope before it could reach a full flame. They needed to find a way to accept each other rather than change each other.

"I would say you're breaking my heart. I would also say I can't be happy if what I'm doing makes you unhappy." She held onto his elbows, her nails digging in deep as if she could hold onto this moment, hold onto him. "Truly, Jose, this is pointless and we both know it. We're only delaying the inevitable."

Even as she hoped he would tell her she was wrong, she couldn't miss the frustration tightening his jaw.

His hands slid from her face to her shoulders. "I think you're the one not being honest with me or yourself. I offer to give you whatever you want and you still turn me down? Who's really afraid of the perfect life?"

His accusation made her gasp, each wording slicing clean through her. It wasn't true, damn it. She'd poured her entire heart and dreams into their relationship. She tipped her head back to blink away tears blurring the stars.

"Shit," he cursed softly.

Just as bullets pocked the ground at her feet.

Chapter 8

JOSE HOOKED HIS ARM AROUND STELLA'S WAIST AND slammed them both against the wall. Gunfire popped from the other side of the building and damn it, he could use some professional distance right now. Even knowing she was a trained agent didn't stop him from wanting to wrap himself around her and insulate her from danger.

But he also had a duty to protect their base, the best way to keep her safe. He whipped his weapon from the holster. A klaxon wailed, waning and increasing, pulsing through the organized chaos. People on foot raced for cover while the armored trucks squealed to a halt as personnel inside went into attack mode.

No enemy forces were in sight. Gunfire and mortars all came from outside the fence in distant tree lines and from behind three crappy trucks. Security forces in the watchtowers returned fire. The too damn familiar sounds of battle swelled.

A whistle sounded, the distinct piercing wail of a...

"Incoming!" he shouted, hooking an arm around Stella's waist a second before the rocket-launched grenade exploded twenty yards away. Concrete spewed into the air like volcanic ash. He tucked Stella closer, debris stoning his back. Even with his body on high alert, still he couldn't help but catch the scent of her hair, the softness of her body.

Damn it, she distracted him, made him weak when he needed to be strong more than ever.

She wriggled in his arms and yelled, "We need to find better cover."

"Roger," he answered, already scanning for the closest door, assessing to see if it would be locked or open.

Fine-tuning his ears, he listened for the direction of the attacking fire. "Stella, the battle's winding down."

"Or they're reloading."

Still, the gunfire diminished, becoming more sporadic by the minute. As quickly as the attack began, it was over. Two of the rusted out trucks beyond the gate now were in flames. The third truck raced away, spewing a cloud of camouflaging dust in its wake.

The siren wailed in the aftermath, and shouts from within the base grew louder along with the echo of something else... Something unexpected. Barking? He peered around the corner and a big-eared mutt streaked out into the open road.

Three airmen sprinted after the blur of reddish brown dog. Shouts of, "Pumpkin, Pumpkin, stop, sit. Come on... Damn it..." made it clear the pooch wasn't new to the neighborhood.

Stella clapped a hand over her mouth, laughing. She sank back on her butt and kept right on giggling and he understood well the need to tap the steaming stress after battle.

Jose eased back out into the street, kneeling until the dog that looked like some kind of mix between a Pharaoh hound and Rhodesian ridgeback barreled into his chest.

An airman wearing a red bandana on his head looped

a makeshift leash around the dog's neck. "Sorry about that. The gunfire freaked him out."

Stella stepped up alongside, still grinning. "You've been hiding a local dog here? That's against regs."

She *would* point out the regs. She probably had the book memorized.

"Yes, ma'am," the bandana-sporting flyboy said with a southern drawl, "but we just couldn't let this little dude starve."

"My wife would kick my ass," said a private who didn't look old enough to go to the prom, much less have a spouse. "We're trying to work through a group that will bring him back to the States."

The flyboy tugged his dog. "We'd better get him tucked away."

"Roger that." Jose took hold of Stella's elbow and steered her toward the hangar. "Things may have died down for the moment, but I'm not feeling the need to stand around here chitchatting."

Keeping his 9 mm in hand, he hoofed it faster, staying close to the buildings until finally he tucked Stella into the safety of the hangar that housed their mobile command center.

He made a beeline straight toward Mr. Smith. "What the hell was that all about outside?"

Mr. Smith normally played life close to the vest, but the guy's regular stony face was downright thunderous right now. The agent reached into his suit jacket and pulled out a roll of antacids and thumbed one into his mouth. "We're still not a hundred percent sure, but actually, those sorts of attacks are commonplace right now." He crunched the tablet, the second already thumbed free and ready. "Rebel forces, separatists, warlords—hell, even al-Qaeda takes potshots at this base. This place needs thicker walls and better intel."

Stella picked away gravel on the knees of her jeans. "What about the cloth? Any luck deciphering it? And what about Sutton's backpack?"

"The backpack had some other relics in it, which we're going over, but no other cloths. We're still working on the kanga with a local translator." Mr. Smith tucked away the antacids. "Once he's through we'll let you know."

"Or I could work with what they already completed," she pressed.

"We'll let you know." Mr. Smith tugged his jacket over his shoulder harness as he left.

Stella's jaw jutted. "Too bad there aren't any trees around here for him to actually mark his territory."

Jose agreed a hundred percent, but firing Stella up further wasn't going to accomplish anything. "You know how intelligence agencies are about working together. He may have saved your ass when you were kidnapped, but that doesn't mean he wants to work with you."

"You're absolutely right," she said with a gleam in her eyes just before she pivoted away.

Aw fuck. She was fired up anyhow.

Jose kept pace alongside her, his boots thudding on the concrete floor. "Where are you going?"

"To talk to the interpreter." She stopped short outside the door, her hand on his chest. "Do you think you can keep Mr. Smith busy?"

If it meant closing this case faster and getting Stella back home safe and sound, he was all in. "How long do you need?"

—◊◊◊—

Samir Al-Shennawi had been in love with Annie Johnson since the first time he saw her a year ago, the day he left Egypt and began his assignment teaching at the East African orphanage school.

Sitting across from her now in the teacher's break room as she graded papers and sipped aromatic coffee, he still couldn't take his eyes off of her. Everything about her mesmerized him like a work of art. Her oval face was creamy and timeless as an oil painting by one of the masters. She wore loose, silky pants suits that shifted and glided against her curves the way his hands ached to do. He wasn't a poetic man, a scientist by trade and nature, yet she made him feel… different.

Even the loose lock of hair slipping free from the thick chestnut mass piled on top of her head tormented him. The barest glint of silver in that strand reminded him they were mature adults, in their fifties. At their age, they should know their wants, their needs. They weren't innocents.

How could she not know he burned to make her his? He shuffled papers to grade, upper level chemistry, watching her out of the corner of his eye, every bit as entranced by her now as he'd been twelve months ago.

Seeing Annie then had caught him by surprise as he had never been one to believe in the whole "at first sight" notion. He was too much of a practical man for that. He'd never had time or the aptitude for romance.

He'd been a bachelor for so long his brother Omari had once pulled him aside and asked about his sexual orientation. Samir had reminded Omari that people didn't question George Clooney or Simon Cowell.

His brother loved American television.

Just because Samir was not a ladies man or Hollywood attractive—or even Bollywood—that did not mean he preferred males to females. He dated quietly. He had sex with women but did not feel the need to brag of conquests. He just had not found the lady he wanted to spend his life with.

Until he saw Annie. So maybe he was a romantic after all.

He wished he could explain what it was about her that drew him, then perhaps he could figure out a way to get over her. Because after a year of attempting to romance her, she had clearly relegated him to the role of friendship.

Something had to change. Because after this long waiting for the right one to walk into his life, he refused to lose her.

After twelve months of failing to win her over, he'd read up on American dating traditions—perhaps they suffered a cultural miscommunication. He thought he had been quite obvious with his offers to walk her to her quarters and hold her chair for her when they sat together at school dining functions. They had even met for coffee and discussed more than just their students.

Yet, her eyes did not light on him the way they should, with a fire that answered the one burning inside him. In fact, she had such solid walls in place, he did not know what she thought and he was growing impatient. Time for a more direct approach and what better moment than now as the only other teacher working this late slipped out the door?

Samir nudged his glasses. "Annie, are you seeing someone?"

She glanced up from her papers and set her pencil down closely, precisely. "Seeing?"

"Dating." There. He'd said it. He'd made his interest in her official.

He felt queasy.

"Sam, you live here on campus just as I do." She cupped her mug of steaming coffee and lifted it to her perfect-as-a-peach lips. "There's no way to keep a romance secret around this place."

"Then do you have someone back at home that I do not know about?" If she did, why hadn't she spoken of him in the past twelve months? Why had she spoken of no one for that matter? It was almost as if she was every bit as much an orphan as the students they taught.

She looked down into her mug. "There was someone… But he died."

Even with her emerald eyes averted, there was no missing the sadness, the loss. And something else… Guilt?

"I am sorry." He wanted to touch her. He settled for resting his hand beside hers. "Was his death recent?"

She looked up with a bittersweet half smile. "No, years ago, and we'd already grown apart because of my job here in Africa, among other things."

"Then you are free." He almost shot from his seat to cheer.

Her smile stretched into a full-out grin. "Sam, are you propositioning me?"

"I meant no disrespect."

"None taken. So?" She tapped his hand lightly with her pencil. "Are you propositioning me or is there someone else you left back in Egypt?"

He thought of the woman he'd dated for a couple of months before moving, a woman who'd made him wonder if maybe it was time to settle for companionship. She'd worked at the chemical research facility with him… and then he'd learned she had been planted in his company by a rival business attempting to steal his work on water purification.

His trust came slower these days, the reason it had taken him a year to make a romantic overture to Annie, regardless of how deeply she moved him. Trusting his own judgment now was even more difficult than believing in others.

"There is no one waiting for me in Aswan." His family had stopped speaking to him when he gave up the more prestigious job to teach. But he was doing good work here too, even if they didn't realize or understand. "I am asking you out on a date."

"A date?" She leaned back in her chair, giving nothing away as she crossed her arms over her chest. "To where?"

She was going to make him work for this. All right then. A fire sparked inside him at the notion of the chase.

"To dinner, downtown, away from the school and curious eyes."

"There's no need to go to the trouble of hiding anything from the rest of the staff. Everyone here thinks we are already sleeping together."

He sat up ramrod straight, enraged. "Who said this?"

"Calm down. They're just rumors because of how much time we spend together. No one seems to believe a man and a woman can have a platonic friendship anymore."

"I will not have people talking about you that way."
Did *she* see their relationship as platonic? Disappointment
seared through him when he'd only just begun to hope.

"You really are old world, old school."

"Old school?"

"Old-fashioned."

A hint of irritation spiked through his frustration. "I
do not think you are complimenting me."

"Your manners are refreshing."

She placed her hand on top of his.

Hot damn, as the Americans said. He linked his fingers with hers.

"Refreshing enough to have dinner with me?"

Her pause doused his enthusiasm, his hope.

She inched her hand free, patting his wrist lightly before twisting her fingers together. "I'm flattered, truly,
but it's not a good idea."

Yes, she had pulled away, but he was certain he saw
disappointment, even regret in her eyes.

So why then did she reject him? Anger fired hotter inside him, unusual to him as he was more used to
an even keeled life. Not knowing how to hold in these
alien emotions, he snapped. "Are you saying no because I am not American? Because my skin is not as
white as yours?"

"Whoa, hold on." She leaped from her chair and rushed
to his side, kneeling. She took his hand in hers and held
his eyes unwaveringly. "First, you know me better than
that and I thought I knew you better because the last thing
I would expect is for you to insult me like that."

Her cool touch against his inflamed skin made it difficult to speak. "I am sorry. And second?"

"Second?" She blinked fast, her pupils widening with a flash of awareness.

"You said 'first,' which implies there is a second point." He very much wanted to know more about her thoughts.

Her eyes fell away, down to look at their hands. "Oh, just that you deserve better than me."

Studying her expression, he realized she truly didn't see or care about the differences in their skin. For some reason this woman perceived a lack inside herself.

"Annie…" He tucked a knuckle under her chin, savoring the texture that was even softer than he'd imagined. And he'd imagined touching her many times as he lay alone in his bed. "Everything I know about you is intriguing. Please do me the honor of having dinner together."

"You think I'm perfect?" She laughed darkly.

He skimmed back the loose strand of chestnut hair, tucking it behind the most delicate ear he'd ever seen. "Not at all. You're stubborn and you have a temper."

"Then why do you want to go out with me?"

Something so very vulnerable in her voice reached out to him, made him wonder who had hurt her. He tossed aside all trust issues of his own and dove straight in. He wanted her. He would have her.

"I want to date you because when you use that stubborn temper to fight for your students, I am enchanted." All in, he reminded himself. "Honestly? When you simply look at me, I am enchanted."

She stayed silent so long he thought certainly she would say no. But then she sighed and leaned closer to him.

"Yes, Sam, I would very much like to have dinner

with you. And as much as I fear you will regret it, I
sincerely hope you continue to be enchanted."

———∿———

Stella angled sideways past a stack of pallets in the
hangar, Jose's footsteps even and reassuring behind
her. When she'd seen the woman working at computer
station five leave for her break, she'd almost broken out
into a happy dance. Of all the stations, that one was positioned the farthest from the entrances—and was blocked
from the view of Mr. Smith's makeshift office by a pile
of newly arrived pallets full of gear.

She glanced over her shoulder at Jose. "Are you sure
you don't mind keeping an eye out for Mr. Smith while
I'm at the computer?"

"Like I would trust anyone else to keep you safe from
that cranky dude?"

The intensity in his eyes brightened the dim and narrow space. Memories of the shooting outside the base
swept through her mind, of that moment he'd wrapped
his body around hers and to hell with anything else. She
could still feel the imprint of his arms, carried the intoxi-
cating scent of him on her clothes.

Of course he would protect her while she worked.
Why couldn't he have the same faith in himself that she
had in him?

Regrets sucked—and wasted valuable time.

She edged around the end of the computer consoles.
"Sorry. Silly question. Thank you."

He pulled out her chair for her. "Be quick about it
though." He pushed her wheeled office chair closer to
the monitor. "I don't like pissing off Mr. Smith types."

Had Jose kissed her on top of the head before he walked away?

The tingling roots of her hair declared hell yes, he had.

She shook off the sensation—or at least managed to dull it enough to work—and logged into the system. Her status with Interpol gave her limited access to the CIA files and the ongoing investigation. Her personal hacking skills would take her the rest of the way in. Keying through the layers of security, she… was… in.

Yes.

Images of the kanga cloth filled the screen, a dozen close-ups of the script. Clicking on each one, she scanned the translations, four in all on this. There was a message on each side, rather than just one down a long rectangular side. Standard stuff she would expect. Caution about the importance of saving money. Warning against chaos. Wisdom about love not seeing flaws.

Lastly, *Dua la kuku halimpati mwewe*. A loosely translated proverb about a chicken's prayers meaning nothing to a hawk. The oppressor not caring about the wants of the oppressed.

Accessing her profile, she merged two programs to plug in the words, cycling through different combinations in hope of finding some rhythm or pattern. Lines and lines scrolled down the screen, and she knew Mr. Smith and all his minions had done the same. Still, she couldn't stop from retracing their steps, hoping they'd missed something obvious. Where was the code? The real message of danger Ajaya had insisted could be found here? It was like she had a puzzle with only half of the…

Ah, damn it.

She sat back in the chair.

Where was the rest of the message? She thought back to taking the cloth from the backpack during their hide-out while waiting for rescue. Smith said they'd already gone through everything in the backpack. Was there something left at the compound?

Had Ajaya realized all of that, knowing they wouldn't find out enough to stop anything? If so, the kid couldn't be trusted.

She stared at the list of traditional sayings, generic, standard ones that could be found in a fortune cookie.

Her mind shuffled through what little she'd learned… Could the sayings on the other piece of cloth be as standard? It was just a matter of stacking the right ones, in the right order, then pick through a sequence of letters to form a coherent message. Tedious, but do-able if she had all the parts.

Made sense not to keep the cloths together. She read the interpreted phrases again, generic, nothing to draw undue attention. Most likely the other half would have much of the same.

She clicked through an Internet search for most common sayings woven into kangas. The more popular, the less likely it would draw attention. Then plugged them into the program and cranked back in the chair…She glanced at the time on the screen and—crap—she'd already been here for nearly forty-five minutes. How much longer did she have? Jose would send up a warn-ing if there was a problem, and quite frankly, there wasn't any reason why she shouldn't be here. Mr. Smith could be territorial all he wanted. She had rights.

It would just be easier if she didn't have to fight for them.

Her eyes scanned along the rapidly scrolling words jumbling and shifting, her mind racing to sort through possible patterns. She narrowed the search and typed in more parameters. She'd learned long ago this kind of work was a mix of science and intuition. That instinct was a higher level of the logical, something needed here as she was looking for a message in a pattern in another language altogether…

A hum started deep in her belly, the kind that told her she was on the trail. Words came together, chemical components, not a full plan but bigger pieces… A date, but no time. A name, but no place. But those parts she could fill in for herself. Just as the kid had said. There were plans to disrupt the vice president's wife visit, during her first day in Somalia.

And while she didn't have all the pieces yet, the chemical sounded a helluva lot like a tetanus bio toxin.

———

Jose found Mr. Smith in the last place he would have expected—out back rolling an unsmoked cigar between his fingers. The CIA operative was in charge of the intelligence angle here; even the military dudes reported up their own chain to him. This guy had some clout for even the base commander to stay hands-off this operation.

The agent didn't jolt or even look around, but Jose could see the second Smith realized he wasn't alone. He stopped playing with the cigar and just held it. Jose pulled up alongside him, the African sun baking the ground so hot it burned clear through his boots.

"Mind if I join you?" Jose pulled his unsmoked cigar from his uniform pocket, looking for an excuse to keep the guy occupied while Stella worked her magic.

Smith shrugged wordlessly, apparently taking a page from Bubbles's silent and grumpy act.

Rolling his cigar between his palms, Jose tried again, "Find out anything new about the attack outside?"

Smith flipped the unlit stogie between his fingers. "Base security caught the truck that drove off, about a mile away. Local authorities stepped in after that."

"Well, that's the last we'll hear of them… until the next time they attack us."

"We do what we can do." Smith shrugged again, stony and stoic as ever. "Once the VP's wife is done here, we'll be able to draw back on our presence. Or rather you will."

Would Stella stay? Yeah, that thought had crossed his mind about a time or fifty while she slept. "I'm just focused on getting through this week. I'll worry about future pirate missions after that."

"Did you need something?"

Shit. His reason for coming out here. "Uh, yeah…" He held up his unsmoked Cuban and pulled the wrapper off. "Just to smoke."

"You don't strike me as a smoker. No nicotine stains under your fingers or on your teeth. No twitchy reach for a pack," Mr. Smith detailed, reminding Jose that every damn move he made was analyzed.

"I've broken the habit for the most part. I hold out for one a month, reserve it for a stressful time." He pulled out a lighter but… held back. "Having Stella captured by separatists hell-bent on torturing her qualifies as stressful."

Smith pulled out his lighter again but didn't light up the cigar. He just flicked the flame on and off, on and off. "I quit a year ago."

Jose watched the dude, not quite able to get a read off him. He didn't hold a cigar right so why did he have one? The question would have to wait because top priority now was keeping the head spook here from walking around the hangar while Stella snooped around.

"I imagine you've got big fat files on me and my team since we've stepped in to help on security."

"Just call me Big Brother," Smith said, but he wasn't laughing.

"Well, since we're playing on the same team here, I'm happy to help out with the profiles, if you need anything."

"Oh really," Smith said, eyeing him as if he already knew this was all a game.

Who the hell cared as long as it kept him outside, away from Stella? Jose shifted through for some benign stuff to share, things that were likely already in their files anyhow, like their call signs.

"You can tell a lot about each guy on the team from his call sign—nickname. Wade Rocha's is 'Brick,' which means rock, like rock, rock head. He's one hardheaded, driven dude. Then there's Marcus 'Data' Dupre because, well, he's just like Stella with the analytical brain. We call Gavin Novak 'Bubbles' because of the irony. We had a team leader named 'Walker,' but he's moved up the chain. Captain Dominic Jablonski's our new one. Jury's still out on him."

The first sign of interest showed in Smith's eyes. "You don't trust him?"

Unease made the hair on the nape of his neck stand

up. That mission at NASA with a corrupt general was a fluke, damn it. It had to be. He wouldn't be able to do this job if he always had to question if his teammates had his back.

He stared up at the sky, jets roaring past in a three-ship formation, striping contrails through the sky. He weighed his words before continuing. "I trust Jablonski in the big scheme of things as far as loyalty to his country and holding his own on the job. He hasn't been around long enough for us to get a sense of his leadership."

"What's *his* call sign?"

"Saint." An odd one they still hadn't quite figured out yet, but he was willing to ponder on it if that gave Stella more time to nose around about translations on the cloth. "There are several rumors about how he got his call sign. His first name is Dominic, so Saint Nic, like Santa. Others say it's because he's holier than thou."

"Not popular with the team."

"I didn't say that exactly." But he'd been thinking it. "He's just—how can I put this?—a really good guy."

"What about the kid, Fang?"

Jose smiled at the tradition. "The acronym says it all."

Fuck, Another New Guy. A new guy needed to be watched until he proved himself—or didn't.

"There has to be more on Sergeant Zane Thomas."

"He's been around awhile." Too long as the newest team member, actually. "It's past time for a new Fang, but government cutbacks and crap... We're making do."

"Stretched thin. I feel you there, brother."

And what the hell? He'd come out here to divert Smith so he didn't walk in on Stella. The last thing he'd expected was a warm and fuzzy bonding moment. "Never thought I'd be on the side of a spook."

"We're all on the same side," Smith said with such a somber air the fella could have been a hundred and ten rather than...

How old? Smith had that ageless look most CIA dudes wore like a suit of armor. Best guess? He must be in his forties. Did he have a family back home? Kids? Or was he married to the job?

"With all due respect to your secret agent awesomeness, since when did you stop marking your territory?"

"Everybody needs a smoke break once in a while."

"Fair enough." Jose tucked away his unused cigar. "What's in your file about me?"

"You're a recovering alcoholic."

Wow, that one came out fast. Smith's first thought about him. Nothing to do with successful missions or training. Just that big albatross hanging around more than his neck. It was chained to him for life.

Then he shrugged off the defensiveness long enough to realize a nuance to Smith's words. "Recovering." Rather than recovered or reformed because those words could never be assumed, not by someone walking the walk. "You know the lingo."

Smith stared at the ground for a moment before answering. "My wife's in the program."

"I'm sorry." Damn, he hadn't wanted this kind of bonding.

"Don't be sorry. It's working." He rubbed his empty ring finger. "She's doing well."

"Glad to hear it."

The missing wedding band didn't mean anything.

Most agents and warriors out in the field didn't wear one, preferring to keep their private life off the grid as much as possible. So why was Smith sharing?

Smith stared straight into his eyes. "Your file says you got your name because you nearly suffered alcohol poisoning from a bottle of Jose Cuervo the day your mother died."

Fuck.

One look at Smith's eyes told him he'd been played. All this sharing and bonding was just an act. Smith had played him, waiting to go for the jugular to get a real read off of him. What did the dude want from him?

How much of what Smith said had even been real? Had the story about the wife been fake, just to get him to loosen up and talk? "What is it that you really want to know?"

"Is your girlfriend through yet?" Smith asked, confirming Jose's suspicions.

Nothing got past this guy. And while he respected the dude for doing his job well—intel kept them all from dying in this crazy-ass, mixed-up world—right now he was damn glad to be on the rescue side of things rather than living in that dark hole of secret ops.

Where Stella lived.

His stare-down with Smith lasted a good sixty seconds before the sound of someone approaching sent them both on alert. Steady footsteps echoed along the side of the hangar, not at all stealthy, which should be a good thing. Bad guys snuck up. Nonthreats just walked.

Still, Jose rested a hand over his 9 mm just as Mr. Smith did the same. The afternoon's attack was still too fresh in his mind, the smell of the mortar exploding, the feel of Stella's heartbeat against his.

The steps came closer and Jose realized he recognized the tread well. So well, it should have unsettled him all the more.

"Stella," he called out, "Smith and I are out here just shooting the breeze."

She probably already knew, but best to be sure.

A second later, she rounded the corner, fire shooting from her eyes. Her arms pumping, her braid swaying with her every determined step, she stalked straight up to Mr. Smith and said softly through gritted teeth, "When the hell were you intending to tell me they're trying to set off a bio toxin in the middle of a diplomacy visit?"

Chapter 9

"Bio toxin?" Jose jerked to attention, his every instinct narrowing to block out anything that distracted him from Stella's words.

Ironic as hell since Stella was a walking, talking distraction by just breathing the same air space.

But for now he blocked out the planes roaring overhead, the sun baking down, the overpowering urge to take Stella somewhere, anywhere, and hide her away safely. Instead, he zeroed in on the moment, one of those instances that battle-honed instincts told him was a crucial, defining instant. She smoothed her palms down the thighs of her jeans, leaving a hint of perspiration before tucking them in her pockets. She tugged the tunic, flipping back her braid nervously.

Shit. If Stella was sweating, this was beyond bad.

An angry tic twitching at the corner of one eye, Smith snapped the cigar in half. He stepped closer, his voice low. "Agent Carson, you're going to need to be more specific with what information you've uncovered and how."

Stella's bracing sigh wasn't reassuring. "I accessed the writing on the cloth and ran them through some programs. I'm assuming your programs didn't decipher the pattern yet or you sure as hell wouldn't be standing around shooting the breeze, taking a smoke. Bottom line, I realized I only have half the puzzle because there's another cloth out there somewhere. But from what I can put together, the separatist group responsible for my capture has a nerve toxin. I believe it's a variation of the tetanus toxin, one so intense a regular vaccination won't do anything but delay the onset of symptoms for a few extra minutes."

Jose closed his eyes for a long heartbeat processing what he'd heard. He didn't doubt her conclusion for a second. They may have had their problems in the romance department, but when it came to her job, Stella was one hundred percent rock solid. He found that brilliant mind of hers sexy as hell most of the time. Right now, he'd wished like crazy that he could be wrong... That *she* could be wrong.

Cursing softly, Smith turned to Jose. "The symptoms of extreme exposure to tetanus are... what?"

Jose's brain shifted into medical mode, but knowledge brought him little comfort. Horrific images filled his head. "Muscle spasms so intense they lead to paralysis, then suffocation."

"Mr. Smith, if that's let loose in a large gathering," she hesitated, swallowing as if her mouth had gone dry, "a large televised gathering..."

The loss of life, the worldwide panic... the consequences were... beyond imagining. He might as well have been cleaved down the middle. Half of him still shouted to get Stella somewhere safe, while the other half of him knew they would both do their jobs and their jobs were going to take them to the core of the threat.

Smith flicked the broken cigar into a trash can. "Smoke break over. We need to roll. Carson, patch a call through to Sutton and see if you can find out more about where he got the kanga. We'll also need to send someone back to the compound to search again." He charged ahead in a blur of generic dark suit, words floating over his shoulder. "And we can talk later about why the two of you felt the need to play me."

———————

Strapped into a CV-22 heading to Mogadishu, nearly a seven-hundred-mile trip, Stella fought down the welling outright panic that had been threatening to swallow her whole since she'd cracked part of the code. The CIA had stepped the operation into high gear.

No cigar breaks.

The bulk of their mobile command unit was being related to Somalia's capital, ahead of the arrival of the vice president's wife. They had limited time to prevent the attack. Attempts to persuade her to abandon her trip fell on deaf ears. Canceling the visit would embolden the very warlords she and the U.S. administration as a whole condemned.

Now it was up to the CIA, Interpol, the Secret Service, and the military to ramp up their efforts to keep the nation's second lady safe.

From what Stella gathered, the rest of the details were on the second stretch of cloth. But the details on the first length of fabric had been chilling enough. The deciphered code contained the formula for a bio toxin.

Ajaya had been warily helpful thus far. From what the teenager had said, the attack was supposed to take place when the vice president's wife made her goodwill visit to Mogadishu—also known as Xamar. The celebrations would be huge, spanning days. There would be everything from a brass band welcome on the tarmac to a speech at a local monument to high profile diners at a convention center. He vowed that he'd only heard about a regular package bomb.

But the code indicated otherwise.

The potential devastation was beyond imagining with so many different scenarios to protect against. An outdoor bomb? An indoors insidious release through the air ducts?

Once Smith had led them back into the hangar, he'd mobilized his CIA team. The PJs were included for on-the-ground security.

Even if they prevented the release of the bio toxin, there was still the potential for panic if word leaked. *Mass chaos.* The PJs' medic skills would be in high demand. With that kind of threat hanging over their heads, Smith had never gotten around to chewing her out for breaking into his intelligence files to get her own private take on that cloth.

The tension in the aircraft was thicker than the humidity. And it was mighty damn dense, carrying the scent of hydraulic fumes and fear. Yes, fear, because she knew something these big badass warriors would never admit. Anyone with sense was afraid at a time like this.

She wanted to reach for Jose, needed the reassurance of his touch, but knew now wasn't the time. Even though they'd worked as a team to give her time in the hangar, they had left so much unsaid.

He'd been here for her again and again, even when she pushed him away, he came through for her. She pressed her leg to his, giving what comfort she could without dinging that male pride. The flex of his thigh against hers told her he noticed even as he continued to sit in his webbed seat, his head resting back, his eyes closed.

How could he be so calm in light of what they were facing? They had scraps of intel to chase down a major terrorist plot likely to take place eighteen hours after they landed. Not much time to defuse things that could change world dynamics forever. She saw Smith on his comm set still chasing down leads about the second kanga.

She looked at the other men on Jose's team, all of them sprawled much like Jose. Catching catnaps? Storing energy, no doubt, which she should be doing. Jose breathed evenly, his eyes closed and his hands folded over his stomach. How many times had she watched him just this way? He always snagged power naps—in a chair, on a train, anytime he had to wait. She'd figured out his body went on autopilot, grabbing rest whenever he could to make up for all the times he pushed himself for days straight in rescue situations.

God, there was so much to admire about him. She felt small and petty right now for pushing him away because he didn't have room in his life for anything more.

For a full life with her.

Bad, bad, bad idea letting her thoughts run that path. No good could be found there. She needed to be smart, focused. Tearing her gaze away, she looked around the belly of the aircraft until her eyes landed on Fang; the junior team member wasn't sleeping at all. His foot was twitching. He looked around at his napping teammates, his gaze and movements jerky. This was big stuff early in the newbie's career.

Big stuff for any stage.

Fang realized she was watching him and he bulked

up, sitting straighter with bravado, then shrugged sheep-ishly. "Can't sleep," he said. "Smells like straight up crotch in here."

A laugh popped free and God it felt good right now.

Bubbles peeked out of one eye. "Lovely, Fang. Lovely."

They could all use a laugh right now. Stella reached into her bag and tossed her fuzzy loofah at Bubbles.

Sgt. Novak flinched back.

Jose laughed. Hard. Wade Rocha pinched the bridge of his nose as he chuckled, and slowly they all settled back to sleep, but their bodies less tensed, less ramped. Well, all but Fang. The baby-faced PJ was still awake, but less tense at least. His hand dropped beside him, reaching under his seat and Stella realized...

Holy crap. The dog from earlier was tucked under there asleep.

The kid looked like Tom Hanks from the actor's early days, with curls and an aw-gosh-golly attitude. He waved a hand. "It's all cleared and official, ma'am. Some folks at the base arranged the paperwork since they care about the dog so much. No worries about the military getting their knickers in a twist."

"Fang," she reached to pat the dog's belly, "somehow I don't think anyone's going to be riding your ass about the mutt today."

"Guess not." Fang scratched his shoulder under the seat harness. "A group in the States sponsored the dog a while ago and since we were headed out, the dog will be swapping over to another plane in Mogadishu. He'll be gone before..." He swallowed hard. "I mean, like, if the worst happens. The dog will be safe."

"Fang, you're going to be okay," she said with a total

conviction she knew he needed to hear. "I've crunched the numbers. I'm the queen of logic, remember?"

He nodded and grinned like a grateful kid before closing his eyes.

The dog scrabbled across the grated floor and tucked in beside Jose. His hand slid down on top of the animal's head and right away she thought of Jose's old commander, the one he'd told her married a lady who worked with therapy dogs for veterans under stress. She could totally imagine how that would work right now.

In fact, she could envision a lot at the moment, that tenderness in Jose that had so drawn her. How could he not recognize that in himself? The part of him meant to nurture…

"Stella," Jose said softly without opening his eyes, just leaning closer to her where no one could hear them, "just because I like dogs doesn't mean I'm primed for domestic bliss. And don't deny you were thinking it."

"I didn't say anything."

"You didn't have to. I can feel your thoughts, lady."

Didn't that just make her point? They were so in tune with each other, it was wrong that he kept denying what they could have together. "You're petting a dog. It's like one of those pictures circling around the Internet of soldiers with pups. It's heart-tugging, all right?"

"Okay. I just don't want you to make too much of it. Yeah, I'm human and the mutt is comforting. You've been kidnapped. You got shot at earlier today. You could get shot at again. I'm rattled, but I'll pull it together before we land."

"I know you will. I have complete faith in your ability to do your job."

"Too bad that confidence in me didn't carry over into the relationship department."

His voice rumbled so lowly it almost blended in with the drone of aircraft engines. But she caught every word all the same. His hand slid away from the dog and the mutt inched on to the next available hand... on to Bubbles, who looked less than pleased to have company, especially fuzzy company. The fuzzy-phobic PJ unbuckled from his seat and guided the pup back to the crate strapped down, although Bubbles chose to sit beside the dog. Softie.

Stella glanced away and back to Jose. Frustration sparked inside her over him laying the whole breakup at her feet. She looked around at the others and they were catching their own catnaps or far enough away where they wouldn't overhear. A part of her winced at having such an intense conversation when they were anything other than alone, but their life was anything other than normal or convenient. They had to grasp moments when they could.

"Jose, you're the one who didn't want me to settle down with a couple of rug rats."

His eyes crinkled at the corner with one of those sad smiles. "Like you would ever settle down."

"If I had kids, I would make changes to my life." And she meant it. "I want to be there for my children. I don't want them to grow up like I did, not if I can help it."

"Moot point for us anyway."

She flinched, reality a cold freakin' splash of water. "We could all die today."

"That's not what I meant, Mary Sunshine." He bumped his knee against hers.

"But it's true. The risk here is off the charts."

He glanced over at the mutt in the crate as if he wanted to haul the dog back out. "I can't walk into missions thinking that way."

"You approach *every* mission thinking that way. *That others may live.* Right?"

He sat up straighter. "You're afraid I'm going to check out on you."

"Is it so wrong to worry you could be killed, living life with that kind of reckless approach?"

"I just didn't expect that from you." He searched her eyes, his forehead furrowed. "I thought you would understand. You signed on for the same thing. Who did you expect to fall for when you hang out with guys like me all the time?"

His words stung, making her sound foolish when she wasn't. She'd just had a plan and he arrived too early. "You make it sound so analytical."

"You're the one who's logical," he reminded her gently.

She sagged back with a sigh. "Apparently not about falling in love."

"You love me?"

He studied her warily, making her all too aware of the pain they'd both felt over their breakup.

"I did."

His hand rested on top of hers gently, but his jaw was hard and set. "I still do."

Oh God, he was breaking her heart here. "That's not fair." She squeezed his fingers. "Especially not now with what we're about to face."

"Nothing between us has been fair." He pulled his hand free, crossed his arms over his chest, and went back to sleep.

Four breaths later, his chest rose and fell evenly, his body lanky and relaxed as if they hadn't just torn each other's hearts out again, damn it. She ached to wrap her arms around the comfort of that goofy looking dog, but surprisingly Bubbles was scratching the mutt's muzzle through the mesh grating.

She *needed* to find peace, resolution, and she needed to find it fast. They would be landing shortly, then go through another debrief with Smith and his intel comrades. Even now, intelligence organizations were following up, gathering data through satellites and drones and human assets on the ground. Those tasked with detail tomorrow would be forced to sleep tonight, to block out the world and recharge their bodies for whatever waited for them when the vice president's wife landed to greet a welcoming crowd of at least a couple hundred. Thousands more gathered outside the airport's secured perimeter.

She was about to launch into the most important mission of her life, one that could send the world into tumult, and still she couldn't help but think about the image of Jose's face when he'd told her he still loved her.

Everything here in Africa had been so intense between them. They'd only had five months together, a month apart. And in less than twenty-four hours, it could all be over. She could actually lose him in a way far more final than any breakup.

Faced with what waited for them tomorrow, she couldn't imagine confronting it with the weight of regrets bearing down on her heart, on her soul. They only had this one last night in lodgings in Mogadishu to themselves before their part of the operation. She couldn't find a single good reason not to spend that night with Jose.

—∿—

Ajaya wondered how much longer they would keep him here at this base. The man who'd questioned him yesterday had left, but one of his friends remained. How often would they make him come back to this room for questions?

At least they let him sleep in a bed in a room by himself. The space had been cool and dark, the shower warm, and the loose clothes soft. But sleep? That had been tough to find, especially after the attack outside the gates. If the people who'd kidnapped him from the school took him back, after he'd been here…?

He would die. Painfully.

His only chance at living was to play this through until he could escape on his own. Because not for a minute did he trust this man in a suit that looked just like the other man who'd questioned him yesterday. The one they'd called Smith had cleared out fast for some reason. This person today, he went by Mr. Jones and wore a cowboy hat like that was supposed to make him look friendlier. His skin was also dark, but not as dark as Ajaya's. But he wondered if they thought he would be more likely to open up because of something as meaningless as similar skin color.

He just wanted to go someplace safe and start a new life.

Mr. Jones sat in the seat across from him, elbows on his knees. "We know you aren't telling us everything, and hey, I can understand why you didn't want to talk before. Mr. Smith is a scary dude. Working for him…" He shook his head, swiping off his cowboy hat and hooking it on his knee. "It's no picnic, let me tell you. I'm glad to have some breathing space now that he's gone."

As if he was stupid enough to buy this man's nice guy act? Ajaya cocked his head to the side, pretending to be the stupid kid they seemed to assume he was. "Picnic? I am hungry."

"Of course. We're happy to bring you anything you want." He waved to an airman in camouflage behind him, a guy not much older than Ajaya. "How about a hamburger? An American hamburger, made right here by our own cooks."

"Food would be nice," Ajaya said, wondering if they would drug him like the pirates who'd taken him had, at first, until they had him so far away from the school he could not run anyway.

Jones smiled, showing off his perfect white teeth, no signs of hunger or worse. "And another soda? Although the fella over there calls it 'pop,' and Mr. Smith calls it 'Coke.' All depends on where you're from. We have little quirks about the way we speak English. It is easy to make a mistake. Maybe you misspoke about something you told us." Mr. Jones tapped him lightly with his outback hat. "But you could correct that mistake now."

Yes, he spoke English very well, and he was not a gullible boy anymore. Gullible—a fancy word he had learned in school. Gullible—what he had been when a teacher introduced him to two men promising money and a job. "You think I am lying? I went to an orphanage

FREE FALL   175

school, with very good teachers who taught me how to speak your English. You can find out."

He stretched out his story to buy himself time to plan, to escape. Because when this Mr. Jones and all his fancy suited friends finished with him, they would throw him away. No one here cared about him. So he had not told them everything then. And he did not intend to now. He needed information to ensure he would not end up unprotected again.

He had not meant to betray his friends at school. He had not meant for them to be taken too because of him. That had torn him apart for a long time.

But now, he would turn on all of them if that was what it took to get away.

———

Jose had twelve hours to sleep before he kicked the enemy's ass—or not.

Towel tied low on his waist, he brushed his teeth after the first shower this week that had lasted longer than ninety seconds. How bizarre that this Mogadishu hotel room looked much the same as countless others he'd stayed in around the world before launching a mission. Brown tile bathroom, a few extra mosaics, and a few less breath mints.

Sleeping away what could be the end of his life seemed like a lame idea, but being anything less than one hundred percent tomorrow would be beyond a bad idea. Tomorrow afternoon, the wife of the vice president of the United States would step in front of the microphones to give a goodwill speech that would be televised live on cable news stations around the globe. On a regular day, people might not even pay much attention to her visit.

But if the world exploded?

The cameras would all be in place, and those small cable stations would have footage of a horror that would terrorize millions.

Unless their information was incorrect. Stella had explained she only had part of the code. They could be chasing ghosts. What if the times, dates, and locations were wrong? The bastards could be as tough to pin down as... toxic fumes.

Damn it, he never had doubts or questions before a mission. He always lived in the moment. Until he'd met Stella.

And he wouldn't be able to sleep tonight until he laid eyes on her. She'd been escorted by local security to the parallel hall, to the rooms for agents, while the military bunked along the other corridor. The best damn protected hotel in Mogadishu.

He tore open the bathroom door, and...

"Damn, Stella." He grabbed his towel before it hit the floor since he'd loosened it reaching for his gun. "How did you get in here?"

Hands behind her back, she stood just inside the door, her hair damp and loose around her shoulders. She looked more like the woman he'd first met in her jeans and black T-shirt.

She held up a hairpin. "I have crazy good lock picking skills. Comes with the job description."

God, he'd missed her. He pulled the toothbrush out of the corner of his mouth and tucked it in his gear bag. "You broke into my room to see me?"

Leaning back against the door, she shrugged. "It seemed a better idea than waiting out in the hall until you finished your beauty regimen."

"I'm glad you're here." He scratched along his bare chest. "The whole calm before the storm feeling has me antsy. I wouldn't have slept well, wondering about you."

Her eyes lingered on his chest. "You sleep anywhere, like today on the flight over."

"You watched me sleep?" He walked to her, thinking about their night in Egypt. How could he not? He stopped short of touching her. "Honest to God, Stella, I'm not in the mood to talk. I think I should get dressed and take you back to your room."

She dropped the pin and reached to touch his chest, trailing one finger lightly back and forth, searing him clean through. "I'm thinking more about what I said earlier. The whole point that we could die a truly gruesome death tomorrow."

"You're really romancing me here, lady." He clasped her wrist, stopping her before his erection dislodged the towel altogether.

"This isn't about romance." She stepped closer until they stood chest to chest, her pulse throbbing faster against his hold. "It's about how if I die tomorrow, I'll regret passing up the chance to be with you again."

"And if we live?" He sketched her damp red hair back, his knuckles skimming along that vital pulse echoing in her wrist, a vitality he would do anything to protect.

"Then I deal with the fallout." She angled closer, her words heating over his mouth. "Can you accept that?"

Her meaning was clear. She wanted to be with him again, just for tonight, and hell yes, he knew she wasn't thinking long term. She was here for all the wrong reasons and he couldn't tell her no.

He slid his arms around her and pressed her flush

against the hard length of how damn much he wanted to be with her. "I can't think of a time I would ever turn down the opportunity to sleep with you."

Chapter 10

MAKING LOVE WITH JOSE FELT LIKE THE ONLY RIGHT thing in a world turned upside down.

She didn't stop to question why she was with him again in spite of how damn hard she'd grieved over their breakup. She didn't have the luxury of time right now. If ever there was a night to live in the moment, this was it.

Sliding her hands down his sides, his skin warm and damp from his shower, she hooked her fingers in his towel and tugged, revealing the rest of his bronzed skin. Her fingers sketched down, down farther until they grazed along the familiar tattoo on his butt—the green footprints were a tradition for PJs, or so he'd told her. But remembering that discussion was for another time. Right now, she was all about the now. And she did so enjoy looking at him, tall and rangy, built for strength and endurance he tapped into for work, for play… and for sex.

"Stella…" His forehead rested against her, his wet hair sliding a drop of water down her temple. "Are we good on birth control?"

They'd used condoms at first until discussing how she'd chosen to have a Norplant because of her job undercover, to protect herself in the event of possible capture… and assault. It couldn't prevent diseases, but at least she wouldn't have to fear pregnancy. "I'm still covered. And I haven't been with anyone since you."

"Me either," he said raggedly, the pain of the breakup unmistakable in his voice.

His body curved into hers, his head angled down toward her. His mouth was only a whisper away from hers, but he didn't kiss her. Not yet. Each heated breath flowed faster over her. The fresh scent of toothpaste and soap seeped through her. Who would have thought Crest and Dial could be aphrodisiacs?

His rich mocha-colored eyes still held hers as she tossed his towel to the floor. She leaned closer into him, the thick length of his erection pressing into her stomach. He hissed between his teeth, and yet still no kiss. She ached to be nearer, as close as she could get.

"Touch me," she demanded softly.

A slow, confident smile spread across his angular face—arrogant man—and she loved it. Soon all that confidence would pour through his bold hands...

On her.

A husky moan crawled up her throat as his palms sketched lightly down her arms inch by inch until he cupped her hips. Her breasts went tight and heavy in the confines of her bra, only brushing his chest with each inhale. She burned to be flesh to flesh against him. But after a month of living with the possibility of never being with him again? No way in hell was she squandering this moment with fast gropes and a quickie before they rolled over and went to sleep.

And from the intensity in his eyes combined with the restraint in his hands rubbing oh-so-lightly into her hips, apparently Jose felt the same way.

Every breath from him, she took into herself and then

gave back, flowing in and out of each other, foretelling the way their bodies would eventually join.

She traced the lines of his collarbone, up the rigid tendons in his neck. "Undress me."

"I will. Soon enough."

Just when she thought he would make her ask again, he plucked the hem of her shirt from her jeans. That simple friction of cotton against tingling nerves sent a shiver over her. Bit by bit he bunched her shirt in his fists, peeling it over her head with total precision, control. In the instant her eyes were covered, her breath hitched in her throat, and the loss of connection with his eyes and their synced up breaths cut through her. Her balance rocked. Then he tugged her shirt free and flung it across the room to land on a stone elephant lamp in the corner.

His eyes captured hers again, and the room faded away. The décor and furniture didn't matter. Just the two of them together, and God, there was something mystical about being here where so much of history began, the timeless connection much like when they'd first made love with the Nile as a backdrop.

His head dipped to brush her shoulder. "Your freckles are the sexiest damn things I've ever seen."

Her head fell to the side as she gave him freer access, her hands sliding to cup his taut ass, every bit of him honed with muscle, the lean body of a marathoner. "My freckles? Really?" Her words rode hitchy gasps. "I think you're stretching it a bit with that one."

A simple twitch of his fingers and he'd unfastened her bra as artfully as she'd picked the lock on his door.

"If that's what you want to tell yourself." His lips

grazed freckle after freckle, lower and lower. "But I'm not budging on this. Counting them, following them... Yep, one of life's greatest pleasures."

His tongue flicked one tight nipple. Her nails dug into his buttocks.

"Call me silly, but I always just enjoyed—enjoy—the way it feels when we're bare skin to skin." Biting her lip, she toed her shoes off. "So if you're going to undress me, my jeans come next."

His laugh rumbled low in his chest, vibrating against her breasts. But hallelujah, his hands moved to the snap of her jeans.

"Remember when we rented that safari cabin for a weekend and at our picnic lunch I painted most of that bare skin of yours with guava jam, then I licked you clean?" He peeled her pants down, underwear, socks, and all. "I was searching for freckles."

His face nuzzled her stomach, his deeply tanned face contrasting with her paler skin in a yin and yang way that made such sense when they were together. She liked it when life made sense and wrestled to find the reason in why she'd been this undeniably drawn to Jose from the start.

She grabbed his shoulders for support. Her legs went wobbly. "We had to swim in the Shebelle River to get clean enough to put our clothes back on. I was certain we would get discovered by someone—or stampeded by a herd of goats."

"The rhinos ignored us, and the place was every bit as secluded as I promised." He pitched her pants to the side. "We had fun together."

"We did." She cupped his face, her heart squeezing

tight in her chest, which made it even tougher to recapture the beautiful flow of energy between them when even their breaths were one. "If I had it all to do over again, I would still want to know you, to be with you, even though I understand why it had to end."

Standing, he hooked his arms under her bottom and lifted her against him. "Don't talk about endings, not tonight."

The kiss.

Yes.

Now.

She slanted her lips over his, her damp hair falling around their faces as if to further insulate them from the world. He carried her toward the bed, the tips of her toes just skimming the carpet. Her flesh pressed to his, her mouth open and hungry, savoring the minty sweep of his tongue.

Turning, he backed toward the bed and she read his intent without hesitation. Her legs wrapped around his waist as he eased onto the mattress, leaning against the headboard. Still face to face, she straddled his lap, his hard-on still between them. She lost track of how long they touched each other, stroked and stoked, taking their time with each other. The lovemaking a process rather than a goal.

Being with Jose had been fun and exciting, and always one hundred percent in the moment. The man was about marathons, not sprints. Why couldn't he see that part of his nature was so ingrained he was meant for the long term? He deserved it.

"Stella," he said against her lips, "stay with me."

That easily he drew her focus back into the moment,

back to the two of them together. How he read her, sensed that her thoughts had been stealing her from this moment together... that scared her. And hurt her. He knew her so damn well.

His hands cupped her waist and he lifted her with ease, positioning her over and lowering her onto his erection. Muscles in his arms bulged with restraint as he took his time bringing them together again, filling her.

Totally.

Tonight wasn't about reinventing the Kama Sutra. No games or gimmicks. Just the two of them, bodies, breath, thoughts connected, not just tantric, but tantra. Sublime.

He moved inside her as she rolled her hips, sweat slicking their skin. She laved along his shoulder to his ear, tasting the salty mingling of them. She took the lobe of his ear between her teeth and tugged, nipped. He thrust deeper again and again, so fully inside her he touched her womb. Desire gathered in her belly, spreading, and she bit back a groan, fiercely, fighting the urge to come and come hard now.

Her head flung back and she stared up at the ceiling with its swirled mosaics, trying to hold on by distracting herself with tiny tiles depicting... what? She couldn't think.

He cupped her face and brought her to him. Looking directly in her eyes. Connecting with her in a way that was far beyond sex. Just like the first time she saw him.

Pleasure slammed through her, pulsing outward with a force so strong she cried out. In a smooth sweep he shifted her onto her back and loomed over her, staying inside her, pumping, drawing out her orgasm until her spine arched off the mattress. Her fingers twisted in the sheets to keep from clawing at him as wave after wave crashed through her.

But she forced her eyes to stay open, to watch him, to bring him with her, not to lose any of their time together. And seeing the intensity of his release, the pulse throbbing in his temple, the flush heating his skin only drew out her release.

The power of it all was so strangely energizing and depleting. She'd given up trying to understand why it was this way between them. His arms gave out and he collapsed on top of her. His breath was hot against her neck, their skin sealed together with sweat.

So in tune with him right now, she could feel him drifting off to sleep, truly asleep, not some micronap on a plane. One of the very rare times, Jose was completely out of it, not simply dozing with an ear fine-tuned to stay on watch.

Her fingers trailed along his back as she turned her head to look out their fourth story window at the harbor leading to the Indian Ocean. For tonight, she would watch over Jose because tomorrow was completely out of her control.

Jose dreamed of guava jam and Stella. Of their bodies tangled up together months ago on a picnic blanket in a private cove by the Shebelle River in one of the most fertile places in all of Somalia. He'd planned the safari-esque escape, minus the hunting, because hell, they got more than enough time with guns on the job. Their time together, eating lunch off of each other's bodies, had nothing to do with work and everything to do with playful sex.

The lush landscape along the Shebelle offered a stark contrast to the scrub brush and cracked dry places of desperation elsewhere in the country. Their jobs were tough enough, brutal even at times. Their mutual time off was rare and finding places to be alone, to shed undercover personas to be themselves? Even rarer. He wanted to show her life at its best when he could.

Except he couldn't escape the feeling that they were transitioning into something... intense. Being with Stella was different. It didn't take a rocket scientist to recognize that their connection was different. Unique. And that had his heart pounding heavier in his chest with a sense that what little time they had together could be racing full-out toward a gut-wrenching crash.

Shit.

He pulled his focus back onto the indomitable woman at his side and thumbed a droplet of perspiration from her forehead. Lime and banana tree leaves rustled overhead but offered minimal shade against the harsh African sun. Her freckled skin started to redden, matching the pink-backed pelican wading along the bank. He tugged a generous edge of the picnic blanket over her body. The handwoven cloth swept around in bright splashes of green and red.

She brushed his hand aside, laughing. "It's no use covering me up. I'll be sunburned all over, but it's a price I'm more than willing to pay." She stroked down his side to his left buttock with the two green footprints tattooed in honor of the early PJs who'd been picked up by a helicopter called the Jolly Green Giant. "And I do enjoy checking out your all over tan."

Ethnicity wasn't something he thought of other than when time came to fill out forms and check the box. He was a U.S. citizen, wore the uniform. But he did have a heritage he was proud of, a grandma who'd put her life on hold to help them out when times got particularly tough with his mother. "My paternal grandmother was born in Cuba. Jose was her father's name and my dad's name."

"Sounds like perhaps your grandmother was more of a maternal influence than your mom."

"She tried until her health gave out."

"Health?"

"She had diabetes, but she put her needs on the back burner to help out when my mother tried rehab… Then Gran was too sick." He'd wanted to be there for her the way she'd been there for him, but he was a kid without a driver's license. He'd jogged to her nursing home eight miles away on weekends when the weather permitted.

The breeze off the Shebelle cooled his skin and hopefully hers too. He was doing his damnedest to romance her, and certainly their dating had been unusual, exotic. But what happened when they returned to real life?

The everyday Jose was a recovering alcoholic with a family so dysfunctional they could eat up a whole season on some Jerry Springer type show. He didn't want to lose Stella, but he didn't know how to keep her. Here, in Africa, their time together was all fueled by adrenaline—sneaking off when she returned from some covert op in a nearby village to ferret out human intel on local radicals. Or after he got back from a mission on the ocean rescuing vacationers from the never-ending flow of pirate attacks.

When he saw Stella, they were either hyped up on the adrenaline of victory or if the mission hadn't gone well, then they came together with an edge of frustration.

Stella smiled up at him, her nose red from the sun. "When we get back home, it'll be a lot easier to grab sunscreen from a nearby drug store. Not that I'm complaining about the picnic, mind you, I have a permanent love of guava jam." She rolled to her stomach and kissed his chin. "I have a permanent love for you."

She was saying exactly what he wanted to hear. She'd said it before.

And every time it sliced him to ribbons inside. "Stella, I love you too."

Fuck. He hated how damn agonized the words sounded when he said them.

She swatted his shoulder. "Jeez-Louise, Jose. You are so damn dramatic. It's going to be okay." She tapped his temple. "Think about it. We love each other. You're just stressed right now, and I get that the kind of work we do is rough on the nerves. We'll get home, indulge in a full week of jam and tantric sex…"

"Stop, Stella." He eased her off him and stood, yanking on his shorts. "Going home will only make things tougher, not easier. The *me* out here in the field, that's the better *me*, and I'm still struggling."

At least she didn't laugh. She quickly pulled on her bra and panties, avoiding his eyes. He sat beside her again, watching her warily as she stared off in the distance.

An ostrich ambled by on lopey legs, staying way clear of the rhinos on the other side of the lake. The smell of syrupy jam clung to her skin and he just wanted to roll her underneath him and make love again. But after four months with Stella, he knew her pensive face and she wouldn't budge until she'd sorted through all the "facts" in her mind.

Finally, she sat again, hugging her knees, her spine so vulnerable, at odds with her indomitable air. "You've spent over five years pushing yourself to the limit in one of the most stressful jobs there is. You've gone overseas, seen combat, natural disasters, and no one would have faulted you if you'd cracked and taken a drink. But you didn't." She searched his face with those too wise and logical green eyes. "You're an expert at running, Jose. Why do you doubt that you can go the distance in your personal life as well?"

"It's not about the pace or the distance." He toyed with the tail of her braid, brushing it along the back of her shoulders. "It's the 'afterward' that has me worried, the everyday life part, the quiet moments. As long as I keep running, I'm good. When I stop, I crash."

"A crash? Why not think of it as a cool down, relaxing and reveling in success? You don't have to keep running until you burn out."

"Maybe. Maybe not." He dropped her braid and scratched his collarbone, itchy from more than jam.

She stayed silent while an albatross flapped low over the water, then sighed hard, a forced smile on her face. "What made you start racing?"

He grasped the subject change with grateful hands. "I was a hyper kid. My grandma would make me run around the outside of the house until I got so tired I wouldn't run around the inside."

"Smart grandma."

"Then I started running in school, especially near the end of high school." He'd stuck around to avoid going home, taking on extra workouts and stints in the weight room.

"When your mom was drinking, after your grandmother got sick?"

"It was simpler for everyone if I stayed busy at school. Dad would swing by and pick me up on his way home. We made it work." He started to stand.

She clasped his hand and tugged him back down beside her. "What about your niece and nephew? Are they into running? How old are they?"

"My niece is twelve and my nephew is eight. Madison is into soccer…" He paused, stuffing painful images to the far corners of his mind. "Michael swims."

"Those are fun ages. My brothers and I were all athletic. Of course, I pretty much had to be if I wanted to keep up with them."

"Paid off for you in the field," he said, his breathing leveling out again as she veered off the subject of his family.

"You're right there. Little did I know, all of our tree climbing to prove I wasn't a scaredy-cat would help in survival and resistance training."

He'd seen firsthand how tough she was in the field and right now he felt like the scaredy-cat, shaking at the thought of her injured, captured… Or dead. "What do your brothers think of your job?"

She crinkled her sunburned nose. "They're under the impression I'm an interpreter for Interpol."

"Good cover story. I guess ignorance *is* bliss."

"I actually thought I might segue back into that field

someday…" She looked at him through her eyelashes. "When I'm ready to settle down and have a couple of rug rats of my own."

Time to veer off that topic ASAP.

He looped an arm around her waist and hauled her close. "Talking about kids when you smell like guava and sex feels somehow wrong to me."

Pressing a hand to his chest, she arched her back. "Are you going to be *that* guy? The stereotypical dude we see in Hollywood movies who's afraid to commit? I really expected more originality from you than that."

Now that stung. "Call it what you want. I have a commander who's on his fourth marriage. Stories like that can give a guy pause."

"How's his fourth marriage going?" She snapped the waistband on his shorts.

Damn, he loved her sass. "I believe he's got a keeper this time," he admitted begrudgingly. "Of course, he's not in the field as much anymore. Good thing, since they have a kid on the way."

"You're not helping your case here. Any other tales of military life misery you want to share to shore up your argument?"

"You're too smart, you know that, right?" His teammates and their wives were producing like rabbits these days. Brick and his wife had a new baby. So did his old teammate Hugh Franco.

"So it can be done," she pressed, her smile tight. "You just don't want to."

"Roger."

"Care to elaborate?"

"Not really." Images of his nephew tormented

him, little Michael scarred for life because he'd been neglected by an alcoholic mom too drunk to hear her child's screams. Bianca had already been through rehab. They'd thought she'd turned her life around.

They'd grown complacent and Michael would pay the price for the rest of his life.

Jose refused to be complacent. Every day he fought the urge to take a drink and yes, so far he'd won. But this was his battle. He'd devoted his life to saving others on the job. How in the hell could he justify the risk of breaking the sacred promise of a parent to protect a child?

Intellectually, he understood from AA meetings that others found a way to rebuild a family life. But that didn't stop the images of Michael for him. Only work offered him complete forgetfulness and he was beginning to realize Stella wouldn't be able to accept that. Hell, she deserved more.

He slid an arm under her legs and lifted her against his chest. "Enough talking. I'd rather take you for a swim."

He waded into the Shebelle River, knowing he'd only delayed the inevitable with Stella. They were headed for the crash…

Holding her sleeping body against him now as the sun rose on a new morning in Mogadishu, he let the memory of that afternoon kick around inside his head awhile longer. They hadn't broken up that day, but it had marked the beginning of the end for them.

Orange gold rays just beginning to streak through the window reminded him their pocket of time—this unexpected last chance to be together—was ending. In less than an hour, he would have to wake her so they could report for duty.

Report in to do their jobs in a world where missions like this one were becoming too frequent, near brushes with the possibility of a cataclysmic attack. How long could they keep dousing these threats? Was he wrong to hold out on committing to Stella because of what might happen when time was already so damn precious?

No, damn it. Because he did love her, too much to risk adding another ticking time bomb to her life.

He kissed her shoulder lightly, whispering against her freckled skin, "Love you."

Easing from the bed to shower alone, he left her.

Annie leaned against the wall in the back of the cafeteria where eight classes of students had been gathered to watch news footage streaming out of Mogadishu today. The broadcast was subtitled. Her stomach knotted. The lingering scent of goat liver from lunch made her nauseous.

The room was packed with wooden tables and chairs, and she couldn't stop the illogical thought of how the number of people would be a fire code violation back in the States. She just needed to keep reminding herself that a school, home, and regular meals were tough to come by for children in this region, much less for orphans. This concrete building with a cracked foundation and peeling paint was a godsend to these kids.

She was making a difference here. Saving lives rather than taking them. And yes, there were days she wanted to rage in frustration over the lost children, the stolen lives, and unbearably poor odds for a free future. However, she couldn't turn away. Teaching here, spending her life, being as much of a mother to these children as she knew how—that was her atonement for the harm she'd caused in the line of duty.

For abandoning her own children.

An arm's reach away, an eleven-year-old girl named Khaali leaned back in her chair. "Why do we have to watch this, Mrs. Johnson?"

Khaali had lost her mother to a post-childbirth infection. Her father left the infant with her grandparents and disappeared. The grandparents were killed in an uprising three years ago and she'd been brought here. She was one of the lucky ones. She'd had a fairly stable, well-fed first eight years and hadn't ended up on the streets after her grandparents were killed.

Luck was a relative thing in a country that stoned women to death.

Annie knelt beside her. "Because I teach you English, I also teach you about English-speaking countries. This is a visit by a very important American woman. She is the wife of the vice president of the United States. Look at all the celebration in place. This is a big deal."

The television screen was filled with images of the pre-ceremonies keeping the crowd entertained while they waited for the plane to land. Dancers performed in regional garb. The colors and sounds of local culture drew Annie now, just as it had when she'd left the States. She loved this country and its people. She turned back to Khaali.

"Boring." The girl tipped her chair back and forth.

"She cares what happens to you." Annie palmed the

back of the chair, gently forcing all four legs on the floor again. "She cares about things that are happening to young girls and boys in this country."

Khaali stared at the television, twirling the edge of her long yellow headscarf between two fingers. "Do you really believe the words from one lady, a lady who just happens to be married to someone important, will bring back our friends, like Ajaya?"

A sense of hopelessness washed over her because no, she didn't think this political visit would make any lasting difference. It was a gesture. She'd been idealistic a long time ago, but not anymore. Now she was a realist. She lived one day at a time, ensuring that for today, these children were fed, taught, loved.

And telling Khaali that would not make her feel in the least secure or loved.

So Annie settled for, "I believe her trip here is a good thing, maybe even a start of something bigger."

"I believe her coming will only start trouble."

Wise child. Then old instincts tugged at her, making her wonder. "Why do you say that?"

Khaali traced a scratched word in the tabletop. "No special reason."

Two rows up, the uptight math teacher—Mr. Gueye—shushed them and Annie rose, stepping back to her post on the back wall, by the rear exit. She bumped against—not a wall.

Gasping, she turned. "Samir?"

She eased away. Public contact between men and women was a tricky thing, even here. But their dinner together last night had been... nice. Really nice.

She'd expected some elaborate wooing, but he'd

opted for a simple dinner he cooked himself, followed by watching a video. The normalcy of that appealed to her on a far deeper level. She'd had delicacies around the world.

Normal was actually more the non-norm for her.

He pressed a finger to his mouth and moved into the hall. She followed without even thinking—because she wanted to be with him. She wanted to sit across the table from him and just gaze at his handsome face with a strong jaw and the most adorable scholarly glasses. Oddly in some ways he reminded her of her husband with his calming quiet manner. But back in her youth she hadn't appreciated that—and then it had been too late. Their marriage crumbled. Her chance to go home was gone. Now he was dead.

"Annie?" he asked, frowning. "What is wrong?"

She swiped a hand over her mouth and realized she'd been frowning too. "This isn't the time. I should stay with the children and I want to hear the speech."

"They're fine with Mr. Gueye and Miss Veronique. You have time. The guest of honor's plane hasn't even landed." His deeply melodic accent washed over her frayed nerves. "Now tell me. What's wrong?"

She surrendered. For now. "I'm not sure."

"What Khaali said bothered you." He touched her elbow so lightly she almost missed the contact as he steered her farther away from the cafeteria. "Why?"

The television grew softer, the low hum from other classes behind closed doors giving a muffled melody of their life, the same year in and year out—until Samir arrived.

She walked alongside him down the deserted corridor,

their students in good hands with the half-dozen other staff members watching over them. "It's just a feeling, like when I knew my children were lying or maybe even just holding something back."

"You have children?"

She stumbled over her own feet. How had she gotten this comfortable with him after one shared meal of beef and rice, followed by watching *Crouching Tiger, Hidden Dragon*? "I did," she answered carefully. "They're gone now."

"Why did you never tell me this?"

Because it was damn stupid to discuss her old life. "It's painful to talk about the past."

He tucked her into a supply nook, away from any possible prying eyes and nestled her among the stockpile of paper, paste, and pencils. "I would like very much for you to talk about your past with me, let me help share the pain so it is less."

"When you speak, it sounds so poetic."

He scowled, his proud cheekbones more pronounced. "You make me sound weak."

"That was not my intention at all." She touched his chest lightly and oh my, the scholar must work out. "It's nice to be around a man who can express what he thinks."

"The father of your children could not?" The scent of musk and sandalwood reached to her.

Exotic. Enticing. She felt so disloyal for wanting this man more than the one she'd married.

Her hand fell away from him and she clenched her fists by her side. "He was a good man and he put up with a lot from me."

Sam cupped one of her hands in his, rubbing a thumb

along the inside of her wrist until her fingers unfurled. "Where is he now?"

"He died a few years ago." She gulped in bracing gasps of air, until the familiar smells of paste and paper helped balance out the scent of this man.

"I am sorry." He squeezed lightly, offering comfort.

She accepted.

"Me too." Any other words about that time in her life lodged halfway up her throat, loyalty and self-preservation holding them back. She needed to get away from Sam, now, before she did something she regretted. But she also needed a moment to compose herself before she faced anyone. "Waiting for the festivities to kick into high gear has the children restless. Perhaps I should get them a snack."

"I will help."

She looked back, guilt tugging her. "I really should stay…"

"Half the staff is with them."

Her hand went back to his chest again. "Sam, I'm not sure this is…"

"I know." He skimmed his knuckles down her cheek in the most sensual caress she could remember experiencing. "I am a poetic man, but I am still very much a man who is aware that you are very much a woman."

Her knees already weak, she didn't even pretend to protest when his mouth sealed over hers. She swayed into him, opened for him in a full-out kiss like she hadn't experienced in… a long time, longer than even before she and her husband split. Sam tasted like cinnamon and felt like unmovable marble. Steady felt so very good after so long in a state of upheaval and fear.

The sharp bolt of desire that shot through her shocked her. She'd known him for a year, and yes, she'd been attracted to him. But this? This out of control, crazy need to tear away his clothes—have him peel hers from her body—the feeling blindsided her.

As much as she wanted to tell herself that her reaction came from years of abstinence, she knew better. Samir Al-Shennawi, the quietly reserved chemistry teacher, was kissing her socks off with a confidence and expertise that had her toes curling.

"Annie," he said against her mouth, his broad hands cradling her face. "We need to stop this, dear."

A cold splash of reality washed over her. Good God, this wasn't the time or the place... She sagged back against the shelves of boxed school supplies. "I don't know what I was thinking..."

"Shhh... I don't mean that at all." He tucked his shirt in quickly. Had she done that? "Someone's coming."

Oh. Damn. She smoothed her hands over her loose muslin pant suit, dimly registering voices swelling louder through the halls, along with the echo of racing footsteps.

"Annie?" a voice called. The school secretary, Veronique, had left her homeland of France for this job, to help in her mother's old hometown. "Annie, Mr. Gueye and I need your help..."

Annie stepped out of the nook, leaving Samir behind her as she fast-tracked down the hall. Hopefully he would take the hint and stay behind rather than stir gossip.

Veronique ran to meet her, unlike the normally collected secretary who fielded childish antics without a wince. "On the television," she gasped, looking every one of her seventy-plus years at the moment, "there's some kind of disruption in Mogadishu. A riot or something at the airport, and the children are terrified. Your class needs *you*."

Her racing heart stopped for a beat before picking up again. Of course the kids were petrified. Most of them had witnessed war. Some had even seen their own families gunned down.

A firm hand settled on her shoulder, slowing her. She looked back at Samir, his onyx eyes sharp, focused. "What's happening?"

Annie shook her head. "Veronique?"

"I'm not sure of the details. Once the plane landed, explosions started. The news people were running for cover." Veronique took her elbow and guided her back toward the cafeteria, obviously too distracted to even question why Samir was here with her. "But there are reports of shooting and tear gas... They say an attack has been made on the vice president's wife."

Chapter 11

THE WORLD WAS SERIOUSLY FRICKIN' CONSPIRING against her.

Stella sat stuck at a computer screen looking at Predator footage of the melee outside her hangar. Someone had set off firecrackers just as the vice president's wife stepped off the plane.

Firecrackers, for God's sake, then just claimed they were celebrating. More likely, the fireworks had been a distraction for the bigger "show."

Damn it. She hammered computer keys in frustration.

Mr. Smith had set up a mobile command center in a small hangar in the area sectioned off for private jets. The setup mimicked the one back at the base, making it easier to pick up where they'd left off in tracking down that bio toxin. Mr. Brown directed tracking data while Mr. Jones directed the collection of human intel.

The fact that this "goodwill" event was still happening in spite of the raised threat level blew her away. But the White House and VP's wife had insisted on the diplomatic necessity. They'd ordered more protection and moved forward.

So how the hell had all that increased security allowed anyone to get by with a pack of firecrackers?

Really?

Clicking the mouse to rewind footage and recheck angles, she shuddered to think of what else had been missed.

Didn't those idiot protestors realize they could have all been shot? Lucky for them security forces had only used tear gas while the VP's wife had been hustled into the airport, skipping the whole opening remarks to the press part.

But then maybe that was what the firecracker toting idiots had been hoping for. She increased the zoom of the first checkpoint, then back to the runway, reviewing the airplane's arrival for the third time.

Even with the Predator surveillance drones circling overhead, she should have been there. On the ground, in the crowd, walking through the masses, gathering human intel on how those firecracker pranksters had gotten through and what else may have slipped past.

Instead, Mr. Hard-ass Smith had parked her behind a computer screen reviewing satellite footage like a newbie recruit. Smith had mumbled something about not being sure she could bring her A-game after the stress of the kidnapping.

She'd bitten her tongue to keep from telling him where he could stuff his A-game.

So here she sat, watching Jose on the screen from earlier as they'd waited for the plane to land carrying the VP's wife. The PJs were pulling guard duty in uniform, the SEAL team lying back farther out and incognito. Jose stood at attention in his uniform, his maroon beret like a beacon to her heart. The way they'd made love last night had been a transcendent farewell.

Transcendent farewell?

When had she gone from being an analytical soul to a lovesick high schooler? Just bring out a prom dress and CD mix of "their" songs. And yes, she knew she was being cranky and irritable because her heart hurt. She'd reconciled herself to a life without the man she loved, and that had been almost bearable when they didn't see each other. But now? After what they'd been through?

What he still faced if she didn't figure out where that bio toxin was hidden? So many unbearable scenarios rolled through her head. Worst of all? What if she'd screwed up? What if Mr. Smith was right and she was off her game? She could have totally misinterpreted the meaning of that cloth—even though they'd run her take through the CIA code breakers. They agreed.

Tuning out the chatter in her headset, she clicked through the different images being fed in, trying to focus less on the man she loved and more on the big picture. She cranked back in her chair and lined up a sequence of images: the plane landing, firecrackers exploding, the guest of honor being hustled inside. She was missing something, damn it; she could feel it.

She accessed additional surveillance cameras inside. The welcoming ceremonies had been shifted inside to the conference room inside the airport. American and Somali flags, along with other African flags, were hastily brought in along with the floral arrangements—the splashes of color from fireball lilies, deep crimson desert roses, and hibiscus brightening the sad little room for such a momentous event. Refreshments had been set up, fruits, cheeses, and a cake bearing both countries' seals. The military honor guards resumed their positions.

The PJs were in place again—*Jose* was in view again.

Anyone watching on television wouldn't see the frenzied caterers, the terse secret service agents, the ragged edges just outside a carefully edited view.

Then the guest of honor stepped up to the podium. Wearing a navy blue flowing dress, the VP's wife had pulled her hair up in a French twist with a whispery scarf over it in respect to local tradition. Setting her notes aside, she spoke…

As much as Stella wanted to listen, she trained her eyes to look around the room instead, searching for where they could have hidden the toxin. Something to do with the flowers? The confined space of the press conference suddenly seemed wrong. Had the stunt outside been designed to maneuver the ceremony inside?

A shout over her headset had her sitting upright. Mr. Smith barked for all eyes to lock in on the motorcade waiting outside. The exhaust from the tailpipes pumped puffy clouds into the air. But that wasn't his worry.

The delivery truck was marked with a bakery symbol. The truck was driving in, when clearly the three-tiered cake was already set up in a corner of the reception area.

Mr. Smith shouted, almost losing his cool altogether. "The bakery truck, damn it. Stop and secure that truck, now!"

Helplessly, she watched as Jose eased from his post inside the conference room. Surveillance feed from the Predators showed his maroon hat—Jose was taller than most people there and he was fast. Crazy fast. Her heart was in her throat as he ran outside, closing in on the white truck, with no windows in back.

A deep fear, deeper than anything she'd felt before, froze her in her seat. He'd worked dangerous missions since they met, but never had she felt this intense, immobilizing fear.

Had he been this insanely rocked when watching

footage of her being held hostage? Of course he had. The full impact of that slammed through her, the toll that both their jobs would take on them, watching each other take on horrifying risks year after year. Knowing the risks for them were tenfold what they were for other couples. She'd been so confident they could make this work; now she wondered if Jose had been right after all, that she was oversimplifying how they would work things out.

How could they both live their lives at this high-octane pace and not self-destruct?

Troops and security shifted with such seamless ease. The ceremony never even paused. Not the least sign showed that they'd even noticed the disruption.

Stella glanced back at the VP's wife quickly just as the woman accepted a gift from a local general's wife. The woman passed over a small flat package wrapped in simple gold paper. Stella started to turn away—then hesitated, something tugging at her, a sense of premonition. The VP's wife set aside the gift wrap and unfurled…

A long length of burgundy cloth. A kanga. A strikingly familiar kanga. She magnified the image but she knew it was the missing code even before her improved view confirmed it.

It was an exact match to the kanga with the coded message.

Oh God. Her gut fell to her feet like the floor of an elevator dropped out from under her. The bio toxin was a diversion. Maybe real, maybe not, but whatever it was, it was meant to draw their attention away from this. The VP's wife was somehow being marked or used to transport the rest of their message, their plan… She didn't know what, she only knew she couldn't let it slip away and she couldn't let Jose walk into whatever trap had been set.

She shot out of her seat, already eyeing the door.

Mr. Smith scowled from beside the big screen, his infamous clicker in hand as he orchestrated the forces closing in on the bakery truck. "Agent Carson, please return to your seat."

"No, sir, I need to talk to you about what's going on in there." She wasn't sure who she could trust and she didn't want to announce her suspicions over the headset to the dozens of listening ears. "If you'll just give me a moment of your time."

"No can do," he snapped. "I'm busy. Sit your ass back down in the chair now. That's an order."

Chain of command be damned. She was out of here. And even as much as she wanted to tell herself she was just a field operative following her well-trained instincts, she also knew she couldn't sit by passively any longer. She had to see Jose.

"Sorry, sir." She tapped the mouth piece with one hand and snagged a New York Yankees ball cap from the station beside hers. "Can't hear you. Going through a tunnel."

She tossed aside her headset, rammed the ball cap over her head, and sprinted toward the door.

—⁓—

Jose whipped open the back doors of the bakery truck.

And—shit. There wasn't so much as a *petit four* in sight. His worst fears were confirmed. A half-dozen large steel canisters lined the inside of the truck. They could be as innocuous as milk containers, but they also looked exactly like vessels for transporting a toxic gas.

Bubbles and the Saint had weapons drawn on the driver and passenger in front. Data was on lookout. Brick and Fang had his back in case anyone leaped from inside the truck. Only one man waited in the back and he kept his hands raised, the bottom half of his face covered in the black head wrap. He seemed to be cooperating, but Jose wasn't lowering his guard. He'd seen too many instances of feigned compliance.

Did the dude have explosives strapped to his chest?

And where were the guys who dealt with hazardous waste? The last thing he wanted to do was inadvertently open the things.

Carefully, he crawled into the truck. "Keep your hands in the air." Gun leveled, he gestured with his free hand in case the guy didn't understand.

Brick edged closer. "Need help?"

"I'm good. It's tight in here." Crouching, he studied the containers, his skin crawling and his mind buzzing with distracting images of Stella. Why the hell had he left her while she slept this morning? "We're just going to keep the truck locked down until the military hazmat dudes arrive."

As if conjured by his words, the guys in hazmat suits jogged forward looking like something out of a *Ghostbusters* movie. Damn, wasn't that an irreverent thought when he knew deep in his gut this was it? A no shit life-or-death moment. Yet he hadn't looked into the eyes of the woman he loved this morning.

He'd faced his fair share over the years—parachuting into war zones, crawling through shaky earthquake rubble to save a couple of kids, the list went on and he remembered every mission, every face. They'd all stuck with him. But he couldn't even imagine the kind of hellish brain stash he would have to wade through if anything happened to Stella today.

He waved the guy out of the back of the truck. "Careful. Hands up."

The man's eyes darted wildly, like a captured beast.

No. No. No, damn it.

"Brick…"

They'd all worked together long enough, words weren't needed. Brick and Fang grabbed the guy's arms and Jose patted him down, forcing himself to stay calm, nerves level in case he found explosives. They had bomb guys. They had everything thanks to the high profile visit.

And… nothing? "He's clean."

From inside the truck, one of the hazmat guys shouted, his voice muffled. "Please clear the perimeter. Our meters are already pinging. Decontamination stations are already being set up."

Already pinging?

Jose exhaled hard. Okay. Bad. But it could have been so much worse. They'd made it before those containers were unleashed on the crowds on the other side of the building.

Bubbles and the Saint hauled the two fake baker bastards from the front seat. Jose grasped the elbow of his prisoner, wind tearing across the concrete stretch, wind that could carry lethal gasses for miles. The gusts slammed harder, whipping his clothes. The wind tore the cloth from around the detainee's face.

Jose stopped short. Stunned. And it wasn't often he

lost his cool. But fiery denial pumped through him as he realized how bad he'd screwed up, everything he'd missed, things that put Stella in danger. Because somehow he overlooked an American traitor in their midst all this time.

He tightened his grip, making damn sure his gun didn't waver as he pointed it at the supposed student hostage, Sutton Harper.

—⁓—

Stella ground her teeth in frustration.

She hadn't made it to the door before Mr. Brown blocked her exit. When she pushed, he reminded her she wouldn't make it more than three steps before he flipped her. She could fight, but with his martial arts training, odds really weren't in her favor.

Mr. Brown and his damn odds. Usually they got along well, feeding off each other's analytical perspectives. Not so much today.

Meanwhile, she was stuck inside the command center, still freaking watching Jose in harm's way and there wasn't a damn thing she could do about it. Her eyes were riveted on his face on the video screen, the camera angle showing the back of the man he'd detained. And given the preliminary sensor readings from their military hazmat experts, those containers were filled with toxins every bit as horrific as she'd originally feared. The details on the cloth hadn't been a distraction. This threat had been horrifically real, which bolstered her fears that the second cloth could hold even more information. If she wanted to get her hands on that, she would have to play by Mr. Smith's rules. And she would.

As soon as she saw for herself that Jose was all right.

The decontamination stalls were already going up in record time. Guys in suits were herding Jose, his PJ teammates, and their captives toward the tents and hoses. Jose was struggling and shouting something that was lost in the frenzy. She wanted to be out there and shout right along with him.

Nobody cared about the fact that the VP's wife may well have wrapped herself in a major message about the current crisis.

She pivoted back to Mr. Brown, the guy who'd usually seemed most open to reason and calm. Yet right now he was not budging.

Reining in her temper, she searched for the logic that had carried her through past cases—had gotten her through her recent hostage horror. "With all due respect, sir, you don't need me here. What harm is there in letting me secure the second cloth? I'm the person who decoded the first one."

"You mean the cloth you decoded through game playing rather than bringing us into the loop right away?" He nudged his glasses, his smile downright condescending.

"The way I see it, bringing you into the loop isn't going that well for me right now. Because quite frankly, I'm not feeling the interagency love."

Where was Mr. Smith? She never thought she would want the help of Mr. Uptight, but right now she felt like she was being torn in two. She needed to find out what was on that pattern—she'd already hedged her bets by asking one of the tech guys to capture up-close images in case she couldn't secure the actual cloth.

She ached to be outside with Jose. She tracked his

progress as he and the guy with him ducked behind the decontamination curtain. Normally they would have just stripped down and hosed off, but the proprieties here made that impossible... made it impossible for her to see him.

She clapped her hand on top of her head, her ball cap still in place. Reasonable, be reasonable. "I just want to be in the loop. I could be wrong. There could be nothing there. But if I'm right? I'm guessing you don't want the hellfire that will rain down on your head if you say no and you're wrong. Sir."

He pushed his glasses up and pinched the bridge of his nose. "Interpol agents... pain in the ass."

"Why thank you."

His glasses slid back in place. "Go see your boyfriend and by the time you get back, I'll have the kanga here for you to inspect."

"Thank you, Brown..." Or whatever his real name was. She sprinted toward the door, then called over her shoulder, "I could use a dedicated computer and a scanner."

"Want, want, want..." He pushed open a side door and waved her through. "Just hurry it up before Smith finds out I let you leave."

"Thanks, really. I owe you." She ducked under his arm and out into the cacophony outside.

Ropes held back the crowds that had waited for hours to watch the festivities. Sirens wailed from an older local police car, lights rippling on top of the other security vehicles. Flashing her badge, she sprinted across, toward the canvas stalls with water flooding underneath. Decontamination units.

Her heart kicked harder in her chest. She jogged

faster, wishing she had Jose's marathon skills. Right now, she felt like she was running on fumes. She'd come to Africa so confident in her ability to take charge of her life, solve the mystery of her mother's death, and bring change to women and children.

Instead, she was nursing a broken heart and barely staying ahead of destruction at every turn.

She held up her badge again to a local soldier. "I'm on the team working with the men in there. I need to check on…" *Jose…* "on my guys."

He eyed her shield more closely, then gestured with his weapon, motioning her through. Splashing through what could well be tainted water, she pushed through to a new set of ropes around the shower stalls. Men in chemical suits sprayed down a row of totally buff men in their skivvies. But she saw only Jose.

Alive.

Thank God, alive.

She soaked up the sight of him, of the lean vitality, the strength of his taut muscles and honey warm skin. His hair turned even darker slicked back. Sun glistened off the water sheeting down his back as he turned, turned, turned, and finally faced her. His deeply brown eyes went wide with recognition as their eyes held.

Just like that first time she'd seen him pulled from the sea into her boat, she felt that spark of something special, of her body acknowledging his. And for a woman of logic, this whole soul mate thing was totally knocking her for a loop. She'd expected to fall for the man most reasonably suited for her.

Not one who battled alcoholic demons and vowed he couldn't give her the kind of forever she craved. But she couldn't imagine living that dream with anyone else. Which left her pretty much confused as hell. All she knew right now was that he was alive. He'd faced the possibility of a horrific death without so much as a blink.

And he would do it again and again and again, because that's the kind of man he was.

Her nose clogged and she hadn't even realized she was crying. Damn it. She swept the back of her hand over her face, smiled at him, and shrugged. Sure, she shouldn't be here and she was probably raising more than a few eyebrows.

He shook his head and shouted, but his words were carried away by the roar of hoses. He swiped a hand over his face and pointed to the other row of decontamination cubicles, the one where the trio from the truck had been taken.

What was Jose trying to tell her?

She looked closer at the third man and… recognized Sutton Harper. Her fellow captive from the compound. A student she'd trusted for her month undercover.

The man who'd carried that length of cloth from their warlord captors.

Jose was running out of uniforms.

His latest uniform was in a toxic waste bin and he'd been given a set of camos without patches until he could get to his own clothes. He scrubbed a hand over his damp hair, his eyes tracking Stella walking along the rope line until finally they met at the end. She flung herself at his chest hard and fast before pulling away.

"You're okay?" She searched his face.

"I'm good. No flesh melting off," he joked—sorta. "We got to the catering truck in time. Exposure appears to be minimal."

But she had to know this already. Maybe she just needed to hear it from him, and God, it felt good to remind himself now that the aftermath of it was hitting him. He touched her shoulder and guided her out of the path of two guards. He thought about taking her inside, but work would intrude a helluva lot faster there. For just a minute, he needed to look at her and let that steady Stella logic ground him.

"Jose, what in the world was Sutton doing in the decontamination booths?"

Didn't she know? He'd called in the student's involvement over his headset, informing Smith right away.

"Sutton was inside the truck with the toxins." And now the student was wearing sweats and walking between two guards escorting him to… hell, he didn't know. He wasn't in that loop. "You really didn't hear that the student turned? I told Smith over my headset as soon as I recognized Sutton."

"I had no idea. He didn't tell me anything." She gnawed her lip for a second. "But then I went off headset for a while. I'm not even really supposed to be out here now."

"I'm glad you came." The way they'd left things this morning, the way he'd walked out on her while she'd slept… Shit. What if he'd died and that was the way their relationship ended? "Stella, I'm…" He wrestled with the right words.

"It's okay. Whatever you're thinking, just hold onto

the thought and we'll talk when there's not so much adrenaline clogging up our brains. Things are moving fast." She cupped his face. "I have to get back to work… things are crazy at the command post. And no doubt the whole Sutton factor complicates everything. We'll have to review everything we heard from him. And there's a second cloth…"

She cut her sentence short, her eyes apologizing.

He squeezed her hand. "It's okay. I don't have a need to know. You do your job. I do mine."

"That's kinda become 'our song.'" Still, she didn't move and neither did he. The worst was over, right? For now. It was a matter of untangling the piece to start nabbing bad guys, which put the ball back in Mr. Smith's court.

He heard his team walking up behind him even though they walked like fucking spooks. He stepped back from Stella.

Brick held out an arm to her like he was some frickin' tuxedoed date. "Interested in your own team of Special Ops escorts back to the command post? We're all headin' that way."

"Thanks; you guys are probably ready to get through your debrief and find food."

Fang trotted alongside, getting ahead then falling back, racing ahead again, puppy style. "I feel like that damn song… should I stay or should I go? This place is crazy. Do they want our help or not?"

Data clipped alongside at an even-measured pace. "The vice president's wife is emphatic on that subject. You can be sure today's events won't send her running."

An odd sense of déjà vu rolled over her. "My mother

said the same thing every time she would leave for her next Peace Corps mission. She would tell me about how little girls here were hurt... She waited until I was fifteen to explain that 'hurt' was a euphemism for female circumcision."

Fang tripped over his overlarge puppy feet. "Shit, Stella. Is it even okay to say those words out loud? Just... *Shit.*"

Data scowled. "In a culture where it's estimated over ninety percent of the females experience that..."

"Argh!" Fang thumped his hands on either side of his head. "Makes me want to kick some pirate ass for all those girls and for that boy we picked up too... Ajaya."

Bubbles cocked his head to the side. "You think the kid's innocent?"

Jose didn't know what to believe anymore, not after Sutton. And now that Ajaya had been mentioned, why hadn't the teen said anything about Sutton's involvement? Perhaps he hadn't known, but it was quite possible he had. How much was truth and how much was a setup? Ajaya *was* the one who'd told Stella about the code in the kanga cloth in the first place.

Her voice pierced through his thoughts as they reached the mobile command center.

"I think he's scared shitless and would do anything to stay safe. I think there are countries that use children as soldiers and weapons for the very reason that we're vulnerable in that arena. We're wired to back off when a kid's involved."

Great. He hitched his hands on his hips. Just fucking great. "I guess this is where we step off. Good luck with that second cloth."

She winced. "Unless I'm about to lead us all on a wild goose chase."

"Hey!" He caught her eyes with his and held firm. "You're a rock star operative who got us here in time to avert a disaster of epic proportions. I have faith in you."

She snorted on a laugh. "Just call me the JLo of Interpol." Stella stepped back, looking at the whole team. "Glad you guys are okay. Good work out there. Jose, I'll bring you in the loop if I can."

Pivoting away, she flashed her badge to the guard, swiped it through the security lock, and disappeared inside. He watched the door close behind her, scratching along the tightness in his chest.

Brick coughed, loudly.

Jose startled and realized—damn it—he'd been staring at the door like a lovesick puppy. Most of the team started hoofing it away before he could bite their heads off and started walking toward the west side of the building, where they would give their statements of what went down.

Brick held back, striding alongside him, one stubborn determined step at a time. Great guy to have guarding your back, but the pigheadedness wasn't always convenient.

"Fine," Jose conceded. "Say it."

"What?"

"Don't play cutesy. You've been giving me that wise old married guy look like you know better than me about everything. So either speak your piece or back the fuck off."

"You're in a mood."

He hadn't fully grasped that himself until just now. "It's been a crappy couple of days."

"You were worried about Stella."

"You think?" He'd been through hell and back, more than once, and now he was screwed, trying to figure out how to make things right with her.

"Why don't you just marry her and put yourself out of your misery?"

His neck itched. Things weren't that simple. "Just because you tied the knot doesn't mean everyone else is cut out for the happily ever after gig with two-point-five kids and a picket fence."

Brick nodded slowly, lumbering alongside. "So you're moving on. Okay then, now that we're clear on that… Who's the new lady in your life?"

"There isn't one and you know it."

"Fair enough. I can help. Sunny has this great friend she met at a recycling fair. A hot babe, truly, blonde with an unbelievably awesome rack. But don't tell Sunny I said that part or she'll kick my ass then serve me those granola bran pancakes of hers." He shuddered. "Anyhow…"

"Quit with the mind games," Jose interrupted, stopping outside their door, the rest of the team already climbing the steps to go inside the concrete building for interrogation. "I'm not interested in seeing anyone else. There? You got what you were fishing for. Are you happy?"

"Why would I be happy, dude?" He clapped him on the shoulder. "I feel bad for you. Because for whatever reason, you keep turning your back on an incredible woman who, honest to God, seems perfect for you."

Brick's hard-hitting truth made heading into a CIA debrief sound like a cakewalk. Jose didn't bother denying a thing.

The words rolled around like acid inside him. "I'm not a total idiot. You aren't telling me anything I don't already know. She *is* perfect. I get that. Man, I really do. She's not the problem. I am."

—~~~—

"Henry Pope, we're very disappointed in you."

Fear gripped the CIA agent in an icy hold at odds with the sweltering sun overhead. Nothing compared to the heat these bastards kept pouring onto him. He hadn't been able to think of anything but the hell they were putting his family through back in the States while he was stuck over here. "I did what you said, damn it. I sent all the transcripts of Sutton Harper's debriefs. I covered his ass when he slipped away instead of leaving the country."

"But he got caught and that could create a real problem for your family."

A scream sliced through the crackling connection. Charlotte. In agony. Oh God, he was going to lose it.

"You bastard, let her go." He hissed, terrified of being overheard by one of the spies crawling all over this place. Even more terrified of what was happening to his wife.

Her scream dwindled to a low moan. Whatever they'd done to her had stopped. She was still alive. For now.

"Daddy," his daughter, Ellie, sobbed hysterically in the background, hiccuping with fear. "Make them stop hurting Mommy. They cut Mommy. Daddy!"

"No, goddamnit, stop!" He wanted to howl out his frustration, to claw his way across continents and oceans to get to his family, vulnerable and alone because of him. He considered just turning himself in, sacrificing his career and even his life for his family.

He'd heard about agents being blackmailed, flipped because of one mistake. He'd never thought it could happen to him. But they were that damn good at finding a person's vulnerability.

"Henry," the mechanical voice came on again. His own personal demon. "Henry, we've been very generous with you. We paid off your gambling debts so you wouldn't lose your job and your family wouldn't lose their pretty house."

Slumping back against a concrete wall, he felt the weight of his own guilt hammer down on him. Even now, the addiction whispered to him, tempting him to win enough money to take his family and hide from everyone forever.

But he owed these bastards too much and they were too well connected to crime syndicates around the world. If he betrayed them, there wasn't a hole deep enough for him to climb into. They would find him, find his family, and slaughter them all.

He dragged his wrist across his damp eyes. "I've done everything you've asked."

"Piddly little tasks to test your competence and your compliance. Dry runs for this mission. We thought you were ready, now we're questioning that assumption. I hope you can come through for us, Henry. Your wife's life depends on you."

His head thudded back against the concrete wall. He had no choice. No way out. Only the hope of buying time. "What do you want me to do?"

"Kill Sutton Harper."

Chapter 12

RAIN HAMMERED THE ROOF OF THE AIRPLANE HANGAR. Rain, of all things. Rare as hell in this part of the world, but choosing today to make her life more complicated.

Stella assessed Sutton Harper as he glared at her from across the interrogation table. She rolled a mango between her hands while Smith and Brown observed the interview from off to the side. She'd been given the lead on this for now since she'd spent the past month with the traitor.

Apparently they'd both been pretending to be a student.

Harper was posturing and he was tough, tough enough to make her wonder how long he'd been involved. He looked so benign in surgical scrubs and wet hair from his decontamination shower—for a toxic bomb he'd brought into a crowded reception. She'd been questioning the treacherous bastard for well over two hours with only minimal success. She could only hope when analysts reviewed his statement that they could detect some thread, some inconsistency that could be traced back further until his story unraveled.

What had she missed before, when she'd been undercover with the students? After weeks cultivating a friendship with him, she should have picked up on something. She was a trained professional, for God's sake, and she'd totally missed she was brushing elbows with a monster who'd joined forces with separatists bent on killing thousands of innocent civilians just to make a statement. At the moment, she didn't feel all that confident in her professional skills.

But she had backup. Smith sat silently like a human lie detector watching every move while Brown took notes on his tablet, doing his standard gig calculating odds—the consummate professionals.

As much as she wanted to be a calm expert here, her stomach was still in knots just thinking of Jose standing in a decontamination booth, how things could have been so much worse. She could have been grieving over his body.

The thought of him dying...

She fought back the urge to scream and focused on her next tack for finagling a misstep from Harper.

"You and that teenager Ajaya really played us when the kid raced out of the woods." She rolled the mango back and forth, steady pace, not giving anything away by pitching faster. "You two must have been laughing the whole time you were pretending to be held hostage. Did you two stage the meet up ahead of time? Or was it just dumb luck?"

"The boy didn't know anything." His hands cuffed, Harper forked his fingers through his blond curly hair, exhaustion straining the corners of his eyes. "Ajaya was too low level to be a part of the plans."

"Plans?" She whipped the fruit from palm to palm. "That's a mighty benign word for killing thousands of people with a bio toxin guaranteeing them a slow torturous death."

"But it would make for great television, press... all those contorted bodies would create such dramatic images. People perk up for drama. They pay attention to drama." His brown beady eyes followed the mango with an almost hypnotic regularity.

Good.

"What message did you want people to hear with your drama?"

He looked up sharply. "Like it would make any difference if I told you. You work for the government."

"So that's it? You're... what? Antigovernment?"

"I'm protesting."

"Easy to protest when you have chemical suits stored in the truck so you don't have to suffer the fallout." She raised an eyebrow. "Yes, our people found them."

"Hey, Stella, don't look at me that way. I'm not a total bad guy. I tried to help you get to that helicopter. I told you to go without me."

And a piece of the puzzle slid into place. "When we were escaping, you fell and freaked out, tripping the land mines. You did that on purpose to slow us down, to make us miss the helicopter."

Shrugging, he worked his wrists inside the cuffs. "I improvised. It all worked out in the end."

He stared back without the least hint of guilt or shame. Damn sociopath.

She leaned closer, damn grateful there was a table between them or it might be impossible to resist the temptation to take him apart herself, piece by piece.

"Harper, you didn't help me get to the helicopter when you tripped those mines. You cost us our flight out, risking a night in the jungle. And you turned in innocent students to be taken hostage." To be tortured. To be murdered.

She pushed images of their faces, people she'd spent weeks with, getting to know them, sharing food and tents. She couldn't let memories of them terrified and in pain distract her, not now. The best way to give them justice and honor the two who'd died? Do her job. Bring this traitor down.

He sneered at her. "Not so innocent after all since you were a plant, a spy. I knew there was a snitch in the group."

No use debating with a mass murderer on the difference between international law enforcement agencies with rules of engagement and warlords slaughtering for profit. She just let him talk, knowing he would eventually dig himself a deep, deep hole.

"I have to give you credit, Stella…" He grinned. "You don't mind if I still call you Stella, do you? Anyhow, I never thought it was you. I actually suspected that anthropology student from Maine. They thought he was just trained well at resistance. Sad to think the poor bastard died for nothing since he didn't really know anything."

She forced herself to keep rolling the mango without so much as a wince. Because that "archeology student from Maine" had been undercover from the CIA and they'd killed him during the interrogation.

Her chest went tight with… She capped the emotions.

Later, she would deal with that information, maybe climb up on a roof and scream out her rage at the top of her lungs. For now, she had to do her job, to put together the rest of the puzzle, pull in the other players responsible for today's attempted attack, because no way did those three men in the truck plan this alone.

Mr. Brown stood, setting aside his tablet. "Agent Carson, I believe it's time for you to turn the interrogation back over to us."

The ominous tone in the agent's voice had Harper fidgeting in his seat. The bastard was fine with seeing people suffer and die for his big stance against "the man." Torture was strictly forbidden, but she knew there'd been breaks in protocol. She wasn't sure she trusted Smith and Brown. They'd brought her in here for a reason and now they were just dismissing her?

"Carson…" Smith nodded toward the door. "I hear you should check your computer. Mr. Jones is waiting to direct you to a place we set aside for you."

Mr. Brown tapped his iPad. Realization kicked in. She set aside her mango. Her computer—images of the second cloth. She had a different role to play, one she felt a helluva lot more confident in: breaking codes.

With one last look at the seemingly innocent face she'd risked her life to save, she swallowed back disgust and angled out the door. Once it clicked closed behind her, she sagged back in exhaustion.

Sure enough, Mr. Jones was waiting, wearing his outback hat and his sleeves rolled up, jacket ditched. The humidity from the rain made the temps worse. "How'd it go in there?"

Stella glanced back at the door. "He's a great liar because he has absolutely nothing in the way of a moral compass. He's into the next thrill—he called it drama. God, when I think about…" She couldn't travel that pathway in her thoughts; she just had to know one thing first. "The team that secured the truck and the toxin—are they okay? Any ill effects after the decontamination?"

"They're fine. Your guy—Cuervo—is fine."

She nodded tightly, giving herself one selfish second for relief before getting back to business. "What about the teenager? Ajaya? Is he here too? Did you get anything more from him?"

"He's in the room next door." He took off his hat and swiped his wrist across his forehead. "The teenager isn't as innocent as he likes to play it. He's still holding back. But do I believe he's responsible for a bio toxin being released at a national media event? No. I think he's a foot soldier."

"That fits." Although so much else still didn't make sense. She didn't have a sense of the big "why" to all of this. What were the warlords or separatists responsible for this attempted attack trying to achieve other than chaos? It didn't make sense. There was always a reason… "I believe Harper when he says Ajaya wouldn't have had access to that level of information. I don't think they would have trusted him with keeping that kind of secret."

"But if they planned on killing the hostages, which I'm sure they intended…" Jones slapped his hat back on his head. "They still would have kept their circle tight in case the teenager got captured."

"Or turned, which he did." Brainstorming with Jones was actually helpful. She liked this guy with his honest eyes and a professionalism that went beyond his Cowboy Troy act. Her gut told her he was one of the good ones—but then her gut hadn't been all that reliable lately. "He's been doling out what little information he could, holding back details for when he needed them. He's smart. But in comparing his statements, I found a place he contradicted himself. He said he was taken by people posing as electricians. Then he said his math teacher—a man named Mr. Gueye—was responsible."

"Maybe they were working together?"

"Could be," she conceded.

"The clock is ticking for us to sort through it all." He gestured toward the row of computers. "Yours is just around the other side, at the end, in a cubicle for privacy."

She'd gotten what she wanted… But for once, work held no allure. She wanted to be a civilian, free to check on the people she cared about. Free to check on Jose.

Mr. Jones tapped his watch and snapped his fingers. "Your cubicle. Go."

Snapped his fingers at her? Really?

She wove her way past the row of computers with CIA and military monitoring Predator feed and recordings of ongoing interrogations. Circling past the end of the row to the sectioned-off cubby where her computer and work waited.

And Jose?

Her feet grew roots as she stared, stunned. She blinked. Looked again. But her weary eyes didn't lie.

Jose sat in her seat, waiting for her.

—⁂—

Jose wasn't sure why Jones had given him the okay to sit here by Stella, but he wasn't arguing. Being with her here in the hangar was better than sleep. As long as he had his eyes on her, he knew she was safe. He couldn't give her what she needed in the long term, but he could damn well protect her now. So he sat and watched while she worked. A low hum of activity swelled over the cubicle walls.

His PJ buddy Data would have understood more about the intricacies of the programs she input. Jose just studied her face and gauged the success of her efforts by every nuance of her expressions. The way she scrunched her freckled nose, furrowed her forehead, chewed on her bottom lip…

Shit, it wasn't going well.

Was there anything even there on that second cloth? Or was this all some crazy coincidence? This part of the world had been in chaos for so long maybe there wasn't a bigger plan. He swiped a hand over his face, then reached for his cup of coffee. Getting philosophical wasn't going to solve anything. Today, his primary goal, his mission, was to keep Stella safe.

He set down his lukewarm coffee. "Any good news to share?"

"I wish." She sagged back in her chair, her red braid swinging. "I've already tried the original code that worked on the first cloth and ruled that out. I've run dozens more, even programs I've written. I'm convinced there's something here. But more complex, which makes me all the more certain I've got a lead, some kind of list. I just wish I had more time…"

"Keep working it." He tugged her braid lightly, then paused to thumb down each curve. "I have faith you'll find the answers."

Her laugh came out choked, stressed. "I wish I had your faith, but my confidence is a little shaky today. I should have known about Harper. Damn it, when I think of you risking your life to get him out of there…"

She squeezed her eyes shut, then turned back to the computer, jabbing keys.

"You did everything you could. We didn't suspect him either. You're the epitome of chill in the workplace. The last thing you should do is second-guess yourself." His hand slid up her braid to cup the back of her neck reassuringly. He could offer her this, now.

"Chill? Hardly." She launched a new scan then turned her chair to face him. "I get upset."

"Like when?" He rested his hands on her knees.

"Well, I didn't much enjoy being held hostage or running away from a building blowing up." She counted down with fingers. "And the whole tetanus bio toxin thing still creeps me out."

"You never showed a sign of nerves through this whole crisis." He squeezed gently. "You've been damn amazing, Stella."

"That would have been a waste of time when seconds counted."

"That's called not losing your cool." He kissed her on the nose, fast, unable to resist her. Hell, when had he ever been able to resist her? "I rest my case."

Her nose scrunched and she pulled her knees away. "I'm a trained professional. It's my job. That's different from being freaked out."

Actually, now that he thought about it, his vision of her shifted. "You're a code breaker. I would have expected you to stay in a vault somewhere listening to clicks and reading bizarre printouts. That's what you're wired for, but you came here to put your mother's ghost to rest. That's admirable."

She looked at the computer, then back at him, half

grinning. "There's no sunlight in a vault. My serotonin levels would be shot all to hell."

He laughed along with her, her smile tapping some of the tension from him. "Things are tough right now, worse than tough. You can take the stress out on me if you want."

"You're propositioning me?" She cocked her head to the side. "I don't know. Seems like maybe I've made this relationship too easy for you."

"What in the hell gave you that idea?" he barked in surprise.

She linked fingers with him. "Our relationship was too simple. I just fell into your arms and told you I loved you."

"What planet are you living on?" Following this woman's "logic" was damn near impossible sometimes. "From where I'm sitting, nothing between us has been simple or straightforward. I still don't understand half of what went down." He lowered his voice to a whisper, talking about so much more than just how they'd met, how they'd fallen love. "The parts I do understand are tearing me up inside."

She squeezed his hand with surprising strength. "Even if I make this easy for you now, it's only going to get complicated again, then we hurt each other. I know that. But after what happened today, when things got truly tough, when I could have lost you…"

Her voice dwindled off with a strangled sob.

He gathered her close to his chest, grateful for the privacy of their cubicle in a corner, but wishing they could be in a room alone so he could hold her all night long while the rain washed away the horror of this day.

Sniffling, she eased out of his arms, swiping a tissue from a box by her computer and blowing her nose. "Sorry to fall apart on you like that. But after what happened today, I'm having a tough time being logical or smart."

He wanted to kiss her so damn bad his teeth hurt. His hands slid up to cradle her face, and yeah, right now he couldn't think of a reason why he shouldn't just go ahead and...

Kiss her.

His mouth covered hers, not in any crazy, out of control way. Not here, where someone could walk up to them at any second. Just her lips against his. He *needed* to connect with her, affirm that they were both alive and on a day like today, nothing else seemed to matter. He drew in the eucalyptus scent of her shampoo, the satiny feel of her skin under his fingertips. *Stella*. It was always about Stella and had been since the first time he...

Ping.

He froze at the electronic chime. Stella jerked back, her eyes wide. She pressed her fingers to her mouth for an instant before she whipped around to look at the computer.

"Stella?" He sat up straighter. "Do you have something?"

"Hold on..." She held up a hand while she hunched closer to the screen, clicking the scroll button as she analyzed data cycling in front of her in what looked like gibberish to him, letters, numbers, and words shifting, realigning into distinguishable lists. Names.

"Oh my God," Stella whispered, horrified.

Shit. On a day like today, there shouldn't be anything

that could shock them. Only something beyond imagining. "What does it say? What's wrong?"

"The words coded into the cloth…" Her hands hovered in front of the screen as if she could gather up the information in her palms. "I've translated them and they're names. When I put those names into the database, it came back a list of U.S. and European operatives in the area. Both alive and dead." Her throat moved a gulp and she reached for a drink that wasn't even there. Her hands fell back to her lap. "I thought at first they had my name on here."

Her words damn near set his skin on fire, to think of her identity out there, exposed. It was one thing for Sutton Harper to have a vague sense of her as an agent in the area. But for enemy intelligence agencies and governments around the world to know specifics, to have her on their radar…

His brain grasped on one bit of hope in her words. "You *thought* your name was on the list? But it wasn't?"

She shook her head, braid swinging like a pendulum. "It doesn't say *Stella* Carson. It says *Melanie* Carson. It's my mother's name."

"Your mother? Why would her name be there?" Unless. Holy crap.

"My mother wasn't working for the Peace Corps." Stella looked from her computer screen straight at him, her eyes hollow with disillusionment. "She was a CIA operative."

―〜〜―

Sam would miss these late night walks with Annie when they came to an end, and he knew they would have to end eventually. His job here would be over once she realized exactly why he wasn't the man for her. For now, he wanted to breathe in the air heavy with humidity from the rain and make the most of every last second with her.

How far was he willing to take that, even knowing it couldn't last? Somehow he'd lost sight of that end result in his yearlong pursuit of her. At some point he'd become so consumed with making her notice him, he'd forgotten there would be a very real expiration date.

After the way they'd kissed at the school earlier, his time to figure out his next move was coming. Most likely sooner rather than later.

Annie tipped her face into the night breeze, moonlight streaming down over her porcelain face, illuminating the freckles along her nose. "The kids recovered quickly from the disturbing news reports. By supper, they were acting like nothing had happened."

"You were good with them in the cafeteria." As they walked onto the playground, he squeezed her hand, a privilege he didn't take for granted. "You calmly talked them through the television report then kept them occupied with all the cookies they could eat."

Her laugh rode the gritty wind that twisted swings until the chains clinked. "They'll be upset later when they realize there's no dessert for the rest of the week."

"We'll add an extra recess." He punted the ball farther, toward the swing set.

"Wearing them out with soccer." She nodded, kicking a stray soccer ball. "Good plan."

"It worked well this evening after supper." He pointed to the row of dark windows along the dorms.

"Worked for most of them." She tipped her head toward his conspiratorially. "Khaali stuffed pillows under her blankets again and hid in the bathroom."

"To read late?" He respected how much she cared for her students, looking after each one like a child of her own.

"Maybe. That's what she says." She dropped into a swing, pushing off with her toe. "But I think she just wants some time to be alone."

He leaned against the metal A-frame. "So she's asleep now?"

"I gave her a flashlight." She pulled on the chains and swung higher, hooks overhead squeaking.

"You broke the rules. I like that about you."

"I'm a rebel at heart, I guess."

He liked that about her too, more than she could imagine. Damn it, this was getting complicated.

Sliding behind her, he palmed the small of her back and nudged her higher. "The staff party this weekend would be a good time to make our dating officially known." Because if their time was limited, damn it, he wanted to make the most of it now that finally she'd noticed him as a man. "We could see each other more openly rather than sneaking a late night walk. I could offer you a proper date."

She glanced over her shoulder and she wasn't smiling. "You're a good cook and I happened to enjoy our movie night."

"Back to the staff party…" he pressed, more determined with each passing second that he was making the right decision. His hand grazed her back again. "Will you go with me as my date?"

She drug her feet along the dusty earth, slowing, stopping. "The staff party would be a sad place to end something that's only just started."

His gut dropped. He stepped around to kneel in front of her. "You want to—what is the English phrase?— break up with me already?"

"I think you are rushing things between us." She trailed her fingers down his cheek.

"I have waited for a year." And he feared time was running out. He clasped her soft hand.

"A year…" She blinked and stuttered. "I…"

"You are speechless for once." He kissed her knuckles. "I am amazed."

"Suddenly you're a comedian." She rested her forehead against his.

"I am a man who has waited a long time for a chance with you." A chance that would very likely be ruined when she learned more about him, about why he left Egypt to come here. But for now, he would allow himself to enjoy what time he had with her.

"You know, an affair would be easier than a relationship."

He choked on a cough. "Pardon me?"

"Does that shock you? We are both adults—more than adults. I may be wrong, but I assumed from your kiss that you find me attractive."

"You know I do." God, he wanted to take her up on the offer, had been thinking the same thing himself.

"Then let's skip the formalities." She kissed him lightly, deliberately. "Come with me to my apartment."

He wanted her, without question, wanted her so much his body ached. And he couldn't imagine spending the rest of his life never knowing what it would be like to hold her in his arms through the night.

But his conscience balked at the notion of being intimate with her when he held back so much about himself. When he knew she could not be honest with him.

She pressed fingers to his mouth. "I am not naïve. I know there are things you haven't told me. There's a look to a person who has secrets. I..." She stuttered for the first time. "I have my own. Maybe that's why we're drawn to each other. And perhaps that's why we can have an affair."

"You make a compelling argument." One he didn't have the strength to argue with.

He pulled her from the swing and into his arms. Kneeling right there in the dusty playground, he kissed her, tasting the lingering sugar and cinnamon from cookies. But more than that, he took in the feel of her, the press of her full breasts against his chest, the silky glide of her hair as he thrust his hands under her scarf. The intimacy of those chestnut strands caressing his skin was almost more than he could withstand.

They needed to move this inside before someone saw them. He wouldn't compromise her reputation or set an improper example for the children. Clasping her by the elbows, he stood, bringing her with him. His body protested the loss of her lips, of her hands on his shoulders even as his mind reassured him soon, soon she would finally be his for as long as they had together.

"Sam," she said, her voice husky with desire. "Your phone."

"What?" His passion-fogged mind wrestled to keep up with words.

"Your phone is buzzing. Can you ignore it?"

His phone. Buzzing. With a message.

Damn it.

Not now, not now, his brain chanted as he hoped the text was something simple. He received countless memos. But this wasn't his regular phone. It was his second, for official business. His instincts told him the news would be bad, and for Annie's sake he needed to know sooner rather than later.

He reached into his pocket and thumbed through the code to read… A series of numbers scrolled across his screen. A code, rather than words, in case his phone was compromised.

A code he knew meant only one thing.

He cursed the timing and his duty. This was not the way this evening was supposed to end. He jammed his phone back in his pack and clasped Annie's arm with purpose rather than passion.

"Sam? What's wrong? Where are we going?"

He couldn't believe all that he was giving up tonight. But he didn't dare look at her right now or he would forget all about his job.

"I don't have time to explain, but I know who you are. Your identity has been compromised. Melanie Carson, I work for Interpol and I need to take you into protective custody."

Chapter 13

STELLA SAT IN THE MIDDLE OF HER BED, LEGS CROSSED, rocking back and forth. A small corner of her brain registered that she was in shock, so she let Jose take over. They'd been lodged at a hotel near the airport, a blah place with plenty of amenities and none of the local flavor.

If she'd been in her right mind, she would have voiced how much she hated it and Jose would have grinned, then offered to distract her. Or checked them both into someplace more exotic. But all of that would have been wasted on her. She was too numb to feel or register anything other than the surreal discovery that everything she'd believed about her childhood, the memories that had shaped her, had all been lies.

He locked the door and closed the blinds, creating a cocoon for her to process, to grieve. She'd come to Africa to find out about her mom, but she'd never expected to find this. Her mind was still reeling with the fact that her mother had lied about everything. Stella forced steady breaths in and out, willing her heart to slow.

Smith had pulled her off the case the second he'd realized her mother was involved. But involved how? What had she been doing here? Stella's image of her mom grew all the more complicated. Her mom hadn't been on Peace Corps missions. Her mother had been serving the government in some capacity. Her mother had been doing exactly what she did, probably since before Stella was born.

And her mother had died in the line of duty rather than on some random road trip from village to village between goodwill missions.

The truth had rocked her to the core.

Jose opened a water bottle and set it on the bedside table before he sat on the edge of the mattress, not talking, just waiting. Giving her space to deal with mind-blowing information at a time when she was already on shaky ground.

How was she supposed to sift through it all? She was such a mess she could hardly lift the water bottle from the end table. Hand shaking, she brought it to her lips. Three gulps later, she wasn't any steadier. The words welled inside her without any organization at all. No surprise since the walls of logic had been blasted away.

"My mom was in and out of my life so often when I was a kid. We made big memories when she was home." She squeezed the bottle, the plastic crackling in her hand, water sloshing up and over. "It was like being with her was always a huge party."

"What about your dad?" Jose took the bottle from her hand. "Wasn't that tough for him, her being the good guy while he managed the daily grind?"

He spoke with an understanding that pierced through her fog, making her think of him as a kid and teenager, taking care of himself while his parents ignored the real problem. The only time he'd had anyone on his side was during that time his grandmother lived with them.

"I honestly don't recall my father complaining." But then she questioned her perceptions today. Big time.

"He really tried. He shared lots of stories about my mom when she was overseas… and after she died… to keep her alive in my mind. She was artsy. My dad kept all her crafts, even after she died."

"He cared about her."

"I believe he did, but tonight I'm not sure I trust my instincts anymore." She pressed her palms to her temples. "I missed the signs from Harper. I obviously didn't have a clue about my own mother…"

He clasped her wrists, thumbing her pulse. "Remember what you said earlier? You're not a robot. You're human and you did the best you could. Your best helped us catch Sutton Harper before he hurt anyone. And your best found the answers about your mom in spite of all the odds. From where I'm sitting, you're mighty damn amazing."

"Then why do I feel like such a failure?" She blinked back the tears and drew the stiff quilted bedspread around her legs. "I love my job. I love serving my country, but…"

"Hey, now, stop." He grabbed her shoulders, his strength so welcome especially now when she was falling apart. "This is adrenaline letdown talking. It's been one of those razor's edge days. Hell, my heart is about to pound out of my chest too."

The tears burned hotter and fuller. "I think I'm done, Jose. The life of a field operative is short for a reason and I'm afraid I've pushed the odds to the limit with this mission."

She needed objectivity and she didn't have it. She couldn't live with the fear that she'd begun losing it after the split with Jose, because that would mean she'd been doing her job at half speed, compromising the integrity of her work. Jose started to interrupt, but she needed to talk this through. To get it all out there.

"I'm ready to move onto another phase of my career working for Interpol… or maybe I'll transfer to a CIA or FBI office." The plan came together, making sense. "Only a small fraction of us do wet work in the field like this. I'm done, damn it. I'm done."

"You say that like you're serious."

"Because I am." She stroked her hand over his hair that had dried sticking up in places from a decontamination shower. "I also understand you're not ready to dry off your feet. Maybe you never will be."

He scowled. "Are you booting me out?"

She didn't know what she was doing other than lashing out, the pain inside her expanding until she had to have relief. "I'm starting to really understand now. You never wanted this to work between us, not really."

"I offered to marry you."

"Offered?" Her eyebrows shot up along with her blood pressure. "Offered? Actually, the way I remember it, *I* proposed to *you*. But hey, let's not quibble when you were so generous. Other than the fact I want kids and you won't even consider it."

"And I want this fucking genetic curse to end with me," he snapped, his patience visibly fraying.

Of course he had almost been taken out by a horrific weapon of mass destruction. But the day had hardly been a picnic for her either. The fury inside her roared louder. "Then adopt."

"I swear to God, if you recite another study about the power of believing in yourself, I'm going to lose it.

Damn it, you know what happened with my sister, to my nephew…"

Oh God, what was she doing here? Her anger deflated in a flash as she thought about the night he'd told her about his nephew, about the horrific accident. "Shhh… Shhh." She leaned forward on her knees, her fingers over his lips. "You're right. Let's not talk about that. I don't want to hurt you, and heaven knows I don't want to fight with you. It makes me get too fired up and the last thing I need to be right now is emotional around you."

He grasped her hand, gripping a hint too tightly, and kissed her fist, hard. The ache in her chest pushed the tears the rest of the way free, in big gulping sobs. Jose hauled her to his chest and she let the tears flow out, along with so many tangled emotions. The horror of a cruel world. The betrayal by her mother. The fear of losing Jose.

She was through. Through chasing ghosts. Through believing in dreams or even hoping for the future. She wasn't going to die in some godforsaken country alone, like her mom, without ever really connecting with anyone in order to keep the job safe. Anonymous.

Screw. That.

She wasn't going to be another statistic spit out by a code-breaking program—a name with no real roots. She wasn't sacrificing the chance at a real family to the almighty job.

Gasping, she gripped Jose's shoulders tighter, her nails digging deep as she soaked his shirt with her pain. She hurt so damn bad and right now his arms were the only thing keeping her from shattering altogether.

His hands soothed along her spine, her braid brushing his wrists. He tugged the band loose and threaded his fingers through, loosening the thick mass, massaging her scalp. Her body melted into his. The sharp edge of her pain found another channel, another outlet.

Desire.

Jose felt the sensual shift in her, and God, he wanted her too. Always.

But he wasn't so sure this was the right time or the right reason. "Stella, you're…"

"Damn it, Jose." She angled back to stare at him, her chest heaving. "Don't tell me about adrenaline letdown or misplaced emotions. I do the same kind of work you do. I've been to all the same training and psych briefings. I get it. And I don't care. I need this. I need you."

She grabbed the hem of his T-shirt and yanked it upward, pressing her mouth to his heartbeat. He'd always taken such care with her, working his ass off to give her all the romance, finesse—hell, foreplay—that he could muster without losing complete control of himself.

Right now, control was tougher than ever to find. He'd been through hell today too. Not because he'd feared dying, but because he'd been scared as hell he might not make it in time to save Stella. So damn all the reasons why this was a bad, bad idea.

They were here, together, alive, and they both needed this. They needed each other.

Stella nipped his earlobe. Hard. "You're falling behind here. Help me undress."

She'd already gotten his shirt off and was well on

her way to tugging down his camo pants. Blood slugged
through his veins, surging below his belt. Stella's touch,
her words, the woman herself set him on fire. He peeled
her tunic away and worked her jeans free, until they
kicked the pants over near their shoes by the door. Her
hands stroked his body with the familiarity of a lover,
lower, cradling him. He gritted his teeth to fight back the
urge to come in her hand.

Then she knelt and took him in her mouth. He
palmed the wall to keep from falling. The sweep of her
tongue, the moist warmth. His head fell back and he
was a second away from losing total control. His hands
fell to her shoulders.

Hauling her up again, he sealed their lips and their
bodies, falling onto the bed. They rolled as dominance
flipped back and forth between them until he pinned her,
kissed his way down her neck, along her shoulder to
the curve of her breast. He captured her nipple between
his teeth, teasing, flicking with his tongue until she
squirmed beneath, her breathy moans demanding more.
He was more than willing to deliver. He reached to the
bedside table and grabbed the water bottle.

Trickle by trickle, he dribbled water between her
breasts. She gasped as the first droplets hit her. She
hissed as he sipped them. He took that as a yes to keep
right on going, down her stomach, between her legs,
tasting until the bottle was empty. He flung it away and
kept right on pleasuring her, which pleasured him.

She gripped his shoulders, tugged at his hair, her
hands frantic until he slid up over her. Into her. And
while he'd enjoyed the hell out of their all night lovemaking in the past, he already knew this was going to

be hard and fast. He could barely hold onto his control now with the warm, moist clamp of her drawing him in deeper. Her legs locked around his waist and she moved with him, her eyes open and telling him she was right there with him, so close to the edge on a day that had brought them both to the brink of a cliff.

The spread and top sheet tangled in his feet, and he kicked them to the floor. Her hands flung back and she grabbed the headboard, arching up to him, crying out as she milked every last pulse from her orgasm. Watching the flush spread up her chest, goose bumps prickling along her flesh, sent a primal wave of satisfaction through him. His hands gripped over hers as he finished and knew he was only one thrust away from jetting his release hot and deep inside her.

And in the most insane thought of his already screwed up life, he imagined filling her with his baby. A growl of denial followed close on the heels of that thought. Even knowing about her birth control implant, he couldn't stop himself.

He pulled out.

Collapsing on top of her, his release throbbing between them, he buried his face in her neck. But he couldn't hide from himself or the knowledge that he wanted to give her more. He wanted to give her everything.

——⁂——

Stella curled up in the armchair, her head against the windowpane as she looked out at the road below, dark other than streetlamps and passing cars. The airport lights blinked two blocks away where the investigation would continue without her. Cop cars were parked at every corner, no doubt a by-product of the near miss with a deadly nerve toxin less than twenty-four hours ago.

She wrapped a kanga around her like a thin blanket, a benign cloth of blues and greens with a message along the border that probably said something like *live long and prosper.* Jose had bought it for her a month ago when they'd snuck away to Kenya for a weekend. Their last weekend together before she'd gone undercover with the students.

God, so much had happened since that memorable, heartbreaking night. Yet it still felt like she'd packed a lifetime of stress into this day.

Her nerves were ragged, totally shot in more ways than one. Apparently all that happened hadn't left Jose unmarked either. She'd sensed an edge to him, a desperation even when they'd been together.

They'd had sex three times tonight. Sex. Not making love. She knew the difference. But that's what she'd asked for from him in bed. In the shower. Then on the dresser as they'd made their way back into the room before collapsing on the mattress, exhausted enough to sleep through the demons that would haunt their dreams.

He slept still, sprawled out with the sheet twisted around his waist. Turning away from the heart-tugging sight of him, she drew the coarse cloth tighter around her, watching the lights blink—still all too aware of the man sleeping just a few feet away. Could she walk away from Jose a second time?

He had damn good reasons for his fears about a commitment, about building a family together. A part of her whispered that she should just give in, take what he offered and be grateful.

Her fists tightened until her fingernails poked holes in the fabric. Damn it, Jose was breaking her heart all over again, just like he'd done a month ago…

"Any idea how long you'll be undercover as a student?"

"Not a clue." Stella looped the blue and green sarong around her again and again, checking in the mirror to make sure she got it just right. She spun back to face Jose. "And if I did know and I told you, then I would have to kill you."

"That's supposed to be my line." He slipped his hands under the edge of the kanga he'd just bought for her from a street vendor.

The Kenyan bed and breakfast by the ocean was a little hokey with its over-the-top safari room. But she enjoyed it all the same—from the zebra skin rug to the mosquito netting around the bed. Even the carved wood animals with a gloss perfection that hinted they might just well say "Made in China" on the bottom.

They had one weekend left before finally she had her chance to blend in with a group of foreign exchange students doing a work study in an area known for recruiting new foot soldiers for anarchy. Jose's stint in Africa dealing with the pirate issue was nearly over, a new team stepping in for the next rotation. By the time she finished her assignment, he would have returned to the States.

And then? They'd both said the big "love" word and maybe it was too early to talk marriage, but was she crazy to want reassurance before they said good-bye?

He hauled her closer, guiding her with him as he backed toward the bed, shouldering through the mosquito netting.

She batted his hands away, plastering a playful smile on her face. "You're bad."

"Not as bad as I want us to be." He tugged again, toppling her onto the bed with him. "Unwrapping you plays a part in more than one of my fantasies."

"You fantasize about me?" She rolled to her side as he kissed her neck, his hands tunneling farther under the wrap. "When?"

"In bed, in the shower, hell," he growled against her skin, "when I'm eating dinner, which can be awkward if there's a mess hall full of people around."

"Oh really?" She liked knowing that he was thinking about her. "What did you do?"

"I sure as hell didn't stand up." His hand trekked over her stomach, cupping between her legs. "I hung out there moving food around on my tray until it was safe to stand up. The smell of mess hall chow still makes me hard."

She appreciated that he was trying to be lighthearted, to ease the tension of preparing to say good-bye while making the most of this weekend. And the way his fingers were toying with her now, she almost forgot her doubts. But it was getting tougher and tougher to play along as time ticked away.

Still, she would try, because the last thing she wanted was to say good-bye with tears or anger. She'd seen that kind of parting too many times with her parents. "Women have fantasies too, you know."

He grinned wolfishly. "Now you're talking." He rubbed small circles, her arousal slicking his fingertips. "What kind of fantasies did you have about me?"

"You would be surprised." Dreams of dinner in a totally nonexotic kitchen that happened to be in a house they owned together. Hopes of children at that table, with precious chocolate stains on their faces… Normal stuff.

Real life.

"Seriously, Stella? You've been holding back?" His erection throbbed against her thigh, his jeans not doing much to disguise how much he wanted her. "I think I would know by now if you had… edgier tendencies."

"That's not what I meant," she said, but not knowing how to tell him.

"Too bad."

Whoa. Wait a second. "Really?"

"Nah…" He stopped teasing and cupped her hip, his eyes dark and serious. "I'm not into pain myself and the last thing I ever want is to hurt you. So, what do you want that you've been hesitant to ask?"

Stella stared back at him, the face of the only man she'd ever loved… and she couldn't say it. She could face down armed gunmen, but she couldn't bring herself to voice how much she wanted happily ever after with Jose. She was afraid he would say no.

Maybe lighthearted was the way to play it this weekend after all. "Do you promise not to laugh?"

"Hand to God…" He clapped a palm over his heart. "I would never laugh at anything to do with you and sex. I take that very seriously."

"A kilt."

His jaw went slack. "What?"

"You promised not to laugh."

"I'm not laughing. I swear. I'm just… stunned."

"Never mind." She sniffed.

"No, hey, I'm not backing down." His arm slid around her back and he pulled her flush against him.

"I'm starting to groove on the whole kilt thing if that's what you want. I just didn't expect it. You're so logical."

"Logical women can't be fanciful?" And have dreams that didn't involve guns and international plots, instead settled into desk jobs where they could serve their country and still have a life.

"What else goes with this kilt?"

A home filled with his babies. "You shirtless, of course."

She swiped the edge of her wrap along his chin. "We could even use a sarong as a tartan."

His brow furrowed and he watched her while cars honked and beeped on the street below. "You really are dreaming big. How did I miss that about you these past five months?"

Suddenly, they weren't talking about sex or playing dress-up games. She couldn't hide her longing for more. "Do you ever wonder what we're doing here?"

"I'm here to save lives. One at a time. How about you?"

"Pursue bad guys around the world, I guess." Uncover the truth about her mother's death. "Except sometimes it's tough to tell who the bad guys are when some seem to keep switching sides back and forth."

He traced the furrows in her forehead. "There's an Arab proverb that goes something like 'People fear time. Time fears the pyramids.' Which I interpret as 'take each day as it comes. There's a picture bigger than us going on.'"

"You're not helping me." Not when she so desperately wanted to talk about the future, their future, not some existential view of the whole freakin' world.

"Okay, how about this one?" He lifted a lock of her hair, rubbing it between his fingers. "'God grant me the serenity to accept the things I cannot change. Courage to change the things I can. And the wisdom to know the difference.'"

His alcoholism. There it was. The big pink elephant in the room, the issue that guided every decision he made regardless of how long he'd been sober.

She accepted that but couldn't understand why he couldn't allow himself to celebrate his success, to move on and have the happiness he deserved. "Where do we fall in that philosophy?"

"Honestly? If I had my way, I would tuck you someplace safe, because thinking about you out there…" He reached into his jeans pocket and tossed a coin onto the mattress where it bounced once before settling.

His five-year sobriety coin.

He stared at her with tortured eyes. "I want to get you the hell out of this place."

A cold chill started in her stomach. She hadn't considered until now that her work, this mission, would be a threat for him, could be a stressor that sent him over the edge.

"I'm good at my job, trained, just like you are." She scooped up the coin and pressed it in his palm, holding on tight. "I'll be okay."

"I get it, Stella, I do. But that doesn't make this feeling go away." His eyes closed, the tendons in his neck straining. "How the hell am I going to make it if something happens to you?"

She squeezed his hand. "I could say the same."

"So this is it," he said against her loose hair. "We're laying it out there on the line, that crazy-ass, unconditional love that tears a person up inside."

She kissed the heavy pulse throbbing in his neck.

"Uhm, I was thinking it's a crazy-ass love that lifts you up, makes you happy. But you don't look very happy. In fact, you look like you want to run."

"I should run, Stella."

Her gut twisted. This wasn't taking the direction she'd hoped.

"Jose, this could be my last mission, then I could step out of the field and take a desk job cracking codes and writing new software. If you're not ready to step out of the field yet, I understand. I want you safe too, but I can wait on that part as long as I know you're coming home to me." She swallowed hard then blurted, "Let's get married."

There. She'd said it.

His cheeks puffed with an exhale, the rest of his body going very still for a heartbeat too long. "Did you just propose to me, woman?"

"Did you just call me 'woman'?" Her heart was still stinging from his hesitation.

"Fuck. I did." He scrubbed his face with his hand. "Sorry. I try to be more enlightened than that. Let's move in together."

It was her turn to pause, to mull over his words and tamp down her disappointment. She tried to reason through the fact that she was likely moving too fast. She should just be patient, logical.

Except her feelings for Jose had nothing to do with logic and everything to do with impulsive emotions. "So you're saying a long engagement?"

"I love you, no question; I want us to get this right. I can't let you down."

That helped—a little. She almost managed to

overlook the panic on his face. "As long as I know we're headed in the same direction, building a life, a family together, I'm good."

"Kids?" His strangled tone left zero room for misinterpretation.

She bolted upright. "You don't want children."

How the hell could she have missed that? She'd heard him talk about his niece and nephew, heard his love for them and just assumed...

Sitting up on the edge of the bed beside her, he stared at the coin in his palm. "It's the alcoholism thing."

Her hand fell to rest on his knee. She had to touch him, to make some connection as she felt him slipping away from her. "Plenty of reformed alcoholics have children."

"It's deeper than that for me." His hand opened and closed around the coin, waves crashing outside their scenic window. "My sister, Bianca, she didn't just get out of the army. She was forced out."

"Because of her drinking?" she prodded carefully.

"In a roundabout way, but not what you're thinking. We all knew about her alcoholism. Hell, once she got old enough to drive, she took the money Dad left for us each day and went out partying with her friends. But she was one of those drunks who just gets sloppy and cracks jokes, so people overlooked it."

"As opposed to the drinker who turns violent?" What kind had his mother been? He'd never indicated beyond mentioning he'd stayed clear of the house as much as possible.

"I'm not saying either kind of drinking is right." He glanced over at her. "I'm only saying the 'jolly' alcoholic tends to get away with it longer, people stick around.

Hitting rock bottom comes later, maybe because folks enable longer. But make no mistake, it still comes."

"As it did for your sister?" And from the weary lines in his face, she feared what would come next, ached for the pain it caused him.

"Her husband was in the military too. When he was deployed overseas, she was stateside with their kids and vice versa. Combat stress along with the pressures of military family life pushed her the rest of the way over the edge. I'm not making excuses. There is no excuse for what she did."

Her gut clenched, but she still asked, "What happened?"

"One night, she started the hot water for the kids' bath and passed out. When Michael jumped into the full tub, it was scalding water." His breath grew ragged, each word forced as if he had to punch them free. "He had burns on eighty percent of his body. My sister was so out of it, she didn't even wake up. My niece pulled her brother onto the bathroom floor and called 9-1-1."

The image he painted, the horror of what had happened to his family, she couldn't wrap her mind around it. The silence roared with the crashing waves and a pain inside Jose so tangible she could swear she heard the rage inside him.

"Oh my God, Jose. I can't even imagine…" Sometimes there just were no words. "Your nephew…?"

"He survived, barely." His voice went raw, his fist so tight on the coin a trickle of blood seeped out. "But he still has scars."

She stroked his hand, carefully prying his fingers open. "It sounds like you all carry scars of some sort from that day."

"In the darker days, I can't stop thinking if I'd helped Bianca that wouldn't have happened."

"You also know your sister would have hit rock bottom another time, another way." She thumbed off the blood on his palm and kissed the tiny wound, a symbol of one so much bigger inside him that had never healed. "And what about your mother? Was she alive then too?"

"She'd died a couple of months before, but she would have only been a drinking buddy. Hell, so would I." He set the coin on the bedside table by the elephant lamp. "Once we knew that Michael was going to live, I went to my commander and told him I needed to go to rehab."

"And you've been sober every day since."

He nodded, his fingers closing around hers. He turned to face her full-on for the first time since he'd started talking about his sister. His brown eyes darkened with intensity. "But I can't do it, Stella. I can't have children. I won't." His voice rang with conviction. "I know I would never be abusive, but damn it all, look at what neglect can do? I can't risk a family, Stella. I just can't."

She did the only thing she could. She wrapped her arms around him and held him, stroking his hair until he stopped shaking. She loved him so damn much, but she felt her dream dying in that moment. Saying good-bye was only a formality. He didn't want marriage. Didn't want a family. Wasn't ready to share in the things that meant so much to her.

She understood now. When he left Africa, he would be leaving her for good...

Stella traced circles on the windowpane overlooking the Mogadishu International Airport, the past and present wrapping around her as tightly as the wrap Jose had bought her a month ago in Kenya, the weekend they'd broken up.

After he told her about his nephew's tragic accident, they'd gone through the motions of finishing out their weekend together. They'd even made love. They'd almost made it back to their quarters before an argument broke out. They'd quarreled over something silly and inconsequential. She couldn't even remember exactly what now, other than it had to do with directions and getting lost for five minutes.

They'd fought, snapping out hurtful words as if that would somehow make it easier to say good-bye. Yet, here they were again, right back in the same painful place with her cocooned in the same wrap, having even fewer answers than before.

Her cell phone vibrated on the bedside table.

She reached behind her quickly, not wanting the sound to wake Jose. Only numbers flashed on the screen, numbers that were code for Agent Smith. Thumbing the on button, she shot to her feet, her legs tangling in the trailing fabric as she made her way to the bathroom.

"Yes?"

"We need you to report back, now," Mr. Smith said with a tense edge that sent a bolt of fear straight through her. This man never lost his cool. Never. "Sutton Harper committed suicide in his holding cell…"

"What? Repeat that, please?" Shock iced through

her—and surprise. She'd been trained to look for signs and Sutton had seemed more the type who would shout his ideology from a jail cell for years to come...

"Harper cut the femoral artery in his thigh. He bled out before anyone noticed."

An injury like that would kill in about five minutes. Her head reeled with the image as she grappled with the need to make sense...

"Carson, we'll deal with the ramification of that later. There's more. Top priority and the primary reason for my call? The list is on the move. We have less than twelve hours to stop the transfer and find those responsible so this kind of leak doesn't happen again. I repeat..."

"Got it. I'm on my way." She disconnected, forcing her training to assume control, an icy focus sliding into place.

They had a lead—and twelve hours to stop the exposure of American agents across Africa and the Middle East. Twelve hours to catch those responsible in the act so every agent wasn't compromised. Twelve hours to protect an intelligence network decades in the making— a network that had somehow failed her mother. Stella pushed that thought aside as she slid back into the hotel room, trying to decide whether to wake Jose or leave him a note.

Moot point. He already sat on the edge of the bed, his phone at his ear and from the narrowed look in his eyes, he'd just gotten the same recall.

Chapter 14

DÉJÀ VU SWELLED OVER ANNIE IN WAVES, AS POTENTLY and vaguely nauseating as the scent of jet fuel in the back of the cargo craft. She'd ridden in countless military transports during her days as a field operative, slipping in and out of countries. Once she'd gone undercover, people hadn't suspected the motherly looking aid worker.

At least not at first.

Even now that her new identity had been ripped from her, she couldn't just become Melanie again—she still thought of herself as Annie, *felt* like Annie. For fourteen years, she'd lived as Annie Johnson, a widowed teacher who poured her energies into her work and her orphaned students. Severing all ties to Melanie Carson had been the only way for her to survive. The only way to keep her sanity after her world exploded. Now, somehow, her real identity had been exposed. Her life could be in danger. Her family's lives could be in jeopardy because of her, even after all she'd sacrificed to keep them safe.

Her worst nightmare had come true.

And the only person she could count on was the man sitting next to her, a man who'd apparently lied to her every day for the past year.

Samir Al-Shennawi.

Looking through her lashes, she checked on him

sitting next to her and thought of that horrible moment
of disillusionment when he'd announced he'd been spying on her the whole time. The way she'd done in her
former life as an operative. She'd understood the truth
of his mission faster than most people might have in
her shoes since she'd lived it often enough. That hadn't
made it hurt any less. But Samir had all the proper cre-
dentials. Intelligence authorities had contacted her and
verified his story.

This CV-22 aircraft packed with U.S. troops erased
any lingering doubts. Red lights tracked overhead
with a hazy glow over people and gear. The nightmare
was real, even though everyone around her seemed at
ease when her world had been turned upside down.
Soldiers slept and listened to music and zoned out
with eReaders. Apparently they were on their way
to an American base in Somalia where she would be
protected until they decided where to relocate her.
Starting all over again at fifty-eight? Saying good-bye
to another man...

She swept a glance at Sam again, engines droning,
filling the cavernous hold until noises from others
faded away.

He met her accusatory look without flinching, already
assuming a bolder persona than before, his shoulders
broader, his strong chin tipped up rather than tucked
down. "I understand that you are angry with me."

"Why should I be mad?" Pride kept her spine straight
and her voice steady.

"I lied to you for a year."

Damn straight he had. But at least he'd been on the
side of a friendly government. What if he hadn't, and

she'd missed the signs that he was working undercover? The children could have been in danger and she was losing her touch.

Yet, she wasn't going to give him the satisfaction of seeing her wince. "You had a job to do. Believe me, I understand all about lying in the line of duty."

Although she'd sure as hell never kissed anyone while undercover. Did he think he was some kind of Egyptian James Bond?

"Yes, my job was to watch over you, although I am not technically a field agent of your level—or rather, your previous level." He sounded so believable, so earnest. "I am a scientist and a teacher. Traveling for my job has facilitated my ability to go where I'm needed. Our governments worked together through different intelligence agencies to protect assets. Very simple."

Could she believe him? Buried professional instincts fired to life and she studied his every move, twitch, and blink. Maybe Melanie Carson wasn't buried as deeply as she thought. "Why did they decide to start watching me this year?"

"You have been watched since the day you assumed the new identity."

His words spoken so matter-of-factly rang true and stunned her silent until a turbulent bump jostled her. *Fourteen years.*

"This whole time? Who?" She searched her mind for all the faces and clues she must have missed. What if someone had been trying to kill her? Would she have seen it coming? And there wasn't a thing she could do about it now except be glad she hadn't exposed her family to the risk. "Teachers or janitors... I guess it's all in the past now. They don't matter, although I don't understand why I matter."

"Melanie…"

"Call me Annie," she said quickly, needing that separation from the past. "That's who I am now. At least they gave me a name that had a part of the old me…" Oh God, she hadn't even considered… "What about you? Is Samir your real name?"

"It is."

Would he even tell her if it wasn't? His eyes looked honest, familiar.

Enticing.

Damn it. "I feel like I don't know anything about you, although I guess you know everything about me."

"The facts." He tapped his glasses in place. "That's all."

"That's *all*?" She laughed—at herself and her whole messed up life. "That's everything."

The more she thought about it, the more frustrated she felt, even violated. Yet, she'd given up her right to privacy when she'd willingly signed on with the CIA.

Sam tipped his head to the side, his eyes curious behind those round glasses. He sat with a zen kind of stillness, but with an edge now. "There are many things I do not know, things I have wondered about you but was not free to ask."

"Such as?"

"What led you to this line of work?"

It had been so long since she made the decision, sometimes she couldn't remember either. She toyed with a bead bracelet Khaali had made in art class and given to her as a gift. "How does anyone land a job? You pursue what you want to do with your life."

"You just walked up to the CIA and asked to be an operative?"

Memories started flooding back. She hadn't allowed herself to think about these things in so long. In the beginning, it had been a matter of survival. Eventually, it had become habit.

"Freelancer. Off the books." At first, but once she'd gotten a taste, she wanted in deeper, envisioned herself changing the world. "I was already active in the area. The aide work was real, not a cover, not in the beginning. After my husband and I graduated from college, we joined the Peace Corps. When our oldest son was born, we tried to keep up the lifestyle, the work. And we managed pretty well even through the birth of our second child—both were born here in Africa."

Her heart ached with memories—the visions of their infant faces, the smell of baby shampoo, the feel of a tiny cheek resting against her chest. She'd tried so hard to be a good mother in spite of feeling ripped in two by a call to action against injustice.

"We had only been back in the States for a few months when the CIA approached us, just a short-term freelancing assignment. My parents helped with the children. And God, we enjoyed it, the adrenaline rush of making a difference in what felt like an even bigger way." Although in the end she'd felt like such a fool for not realizing the mammoth gift of a sticky hug from her child. She'd learned too late to appreciate what she'd lost.

"What changed?" he asked, even though he had to know from her file.

Still, it felt good to talk about the past, not to guard

every word out of her mouth. "We found out I was pregnant again. My husband said he wasn't into the whole 'Kumbaya' lifestyle anymore. He wanted a regular roof over our heads and meals at a family table."

"So you relocated back to the States permanently."

"We did. I went back to work in the classroom, had another child, our only girl. And I tried, I really tried to tell myself I could wait until the children grew up to help over here…"

An air crewman walked by on his way to the back and she paused until he passed.

"Until one day," she continued, "during a parent-teacher conference, I was talking to a student's mother and she mentioned her husband's work overseas. He was in the Army. For weeks I thought about that father fulfilling his call to serve, and I couldn't deny the strong desire I felt to go back again. I needed to make a difference in the world."

"What did your… husband say?"

She tried not to read too much into the way he seemed to stumble over the word *husband*. She was overanalyzing, just wishful thinking.

"He told me I was being selfish. That I was screwing up our family, that I was breaking the agreement we'd made when we got married." That awful argument, the rage in his voice, the pain she'd caused, all came back to her as real as if she'd just walked out the door of their little red brick house. "We'd promised each other we were a team. Where one went, the other would go."

"Yet you left anyway."

After all the angry—but logical words—he'd shouted at her, it was the strangled pain in his final question that haunted her most to this day. *Who the fuck's gonna braid Stella's hair?*

"Freelancing was our compromise." A brittle peace settled between them. "I wouldn't take it on as a full-time job."

"He was not happy."

Not by a long shot. "Neither of us was, but we made it work until Stella was fifteen."

"And then you 'died.'"

There was an implied question in his tone she couldn't miss. How did Sam manage to get her to share so much so quickly when by all rights she should still be reeling from the hurt of how he'd played her? Maybe a part of her believed she deserved any and every bad thing that came her way as retribution for the pain she'd caused her family.

"You're wondering if I used my faked death as an out to abandon my family."

"I did not say that." But still the hint of a question remained.

Although oddly, she found no condemnation. Either he really didn't blame her—or he was that good of an actor. With nothing to lose anymore, she kept on talking, needing to pour out the words she'd kept bottled inside for so many years.

"But you're thinking it. Believe me, I've questioned myself on that more times than I can count. In my head I know I didn't have a choice. My identity had been compromised in a major way in southern Africa, and I needed to assume a new life to keep my family safe."

She'd opted to stay in Africa for two reasons. She wanted to minimize the temptation to seek out her family anyway, even for a glimpse. And she still wanted to help. Funny how in the end she'd found returning to her roots in more of a teaching and aide manner brought her far more satisfaction than any large-scale mission.

Sam nodded slowly as if processing. "Annie Johnson was born."

"Such an innocuous name... Smith. Jones. Brown. Johnson. Jane or Anne or Mary. I could take my pick mixing and matching."

"Why did you choose to leave your family behind? It is my understanding witness protection will keep a family together."

His words made her realize she cared what he thought of her, deeply. She wanted him to know she'd truly tried her best. "My sons were already heading off to college. And my daughter... I had to keep her safe. Staying out of all their lives was the best way to do that." But in her heart she'd harbored doubts. Even though she'd missed them every single day, she feared that she'd made a self-ish choice to stay in Africa. Life wasn't clear-cut with simple answers. But she'd known one thing for certain. Living on the run? That was no life for a child.

"And your husband agreed?" Sam's stern tone made it clear he wouldn't have made the same call.

Something stirred in her stomach, something that felt strangely like... butterflies? At her age? Just because this man hinted with a tone of his voice that he would have fought to keep her?

She hadn't given her husband that chance because she'd already known his answer. He loved her, but he would have let her go, given the choice. So she'd saved him the pain of deciding. "He was told I was dead. The agency even found an unclaimed body at the morgue that looked enough like me and with such extensive injuries to that body, no one looked too close or questioned. That was for the best. I didn't want to tie up his life with my mistakes. The agency assured me that I was dead, legally, so there were no repercussions if he decided to remarry…"

Except he hadn't. The agency had told her that much in one of the few times they'd contacted her— after his death. She had mourned him despite all the ways they'd hurt each other. Mourned the lost chance at happiness they might have had together bringing up their children. They'd shared some big dreams at one time, but somewhere along the way they'd drifted apart. Still, she had grieved for all he'd given up for her and all the ways he'd carried on without her. She'd owed him better.

But that was in the past. Annie Johnson's quiet life of hard work had been part of her healing.

Sam folded his arms over his chest, his face foreboding in the hazy red glow of the lights lining the ceiling. "I would not want those choices made for me without my consent."

The censure in his voice set her on the defensive. "I did the best I could then… Would I make the same choices now? I don't know. At the time, I was in so much pain…"

"Pain?" His arms slid down, his judgmental air easing.

"My cover was blown when I was kidnapped along with two others I worked with. The local warlord who took us had international black market connections. He was an evil man and…" She forced her voice to stay steady. "He was a harsh interrogator." He was a rapist. "The other woman in our group broke, told him everything."

She'd been damn close to breaking as well. When she'd thought she couldn't take anymore, she'd found an opening to kill the lead interrogator. She'd escaped with the other remaining hostage.

As she thought back to those harrowing moments, she realized he hadn't said anything.

"Didn't my file mention any of that?"

She could read in his eyes that it had. A fast pulse throbbed in his temple, his fists clenched as he just let her talk. He'd somehow known she needed to share all of this that she hadn't been allowed to discuss with anyone.

Had he kept things so platonic between them for so long because he worried about her?

Or because he saw her as defiled? She'd thought he was holding back from physically comforting her now to give her space… That he might see her as untouchable…? That thought was beyond bearing.

She'd dealt with the attack as much as anyone could. She'd found her own peace to move forward with her new life. But she understood rape was perceived differently in this region of the world. Archaic views still prevailed, that the woman was damaged goods, somehow to blame.

"Once I was rescued, I could only think of them taking my children… my daughter…" Her voice choked off and she struggled for control, looking around the plane and seeing that no one here even really noticed she existed. She was just one of a number of passengers on a noisy transport plane. "Once the decision was made, there was no going back."

Although now that she looked back, perhaps she hadn't been in the best state of mind to make decisions that large, that fast.

She looked down and realized at some point, Sam had placed his hand on top of hers. She'd been so wrapped up in the past, she hadn't noticed, just like he'd slipped past her defenses this past year. He had a way about him that made it easy to simply… exist. And maybe that was a part of his undercover training, low level or not, but at the moment, she decided to go with the flow and continue talking.

How much more could she be hurt anyway?

"Every child I saw, I thought of mine at the same age and wondered what they were doing. I hoped they were thinking of me, remembering memories we'd made. When my daughter was eight, I rented the movie *Out of Africa* to give her a sense of where I went when I left home. She would draw pictures and mail them to me—pictures of me passing out mosquito nets to children. And she always drew herself as well, standing beside me. I was supposed to get rid of everything from my prior life, but I kept one of those pictures."

With that last confession she ran out of words. She was emptied out, exhausted. This time in the CV-22 with Sam was all the indulgence she could allow herself. She didn't know what would come next for her or if she would even see Sam again. If this relocation was anything like the last, the coming couple of days would move quickly and radically. She needed to get her head together, because all too soon they would be on the ground and things would be out of her control.

In fact, the aircraft was starting to slow. The CV-22's

loud rotors cranked into motion, shifting the blades to an upward helicopter position for landing. Still, Sam held onto her hand. Why hadn't she thought to ask more about him?

Because she didn't trust yet that he would tell her the truth. She didn't want something to be said, more lies told, that she couldn't overlook. After living through some of the worst experiences life could dole out, somehow knowing that Sam hid his identity to protect her didn't feel like an unforgivable sin…

The CV-22 settled on the ground with a light thump that echoed in her stomach. Her hand clenched around Sam's. This was it. When the hatch lowered, life as she'd known it for the past fourteen years would be officially over. Could Annie Johnson handle the upcoming intelligence meetings? The reorganization of her life?

She couldn't screw up much worse than Melanie Carson had.

And she was older now, stronger. Tougher. She let go of Sam's hand and tried not to think about how much she wanted to hold on and drag him into her next incarnation.

Shoulders squared, she walked down the load ramp, dry wind funneling around tan military buildings and whipping her loose pant suit around her. She was ready, damn it. Prepared for anything…

Except the sight of her daughter standing only twenty yards away.

Stella's gasp sent Jose's protective radar on high alert.

He scanned the troops off-loading from the CV-22

at the airport in Mogadishu, wondering which one was Smith's new contact and why Stella was so upset. She staggered back a step and he caught her, steadying her with a palm to her spine. Smith had brought them all out here for the arrival of some new intel contacts, but beyond that, the lead agent on this had been damn tight-lipped about where he thought the list of operatives was about to be exposed.

Or why the coded cloth had been draped on the VP's wife.

Irritation was running high. He'd always been able to stay detached during an operation, but with Stella involved, the stakes for him became all the more personal. Her moods fed his and that was a scary thought.

He wanted to pin Smith and demand answers for Stella. Now. No more jerking her around. If the guy didn't want to talk, why the hell had he dragged them out of bed?

Jose ducked his head to her ear. "Are you okay?"

Eyes wide and stunned, she shook her head, pointing. "The woman there, one of the last off the load ramp... That's my mother."

"Your *what*?" Squinting into the late morning sun, he scanned the stream of people pouring off the CV-22, a mix of soldiers and civilians.

He followed the line of Stella's attention to a couple trailing the rest. A dark-skinned man dressed in local garb stood beside a fair-skinned woman in a loose linen suit and a scarf that almost managed to hide her brownish-red hair. "You mean that lady looks like your mother?"

"No. That woman *is* my mother."

Stella's mother was *alive*? *This* was Smith's special contact they'd been brought out here to meet? The implications of this woman's name being on the list of operatives in the area took on a whole new complexity now.

She pivoted hard and fast toward Smith, anger vibrating from her. "You knew. Why the hell didn't you warn me?"

Smith didn't even wince, his craggy face unapologetic. "I was curious to see if you already knew she was alive, if she'd broken the terms of her agreement and contacted her family after all. That information could have provided a lead to how this list leaked out."

"Well, trust me. Even I'm not that good of an actress." Stella's mouth tightened into a grim line.

Across the stretch of asphalt, the woman in question had her eyes locked on their small group as well. She'd gone white as a sheet. Her feet moved forward in something close to slow motion. The man at her side adjusted his pace to stay right by her until the couple stopped.

No one spoke. The aircraft engines rumbled and other base noises echoed—trucks, loudspeakers, people going about the business of parking and servicing planes.

The two women continued to stare at each other. Now that they were closer, the resemblance was unmistakable, right down to the freckles on the nose.

There were minor differences—Melanie Carson had more of a brownish tint to her hair and time had brushed some lines on her face. What did Stella see when she looked at the mother she thought she'd lost, a mother who'd walked away? He wanted to scoop Stella up and hold her, insulate her against the pain.

Stella stepped nearly nose to nose with the woman without reaching out. Her arms stayed stiff and straight at her sides. "I hope to God you've had amnesia for the past fourteen years, otherwise I'm going to have a tough time getting past this."

Melanie Carson shrugged wryly. "No amnesia. Sorry, Stella."

Smith interjected, "Touching as this is, the rest of this reunion will have to wait." He gestured to Agent Jones. "If you'll show Mrs. Carson and Mr. Al-Shennawi to the briefing room, I need a few moments with… Stella."

Interesting. Melanie didn't know about her daughter's job, because otherwise why would Smith purposefully avoid calling her Agent Carson?

Smith charged ahead, orders given.

Apparently now that he'd gotten his shock value test to read mother and daughter he was ready to move this little party inside the hangar. Jose kept his hand on Stella's back and to hell what anyone else thought. Rage and pain damn near radiated off her in waves, stirring every protective impulse in his body. He was staying by her side until he received a direct order to the contrary.

Once inside the hangar, Smith guided Stella to the door. Jose stayed with her every step of the way. Smith just lifted an eyebrow but didn't argue.

"Sergeant James, this actually will be of interest to you," the agent said as if it had been his idea to include Jose. "Mr. Brown, stay with us."

Stella took a place at the long table, chairs, and a smart screen with a map of the region running feed in all four corners. Really? They were going to have a brief while Stella thought of her mother on the other side of the wall? Smith was a fucking sadist.

The senior agent leaned a shoulder against the wall by the screen. "We got the reports back on the bio toxin in the container."

Jose sat up straighter. Hell, that seemed like years ago now. "And?"

"All exposed can enjoy a sigh of relief." He thumbed a remote in his hand, bringing a report onto the screen. "The toxin levels were high enough to set off our sensors, but not enough to do more than make people sick—which explains how it flew under our radar. We would have caught the movement of chemical sales large enough to create a weapon of that magnitude."

"A hoax?" Stella inched forward in her seat, her face overly controlled. "To cause chaos?"

"Apparently that's what Harper and the warlord's troops that brainwashed him intended." Smith clicked through slides with images of the compound, the captors, Stella… the rescue.

Smith paused on a picture of the stolen artifacts, with the folded kanga Harper had stuffed in his backpack. "Their goal has never been order, but rather more anarchy so they can continue with their illegal trades."

And now Sutton Harper was dead, a casualty of someone else's larger plan.

Stella pointed at a new image. "Why did they drape the list on the VP's wife?"

Brown took notes on his iPad. "To send a message? Or arrogance? My money's on the former."

Stella rubbed the back of her neck. "Or could she be involved?"

Brown looked up fast. "Did you really just say that, Carson?"

"It had to be said," Stella answered. "True, Mr. Smith?"

Agent Hard-ass wasn't giving anything away. "All scenarios have to be taken into consideration. But we must always—always—protect the families of our leaders without hesitation." His eyes lasered in on Jose, finally coming around to the reason he'd been allowed in the brief. "We'll sort it all out regarding possible high profile involvement once the dust settles."

The official orders may not have come down yet, but it was clear even without Smith's veiled mention. Special operations forces would be a part of the security detail and since his was already in the region, that put them at the top of the list. Jose knew his job and the best thing he could do for Stella was keep his focus, get through this nightmare scenario. He tuned in as Smith continued.

"We circulated a story that the cloth was promptly packaged up and mailed back to the States. Initially, we hoped they would try to track our decoy package. However, our intel on the ground indicates there will simply be another transfer that will take place tonight at the state dinner honoring the vice president's wife. I don't need to spell out how many years of operations— how many lives—will be in jeopardy if the list of our human assets becomes public knowledge. The balance of power and peace is already so unstable in this region."

If intelligence agencies and special operation forces were compromised, unable to help stem the flow of pirates, warlords, separatists, terrorists, too many unstable factions to count, there would be nothing left to stop them—except war.

Fang's words from earlier rolled around his head, how the kid had half-jokingly asked... *Should I stay or should I go?*

Jose glanced at Stella and saw the answer in her eyes. There was no question for people like them, intel, and special ops. They were here for a mission and they had to see it through to completion.

He'd always understood that part of his mission.

But this need to take Stella and tuck her away somewhere—anywhere—safe and to hell with the cost to everyone else? That distraction was a hundred percent new.

"Henry, we have one final mission for you and then your debt will be paid."

Cell phone pressed to his ear, he watched Jose James stand guard outside the room where Stella Carson spoke with her mother. James's determination, his protectiveness damn near vibrated through the air.

He understood the feeling well. There'd been a time he'd thought he could protect his family from anything by sheer force of will.

"Hold on. I need to get somewhere I can talk." Henry marched toward the hangar exit, trying to give off the air that he was working and to back the hell away.

Shoving through the door, he blinked at the harsh sun. God, he missed his little house in Virginia, the snowy winters, all the shit he'd griped about, taken for granted. "Why should I believe this is ever going to stop? That I'll ever be free?"

"Because you'll die on this mission, Henry. You won't be a danger to your family ever again."

He squeezed his eyes shut, holding onto that image of building a snowman with his wife and kid. "Or I could eat a gun now."

"Henry, you don't want to do that."

"Why the hell not?"

"We can't let it be that simple for you or word will spread and others might get the same idea to escape their obligation to us," he spoke patronizingly—and without the voice distorter. This truly was the end if he wasn't worried about his voice being recognized. "Do what we ask and your daughter will live as a sign to others we keep our word—as long as you follow our orders."

His throat clogged with the truth he already knew but had to ask. "And Charlotte?"

"Your wife's already gone."

He doubled over, grabbed his knees, and fought back the urge to vomit.

"But your daughter can walk away from this alive. Little Ellie can grow up with her cousins in your sister's home where no one gambles with her future."

Like he needed the reminder this was all his fault, how he'd justified his addiction, then justified the things he'd done to hide his secret. "What do you want me to do?"

"You will shoot the vice president's wife. She doesn't have to die, but an injury to her will create chaos. And continued chaos in that region equals free trade of goods and information. We don't need to get into the gory details. You're a smart man, Henry."

A smart man? More like a dead man walking.

Stella squeezed the doorknob and searched for the will to pull the door open. Her mother waited on the other side and Smith had given them ten minutes to "talk" before they went to work. The reality still hadn't settled in her brain. She'd barely had time to process her "dead" mother had worked for the CIA. Then to learn in such a shocking fashion that her mother was still alive? She should be rejoicing... if it weren't for the searing betrayal. They'd even been given a body to bury...

What the hell had Melanie Carson been doing for the past fourteen years while her family grieved for her?

Anger fueled Stella's feet. She opened the door and charged inside. Her mother sat alone in an industrial metal chair, the hangar walls and beams stark around her. Memories of a trip to the beach sucker punched her with the scent of peanut butter sandwiches and sunscreen.

She should sit. Should. But she stayed against the door instead. "Mr. Smith says we have ten minutes, so let's cut straight to the chase. You've been alive this whole time."

"Yes, Stella, I have," her mother said, her voice a bit lower pitched than Stella remembered, but still familiar.

The last time she'd talked to Melanie, they'd gone to the mall, shopping for Stella's school clothes. She'd tortured herself for years regretting her last words to her mom had been *I hate you*. Now to learn all this time her mother had been alive?

How dare she sit there so poised and regal as if they were simply meeting for lunch? "A postcard would have been nice."

"I'm sorry, but I couldn't communicate with anyone in my former life." Her mother swept her scarf off her head, fully uncovering her chestnut hair—and strands of silver that caught Stella unaware.

She pushed back distracting emotions, sliding into a chair, her shaking knees close to betraying her. "Are you telling me you were in witness protection?"

"In a sense, but deeper."

Willing her heart out of her throat, Stella counted bolts in the beams…

Melanie smiled. "What are you counting?"

"What?" She sat up straighter, startled.

"You always did that when you were little, counting to calm yourself… crayons, stairs, roadside signs."

Stella's already thread-thin control snapped. "How would you know what I'm like anymore?" She smacked the table, leaning forward. "You haven't bothered to speak to me since I was fifteen years old."

"Would you believe me if I said I did it for your own safety?" She twisted the headscarf between her fingers.

That took a little wind out of her sails and made sense. Her mother had been an agent, and so many things could go wrong for operatives that would change life forever. But damn it, she didn't want to feel sorry for her mother. "Where have you been all this time?"

"Teaching at an orphan school, here in Africa."

"Of course. You always did love this place." She couldn't help the bitterness in her voice. Her mom had cared more about this country and its people than her own family.

"Stella, I'm sorry I had to leave you." Her mother's hand inched across the table, close but not touching.

"And Dad and the boys."

"All of you. I thought I could have this job, stay in the

field, and have my family too. For a while it worked."
Her green eyes took on a faraway look. "Until my cover
was blown and the only way I could ensure our family's
safety was to disappear."

"I wanted to come with you." Their fight at the mall
came roaring back, the ache of abandonment. "Did you
ever think of offering us the option to join you when you
built your new life?"

"Even if I could have justified putting you at risk,
your brothers were in college. And what would have
happened if you said no? Once you knew I was alive,
I would have placed you in danger for the rest of your
life." Her shoulders braced again. "I made the decision
and you can be angry with me. Blame me. Hate me. But
I will always believe I made the best possible choice
under the worst possible circumstances. Think logically,
think like the agent you are, sift through it, and you'll
come to the same conclusion."

Her mother's words made total sense in a heartbreaking way. Melanie Carson—Annie Johnson—had
made her choice: the job. Her mother was the kind of
agent she would never be, the kind she didn't want
to be.

Stella squeezed her eyes closed and… accepted.

"What do I call you?"

Her mother might have chosen the right course of
action—logically. That didn't mean Stella had to like it.
Right or not, the decision hurt immeasurably.

"My name has been Annie Johnson for fourteen
years. I don't know who I will be after this."

"Okay, then." She shoved her chair from the table
and walked to the door. Pausing without facing her

mom, she said, "For what it's worth, Annie, Melanie, whoever you are, I forgive you."

Stella slipped out of the door past her mother's Egyptian bodyguard and back to her final mission.

Chapter 15

SITTING ON THE EDGE OF THE BED, JOSE TUGGED OFF his combat boots. He and Stella had twenty minutes—tops—to change into more formal gear and get back to work security for the outdoor festival. Her head had to be reeling after the confrontation with her mother, but Stella had stayed silent during the bus ride from the airport to their quarters.

Not that he'd expected her to talk about it in front of his team and other operatives. And now that they were alone? She was still putting up walls, and he needed to get through to her before they launched this last phase of the mission. Especially when she'd made it so clear she was ready to be done.

Frustration simmered on so many levels. Somebody should have his head examined for planning an outdoor celebration in this volatile region. But he went where he was sent, carried out the assignments he was given. He didn't know any other way to live. He was fast realizing he didn't know how he could live without Stella in his life. These past days together again had to mean something to her too. Why couldn't she recognize that?

He thumbed the buttons on his sweaty ABU—Airman Battle Uniform. He would change back into the same digital camo uniform, but a clean version with a bulletproof vest and his maroon beret. His role dictated he stand out as a security force. Stella, on the other hand, would be blending in.

She pinned her braid into a bun on the back of her head. She wore her standard black pants and tank top, her bulletproof vest, and a kanga resting beside her on a chair. He recognized that length of cloth well. He'd bought it for her on their last date.

God, how could they be so good together and so wrong for each other? But without a doubt, he couldn't miss the sadness on her face. He pulled off his sweat-stained uniform and reached for a fresh set, tugging on his pants, his eyes never leaving her.

She reached for her Kevlar vest and stopped short. "Is there a problem?"

"Problem? Hell yes, there's a problem." He closed the two feet between them, taking the vest from her hand and tossing it aside. He cupped her face. "I don't know how I'm going to walk away from you again."

She blinked in surprise, then more of that sadness flooded her green eyes. "Maybe we were destined to fail from the start since we're so different. You get along with everyone, and I don't know how to be anyone's friend."

Surprise rocked him to his socks. "Why would you say that?"

"Forget about it." She eased his hands down. "Could you please stop trying to be so nice? We can't just pretend to be friends, or even just pick up where we left off. And I'm in a crummy place today after talking to my mother, too bad a mood to fake it."

There she went putting up those walls again. "I know. And I want to be supportive."

She tugged on her bulletproof vest like armor against him as well as the rest of the world. "The best thing you can do for me is to back away."

He touched her shoulder.

She shrugged his hand aside. "You're not listening to me. I. Need. Space."

"Damn it, Stella, let me spell it out for you." An image of her out there in the line of fire in her current unsteady state scared the shit out of him. "I care about you. I'm worried about you going in the line of fire in this mood. This region isn't safe, so you don't have the luxury of 'space.'"

"You forget I'm a trained agent." She strapped on her 9 mm for easy access and a right-hand draw.

"Lot of good that did when you got taken by warlords and had to call me to save your ass."

"That's not fair."

Gut-twisting fear for her safety pushed him past the point of measuring his words. "Nothing that's happened between us has been remotely fair. Our relationship feels like one big cosmic irony, a guy who never wants to get married falling for a woman craving a white picket fence and babies."

"Don't you dare mock me," she said, standing toe to toe with him.

"Mock you? I'm trying to help you because I love you." The words burned like raw alcohol in his gut. "You don't seem to get it. You broke my heart. Not some flowery, romantic sob story. It's messy and painful. Let me say it again, clearer. You broke my fucking heart."

"Oh God, Jose, I'm sorry." Her face softened and she swayed toward him. "You know that I love you too."

"Fine." Like that made a bit of difference.

"You don't believe me?"

"Oh, I believe you." His laughter hurt. Hell, even his toenails hurt. "I thought we were going to be together for the rest of our lives. My world made sense for the first time, and it felt good, so damn good to think past one day at a time. To think beyond just making it to the end of the day without taking a drink."

Sighing, she clapped a hand over her face. "Jose, haven't we torn each other up enough already?"

"Apparently not."

She scrubbed her wrist over her eyes. "You know what I think?"

"It sure would be nice for you to tell me for a change, instead of making me guess." Frustration chewed a fresh hole in his gut.

"Nice, love the sarcasm," she said tightly. "Really helps maintain constructive lines of communication."

"Constructive lines of communication?" His frustration reached the breaking point. "Could you just speak English?"

She sagged back against the wall next to a corny stock painting of an elephant. "I think you keep pushing me away because for some sad reason you seem to have decided no family is better than losing one again."

Her words struck deep and true, but then that's what happened with people who knew each other too well. "You're one to talk with your expectations of a perfect family that doesn't exist."

He regretted the words the second they left his mouth, knowing they would cause her even more pain on a day that had already handed out too much. But he still believed every bit of it.

"You're wrong," she answered defiantly, snatching

the kanga from the chair. "What about your friends from work and their wives? They're happy and building great lives together."

He didn't even have to think. He already knew. "Give them time."

Stella clutched the blue-and-green kanga to her chest and stared back at him with finality.

And pity.

"Jose, I really wish I'd had the chance to prove you wrong." Turning her back on him, she wrapped the cloth around her, over her gun and vest.

The finality of her tone and the brace of her shoulders went beyond anger, beyond a regular fight. This was really it for her, and he knew it. They were over, no going back, no more making love or pretending they could keep living in limbo. There was nothing left for him but to keep her alive so she could go home and build that fantasy life with some other man.

—ww—

One look at Annie, and Samir Al-Shennawi had a pretty good idea how the meeting with Stella went. He closed the door behind him, sealing him in the small interrogation room with Annie. He'd spent the past year reading every nuance of her face, both as her protector and as the man who loved her.

And today? He would have to continue as the man who protected her, here in a stark cubicle of a room at the airport. The agent in charge—Smith—wanted her tucked away until they had completed damage assessment. Meanwhile, Smith would keep things secure at the big shindig political dinner downtown.

He had his job keeping Annie safe here while the powers that be figured out where to relocate her.

Sam stopped alongside her. "Would you like to take a walk?"

Her wariness changed to surprise. "I thought I was under house arrest."

"You are," he confirmed, too aware of how she'd been keeping her distance. She may have told him everything, but she had still closed herself off from him. "But they need this space for questioning, and I found an unused office with an incredible view. I had food sent up for you. There is even a sofa if you need to rest."

Her smile didn't reach her eyes. "As if I have any choices these days."

Neither of them did. He opened the door and gestured her through into the sparsely populated corridor. His hand rested over his weapon, his eyes tracking the length of the hallway. Transfers were always the most dangerous, even in a locked-down-tight facility. Four doors down, her room waited. Uniformed and armed military guards were stationed at every corner.

Those few steps seemed like miles as he escorted her past framed posters about touring historic Mogadishu. Her steps against tile seemed so dainty, so vulnerable. He understood she had training and could protect herself. During past missions, he had trusted female agents. But Annie wasn't just any agent. After listening to her talk about her capture and what she'd endured, hearing her voice give life to facts he'd read…

He couldn't let her out of his sight now. Maybe ever. Which made that emotional wall she had put up between them cursedly inconvenient.

A dozen steps later, he finally had her in the new room, one he'd chosen just for her to make this lockdown more bearable. During the past year, he'd made it his mission to learn everything about this fascinating woman. He knew she liked wide open spaces. Even at the school, she taught outdoors whenever possible.

So he'd picked this office with care. A wall of windows—bulletproof and tinted—overlooked the runway, but more importantly a distant view of the Indian Ocean.

She raced across the room and pressed her palms to the glass. Airport lights created a bubble of light in the dark night. Fireworks split the sky, just a few, more like amateur stuff before the big show at the end of the ceremonies later.

Her back rose and fell with deep breaths. "Thank you for bringing me here. I was about to scream from being stuck in that claustrophobic room." She glanced over her shoulder. "But I'm guessing you knew that."

He wanted to know more about her, everything and anything he needed to keep her safe. "I take it things did not go well with your daughter."

"Not as I would have hoped, but as I predicted," she said with a deep sadness in her eyes. "She forgives me but she's upset, hurt, distrusting, and that's completely her right. I didn't expect hugs and tears."

Pain, loss, and regret all radiated off her in waves. He walked past the covered meal to stand beside her, crossing his arms behind his back as he stared out at planes taxiing. "Seems to me since she is also an agent she might have a little understanding for the difficult decision you had to make. You sacrificed a lot to keep her safe."

"Don't make excuses for me." She pressed a hand to her throat. "You don't have to pretend to be nice anymore."

"You think I was pretending?"

"It was your job to get close to me, to do whatever it took, to be whomever you needed to be to get under my skin so you could watch me. I get it. Now the need to playact is over."

Playact? She thought he was pretending to care about her? He couldn't let her go on believing that, but he wasn't sure how much she was ready to hear.

So he just touched her arm lightly, but even that brought back memories of their kiss and how much more he wanted from her. "Not everything is an act. You should also know the best covers for agents are the ones that blend the truth in with the fiction. That makes it easier not to trip up."

Her chin tipped proudly, but he could have sworn her eyes held a tentative hope that fired him to clasp both her hands and continue.

"If I had just wanted to get close to you, the simplest way would have been to pretend I was in love with someone else, perhaps a heartbroken widower who could never love again." He'd played that role before on a prior mission in Cairo. "I would have created a back-story to keep you at arm's length romantically while still staying close to you."

"Instead, you chose to be my friend for a whole year?" She glanced down at his hands holding her. "Friends don't kiss."

Why was she making this difficult? Perhaps because she did not want the same thing? Or he had missed his chance by being too cautious? Too honorable?

Frustration chewed at his already overtaxed self-control. "That's because I do not want to be your friend, damn it, and this may not be the best time to tell you, given all you have been through today." His hands slid up her arms to hold her shoulders. Finally, he allowed himself to vocalize his deepest wish since he'd first seen her. "But I want to be with you, romantically. I always have."

"Oh." Her eyebrows shot upward as quickly as the plane outside climbed into the night sky.

"Oh? That is all you have to say?" He had bared his pride to her, and she could only say… "Oh?"

"It's the always part that I'm stuck on." More light powered on outside, casting beams across her incredulity. "Always?"

The power of that first meeting with her surged over him again, the sense that he had been waiting for her his whole life. "From the moment I met you. You were sitting in your classroom putting together some kind of project for a bulletin board. You had the saddest look on your face. All I wanted in that moment was to make you smile."

He still did.

"I remember the day you arrived, that moment you introduced yourself." She angled her head to the side, her beautiful face so dear to him, every freckle imprinted on his memory. "I was thinking about my daughter and how we used to make art projects together when I came home—things to hang on the wall or even use as a doorstop. I needed to know that I'd left a part of myself with her whenever I left."

Guilt creased deep grooves into her face, weighting down her words. More of that pain swelled from her and he realized *that* was the wall between them. She couldn't allow herself to be happy. "Annie, I know you and I am certain you tried your best."

Tears welled in her dark green eyes. "All of that doesn't matter. The reality is, I let her down. I let my boys down... my husband too." She looked at him with those sad eyes again, just like she had the first day he met her. She blinked and two fat tears rolled down her cheeks. "I don't think I could live with myself if I failed again."

"Annie..." His voice came out strangled and hoarse. He gathered her against his chest, breathing in the familiar scent of the hand lotion. So many times he'd walked by that bottle she kept on her desk and resisted the urge to lift it to his nose. "I meant what I said. My feelings for you have never been an act."

"Still? Even after everything I've said?" she asked, all the self-doubt in her voice tearing him up inside. "The kind of person I am—a woman who could leave her husband and her children?"

Decades ago when he'd begun his undercover career, he might well have judged her, back when he'd been stuck in very narrow views of right and wrong. He'd seen too much since then to live that way anymore. Life was far more complicated.

"Annie, you are not perfect. Neither am I. No one is. This is likely the worst possible time to tell you, but I loved you the first time I saw you. Each day, as I got to know you better only made me love you more. It made me want to leave behind my old job and teach by your side in reality. To have the privilege to keep right on loving you."

More of those tears flowed from the strongest woman he'd ever met. "Sam…"

He touched her mouth. "You are not alone anymore."

She swayed into him, her mouth opening to speak, but he stopped her again. "Just think about what I said. I do not want an answer now when so much is turned upside down in your life. I only told you so you would know, you are not alone anymore."

She kissed his fingers lightly, then held his hand to her chest. "It's that simple for you to commit?"

"Not simple at all. But it is true and I have had much longer than you to think through this."

Her pulse raced against his hand pressed to her heart, a tentative smile pushing through her tears. "Sam, I want to believe I can have that kind of happiness again. The picture you paint of us teaching together is incredible. I want to be with you, if that's possible once I find out if I even have a future…"

The beautiful smile on her face faded into a frown, her eyes drifting from him to the window, then widening with confusion, then outright fear.

She pointed toward the tarmac outside, toward the halo of halogen lights. "That's Ajaya, from the school. And one of those agents wearing a dark suit has a gun pointed at him." The light gleamed off the agent's cowboy hat. "He's forcing Ajaya onto an airplane."

—⁂—

Ajaya didn't know who to trust anymore.

The American agent, Mr. Jones, acted like his friend, but he had a gun out, his hat in place like he was some African American cowboy. He said leaving was for his protection, but he wouldn't explain why they were getting on an airplane. How much longer would his life be out of his control? When could he become a man and take charge of his own life, his own destiny?

Except he could never have the one thing he wanted most.

To go back. To live with his family and be a child again. The one thing he could never have.

The night wind full of dirt grated against his skin, carrying the sounds from the festival close by. The familiar music and scent of grilling meat reminded him of home. So much so he could swear he heard his mother calling his name.

"Ajaya…"

Mr. Jones pivoted on his heels, weapon leveled.

"Ajaya…"

It wasn't his imagination. Someone was shouting for him. He looked and couldn't believe… "Mrs. Johnson?"

Somehow, impossibly real, his English teacher ran toward him. His chemistry teacher Mr. Al-Shennawi trailed protectively behind her. Ajaya didn't understand how it could be true. But Mr. Jones was already lowering his weapon. They were all on the same side. He was safe.

For the first time in longer than he could remember, Ajaya wasn't alone anymore.

───◈───

Stella winced as another firework exploded in the sky.

The courtyard celebration was already a security nightmare, full of people in thick layers of clothes that could hide an assortment of weapons—as her kanga hid her gun and the knife strapped to her leg.

Too bad there was nothing to protect her from letting Jose break her heart all over again. She was the smart, logical type. Except when it came to him. She tried to keep her eyes off Jose and his team as they stood in a protective row in front of the dais, red berets a perfect blend for the festive colors.

Her eyes betrayed her and skated front anyway, right to her pararescueman, the tallest one standing lean and strong in the middle. The loss burned over her, almost sending her to her knees. She'd pushed him away, but what choice did she have? Why did she keep setting herself up for this pain again and again?

She couldn't afford to figure that one out now, not when she needed to focus every ounce of energy on the celebration around her. If they could get through this evening without incident, they might not have answers, but they would have time and space to follow up leads without fear of a national incident involving a major political figure.

Her earpiece chattered with voices from the command post, agents and military guys discussing surveillance. She was on the ground to gather human intel rather than sitting behind a computer. Mr. Smith had gotten past parking her behind a monitor. Not that any of them knew what they were looking for. They were shadowboxing with a ghostly enemy.

Hundreds of guests dressed in ceremonial clothes filled the tents with color—a mix of flowing robes to tuxedos. Women covered their hair with everything from simple headcloths to colorful hijabs. Jewelry, beads, and gold glinted in the lights, creating one distraction after another as she searched for guns, knives, and any other possible weapons. Even the display on the dais containing a case of African artifacts reminded her of how easily she'd turned similar remnants into tools to survive in the warlord's compound. Except she hadn't needed them because Jose had come for her. At the compound, he'd pushed through the doorway wearing his full battle-rattle, face streaked with camo paint.

But she'd recognized him without hesitation.

She forced her thoughts away from how she'd known him so instinctively.

More fireworks popped overhead, but otherwise the skies were empty. All flights had been canceled until after the guest of honor made her speech. The airspace would stay clear, no risk of threats from above.

Meanwhile, the invited guests and dignitaries partied on, picking at falafels, fried plantains, the spongy sour cake-like injera, meats, fruits, all local but surprisingly not overdone. In a country full of starving people, excesses would have been wrong—not to mention bad press.

Her mother had fought and sacrificed her entire adult life to help others here. Just as Jose sacrificed his life for others? Was it somehow her fate to love people who gave up a family for some higher calling? What was the answer for her?

A part of her wanted to shout at the Melanies and Joses of the world that this fight was futile. They couldn't win and they were forfeiting a personal life for nothing. She pressed a finger to her earpiece, sifting through all the chatter. So much going on at once.

Mr. Smith monitoring the placement of security forces as the vice president's wife took the podium.

Mr. Brown calling in from the entrance checkpoint.

Mr. Jones escorting Ajaya to a secure location.

Voices in her headset competed with the music swelling through the air, played on instruments that were works of art themselves—bamboo flutes, xylophones, kettle and clay pot drums, a kora harp. And those were only the ones she recognized.

Her earpiece filled with the cool logical tones of Mr. Brown. "Heads-up. Suspicious activity in the west corner of the park. Two persons of interest from a student rebel group. Wearing green hats. I repeat, west corner of the park."

Smith came on the line, barking out orders shifting his security around. Stella angled sideways through the crowd, arching up on her toes for a better view. Damn it, she needed a clearer vantage point. Period.

No one questioned how Brown could remember faces from thousands in a registry of suspicious persons. The man had a photographic memory and a careful attention to detail. And the timing lined up for some kind of move to be made. The vice president's wife was giving her statement about women's rights in the region. Gifts were being exchanged, including a doll passed from a local official's daughter. Beads on the doll's dress gleamed in the morning sun.

Stella grabbed a light pole and stepped up onto the ridged edge, searching the crowd—until, yes, there were two men walking side by side, both wearing hats that matched agent Brown's description. But where was he? She searched for his dark suit in the splash of color, careful not to linger on the PJs still creating a wall of strength in front of the dais. She found Smith an instant later, just past the stage.

Jones would have been easy to find with his outback hat, but he was at the airport taking Ajaya into protective custody so he could be moved to the States. So why wasn't there a dark suit on the west side of the park? Only military uniforms converging for protection as ordered.

Hanging onto the lamppost, she angled around, looking off to the east, which didn't make sense. Mr. Brown was in the back, watching the west. Except he wasn't. She saw his dark suit and short ginger hair, spiky on top. Okay, so he wasn't in his assigned position and he'd called in a report that shifted the bulk of security to the other side of the park. Could be explained away by something as simple as him finding a better vantage point as she had.

No big deal. She was just looking for trouble because of hints of a mole. And there were always rumors and fears of a leak in intelligence.

She glanced back at the rear entrance to see who'd taken Brown's place...

No one. She slid off the lamppost and back to the ground. Her feet carried her toward the east side of the park, where she'd seen Mr. Brown on the edges of the party.

Brown didn't make mistakes. He was Mr. Logical, like her. Except right now she wasn't thinking logically. She was thinking that her every instinct screamed something was wrong about Mr. Brown. That he was the kind who could have cracked codes to get his hands on the list of agents. That he was the kind who would have the aptitude to encrypt the information.

Him and hundreds of other people.

Except he was here and she had questions with very little time to waste waiting for answers. She pushed through the crush of bodies, applause and cheers reverberating over something in the speech. Damn it, she needed to move faster. If she voiced her suspicions over the headset to Mr. Smith, she could divert security in the wrong direction—and Mr. Brown would hear her.

This was a no-win.

Finally, the crowd thinned and she spotted Mr. Brown on the sidelines. Approaching him in the darkened corner didn't feel right. And when the hell had she started going so much on "feelings"?

Since Jose.

She looked closer. Brown's spiked ginger-colored hair shone… along with the glint of his gun.

Gun?

Why the hell did he have his weapon drawn? She palmed her 9 mm. Damn, damn, damn, a shoot-out here would be a very bad thing. And maybe his intent was benign. Even so, she couldn't stay quiet any longer.

She brought her sleeve up to her mouth and spoke into the mic. "Carson here, east side of park. Mr. Brown, why do you have your weapon drawn? Over."

Mr. Smith hissed over the headset. "Draw down. Now. That's an order."

Brown pivoted, fast and sharp on his heels, facing her for an instant. His eyes blared the worst message of all. Desperation.

As if in slow motion, she saw his gun arm swing back toward the stage. Toward the vice president's wife.

"No!" she shouted, whipping her 9 mm from under the folds of her wrap.

Sprinting, she wished like hell she had Jose's speed. Her heart leaped in her throat. Her ears roared so loudly she couldn't have heard a gunshot or screams. She caught a flash of red out of the corner of her eyes. Blood? No. Jose's hat as he vaulted onto the stage to protect his charge. She ran faster, closing the gap. And thank God the few people in her way dropped to the ground, giving her a clear shot at Agent Brown.

A man she'd worked with for the past six months.

She squeezed off two shots without hesitation, catching him in the shoulder. Ten feet away, Brown spun around from the impact. His fist still gripped his gun.

Pain exploded in her leg. In her head. She stumbled forward toward her target.

Then she smelled it. Blood. Her own. Dripping in her eyes and down the sides of her nose. She fell to her knees and shot Brown again, blasting away his kneecap. Howling, he fell to his side. His gun skittered away. And finally, she let herself sag the rest of the way to the ground.

As she lay on her side, she looked into the eyes of a man she'd trusted with her life and asked, "How could you?"

Sweat rolled down his face, his mouth twisted in agony. "Wouldn't you do anything to protect your family?"

Her family? Images of her brothers, her father, her mother all scrolled through her mind in the fast-track life review. But then the reel slowed and focused on one face, one man.

Jose. Her family. And she'd foolishly pushed him away. Love and loss seeped through her as tangibly as her life's blood leaving her body.

Chapter 16

JOSE WAS IN HELL.

Draped over the vice president's wife, he needed to be with Stella. Each gunshot echoing in his ears ripped a roar of denial from him. He'd done his job, protected the vice president's wife, but at such a high cost. Stella had been shot. She'd defied the odds to stop an all-out massacre, and he doubted he could have done anything more.

The fact that they'd both been doing their jobs was piss poor comfort. His heart hammered in his ears. Where the hell were his objective instincts from years of training?

A hand clamped him on the shoulder. He jerked, looking to find Bubbles crouched beside him. "I've got things here. The Saint too. Go treat Stella. Go."

He didn't need to be told twice. Jose launched off the stage into the mayhem below. Jose pushed past a couple shoving back against him, desperate to get away. His eyes stayed locked on Stella, the world around him a peripheral blur.

Security had their hands full restoring order. Fang loped up alongside him, medical rucksack in hand that carried enough supplies to treat up to three patients. How fucking ironic that Stella and Brown would be sharing lifesaving gear. Fang kept pace as they dodged musicians huddled by a bandstand. There was no discussing who would treat Brown and who would take Stella.

She was his, damn it.

Fang could care for the traitorous bastard.

A trio knelt around Stella, and he could only see her feet and a trailing edge of the kanga he'd given her. If she was dead… Even thinking it threatened to knock the ground out from under him. He could rub that sobriety coin all damn day and nothing, *nothing* would get him through if he lost the most important person in his life.

"Move," he shouted, to hell with control and calm, "medic coming through."

The wall of people parted and… Oh God. The streetlamp bathed her in stark light that revealed everything, too much. Stella lay stone still, her eyes half-open and glazed with pain. A wad of bloodied handkerchiefs lay beside her head, no doubt someone's attempt to help.

Blood streamed from a scrape along her temple. Most would have gone for that first, but he evaluated fast and ranked it as the least of their worries.

Her thigh wound pumped blood from the femoral artery. She could bleed out in about five minutes.

"Hang on, Stella." Dropping to the ground, he slapped a hand to her leg and pushed hard while tearing into the medic pack with the other.

He had gear for a splint, tracheotomy, intubation, and countless other lifesaving measures he prayed he wouldn't need. Finally, thank God, finally his body went into autopilot. A tourniquet for her leg. Bandages. IV antibiotics.

Beside him, Fang treated Agent Brown who kept groaning, *"Let me die, let me die."*

Fang muttered, "Not a chance. You'll face your firing squad."

How fucking ironic—and unfair—that Stella had aimed to maim when her enemy had shot to kill.

Her fingers clamped his arm weakly. He looked into her eyes again. Bad, bad idea. Professional distance crumbled.

Her lips moved but nothing came out other than a faint whisper he couldn't understand.

"Shhh," he soothed, checking her vitals, willing his hand not to shake as he counted her pulse, simultaneously monitoring the drip on the IV. "You're going to be fine, Stella. I'm that damn good at my job."

She blinked up at him. Alive. Awake. For how long?

He shouted over his shoulder, rage and desperation chewing through his gut. "We need medical transport. Stat!" He looked back at her, adjusting her elevated feet. "Stella, stay with us. You're going to be fine. A transfusion or two and you'll be kicking ass again. I promise."

As he checked her pupils he realized... she was blinking in a pattern.

"Morse code?" he asked, focusing on her while listening for updates in his earpiece. Where the hell was the ambulance? "Are you trying to tell me something?"

Yes, she blinked. *Agent Brown.*

"Agent Brown. We know. We've got him. You got him, wounded but not dead. You kept him alive for interrogation." A siren wailed in the distance. "You did great, Stella. Help's coming."

She squeezed his arm again. *Love. You.*

"Love you too." And he meant it, with every cell in his body that screamed for her to hold on. Not to give up.

Come hell or high water, if she lived, he would do

anything to make sure he didn't lose her again. He'd thought he was protecting her by staying away, but she was right. He'd only been shielding his heart from the possibility of losing another family. Yes, he carried a genetic flaw and he couldn't forget that, but he'd made different choices for his life than his sister and mother. He sure as hell refused to be like his dad, enabling, avoiding.

Jose monitored her thready heartbeat and willed her to stay with him. He and Stella deserved a life together.

Without her, he had no future. "God, Stella, you can't die, damn it. I want to spend my life with you."

But he'd waited a second too long to tell her. Her eyes stayed closed, no more blinking messages.

She'd passed out cold.

—ᴍᴠ—

Pain hovered just below the surface under a blanket of drugs.

Part of Stella wanted to stay under the numbing fog, and another part of her insisted she needed to wake up, even if that meant facing the agony of… gunshot wounds.

The hellish scenario flashed through her mind in fragments. Brown's betrayal. Shooting him. Him shooting her.

Jose's shout of horror piercing her headset.

Her memory filled with the sight of him leaning over her, treating her, pleading with her to hang on. The fear in his eyes had let her know just how bad her injuries were. By that time, she'd been floating in a cottony cloud of shock.

Was she alive now? Or hovering in a limbo state?

She drew in air and could swear she was actually

breathing, except there was no antiseptic scent of a hospital. Her body felt so heavy, anchored by the crisp weight of a thin blanket.

A sheet? She forced her hand to grip the sheet, then move to her face where tubes pumped oxygen to her nose. No wonder she hadn't detected the standard hospital smell.

At least she was alive. Knowing that, she fought through the hazy pain, fought her way back so she could see Jose and tell him how much she loved him. She wasn't missing out on that chance again.

Her eyes opened and a chair screeched back against the floor. She turned her head on the pillow and found… her mother.

A smile of relief spread across her mother's face. "Good morning, kiddo. How do you feel?"

"Mom?" she croaked, then coughed.

Her mother passed her water to sip through a bendy straw just like when Stella had the chicken pox at five years old.

How could she have forgotten that?

Annie set the cup on the bedside table. "I'll call for the nurse."

"No, please." Stella gripped her wrist. "Wait. Tell me what happened first."

"You're in a hospital. You were shot twice. One bullet grazed your temple. The other hit a major artery in your thigh." She squeezed her hand. "But you're going to be fine. Jose treated you on the scene while you waited for the ambulance. The doctor said Jose saved your life."

Her voice trailed off and she pressed a palm to her

chest. Annie blinked back tears that spoke louder than words of how close she'd come to dying. She owed Jose so much. "And the list, the names?"

"Agent Brown was the leak. It appears he was turned traitor when he built up gambling debts. An enemy exploited that weakness. I'm not privy to all the details, but I'm guessing they may offer him his life in exchange for all his contacts. Regardless, the leak has been plugged."

Annie clicked through the high notes like the seasoned professional she was and Stella felt an uncanny sense of looking in the mirror. How humbling to think she was so much like this woman whose choices frustrated the hell out of her.

She would get the rest of the details later, once she could link up with her contacts at Interpol. She intended to press hard for the right to sift through every piece of data the analytical Mr. Brown recorded, check and recheck each piece of paper he touched. If he'd falsified so much as an order for candy bars, she would find it.

And she couldn't help but wonder if she might have been more effective from the start if she'd stuck to what she did best.

Analyzing data.

"Uhm, Stella?" her mother asked, uncertainty looking so alien on her confident mom. "You need to know I'm coming back to the States."

Pain meds dripping through the IV tube fuzzed regular details like the sun shining through the window and the bedpan on the rolling table.

Sifting through her mother's words made her head

throb. She pressed her fingers against her temple—and winced as she touched the bandage. She'd come that close to dying from a bullet to the brain.

Stella thumbed the remote and raised the head of the bed, wincing at the stab of pain as her leg moved all of a couple of millimeters. "What about your whole witness protection program?"

"A lot of years have passed since I was in the loop." She smoothed back her silver-streaked hair. "I haven't been an active agent in so long anything I know is outdated. Maybe I've been hiding out here in Africa, afraid to face you and your brothers. Afraid to face myself."

"Wow, I don't know what to say." She reached for the cup and sipped more water to clear her throat and her thoughts.

"I don't intend to camp in your front yard, if that's what you're worried about."

"That isn't what I said." The thought of spending more time with her mother was scary, yes, but also... amazing.

"Sorry to be defensive." She rubbed her bare ring finger where she'd once worn a plain gold wedding band. "I haven't put together my whole plan, but knowing that you almost died out there and I could have missed the opportunity to see you again? I just want the chance to get to know you and your brothers again."

"I can understand that." She felt the same way. Second chances were rare in life. "If you need help, just let me know."

"I'm a teacher. I can support myself, and sadly, there's no shortage of orphan schools in the United States as well.

I've been thinking about that a lot as your agency friends work on placing Ajaya somewhere in the States."

"What about your, uh, boyfriend?" She hadn't missed how Mr. Al-Shennawi never left her mother's side—except for now.

Annie smiled, as if reading her thoughts. "He's just outside the door. We've talked about taking teaching jobs at the same school, maybe lead a beautifully boring life together."

Stella reached a hand out to her mom, knowing all too well how much courage it took to hope for a happy ending. "I hope your dreams play out for you, Mom, I really do."

Her mother looked at her extended arm, an olive branch, and her eyes filled with tears. Annie squeezed her daughter's hand. A sense of peace filled Stella, a lot more soothing than any painkiller dripping from that bag on the IV pole. She and her mother still had plenty to talk through and fences to mend, but they'd made a good start.

"Hey, Mom? Could you do me a favor?"

"Anything. Just ask."

"Could you find Jose? I really need to talk to him."

Reaching out to her mother had been a good first step in putting her life back together. But nothing would be okay again until she made things right with Jose. The love she'd seen in his eyes when he'd treated her back at the festival gave her hope. She just prayed she hadn't been hallucinating from blood loss.

Because the pain in her brutalized leg was nothing compared to the agony she would feel if she lost Jose for good.

———~~~———

Jose stared into the steaming cup of coffee his buddy Bubbles kept refilling. The big lug sat beside him on the cracked leather sofa, offering silent support.

The night had been the longest of his life. Hands down. Once he'd stabilized Stella at the scene, he'd been left with no choice but to turn her over to paramedics. Fang had held him back as he'd tried to force his way into the ambulance. Only Mr. Smith's promise to keep him in the loop had managed to calm him down enough to keep him from getting arrested.

The bastard Brown had survived and was under guard on a different floor of the hospital. Jose had ditched his bloodied ABU jacket, but refused to leave the hospital. He waited, in his camo pants, boots, and T-shirt. The doctor sounded knowledgeable, but trusting Stella's care to someone he didn't know in a third world country hospital was tough, to say the least.

Normally he would have flipped his sobriety coin. God knows the painful crawl of hours waiting for word on Stella had been beyond stressful. He glanced at Bubbles. "Thanks for hanging out here with me."

"No problem. It's what we do for each other."

The words resonated, reminding him of how he'd said the same thing to his teammates in the past. They all said it. His team had been like a family to him, helping him keep his head above water, just as he liked to think he helped them.

How much better would it be in a rock solid family? With Stella? Because he knew now. He was in for the long haul. He was a marathon man, after all.

Soft footsteps whispered down the hall, coming closer, around the corner. Stella's mother walked into the waiting room.

Jose stood, fast, sloshing hot coffee onto his finger. "Stella?"

Exhaustion stamped its mark on her face, her clothes wrinkled from sleeping in a chair. She looked like... a worried mother. "She's awake and asking to see you. The doctor's checking her over now."

Thank God.

The knowledge that she was out of the woods damn near took his knees out. Annie must have known because she reached for him, giving his arm a simple squeeze.

Then it hit him. If he married Stella, he got a family along with her. And what do you know? The thought didn't scare him. It felt... kind of right.

"Thank you." He offered her his coffee. "I haven't even touched this yet."

"Thanks." She smiled her gratitude.

Her eyes shifted from him to across the hall where her Egyptian friend stood at the nurse's station. She patted Jose's hand, leaving him to go to Stella.

Ten steps past the nurse's station and a rolling cart with lunch trays, he reached Stella's door as the doctor walked out.

"She is a lucky woman," the doctor said in broken English before moving on to the next patient.

Right now, he felt like the lucky one.

Jose pushed open her door and God, she was beautiful. But so damn pale her freckles stood out all the more. At least the heart monitor beeped a steady reassurance, even if the bandages on her head and her leg struck a fresh bolt of fear through him.

"Stella, what the hell were you doing out there?" Shit, that wasn't what he'd meant to say.

But she didn't bristle. She simply rolled her eyes at him, understanding too well, probably more than he deserved. He charged across the room and kissed her forehead, taking in the warmth of her. Alive. Thank God, alive.

Her fingers stroked the back of his neck. "I was doing my job. Which included saving your ass."

"You're a code breaker. A data techie. That's your job." He angled back, looking into her glittering green eyes that reminded him of the dewy morning grass of home. "Leave that shoot-out stuff for us security dudes."

"But I knew something was off when Brown told everyone to go west and he went the other way." She frowned at the memory, her well-ordered brain always ready to catch a piece of a puzzle that didn't fit. That was one of many reasons she was so damn good at her job.

"You found the mole and kept sensitive information safe. I would wholeheartedly approve if you hadn't gotten shot in the process." The kick to his gut was so damn sharp it was like seeing it happen all over again. "You took doing your job to a whole new level."

Her hand slid around to caress his unshaven cheek. "My job is to love you, Jose James. That's the only thing I care about. But you know I've spoken before about focusing my work life on code breaking, the desk type, out of the field."

She was making this too easy for him, which also

made it tougher because he wanted to earn her, to be worthy of this amazing woman who'd given him her entire heart.

"Loving you is the scariest damn thing I've ever done, Stella." He kissed her forehead again, then her freckled nose, her mouth, quickly, carefully. "And I do, I love you… so much."

That point had been hammered home to him in the month he'd spent without her. He'd known then that he wasn't ready to let her go. But this last week together had been the pressure cooker that stripped everything else away—all his dumb defenses and all his half-baked notions about what he wanted for his future. The only thing that was left was his love for Stella and faith in her. Hell, if this smart, kick-ass woman saw him as a stand-up guy who could take on a family, then by God he could.

"I'm glad to hear it." She stroked her thumb over his mouth. "I wondered if I was hallucinating when I heard you say that last night."

No more wasting time. No more running. He was ready to take on the future, with Stella. "Let's get married."

She looked at her IV bag quickly, then back at him. "Did I hear you say what I think or are the pain meds messing with my head?"

"Stella, I mean every word. I want us to get married and if you're not ready to talk about that now, I'll wait until you're feeling better. Hell, I'll wait however long it takes because I'm not giving up on us again."

"What about your concerns? You have some very real worries and while I believe in you, I don't take those lightly." Wary hope flickered through her eyes and he hated that she had to wonder or doubt him.

He lowered the bed rail and sat beside her, cautiously so as not to jostle her. He checked the half-empty bag of fluid and the machine blipping her vitals. Satisfied she was okay, he settled beside her. "I want to be with you. Period. I'm fucking miserable without you."

"So romantically spoken." She rested her head against his shoulder, toying with the chain on his dog tags until they slid free from under his T-shirt.

"But from the heart. And actually, it's the logical, practical truth, just the way you like it." He clasped her hand and pressed it against his chest right over his pulse pounding for her. "When I'm with you, I don't fear the future anymore. I want it all, as long as we're together."

She started to answer but he needed to tell her everything. He wanted her to understand how much peace she brought him.

"Before you say anything, I'm willing to revisit the issue of kids."

Her eyes went wide with shock, and she wasn't blinking anything, much less Morse code. "I'm listening."

This part was still tough for him to wrap his brain around, but it was getting easier. And he had faith now that he could be a part of a healthy relationship, with Stella. "I would just ask that we wait to have children until I'm out of the field so there would be less pressure on... our family."

Was it wishful thinking, or did some color flood back into her cheeks? She looked so damn happy she practically glowed.

"That sounds good, really good." Her fingers caressed along his heart, grasping a handful of his shirt. "After what I've been through with my mother, you won't hear any argument from me on that part. Are you sure, though? I don't want you to make spur-of-the-moment promises because of what happened last night."

"It's not spur-of-the-moment. It's been a slow and steady build to the realization that I'm not my mother or my sister. I've been through the worst stress imaginable in the last month and a half, and I haven't thought of taking a drink." He rubbed his cheek gently against the top of her head on the uninjured side. "I've only thought of you and how to make you happy."

"You do make me happy, Jose." She looked up at him, and he knew he wanted to stare into those eyes forever. "And I have total faith in you."

"Besides, any leftover doubts I had got kicked in the ass yesterday. This has been the kind of time that makes a person reevaluate life. I want to spend mine with you. You're going to be an amazing mother someday and I want to be a good dad."

"We're going to make it work, Jose. Forever." She tugged his dog tags, bringing him closer for a kiss to seal the deal.

Sealing their future together.

And making him the happiest flipping man in the world, because he wasn't letting her go.

Epilogue

WHEN STELLA CARSON WAS EIGHT YEARS OLD, SHE made a scrapbook from magazine photos, collaging the "perfect family" and a monstrously big wedding. Reality was a thousand times better than any of her childhood fantasies.

Never in a million dreams could she have envisioned getting married on a sailboat, anchored in a scenic cove along the Nile River. Best of all, her mother stood with her below deck in a tiny cabin, pinning white jasmine blossoms in her daughter's long, loose hair. Stella watched in the oval mirror, Annie's face reflected beside hers like a picture in that long ago dream album.

Her mother smiled. "You look beautiful, sweetheart."

"Thanks, I'm just so very happy to have gotten this right, to have been this lucky."

Peace flowed through her without even a hint of pre-wedding jitters. She and Jose were meant to be together and today was the fulfillment of the first time she'd seen him emerge from the Gulf of Aden.

After their mission in Africa had wrapped up, she'd taken a leave of absence from her job with Interpol to spend time with Jose in Georgia where he was stationed at Moody Air Force Base. She'd struggled at first with what to do with her life and took a job at a local college to pay bills, only to find she enjoyed the hell out of the intellectual challenge. Life was funny sometimes in the way she found her best answers in the surprises.

Like her unexpected meeting of her Mr. Right the day Jose had pulled himself up into her boat and changed her world forever.

Stella passed another flower and bobby pin over her shoulder. "I'm glad you and Sam could be here with us today."

The couple would serve as their only witnesses, Sam and Annie having eloped five months ago.

Annie clipped the final bloom in place. "I wish I could have been there for so many other important moments in your life."

"You're here now." Stella clasped her mother's hand over her shoulder and turned to face her.

Annie's face radiated contentment, her restlessness having finally eased. "Ajaya has given me a do-over of sorts."

Sam and Annie had sponsored his immigration to the United States and served as his legal guardians. He'd been placed in a boarding school for teens with troubled pasts, but he would spend all holidays with Annie and Sam.

"And now I have another brother." Her biological brothers were slower in warming up to their returned-from-the-dead mother, but time and patience seemed to be easing the path.

Life was too short to waste on anger. Too easily they could have all died six months ago. Thank God the guilty had been brought to justice.

Mr. Brown—Henry Pope—had been arrested and

was currently standing trial for treason. Yet, he'd never once spoken about his crimes or given evidence. At one point he'd been placed on suicide watch, but never tried to end his life—unlike the teacher Mr. Gueye who'd hung himself rather than face justice for selling his students. Profilers could only deduce that Pope had chosen to live for his daughter, who was being brought up by her mother's sister.

The warlord responsible had been traced through the bio toxin, a formula so specific it might as well have left a signature. He'd been taken out by his own troops before he could be arrested. And another warlord stepped into the power vacuum. It seemed a never-ending battle, but with defenseless boys and girls lives in the balance here? Turning away just wasn't an option.

Music drifted through the open hatch, a lute and harp lightly calling her to shake off the thoughts of work for now. The time had come to join her life with Jose's.

Annie picked up the lotus bouquet and offered it to Stella. "Are you ready?"

"Absolutely," she answered without hesitation.

"He's a great guy."

"You don't have to convince me." Stella laughed lightly. "I've known he was the one since the first time I saw him."

Clasping the fragrant flowers, Stella started up the steps and into the shining sunlight. The rippling breeze teased her simple eyelet cotton gown around her ankles. Date trees and palms rustled along the bank, reminding her of another time here with Jose.

And the love of her life stood waiting on deck beside a military priest. The sight of Jose, tall and steady in his uniform, made the breath catch in her chest. The sunlight glistened along his jet-black hair, the familiar angles of his handsome face so dear to her. She'd found her family, found her home in Jose.

He held out a hand to her and she joined him, his touch familiar, stirring. He squeezed her hand, the love in his eyes speaking as tangibly as words. Her smile answered him right back before she turned to the military chaplain as her mother moved to stand by Sam, hooking her arm with his.

Stella held hands with Jose, the sailboat rocking gently by the Nile River. His voice rumbled low and firm as he spoke his vows with a firm conviction that tingled through her. And then it was her turn.

"I, Stella, take you, Jose, to be my husband…"

She and Jose had decided to keep the wedding simple and celebrate later with a larger party in the States. Today, this moment, was just about the two of them, affirming their love and their future by each placing a simple gold band on the other's ring finger.

"…to have and to hold, from this day forward."

Thanks to Jose and his fearless rescue, she was alive to enjoy that future.

"For better or worse…"

They'd been through so much and survived so much already this past year, coming through it all stronger. Life wouldn't always be easy, but together? They were rock solid.

Stella continued, "For richer or poorer. In sickness and in health."

She'd started attending Al-Anon meetings, arming herself with the knowledge to better understand his recovery and the challenges they could face. And each day made her all the more certain she wanted to spend the rest of her life with him, as his wife.

"...to love and to cherish from this day forward, 'til death do us part."

And before the chaplain could even finish with his official blessing, Stella arched up to kiss her husband. Warm anticipation curled deliciously through her veins, along with love. So much love.

She'd been wrong about one thing that day they'd met. She'd thought the timing was off. But she'd fallen for the right man at the right time, and looked forward to falling for him all over again every day for the rest of their lives.

If you enjoy sizzling thrill rides of action and attraction, check out the pulse-pounding romance in the rest of Catherine Mann's Elite Force series.

Read on for excerpts from:

COVER ME

HOT ZONE

UNDER FIRE

Available now from Sourcebooks Casablanca

From COVER ME

IT WAS A COLD DAY IN HELL FOR TECH SERGEANT Wade Rocha—standard ops for a mission in Alaska.

He slammed the side of the icy crevasse on Mount McKinley. A seemingly bottomless crevasse. That made it all the more pressing to anchor his ax again ASAP. Except both of his spikes clanked against his sides while the underworld waited in an alabaster swirl of nothingness as he pinwheeled on a lone cable.

Wade scratched and clawed with his gloved hands, kicked with his spiked shoes, reaching for anything. The tiniest of toeholds on the slick surface would be good right about now. Sure he was roped to his climbing partner. But they had the added load of an injured woman strapped to a stretcher beneath them. He needed to carry his own weight.

Chunks of ice and snow pelted his helmet. The unstable gorge walls vibrated under his gloved hands.

"Breathe and relax, buddy." His headset buzzed with reassurance from his climbing partner, Hugh "Slow Hand" Franco.

Right.
Hold tight.
Think.

Focus narrowed, Wade tightened his grip on his rope. He'd earned his nickname, Brick, by being the most hardheaded guy in their rescue squadron. Come hell or high water, he never gave up.

Each steady breath crackled with ice shards in his lungs, but his oxygen-starved body welcomed every atom of air. Lightning fast, he grabbed the line tying them together and worked the belay device.

Whirrr, whippp. The rope zinged through. Wade slipped closer, closer still, to Franco, ten feet below.

"Oof." He jerked to a halt.

"I got ya, Brick. I got ya," Franco chanted through the headset. Intense. Edgy. Nothing was out of bounds. Franco would die before he let him fall. "It's just physics that makes this thing work. Don't overthink it."

And it did work. Wade stabilized against the icy wall again. Relief trickled down his spine in frosty beads of sweat.

He keyed up his microphone. "All steady, Slow Hand."

"Good. Now do you wanna stop horsing around, pal?" Franco razzed, sarcastic as ever. "I'd like to get back before sundown. My toes are cold."

Wade let a laugh loosen the tension kinking up his gut. "Sorry I inconvenienced you by almost dying there. I'll try not to do it again. I'll even spring for a pedicure, if you're worried about your delicate feet chafing from frostbite."

"Appreciate that." Franco's labored breath and hoarse chuckle filled the headset.

"Hey, Franco? Thanks for saving my ass."

"Roger that, Brick. You've done the same for me."

And he had. Not that they kept score. Wade recognized the chitchat for what it really was—Franco checking to make sure he wasn't suffering from altitude sickness due to their fifteen thousand foot perch. They worked overtime to acclimate themselves, but the lurking beast could still strike even the most seasoned climber without warning. They'd already lost one of their team members last month to HACE—high altitude cerebral edema.

He shook his head to clear it. Damn it, his mind was wandering. Not good. He eyed the ledge a mere twenty feet up. Felt like a mile. He slammed an ice ax in with his left hand, pulled, hauled, strained, then slapped the right one in a few inches higher. Crampons—ice cleats—gained traction on the sleek side of the narrow ravine as he inched his way upward.

Slow. Steady. Patient. Mountain rescue couldn't be rushed. At least April gave them a few more daylight hours. Not that he could see much anyway, with eighty-mile-per-hour wind creating whiteout conditions. Below, his climbing partner was a barely discernible blur.

Hand over hand. Spike. Haul. Spike. Haul. He clipped his safety rope into a spike they had anchored in the rock on the way down. Scaled one step at a time. Forgot about the biting wind. The ball-numbing cold.

The ever-present risk of avalanche.

His arms bulged, the burden strapped to his harness growing heavier. *Remember the mission. Bring up an unconscious female climber. Strapped to a litter. Compound fracture in her leg.*

His job as a pararescueman in the United States Air Force included medic training. Land, sea, or mountain, military missions or civilian rescue. With his brothers in arms, he walked, talked, and breathed their motto, "That Others May Live."

That people like his mother might live.

Muscles burning, he focused upward into the growl of the storm and the hovering military helicopter. A few more feet and he could hook the litter to the MH-60. Rotors *chop, chop, chopped* through the sheets of snow like a blender.

The crevasse was too narrow to risk lowering a swaying cable. Just one swipe against the narrow walls of ice could collapse the chasm into itself. On top of the injured climber and Franco.

On top of him.

So it was up to *him*—and his climbing partner—to pull the wounded woman out. Once clear, the helicopter would land if conditions permitted. And if not, they could use the cable then to raise her into the waiting chopper.

Wind slammed him again like a frozen Mack truck. He fought back the cold-induced mental fog. At least when Hermes went subterranean to rescue Persephone from the underworld, he had some flames to toast his toes.

Wade keyed his microphone again to talk to the helicopter orbiting overhead. "Fever"—he called the mission code name—"we're about five minutes from the top."

Five minutes when anything could happen.

"Copy, the wind is really howling. We will hold until you are away from the crevasse."

"Copy, Fever."

The rest of his team waited in the chopper. They'd spent most of the day getting a lock on the locale. The climber's personal locator beacon had malfunctioned off and on. Wade believed in his job, in the motto. He came from five generations of military.

But sometimes on days like this, saving some reckless thrill seeker didn't sit well when thoughts of people like his mother—wounded by a roadside bomb in Iraq, needing his help—hammered him harder than the ice-covered rocks pummeling his shoulder. How damned frustrating that there hadn't been a pararescue team near enough—he hadn't been near enough—to give her medical aid. Now because of her traumatic brain injury, she would live out the rest of her life in a rehab center, staring off into space.

He couldn't change the past, but by God, he would do everything he could to be there to help someone else's mother or father, sister or brother, in combat. That could only happen if he finished up his tour in this frozen corner of the world.

As they neared the top, a moan wafted from the litter suspended below him. Stabilizing the rescue basket was dicey. Even so, the groans still caught him by surprise.

The growling chopper overhead competed with the increasing howls of pain from their patient in the basket. God forbid their passenger should decide to give them a real workout by thrashing around.

"Franco, we better get her to the top soon before the echoes cause an avalanche."

"Picking up the pace."

Wade anchored the last… swing… of his ax… Ice crumbled away. The edge shaved away in larger and larger chunks. *Crap, move faster.* Pulse slugging, he dug deeper.

And cleared the edge.

Franco's exhale echoed in his ears. Or maybe it was his own. Resisting the urge to sprawl out and take five right here on the snow-packed ledge, he went on auto-pilot, working in tandem with Franco.

Climbing ropes whipped through their grip as they hauled the litter away from the edge. Franco handled his end with the nimble guitarist fingers that had earned him the homage of the Clapton nickname, Slow Hand. The immobilized body writhed under the foil Mylar survival blanket, groaning louder. Franco leaned over to whisper something.

Wade huffed into his mic, "Fever, we are ready for pickup. One survivor in stable condition, but coming to, fast and vocal."

The wind-battered helicopter angled overhead, then righted, lowering, stirring up snow in an increasing storm as the MH-60 landed. Almost home free.

Wade hefted one end, trusting Franco would have the other in sync, and hustled toward the helicopter. His crampons gripped the icy ground with each pounding step. The door of the chopper filled with two familiar faces. From his team. Always there.

With a *whomp*, he slid the metal rescue basket into the waiting hands. He and Franco dove inside just as the MH-60 lifted off with a roar and a cyclone of snow. Rolling to his feet, he clamped hold of a metal hook bolted to the belly of the chopper.

From **HOT ZONE**

THE WORLD HAD CAVED IN ON AMELIA BAILEY.

Literally.

Aftershocks from the earthquake still rumbled the gritty earth under her cheek, jarring her out of her hazy micronap. Dust and rocks showered around her. Her skin, her eyes, everything itched and ached after hours—she'd lost track of how many—beneath the rubble.

The quake had to have hit at least seven on the Richter scale. Although when you ended up with a building on top of you, somehow a Richter scale didn't seem all that pertinent.

She squeezed her eyelids closed. Inhaling. Exhaling. Inhaling, she drew in slow, even breaths of the dank air filled with dirt. Was this what it was like to be buried alive? She pushed back the panic as forcefully as she'd clawed out a tiny cavern for herself.

This wasn't how she'd envisioned her trip to the Bahamas when she'd offered to help her brother and sister-in-law with the legalities of international adoption.

Muffled sounds penetrated, of jackhammers and tractors. Life scurried above her, not that anybody seemed to have heard her shouts. She'd screamed her throat raw until she could only manage a hoarse croak now.

Time fused in her pitch-black cubby, the air thick with sand. Or disintegrated concrete. She didn't want to think what else. She remembered the first tremor, the dawning realization that her third-floor hotel room in the seaside Bahamas resort was slowly giving way beneath her feet. But after that?

Her mind blanked.

How long had she been entombed? Forever, it seemed, but probably more along the lines of half a day while she drifted in and out of consciousness. She wriggled her fingers and toes to keep the circulation moving after being so long immobile. Every inch of her body screamed in agony from scrapes and bruises and probably worse, but she couldn't move enough to check. Still, she welcomed the pain that reassured her she was alive.

Her body was intact.

Forget trying to sit up. Her head throbbed from having tried that. The ceiling was maybe six inches above where she lay flat on her belly. Again, she willed back hysteria. The fog of claustrophobia hovered, waiting to swallow her whole.

More dust sifted around her. The sound of the jackhammers rattled her teeth. They seemed closer, louder, with even a hint of a voice. Was that a dog barking?

Hope hurt after so many disappointments. Even if her ears heard right, there had to be so many people in need of rescuing after the earthquake. All those efforts could easily be for someone else a few feet away. They might not find her for hours. Days.

Ever.

But she couldn't give up. She had to keep fighting. If not for herself, then for the little life beside her, her precious new nephew. She threaded her arm through the tiny hole between them to rub his back, even though he'd long ago given up crying, sinking into a frighteningly long nap. His shoulders rose and fell evenly, thank God, but for how much longer?

Her fingers wrapped tighter around a rock and she banged steadily against the oppressive wall overhead. Again and again. If only she knew Morse code. Her arm numbed. Needle-like pain prickled down her skin. She gritted her teeth and continued. Didn't the people up there have special listening gear?

Dim shouts echoed, like a celebration. Someone had been found. Someone else. Her eyes burned with tears that she was too dehydrated to form. Desperation clawed up her throat. What if the rescue party moved on now? Far from her deeply buried spot?

Time ticked away. Precious seconds. Her left hand gripped the rock tighter, her right hand around the tiny wrist of the child beside her. Joshua's pulse fluttered weakly against her thumb.

Desperation thundered in her ears. She pounded the rock harder overhead. God, she didn't want to die. There'd been times after her divorce when the betrayal hurt so much she'd thought her chance at finally having a family was over, but she'd never thrown in the towel. Damn him. She wasn't a quitter.

Except why wasn't her hand cooperating anymore? The opaque air grew thicker with despair. Her arm grew leaden. Her shoulder shrieked in agony, pushing a gasping moan from between her cracked lips. Pounding became taps… She frowned. Realizing…

Her hand wasn't moving anymore. It slid uselessly back onto the rubble-strewn floor. Even if her will to live was kicking ass, her body waved the white flag of surrender.

—◦◦—

Master Sergeant Hugh Franco had given up caring if he lived or died five years ago. These days, the air force pararescueman motto was the only thing that kept his soul planted on this side of mortality.

That others may live.

Since he didn't have anything to live for here on earth, he volunteered for the assignments no sane person would touch. And even if they would, his buds had people who would miss them. Why cause them pain?

Which was what brought him to his current snowball's-chance-in-hell mission.

Hugh commando-crawled through the narrow tunnel in the earthquake rubble. His helmet lamp sliced a thin blade through the dusty dark. His headset echoed with chatter from above—familiar voices looking after him and unfamiliar personnel working other missions scattered throughout the chaos. One of the search and rescue dogs aboveground had barked his head off the second he'd sniffed this fissure in the jumbled jigsaw of broken concrete.

Now, Hugh burrowed deeper on the say-so of a German shepherd named Zorro. Ground crew attempts at drilling a hole for a search camera had come up with zip. But that Zorro was one mighty insistent pup, so Hugh was all in.

He half listened to the talking in one ear, with the other tuned in for signs of life in the devastation. Years of training honed an internal filter that blocked out communication not meant for him.

"You okay down there, Franco?"

He tapped the talk button on his safety harness and replied, "Still moving. Seems stable enough."

"So says the guy who parachuted into a minefield on an Afghani mountainside."

"Yeah, yeah, whatever." Somebody had needed to go in and rescue that Green Beret who'd gotten his legs blown off. "I'm good for now and I'm sure I heard some tapping ahead of me. Tough to tell, but maybe another twenty feet or so."

He felt a slight tug, then a loosening, to the line attached to his safety harness as his team leader played out more cord.

"Roger that, Franco. Slow and steady man, slow and steady."

Just then he heard the tapping again. "Wait one, Major."

Hugh stopped and cocked his free ear. Tapping, for sure. He swept his light forward, pushing around a corner, and saw a widening cavern that held promise inside the whole hellish pancake collapse. He inched ahead, aiming the light on his helmet into the void.

The slim beam swept a trapped individual. Belly to the ground, the person sprawled with only a few inches free above. The lower half of the body was blocked. But the torso was visible, covered in so much dust and grime he couldn't tell at first if he saw a male or female. Wide eyes stared back at him with disbelief, followed by wary hope. Then the person dropped a rock and pointed toward him.

Definitely a woman's hand.

Trembling, she reached, her French manicure chipped, nails torn back and bloody. A gold band on her thumb had bent into an oval. He clasped her hand quickly to check the thumb for warmth and a pulse.

And found it. Circulation still intact.

Then he checked her wrist—heart rate elevated but strong.

She gripped his hand with surprising strength. "If I'm hallucinating," she said, her raspy voice barely more than a whisper, "please don't tell me."

"Ma'am, you're not imagining anything. I'm here to help you."

He let her keep holding on as it seemed to bring her comfort—and calm—while he swept the light over what he could see of her to assess medically. Tangled hair. A streak of blood across her head. But no gaping wounds.

He thumbed his mic. "Have found a live female. Trapped, but lucid. More data after I evaluate."

"Roger that," Major McCabe's voice crackled through.

Hugh inched closer, wedging the light into the crevice in hopes of seeing more of his patient. "Ma'am, crews are working hard to get you out of here, but they need to stabilize the structure before removing more debris. Do you understand me?"

"I hear you." She nodded, then winced as her cheek slid along the gritty ground. "My name is Amelia Bailey. I'm not alone."

More souls in danger. "How many?"

"One more. A baby."

From UNDER FIRE

Patrick Air Force Base, Florida

"KILL ONE. SCREW ONE. MARRY ONE."

Major Liam McCabe almost choked on a gulp of the Atlantic as his pararescue teammate's words floated across the waves. Today's two-mile swim was pushing toward an hour long. A light rain pocked the surface faster by the second. Still, there was no reason to think one of his guys had gone batty.

Liam sliced an arm through the choppy ocean, looking to the side. "Wanna run that by me again, Cuervo?"

Jose "Cuervo" James swam next to him, phrases coming in bursts as his face cleared the water. "It's a word game. Kill one. Screw one. Marry one. Somebody names three women…" *Swim. Breathe.* "And you have to pick." *Swim. Breathe.* "One to marry. One to kill. One to—"

"Right," Liam interrupted. "Got it."

He would have sighed and shaken his head except for the whole drowning thing. At moments such as these, he felt like a stodgy old guy more than ever.

"So, Major?" Cuervo stroked along and over the rippling waves. Storm clouds brewed overhead. "Are you in?"

On monotonous swims or runs, they'd shot the breeze plenty of times to take their minds off screaming muscles. The distraction was particularly welcome during intense physical training.

This word game, however, was a first.

A quick glance reassured him the other six team members were keeping pace with him and Cuervo. Each held strong, powering toward the beach still a quarter of a mile away.

Feet pumping his fins, Liam shifted his attention back to the "game." His body burned from the effort, but he had plenty of steam left inside to finish up. He was their team leader. Their commanding officer. He would not fall behind.

"How about I just listen first?" Water flowed over his body, briny, chilly. Familiar. "Let one of the others start off."

"Sure, old man," huffed Cuervo, spewing a mouthful to the side. "If you need to save your breath to keep pace. Okay, Fang, you're up."

Fang, the youngest of the group and the one most eager to fit in, arced his arms faster to pull up alongside. "Bring it on."

"Topic for first three. Brad Pitt's women," Cuervo barked. "Gwyneth Paltrow. Jennifer Aniston. Angelina Jolie."

"Jennifer's hot." Fang spewed water with his speedy answer. "I would do her in a heartbeat."

Liam found an answer falling from his mouth after all. "I'd marry Angie."

"Too easy." Cuervo snorted. "You've been married three times, Major, so that's not saying much for Angie."

Which just left... poor Gwyneth.

But then he'd always had a thing for brunettes. And

redheads. And blondes. Hell, he loved women. But he
really loved brunettes. One brunette in particular, the
one he *hadn't* married or slept with or even made it past
first base with, for God's sake.

Focus on the swim. The team.

The damn game. "Cuervo, are we playing this or not?"

"Next trio up… topic is singers," Cuervo announced.
"Britney Spears. Christina Aguilera. And Kesha."

Huh? "Who the hell is Kesha?"

"Are you sure you're not too old for this job?"

"Still young enough to outswim you, baby boy."
Liam surged ahead of Cuervo. Swims were a lot easier
on his abused knees than parachute landings or runs.
But a pararescueman needed to be ready for anything,
anywhere. Any weather.

Thunder rolled like a bowling ball gaining speed, and
his teammates were the pins.

All games aside, this little dip in the rain was about
more than a simple training exercise. More than team
building. He needed his pararescuemen in top form
for a mission they usually didn't handle—the external
security for an upcoming international summit being
held at NASA. Not normal business for pararescuemen,
but well within their skill set to act as a quick-reaction
force if anything went down. After all, isn't that what a
rescue was? A quick reaction to something going down?
Trained and prepared to fight back enemy-combatant
forces if necessary to protect their rescue target.

This made for a tough last assignment. His final
hoo-uh, ooh-rah before he said good-bye to military
life. Since he was eleven years old watching vintage
war movies on a VCR with his cancer-stricken mama,

all he'd wanted was to be that man who took the hill and won the woman. His mother had lost her battle. But Liam had been determined to carry on the fight by putting on that uniform.

Damned if he would go out with a whimper.

Fang slapped the water. "Can we get back to the fuck-me game?"

"Hey," Wade Rocha's voice rumbled as deeply as the thunder, "no need to make this crude."

"Oh, excuse me," Fang gasped. "Now that you're married, you're all Sergeant Sensitivity." *Gasp. Stroke.* "I guess we'll call this… kill one, marry one…" *Gasp. Stroke.* "Make sweet, flowery love to one."

Rocha muttered, "You're just jealous, smart-ass."

Fang chuckled and spluttered. "Not hardly. Monogamy until I'm in the grave?" He shuddered. "No thanks. Not into that."

But Liam was.

He'd tried his ass off to make the happily-ever-after thing work. Tried three times, in fact. Problem was, he had a defective cog when it came to choosing a woman to spend his life with. Didn't help that he'd always put the mission first, something that hadn't sat well with any of his wives. A small fortune spent on marital counseling hadn't been able to fix the relationships or him.

And still, he couldn't get that one woman—that one brunette—out of his mind, no matter how many times he chanted, "*Old patterns, not real, get over her.*"

He was a romantic sap who fell in love too easily. He kept looking for that classic silver-screen ending. Guy gets girl. Roll credits.

If only he could have persuaded Rachel Flores to go

out with him once they'd returned to the States. They'd worked together rescuing earthquake victims in the Bahamas six months ago. Had become good friends, or so he'd thought. After they got back, she never returned his calls.

Sure, if they had dated, the relationship would have self-destructed like all the rest. Then he could have walked away free and clear, no regrets, no lengthy explicit dreams that woke him up hard and unsatisfied. Now he was stuck with images of Rachel rattling around in his noggin until he wouldn't even notice another woman if she were waiting on the beach ahead wearing nothing but body glitter and a do-me smile.

Except there wasn't anyone on the beach. Just a stretch of sand and trees and a five-mile hike waiting to set his knees on fire after he hit the shore.

His life had been about training and service since he'd joined the army at eighteen. Became a ranger. Then got his degree while serving, became an officer, and swapped to the air force and pararescue missions.

Training. Honing. Brotherhood.

He'd sacrificed three marriages and any social life for this and would have kept right on doing so. Except now his thirty-eight-year-old body was becoming a liability to those around him.

One week. He had one week and a big-ass demonstration left. Until then he would do his damnedest to keep his team focused and invincible. He wasn't going to spend another second fantasizing about a particular sexy spitfire brunette with as much grit as his elite force team.

Liam narrowed his eyes against the sting of salt and

the pounding rain pushing through the surface like bullets. "I've got a new game, gentlemen. It's called Pick Your Poison." *Stroke. Breathe.* "If you've gotta die in the water…" *Stroke. Breathe.* "Would you choose a water moccasin? An alligator? Or a shark?"

Rachel Flores learned to break into cars when her mom rescued animals from locked automobiles. But she'd never expected to use that skill to lock herself and her dog *inside* a vehicle.

Checking over her shoulder, Rachel searched for military cops or a suspicious passerby around the tan concrete buildings on Patrick Air Force Base. The dozen or so camo-wearing personnel all seemed preoccupied with getting out of the Florida storm and into their cars at the end of the workday. Everyone was in too much of a hurry to spare a glance at her. Or maybe she was just that good at pretending she and her dog belonged here. Even though they totally didn't.

Death threats offered up a hefty motivator for her to circumvent a few rules.

Raindrops slid down her face, her hair and clothes slicked to her skin. She'd wasted valuable minutes trying to pick the lock, but the car was darn near pickproof. Which was actually a waste of technology, when combined with a vulnerable ragtop.

One way or another, she would get inside Liam McCabe's vehicle.

How ironic that after six months of fighting the damn-near-crippling urge to return his calls, now she was literally throwing herself in his path. Was that fair

to him? No, but God, she was scared to death and Liam
was a rock. If it were only her life at risk, she could have
fought her own battles. But with other lives at stake,
and given the explosive mess she'd landed in… she had
nowhere else to turn.

Stifling her conscience and vowing to repay him for
the damage, she shielded her hands from view with her
body as she slid a penknife along the Jeep's canvas roof.
Not a long slice. Just enough to slip her fingers inside
and reach… for…

The lock popped. She secured her hold on her
Labrador retriever's leash and pulled open the door. If
all went according to schedule, Liam would finish work
within a half hour, according to Wade Rocha's wife,
when Rachel had risked calling to ask.

At least she'd been able to get on base easily, thanks
to her work supplying therapy dogs to PTSD patients
at military hospitals throughout Southern Florida. She'd
wanted to drive straight to Liam's house off base and
wait for him there. But once she'd realized she was
being followed, her plans had changed. Going on base
got rid of the car trailing her.

Temporarily.

Acknowledgments

Around my house, we have a saying: "It takes a village… to write a book." Lucky for me, I have an awesome "village" populated with talented and supportive folks! A great big thanks to my editor Deb Werksman and the whole Sourcebooks team. And endless appreciation to my agent, Barbara Collins Rosenberg. (I'm a lucky author to work with all of you!)

I don't know what I would do without my critique partner, Joanne Rock, who provides such brilliant insights e-mailed and phoned at a moment's notice. (Truly, you've got to move closer! I miss you, BFF!)

Thanks to my dear friend and amazing beta reader, Zo Carlson, for her eagle eye and the celebratory dinners out. (You're a gem!)

As always, I'm so grateful to my flyboy husband Rob for sharing his military knowledge. (Thanks, too, for the patience and love! Right back atcha!) Hugs and love to our four vastly entertaining children. (Special soup for all of you!)

But most particularly, thanks to our youngest, Maggie, who saved my sanity during this deadline by cooking dinner, cleaning the kitchen, and reminding me to shower. (Maggie, you rock!)